ID0937996

ALSO BY JAMES J. SCHNEIDER

The Structure of Strategic Revolution:
Total War and the Roots of the Soviet Warfare State

GUERRILLA LEADER

GUERRILLA LEADER

*T. E. Lawrence
and the Arab Revolt*

JAMES J. SCHNEIDER

FOREWORD BY
THOMAS E. RICKS

WITHDRAWN

BANTAM BOOKS · NEW YORK

Copyright © 2011 by James J. Schneider
Foreword copyright © 2011 by Thomas E. Ricks
Map copyright © 2011 by David Lindroth, Inc.

Published in the United States by Bantam Books, an imprint of
The Random House Publishing Group, a division
of Random House, Inc., New York.

BANTAM BOOKS and the rooster colophon are registered trademarks
of Random House, Inc.

Library of Congress Cataloging-in-Publication Data
Schneider, James J. (James Joseph).
Guerrilla leader : T. E. Lawrence and the Arab revolt / James J. Schneider;
foreword by Tom Ricks.
p.   cm.
Includes bibliographical references and index.
ISBN 978-0-553-80764-6 (acid-free paper) — ISBN 978-0-345-53020-2 (eBook)
1. Lawrence, T. E. (Thomas Edward), 1888–1935—Military leadership.   2. World War,
1914–1918—Campaigns—Middle East.   3. Arab countries—History—Arab Revolt,
1916–1918.   4. Command of troops—History—20th century.   I. Title.
D568.4.L45S34   2011
940.4'15092—dc22   2010054141

Title-page image copyright © iStockphoto.com / © pop_jop

Printed in the United States of America on acid-free paper

www.bantamdell.com

2 4 6 8 9 7 5 3 1

First Edition

Book design by Victoria Wong

I had believed these misfortunes of the Revolt to be due mainly to faulty leaders, or rather to lack of leadership, Arab and English. So I went down to Arabia to see and consider its great men.

—T. E. LAWRENCE, *Seven Pillars of Wisdom*

Contents

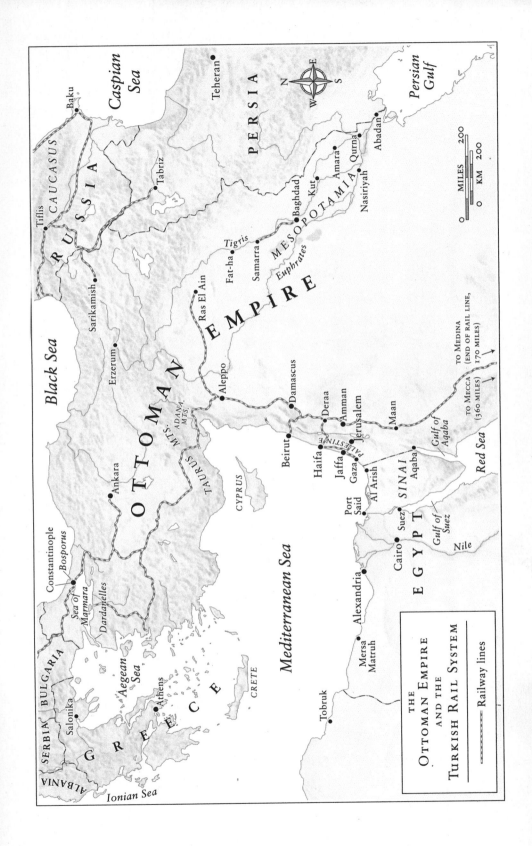

THE
OTTOMAN EMPIRE
AND THE
TURKISH RAIL SYSTEM

▬▬ Railway lines

Speaking for the Dead

This Work Is Respectfully Dedicated to the:
SOLDIERS

Look: toward the west . . . toward the west . . . to the land of Cochin,
Where, through endless clouds of rust-hued dust we plod.
Down eternal, emerald, jungled halls we slogged.
Toward the blazing maelstrom . . . into the crucible . . . we trod;
Not to victory,
But to our destiny.

Unseen, unheard, unremembered strong-armed men—
from un-named, far-off, time-less battle-fields—stood nigh
As we marched by.
In burnished, bronze bucklers, in helms of nodding horse-hair plumes,
In khaki-colored shirts, in strange black iron tombs;
Yet from their brilliant, incandescent visage a curious,
Caring glance was cast
As we marched past.

Then just ahead . . . the sky was red:
Burning, cloying, smoking, hell-evoking
Where in the dusky shadows lurked the demons of despair,
At our hearts and minds they tear.
Inexorably, towards the fiery forge we storm to find:
That final terror, death's dark fear,
Now in its grip, our souls to sear.
Our years of youth, like timeless tracks of tears are shed
Until all hope is gone, is dead.

.   .   .

Like the hammer of Hephaestus, the shot and shell explode.
Amidst the screaming anguish, our minds corrode.
Like stentoric bellows, the cannons roar
And searing sparks, like tracers soar.

A brief glimpse, a yellow face appears: once our enemy
Now, like us, a victim of his destiny.

As though mere ashes, our naked souls are strewn.
Placed upon battle's anvil, new men are hewn.
Blow upon blow, war's hammer forges the metal of our soul.
The metal, some base as brass, but only iron the battle-test can pass.
Only iron—the essence, the virtue of our souls, our selves—can last.
At last, fire-quenched, our steeled soul is tempered true,
Through . . . and . . . through.

Metamorphosed, quantum-like, life and death seemed one.
And now it looked as if a vision did appear:
The Christ and His squad of twelve drew near.
Upon his face was sadness filled.
Yet, bringing quietude, the battle stilled.
His voice, soft as the air itself, we strained to hear.
But what he said at once was clear:
"Man! You are born to war.
Your birth-cry is your battle-cry;
Avenging all, defending nothing.
The flame of hate burns within.
It fascinates . . . entices to destroy.
Into the streets like blood it spills; its evil armies to deploy.
Throughout your cities, through the land
Hate makes its final, murd'rous stand.
Brilliant, ingenious, the conquered stars are yours,
But unconquered still is your fear to love.
I say to you: You will be left on Megiddo's field,
unburied to rot—your fate,
To putrefy in your shroud of hate.

Hell's maggots will carve out, in your stinking carcass, epitaphs
Unless from this place you can return; from these smoking depths
To sunny reaches up above, bearing simple human love."
A fleeting smile across His face came now,
To chase away the clouds of sorrow upon his brow.
Then with a final glance, the Prince of Peace was gone;
And the Light of Love went out.

Then the din of hell returned in fury,
Trying all the while our souls to bury.
Vulcan now our tempered souls did take,
Like links to forge; a chain to make:
In self-sacrifice and comradeship, love's bond was made.
A band of love and Man that could not break.
At last . . .
At last . . . the paradox resolved.
Of all the hate, we were absolved.

Out of this hopeless abyss we came,
Bearing the sacred mem'ry of comrades once beloved,
Friend and foe, whose lives like a fragile flame, were quenched.
After a year, to our homes we went
To be met—not by pomp—but stony stares and icy gazes:
Our hearts were rent.

Since then, a secret, smoldering silence we have kept.
For men, strong-armed, cannot of love bespeak
For fear that others would think us weak;
Nor of the sight and sound of broken minds and limbs,
of shattered dreams
And sleepless nights, of broken lives and broken hearts—
Of comrades once held dear;
Nor of the hate, still its ugly head does rear.

With unseen, unheard, unremembered strong-armed men—
From un-named, far-off, time-less, battle-fields—we stand nigh
As the thankless shuffle by.

In burnished, bronze bucklers, in helms of nodding horse-hair plumes;
In mottled, emerald casques, in khaki-colored shirts,
In strange black iron tombs;
And from our brilliant, incandescent visage a curious caring
glance is cast,
As the unseeing, unknowing to their fate walk past.

Lonely sentinels, shoulder-to-shoulder, shield-to-shield,
our ranks stand fast.
In a timeless cry, a sacred pledge, our muted voices shout:
"Seize this day; let the Prince will out.
End this hate; within your hearts, quiet war.
And give us rest . . . eternal rest . . . fill these ranks no more!"

JJS
FIRST INFANTRY DIVISION
VIETNAM, 1966–67

Foreword

THOMAS E. RICKS

In this provocative book, James Schneider gives us a refreshing new look at T. E. Lawrence, one of the most interesting and romantic figures of the twentieth century. The Lawrence that Schneider gives us is not the familiar one we think we know, the person that has previously been presented. Here he is examined as a military leader and innovator. We see him first as a smart newcomer, then as a small-unit tactical leader, and finally, in the last phase of World War I in the desert, as an operational commander overseeing subordinate efforts.

Schneider argues—persuasively, I think—that Lawrence's greatest achievement was an intellectual act: "Lawrence was the first theorist and practitioner to revolutionize the guerrilla within the broader context of modern industrialized warfare." He was able to discard the dominant military paradigm of his day and forge a new one that combined age-old raiding techniques with industrial-era weaponry and targets. That dominant paradigm, which focuses on the destruction of the enemy, is still with us today, and is a major reason that the United States military has had such a difficult time in Iraq and Afghanistan. It was only several years into those wars that our senior leaders began to consider the possibility that killing the enemy was not perhaps always the best answer, or even the default mode of warfare.

Lawrence's great insight early in his time with the Arab tribesman in the north Arabian desert was that victory did not lie in the physical destruction of his foe. "A dead Turk was a man who could no longer eat and remain a logistical burden," Schneider writes. "A dead Turk was a man who could no longer fear and spread the virus of terror among his living comrades: Lawrence wanted a living demoralized mob, not an army of dead heroes." And even though his forces incessantly attacked the Hejaz railway, he sought only to squeeze that key Turkish line of supply, not to destroy it. As Lawrence put it, "Our goal must be to keep the railroad working, but just barely while inflicting maximum loss and discomfort on the Turks." He was imposing costs on the enemy, tying up his troops, bleeding him rather than decapitating him.

Schneider also shows us that in another departure that remains heresy in Western militaries even today, Lawrence put the men before the mission. That is, he would rather fail in the mission than lose his fighters.

In depicting how Lawrence took that mental leap away from the dominant Western paradigm of annihilation, Schneider insightfully takes us deep into the man's personality and quirks, looking at how his rare, even unique, qualities, enabled his achievement but likely also made him vulnerable to mental collapse at his moment of triumph. Leading men in combat is an extraordinarily stressful task. How, Schneider asks, was it possible for this introverted, otherworldly Englishman to help spur a revolt in a foreign land, to lead bands of warriors alien to his culture? Moreover, how did he manage to adapt nineteenth-century guerrilla warfare to the twentieth century, discovering how to carry it out in the industrial age?

Like many good military leaders, Lawrence had an ability to grasp quickly the heart of the matter, the essential element. And like the best strategists, Schneider notes, Lawrence was a "master learner," endlessly curious and reflective to a fault. Also, his background in military intelligence gave him an advantage in prosecuting a campaign of irregular warfare, in which information usually is more important then action.

But most of all, Schneider shows us that it was Lawrence's extraordinary empathy that enabled his achievements. This ability to identify with others, to grasp their hopes and fears and understanding of events about them, was key in the sort of campaign he conducted. "In an insurgency, empathy plays an especially crucial role," Schneider writes. "It places the leader inside the hearts and minds of his own men." In an interesting aside, Schneider also observes that it enabled Lawrence to understand his superior, General Edmund Allenby. This question of understanding the thoughts of a superior is a little-studied area of military command, but it is especially important when, as with Lawrence, one's own commander is distant and difficult to reach, and the barest strategic intent is all that one has to go by.

It was because of these qualities that Lawrence came to understand and use the centrality of narrative to Arabic culture, studying the stories that each tribe told about itself. I would argue that narrative is just as important in our culture, and that Western militaries have been slow to grapple with its use. Indeed, the United States Army seems almost to pride itself perversely on having inarticulate leaders who present themselves as "muddy boot sojers."

Yet because of all these qualities, Schneider shows us, Lawrence also was extremely vulnerable to traumatic stress. Months of combat, several woundings, and the loss of close comrades wore the man down. Invoking the work of the pathbreaking psychiatrist and veterans counselor Jonathan Shay, he illustrates how the betrayal of the Arab cause of independence by the British and French, who had colonial designs on the remnants of the Ottoman Empire, also undercut Lawrence's stability and eroded his character. Near the end of the war, outside the village of Tafas, Lawrence for the first time personally gave the order, "Take no prisoners." Schneider says that, "At that instant, . . . Lawrence stopped being a leader, his moral compass gone." By age thirty-one, Lawrence had made his great achievements, but psychologically was a dead man walking. The remaining seventeen years of his life were only a slow unraveling.

Preface

This [leadership] at bottom is the wish and prayer of all human
hearts, everywhere and at all times: "Give me a leader, not a false
sham-leader; a true leader, that he may guide me on the true way."

—THOMAS CARLYLE, *Chartism*, 1839

In the nineteenth century, a noted fellow soldier and countryman of
T. E. Lawrence, Sir William Francis Butler, wrote: "The nation that
will insist on drawing a broad demarcation between the fighting man
and the thinking man is liable to find its fighting done by fools and its
thinking done by cowards." Butler's quote stands to emphasize the
importance of the intimate and dynamic connection between learning
and leading and serves as the leader's most important antidote to the
consequences of interminable war. We have learned the hard lesson
from Vietnam that education is an important inoculation against
post-traumatic stress disorder. Hard learning strengthens the mind to
resist the shock and trauma of combat.

The influence of Lawrence on military leadership of the last century and into the present one has been largely ignored, forgotten, or
misunderstood. His literary and intellectual influence on Western
thinking in general, however, has been more broad and profound,
especially in the twentieth century. His writing, most significantly
Seven Pillars of Wisdom, though often overwrought, obscure, and
self-serving, is always gripping, powerful, and poetic. To the extent
that Lawrence had any kind of impression among the military—any

military—it was when he resonated with a particular kind of rare officer: the military intellectual who saw *Seven Pillars of Wisdom* and other writings as a psychological and intellectual window into the mind of a desert warrior and guerrilla leader.

For the average reader, the brush with Lawrence was perhaps through David Lean's motion picture *Lawrence of Arabia,* starring Peter O'Toole. The movie captured the essence, though not the whole truth, of Lawrence's desert epic and offers some grainy insight into the role of Lawrence as a leader of the Arab Revolt. Though many might argue that leaders are made, not born, Lawrence's case suggests a delicate balance between nature and nurture in the development of any great leader.

Leadership is perhaps the most important human imperative: without leaders—without purpose, direction, and motivation— society as we know it could not function. Leadership is a fundamental birthright that at one time or another we are all called upon to exercise, whether as leader or follower. Yet in both roles, personal character and professional competence are demanded. The actual expression of the two is always defined by the unique social and historical circumstances of the striving group.

In modern war, it becomes axiomatic that the greatest demoralizing force—next to the shock and loss of comrades in battle—is the unschooled, intellectually incompetent leader. The glassy-eyed gaze of terror and incomprehension on the face of a combat leader is an expression that haunts surviving soldiers to their graves. Increasingly, as modern war continues its swift evolution into the twenty-first century, soldiers will look to their leaders not only for hard answers, but also for a whole array of real-world solutions, whether in Iraq, Afghanistan, or some other dimly imagined battlefield of the future.

The Middle East is the center of gravity of the twenty-first century: commotion and upheaval in that region move the rest of the world along with it. For good or ill, this influence will continue for the next hundred years. The recent rise of the Middle East in world history began with World War I, and one of the key players in that ascension was Lawrence. This book examines Lawrence's crucial role in the early transformation of the Middle East while leading an Arab revolt against the Turkish Empire.

Bibliographic Note

Although the book is based on extensive research in primary and secondary sources, I have dispensed with the normal scholarly apparatus of lengthy footnotes, disputations, tables, and the like for the sake of readability. Lawrence's journey to the pinnacles of leadership is an intensely personal narrative that should be read as a seamless story insofar as is practicable. This has been my chief objective as a matter of writing style. The only exception concerns Lawrence's own words, in which case I have provided footnotes to the appropriate sources. Readers interested in more bibliographic details are invited to consult the extensive bibliographies found in Jeremy Wilson, *Lawrence of Arabia* (New York: Atheneum, 1990), and Michael Korda, *Hero* (New York: HarperCollins, 2010).

As regards Arabic spelling, I have used Lawrence's usage unless superseded by a more common convention.

Dramatis Personae

Abdullah ibn Hussein (1882–1951): King Hussein's middle son and initial spark plug of the Arab Revolt. His great political instincts made him a natural revolutionary, though he was less successful at conventional military operations. He was appointed emir of the Trans-Jordan in 1923 and later assassinated in Jerusalem.

Ali ibn Hussein (1879–1935): Hussein's eldest son, though the least capable leader. More on the bookish side, he was studied in Muslim law and found combat a bitter experience. After his father was deposed in 1926 by ibn Saud, Hussein's titles fell to Ali.

Allenby, Edmund Henry Hynman (1861–1936): A consummate cavalryman, Allenby commanded British forces in Palestine from June 1917 until the end of World War I. He developed a close working relationship with Lawrence and found the Arab insurgency readily adaptable to his long-term strategic designs aimed at defeating the Turks. His name, Allenby, transliterated into Arabic as "the Prophet of God," making his dramatic entry into Jerusalem in December 1917 a harbinger for Arab victory.

Auda abu Tayi (1874?–1924): The quintessential tactician of the Arab Revolt. Skilled in raiding, tracking, ambush, and deep strikes, the sheikh commanded the eastern Howeitat, the abu Tayi. Auda was essentially the tactical linchpin during the raid on Aqaba. His skill and determination exploited the natural fighting abilities of the Arab raider. Auda was prominent again during the final drive on Damascus in September 1918 that sealed the fate of the Ottoman Empire.

Brémond, Eduard (1868–1948): A French artilleryman, wounded in France, sent to Palestine to command the French military mission in August 1916. He arrived in the Hejaz a few months before Lawrence, who immediately realized his purpose was to spy on the Arab Revolt for the French, ever wary of their interests in Syria. He was sent home in December 1917.

Clayton, Gilbert Falkingham (1875–1929): An artilleryman by training, Clayton made his successful career as an intelligence officer commanding military intelligence at British Army headquarters in Cairo during the early stages of the war. He worked very closely with Lawrence in developing a robust intelligence picture of the Arab Revolt. Clayton ended the war as chief political officer of the Egyptian Expeditionary Force from 1917 to 1918.

Fakhreddin "Fakhri" Pasha (1868–1948): Turkish commander sent down in late spring 1916 to defend Medina. He became a tenacious foe of Lawrence and the Arabs during their struggle to claim the Hejaz.

Feisal ibn Hussein (1883–1933): Youngest son of King Hussein, Feisal became the national leader of the Arab Revolt when his leadership potential was first identified by Lawrence in late 1916. Feisal's motivational talents quickly emerged on the national level as he sought to harmonize the various and disparate factions of the Bedouin toward a common Arab undertaking. Feisal was with Lawrence during their triumphal entry in Damascus and the subsequent efforts to establish a national government.

Georges-Picot, François Marie Denis (1870–1951): A French diplomat who signed an agreement with the British Mark Sykes that carved up the Ottoman Empire into French and English spheres of influence. Later, Russia and Italy were brought into the compact.

Hussein ibn Ali (1854–1931): Sherif of Mecca from 1908 to 1917, when he was proclaimed king of the Hejaz and assumed nominal leadership of the Arab Revolt. Crafty, ambitious, and jealous, he became the international figurehead of the Arab Revolt.

Kitchener, Horatio Herbert (1850–1916): Became secretary of state for war at the beginning of World War I. He was killed by a German naval mine near the Orkneys while aboard a battleship traveling to Russia. His initial strategic vision shaped the early dynamics in the Middle East.

Liman von Sanders, Otto (1855–1929): German officer who received command of combined Turkish and German forces in Palestine, replacing Erich von Falkenhayn in February 1918. Understood well the Turkish soldier, but his appointment came too late to overcome his desperate odds.

Lloyd George, David (1863–1945): The first strategist and war leader since Abraham Lincoln who understood the nature and dynamics of modern protracted war. Elected prime minister in December 1916, he laid the grand strategic groundwork for the ultimate success in Palestine and the overthrow of the Ottoman Empire.

Murray, Archibald James (1860–1945): An infantryman, Murray was given command of the Egyptian Expeditionary Force in January 1916. Initially skeptical of the Arab Revolt, Murray became a supporter after considerable urging by Lawrence, Clayton, and others. His fate was sealed after several tactical defeats in Palestine near Gaza.

Robertson, William Robert (1860–1933): Appointed chief of the Imperial General Staff in January 1915, Robertson was a vigorous advocate for a victory on the western front. He saw efforts in the Middle East as a waste of strategic resources that only delayed the end of the war.

Shaalan, Nuri (1845?–1927?): Led the large contingent of Ruwalla in the northern Arabian Peninsula. Shaalan rode the fence until well into the Arab Revolt, trying to convince both the British and the Turkish of his loyalty. By the middle of 1918, he threw off all pretenses and moved decisively against the Turks. After ibn Saud and King Hussein, Shaalan was the most powerful Arab sheikh.

Storrs, Ronald Henry Amherst (1881–1955): Regarded by Lawrence as "the most brilliant Englishman in the Near East, and subtly efficient, despite his diversion of energy in love of music and letters, of sculpture, painting, of whatever was beautiful in the world's fruit. . . . Storrs was always first, and the great man among us." He played the key role in persuading Hussein to initiate the Arab Revolt.

Sykes, T. B. Mark (1879–1919): British diplomat who was primary signatory to the Sykes-Picot Agreement. He died later in Paris of the Spanish influenza during the peace negotiations following World War I.

Wemyss, Rosslyn Erskine (1864–1933): British naval commander who as head of the East Indies and Egyptian Squadron supported Lawrence's Arab Revolt in the Hejaz. Wemyss became first sea lord in December 1917. He was noted for his creative use of naval forces in support of an insurgency.

Wingate, Francis Reginald (1861–1953): British general who administered Egypt and the Sudan through World War I. Wingate was constant in his support of an Arab uprising offering logistical aid often beyond his means to deliver.

GUERRILLA
LEADER

CHAPTER ONE

Arrival

All men dream: but not equally. Those who dream by night in the dusty recesses of their minds wake in the day to find that all was vanity: but the dreamers of the day are dangerous men, for they may act their dream with open eyes, and make it possible. This I did.

—T. E. LAWRENCE, *Seven Pillars of Wisdom*

In the fall of 1946, two men sat facing each other across a green, felt-clad library table.[1] The location was Hanoi, in French Indochina. The first man was General Raoul Salan, sent as part of a diplomatic mission to negotiate the return of French authority to the land that would be known to history as Vietnam. The other man gazing across from Salan was the wily Vietnamese guerrilla leader Vo Nguyen Giap. The leaders conducted a wide-ranging discourse that lasted several hours into the waning afternoon. Toward the end of the meeting, discussion turned toward Giap's success in resisting the Japanese occupation of Indochina since 1940. Salan wanted to know the source and inspiration of Giap's success. Without hesitation, Giap reached behind his seat and withdrew from a shelf a heavy book and laid it before Salan, who recognized the author immediately. Giap gestured toward the book, saying, "My fighting gospel is T. E. Lawrence's *Seven Pillars of Wisdom*. I am never without it."

Salan became intrigued and wondered aloud how a book about guerrilla warfare in the desert could possibly find expression in the jungles of Vietnam. "Ah," Giap replied. "Is that your assessment of Lawrence?" Salan nodded a casual affirmation: "Of course." "Then you have missed the whole point of Lawrence," said Giap. "He is less about fighting a guerrilla war than leading one. And *leadership,*" Giap emphasized, "is applicable in any context: desert or jungle, military or civil." Perhaps, thought Salan . . . but the hour was growing late and there was much work to be done. In parting, the two vowed to continue the dialogue about Lawrence and his leadership at the next opportune time, but that time would never arrive. In the end, Giap would continue his application of Lawrence's methods against an even more implacable foe than the French; the United States would learn—and forget—many of the same lessons as the French, though the outcome would be the same.

LIKE MANY NOTABLE leaders, T. E. Lawrence appears to have been a child prodigy. He could read before he was five. Recollections of family and friends describe an active boy who enjoyed running and climbing trees. He was also "frightfully bossy; he used to order us about, but in a very nice way." There was also a sense of aloofness, another leadership quality: of being in a group, but also above it. Lawrence was never good at group games, not because he disdained their irrelevance, but because he had to be the leader in all things. The element of aloofness was perhaps reinforced by a pervasive aura that "there was always something he was not satisfied with, even as a child . . . a secret something of unhappiness."

When the family relocated to Oxford, they moved into a red-brick, typically Victorian home at 2 Polstead Road in a middle-class neighborhood on the outskirts of town. In this new environment, Lawrence began to develop and demonstrate key qualities of a dynamic military leader: extraordinary energy, personal courage, profound curiosity, keen powers of observation, and an aptitude for novelty and innovation.

The powerful amalgam of energy, courage, and curiosity became the lifelong source of Lawrence's leadership abilities. Since leadership is fundamentally a careful blend of character and competence, energy, courage, and curiosity as character attributes bear especially on a leader's competence, because they generate the desire and need to learn in order to overcome *in*competence. For Lawrence, an initial curiosity about the Middle Ages led him to delve deeply into the military art, architecture, and organization of the period. He also used the character and qualities of the medieval knight as a kind of role model that continued to evolve with his learning and practical understanding.

Psychologically, the energy and curiosity served his appetite for excitement in the discovery of new things. It also served his sense of humor, as his exploring curiosity directed him into corners of mischief. In Lawrence's day, the chief outlet for the curious mind was found in books. From about the age of sixteen, Lawrence unharnessed his voracious reading appetite on the broader study of military history. Here he began a more formal and systematic study of not only the Middle Ages—castles, armor, uniforms, heraldry, religion, original manuscripts, artifacts, coins, and the languages of the period, Latin and Greek—but also the lives of the great generals, especially Belisarius, Maurice de Saxe, and Napoleon. Placed in a larger military context, the investigation led to his deeper understanding of the feudal, romantic, and chivalric traditions and outlook of the culture that would lead to his particular fascination with the Crusades and the heroic leader. Out of these early studies grew a self-motivating desire to "free a people."

The great gear that drove Lawrence's personal motivation began to turn during his formative adolescence. "I had dreamed at the City [High] School in Oxford, of hustling into form, while I lived, the new Asia which time was irreparably bringing upon us." The "new Asia" was the emergence of what we now know as the Middle East. The development of such a yearning in most people would merely have remained a curious fantasy, but with Lawrence this fantasy became a motivational reality.

Lawrence's progression as a military leader began with what we might term "the militarization" of his mind. By the time he completed studies at Oxford, he had written a highly original contribution to the history of medieval military architecture entitled "Crusading Castles." Lawrence's development during the period can be understood as two interrelated phases. The first concerned his three-year immersion into the literature and culture of the medieval period; the second phase embraced his periodic research travels that culminated with his journeys through the Middle East before the war. During these years, Lawrence developed the rarest of leadership skills: the ability to lead people from another culture. He developed a capability to use his knowledge and understanding of other peoples to move beyond his own cultural framework and biases and embrace an alien reality.

For Lawrence, medieval (mostly French) literature opened a whole new vista. As a form of interest it also became a means of escape, a kind of epic fantasy world that would be the wellspring for such post–World War I writers as J. R. R. Tolkien, C. S. Lewis, and E. R. Eddison. His interest in the material was intense. From his study of the medieval knight culture, Lawrence developed a portrait of courtly society where romantic interests could flourish, refinements of life could emerge, and the embodied martial character could grow. After three years of extended study, Lawrence's interests began to disrupt his university work in general. He confronted the reality of having to complete his degree, and since his field was history that meant a substantial research project. And the topic was obvious and simply a continuation of his chief military interests.

During his early adolescence, Lawrence began touring English castles and churches with his father by bicycle. Later he would often travel alone or with a friend or family member in tow. By the end of the year, Lawrence had seen all the English castles of note, including the great twelfth-century fortresses built by Edward I in Wales. He soon decided to carry his explorations to France. A summer month was spent in 1906 as an initial excursion that included visits to old family friends in France but ended up with visits to castles in Brittany, at Saint-Malo, and in Dinant. During Easter 1907, Lawrence went back to north Wales to visit castles like Conwy and Caernarvon. Around his nineteenth birthday, he went along with his father to photograph and sketch the castles of the Loire Valley in France. The following year he began his first exploration of French medieval architecture with the express purpose of gathering research material for his undergraduate thesis. Here he covered most of southern France by bicycle in one great circle. He contracted malaria when he reached the Mediterranean Sea. During the course of his touring through

France, Lawrence logged several hundreds of hard miles by bike. The toughening process that molds any good leader would continue its work throughout the rest of Lawrence's life. He was less spartan than some kind of fighting monk—for Lawrence, like the Crusading monk, valued the role of learning and intellect as central to his avocation as a leader.

In letters from France, he began to display the great descriptive powers that he would later express in *Seven Pillars of Wisdom*. He married his literary qualities with highly developed photographic and graphic skills: all three would place him well in advance of most staff officers in his day. The conjunction of Lawrence's creative qualities was drawn together in France through his keen focus on the stone and mortar of military architecture. He saw the strengths—and weaknesses—of fortifications as well as the importance of geography and logistics in the conduct of military operations. He would carry all these insights with him as a leader through an exquisite realization of his self-motivation.

IT IS NOT precisely certain when Lawrence chose his thesis topic. Certainly by the end of 1908 at the age of twenty, he decided to study the role the Crusades played in influencing Western European military architecture. It had generally been accepted that the Crusades carried architectural influence back to Europe from the Middle East. Lawrence challenged the accepted view by arguing that the Europeans modeled their castles on preexisting, pre-Crusade Norman structures that evolved simply to suit the needs of the designers. Lawrence found little marked influence from the Crusading East, where the builders simply carried the Norman designs with them to the Holy Land and made basic modifications accordingly. The thesis, however, meant a difficult comparative study. It further entailed that Lawrence, who had already surpassed most standards of undergraduate field research, must now go to the Middle East to study the Crusader castles as well.

Lawrence's journey began in the middle of June 1909 aboard the steamship *Mongolia,* taking him through the Straits of Gibraltar into the Mediterranean and the ports of Said, Jaffa, and Beirut. He would spend the next four months traveling on foot through the region he

had long dreamed and fantasized about. Although ostensibly studying the area for its Crusader architecture, Lawrence for the first time
became acquainted with an alien yet romantic culture that in many
ways remained unchanged since the days of Richard the Lion-Hearted
and Saladin. The Arabs, especially the desert Bedouin, captured Lawrence's imagination completely.

He arrived in the Middle East at Port Said around July 4, also
visiting Beirut before heading south by foot on July 6 to Sidon and
across the Jordan to Banias. Upon reaching Safed, he headed south
along the Sea of Galilee to Tiberias. After a short rest, he headed west
to Nazareth and tracked across Mount Carmel to the sea. A brief
stop on the coast placed Lawrence on his way again north through
the great Crusading towns of Haifa, Acre, and Tyre and on to Beirut,
where he completed the circle in early August. The swing through
Palestine was a prelude to the next and most ambitious leg of his
journey as he plied his way ever northward into Syria and visits to the
famous military sites at Tripoli, Latakia, and Antioch. He reached the
strategic fortress of Aleppo at the beginning of September. After a
short break, Lawrence headed by car to Urfa and the gateway into
Mesopotamia. On September 30, he was on his way to Beirut by
train. A few days later, he was back on board ship for the long journey home. During his travels, Lawrence logged over eleven hundred
miles alone and mostly by foot.

In preparation for his trip while still at Oxford, Lawrence, in his
usual fashion, spared no pains in immersing himself in the region. He
began by learning to speak Arabic before his departure from Oxford.
Although his vocabulary was small—he admitted to one of his biog-
raphers of knowing eighty or so words of Arabic—Lawrence possessed a natural knack for learning languages that he had fostered
initially while traveling throughout France. During his Middle Eastern sojourn, he stayed with many private families throughout the
area and was deeply affected by the simple and sincere hospitality of
the local people. On August 15, he wrote to his father from Tripoli:
"This is a glorious country for wandering in, for hospitality is something more than a name: setting aside the American and English mis-
sionaries, who take care of me in the most fatherly (or motherly)
way:—they have all so far been as good as they can be—there are the

common people, each one ready to receive one for a night, and allow me to share in their meals: and without a thought of payment from a traveler on foot. It is so pleasant, for they have a very attractive kind of native dignity." As always, his letters are filled with meticulous details and accounts of everything he encountered, including the people and their culture, as well as his bouts with malaria and a potentially deadly incident with local highwaymen who robbed and nearly murdered him.

This perceptive acumen went beyond the ability to see the tangible; it permitted him to see the invisible: in the case of the Arabs, their fears, habits, beliefs, customs, and tribal relationships. He saw things as assemblages and systems, not as pieces and parts; not as puzzles and events, but as problems and processes. He saw their social and cultural edges, their patterns and points of leverage. Lawrence began to see the Arab world in a new way and would soon come to believe he could move and bend it to his will: that his Crusader musings were more than an adolescent fantasy.

LAWRENCE'S EDUCATIONAL EXPERIENCE at Oxford, which culminated in his "Crusading Castles" thesis, was pivotal and became the firm cornerstone of his leadership. It was Oxford that ultimately produced the leadership fusion of character with competence.

The "Oxford method" of learning, which predominated around the time of Lawrence's formal education, comprised the following: First, there was a very close master-apprentice relationship between the university don, who acted as a kind of tutor, and his student. The don tailored the instruction to best suit the educational needs of the individual student. Second, the master-apprentice relation was supported within a strong social network bounded by the various colleges within the university proper. The collegiality reinforced and encouraged dialogue and debate among the dons and students to make learning a way of life. Third, learning resources—libraries, museums, lectures, textbook material, chaired professors—were among the best in the world. In Lawrence's day they *were* the best. Fourth, the program of instruction grounded its central tenets of learning in the idea of a liberal education. The carving up of knowledge into discrete territories with inviolable disciplinary boundaries had not yet occurred in Lawrence's time. All that mattered was excellence in learning and the removal of impediments along the student's path to knowledge and self-understanding. Finally, it was always recognized that the burden of learning rested with the student: this was taken seriously by the student as his primary moral responsibility while at university. The approach placed a large emphasis on student curiosity and his reliance on the socialization of learning in a university environment, where he was expected to learn as much from his peers as from his mentors.

During the period of Lawrence's matriculation at Oxford, a unique climate of inquiry existed. By 1910, it was recognized that the next five years of British history would eclipse the last fifty in terms of the practical demands it would place upon its students. This outlook consequently reinforced the idea that student higher learning would continue to be self-directed, personalized, and, especially, problem oriented. Lawrence's in-depth study of the Crusader castles is a prime example of what we now understand as "problem-based learning."

Very briefly, this approach to education centers around real-world problems, yet the learning is more important than the solution to the problem itself. In Lawrence's case, the problem he tried to resolve was, on the face of it, purely academic: whether or not the Crusaders brought their design influence *with* them to the Holy Land or brought the influence *back* with them to their Western kingdoms. Still, in its resolution the issue had profound practical and real *learning* implications in its solution, as we have already seen. In his learning, Lawrence had to identify clearly what he needed to know, how to find it out, how to share it with his colleagues in his written thesis, and finally how to apply the new knowledge through the discipline of military history. In the process Lawrence was encouraged to explore learning independently outside the classroom and thus gain a deeper understanding of the material instead of a simple superficial overview. In practice this meant he was able to explore the gaps in his own understanding and discover knowledge that was directly and personally meaningful to him. In this way, understanding becomes a personal construction that is always unique to the individual, not dependent on the context of a given body of curriculum. Here the mentorship of the college don was important because he understood how the learner's goals, the context of his interests, and his own experience are all woven together to become part of the student's character.

The chief premise of problem-centered learning resides with the motivational aspect of education in its recognition that *puzzlement is the primary factor that motivates the learner to learn.* Obviously, any student with an innate curiosity—a student like Lawrence—would respond very well to this approach, and part of the don's skill lay with his ability to recognize that curiosity in his students and challenge them with the possibilities of puzzlement.

Without full intention, places like Oxford created the sort of curious mind that could thrive in the kind of complex environment that would be characteristic of events like the Arab Revolt: a highly unstructured problem that would instill a sense of motivation, a feeling of satisfaction, and a personal sense of ownership in the solution that was also unconfined by conceptual bias and intellectual boundary.

WHEN IT CAME time for Lawrence to serve his internship or—better—clinic in leadership, two things are striking: He likely never realized it was an apprenticeship as such; nor did he serve his basic course in leading with a military unit. Instead, he spent over three years on an archaeological dig at the ancient Hittite city of Carchemish, located in a region of modern south central Turkey. After his graduation from Oxford in June 1910, Lawrence made three more trips to France, this time working for the famous Ashmolean Museum in Oxford under David Hogarth, one of his mentors. Hogarth was able to obtain a four-year traveling scholarship for Lawrence through Magdalen College. Lawrence wrote: "Mr. Hogarth is going digging: and I am going out to Syria in a fortnight to make plain the valleys and level the mountains for his feet:—also to learn Arabic. The two occupations fit into one another splendidly." He arrived in Beirut just before Christmas 1910 and left for Jebail to begin an intensive two-month study of Arabic under the keen tutelage of Miss Fareedah el Akle.

Sixty years later, Lawrence's perceptive Arabic teacher could still recount specific details and impressions of the period and offer direct insight into his qualities as a leader. One of the most important is mental strength sustained by a deep spiritual source. She wrote of

Lawrence that he "did not speak of religion much, but he lived a religious life. He was a man of the spirit and lived rather in the spirit than in the body. . . . Once, talking to Lawrence about an important matter, I asked him a question and he said, 'Help comes from within, not from without.' This seemed to me to reveal the secret of his inner life. He seemed to be a man guided by a dynamic power in him: the power of the spirit." A century earlier, the great Prussian military philosopher Carl von Clausewitz had written emphatically: "If the mind is to emerge unscathed from this relentless struggle [in battle] with the unforeseen, two qualities are indispensible: *first, an intellect that, even in the darkest hour, retains some glimmerings of the inner light which leads to truth; and second, the courage to follow this faint light wherever it may lead.*"

After completing language studies and a tour of the region, Lawrence arrived at the dig site in early 1911. He immediately began to immerse himself in his new world, where his main responsibility was to "direct the men" in their digging. But his work also included technical responsibilities like the drawing of sculptures, the recording of inscriptions and photography, and any catchall "other duties as assigned." The digging was extremely arduous and often entailed the movement of tons of rock and stone by rope and brute force using teams of sixty men straining and pulling in the Mesopotamian heat. By night, Lawrence's time was "filled up with odd jobs that might have been done in the day, squeezing and copying inscriptions, writing up pottery and object lists, journals, etc. Also it gets colder after sunset, and we go to bed early (about 10 or 11 as a rule), to avoid it."

The digging season ended four months later in July, when Lawrence began a thirty-day tramp through the Euphrates area on foot to study the local castles and seek further Hittite artifacts. Along the way he contracted dysentery and suffered more attacks of malaria. Still feeling ill, he returned to Great Britain in August. Resumption of the digging season the following spring of 1912 was delayed owing to legal squabbles over railroad rights and ownership of the archaeological site. These issues were finally resolved on March 17.

By now, the famous archaeologist Sir Leonard Woolley had arrived to take charge of the operation. With Woolley on site, many visitors took note and began periodic visits to the location. One of these was the wife of the British consul in Aleppo, Winifred Fontana. She had met with Lawrence the previous year and upon her return noticed a visible change in him. He had sloughed off "much of his absorbed and discomforting aloofness with his visiting clothes and clad in shorts and a button less shirt held together with a gaudy Kurdish belt, looked what he was: a young man of rare power. . . ."

As time passed by, Lawrence became more competent with his Arabic, and as he became more competent his confidence grew and prompted him to take a more active role in the social relations among the diggers, as they recognized his personal concern for them as well as his easy style in handling their problems. In consequence he became a popular feature on the local landscape. A typical example of this aspect of Lawrence's leadership occurred in June: "Today I cured a man of compound scorpion-bite by a few drops of ammonia: for that I have a fame above Thompson's as *hakim* [doctor] and as a magician who can conjure devils into water. . . ." His role as camp physician would be put to good use, for in June 1912 a severe outbreak of cholera struck the Aleppo area and saw Lawrence helping the local population deal with the problem through the remainder of the summer. More language training ensued in August back at Jebail. In September, work at Carchemish was interrupted by the encroaching Baghdad railway then being built by German engineers. After six weeks of leave in England, Lawrence returned in January 1913 for another campaign of digging.

The excavations that began in earnest in March were to be the most successful during Lawrence's participation. By the end of the year, Lawrence had gained the reputation and authority among the Arabs equal to that of a local judge and elder: "He became thoroughly conversant with the intricacies of their tribal and family jealousies, rivalries and taboos, their loves and hates, and their strengths and weaknesses. It was this carefully garnered knowledge, together with his remarkable ability to identify with the feelings and personal priorities of individual Arabs, to know the emotions and concerns upon which their self-esteem, security, power and prestige were based, that enabled Lawrence to win the confidence and acceptance of the Arab people. . . ." For Lawrence, the experience among the Arabs was just another schoolhouse, another kind of learning that had to be mastered, and quite simply it was his innate curiosity that made him a natural and expert learner.

A close friend of Lawrence's at the time, Ernest Altounyan, understood his quality as a master learner. He wrote: "Students of his life cannot but be impressed by his persistence as a learner. Nothing could master him, but he proved a brilliant pupil in each successive school; until once more driven to tyranny by his unique sense of proportion. This quality has seldom met with due regard in human history." Years later Lawrence would admit to Altounyan, "I haven't had much kick out of life; those days at Carchemish were the best."

The final lesson of Lawrence's prewar education began in January 1914, when he and Woolley were assigned to conduct a geographic survey of the area of Wadi 'Araba from the port of Aqaba to the ancient city of Petra and the eastern Sinai in the region known in the Bible as the Wilderness of Zin. The survey was sponsored by the Palestine Exploration Fund and had a purpose serving strategic intelligence; the geographic intent became the "cover" to conceal its political and military aim. The strategic object was to map the entire region because of its political location on the border between Egypt and the Ottoman Empire. After completing the project, Lawrence returned briefly to the dig, which he closed out in June, and then he made his last peacetime journey home to England.

BY THE END of his apprenticeship among the Arabs, Lawrence had developed all the requisite leadership skills needed to lead a people's revolution. Lawrence also saw that a leader must provide purpose and direction, as well as motivation, to his troops. Such leadership, that of an insurgency, demanded a rare kind of leader with a vision and special imagination, a *dreamer*: "All men dream: but not equally," he wrote. "Those who dream by night in the dusty recesses of their minds wake in the day to find that all was vanity: but the dreamers of the day are dangerous men, for they may act their dream with open eyes, and make it possible. This I did. I meant to make a new nation . . . to build an inspired dream-palace of [Arab] national thoughts. So high an aim called out the inherent nobility of their minds, and made them play a generous part in events. . . ."

By his will and leadership, Lawrence seized the Arab Revolt like an archer grasping his bow: Arabs like Auda abu Tayi were his arrows; Feisal was the quiver. With great physical and intellectual strength, Lawrence flung the shafts of insurgency across the desert toward Aqaba, Damascus, and beyond. This is his story; it begins with the world on the terrible brink of its first great war.

CHAPTER TWO

Pale Rider

Certain men . . . come to be accepted guardians and transmitters—
instructors—of established doctrines. To question the beliefs is to
question their authority; to accept the beliefs is evidence of loyalty
to the powers that be, a proof of good citizenship. Passivity, docil-
ity, acquiescence, come to be primal intellectual virtues. Facts and
events presenting novelty and variety are slighted, or are sheared
down till they fit the Procrustean bed of habitual belief. Inquiry
and doubt are silenced by citation of ancient laws. . . . This attitude of mind generates dislike of change, and the resulting aversion
to novelty is fatal to progress. What will not fit into the established
canons is outlawed; men who make new discoveries are objects of
suspicion and even of persecution.

—JOHN DEWEY, *How We Think*

When Lawrence returned to the Middle East and to Cairo in
December 1914, World War I was already four months old.
Though the shooting had begun in August, the seeds of regional dis-
cord had been sown much earlier. As the Ottoman Empire entered the
nineteenth century, the Arabs of the region were united by a common
tongue and a common religion. One would have imagined a strong
nationalist sense to emerge as was developing throughout much of
Europe. Instead, most Arabs sided with the long-suffering Turks and
began to fear the encroaching European Christians more than their
befuddled imperial masters, especially after the British occupation of

Egypt in 1882. This sense of uneasy solidarity was suddenly called into question in July 1908 when a group of radicals calling themselves the Young Turks seized control of the Turkish government. Like many of the disenchanted Arabs, the Young Turks sought relief from the yoke of imperial repression. They had grown up among Turkish expatriates in Europe, where ideas of revolution carefully stoked their radical thoughts of reform. When they came to power in Istanbul through a bloodless coup, the people received them with hope and joy.

Through their political arm, the Committee of Union and Progress, the Young Turks sought to implement a secular worldview and rabid nationalism called Pan-Turanism. The latter view, exploiting Turkic roots among the Tartars, attempted to elevate the heathen conqueror Genghis Khan; Batu Khan, his grandson; and others to the position of Turkish forefathers. The secularization program was essentially anti-Arab and even anti-Muslim in its effort to translate the Koran into Turkish and to nationalize Arab schools. A backlash led to the establishment of various Arab nationalist secret societies and to a general movement of passive resistance throughout the Ottoman Empire. On April 13, 1909, a counterrevolution erupted led by disgruntled army officers and Islamic religious students. The counter-coup soon slopped over into a full-blown genocide against the largely Christian Armenians in the Turkish province of Adana, where the military generally watched idly by, and even participated, as the reactionaries wasted the region. Believing the Armenians to be supporters of the Young Turks, the rabble killed up to thirty thousand of them. Meanwhile, the massacre in Adana was not lost upon the Arabs. The possibility of violent retribution against a non-Turkic ethnic group and the encroachment of a seemingly Christianizing Europe kept even the most virulent Arab nationalists loyal to the empire.

In contrast with the internal situation within the Ottoman Empire, the political outlook among the international rivals was equally fragmented. Both Germany and Great Britain maintained a bifurcated and flawed understanding of the fundamental issues that motivated the Turks and Turkish political existence. The two countries saw internal revolution as both a danger (Germany) and an opportunity (Great Britain). In 1905, when Kaiser Wilhelm II considered a

European war a real possibility, he was adamant in securing his eastern flank against a viable Turkish bulwark. The British saw Arab unrest as a fulcrum point, where the lever of revolution would dislocate that bulwark. But both assessments were based on an exaggerated misperception of pan-Islamism and the Muslim community, which saw Islam as a monolithic entity under the guiding and benevolent hand of Muhammad's religious successor, the caliph in Istanbul, and whoever controlled the caliph would command the Muslim world.

Because of the vital economic and strategic role of the Suez Canal, the British window into the Muslim world and into the Ottoman Empire was through Egypt. This perspective gave a natural but biased geostrategic outlook that ranged upon the Arab question. In 1911, Lord H. H. Kitchener, the conqueror of Sudan (1898) and Britain's most revered living hero, became consul-general in Egypt. His long service in the region led to a fully developed policy toward the Turks. He was acutely aware of the recent Turkish turmoil in the Balkans and especially the loss of Libya at the hands of Italy during 1911. The loss of Libya to a Christian nation like Italy caused special outrage among the Arabs of the province and throughout the empire. Kitchener believed that the Ottoman Empire was slowly sliding toward collapse. In his view, the only way Turkey could save itself was through an accommodation with Germany. For their part, the British ought not to aid the Turks so as to foster their eventual demise. He believed that the collapse would begin through an incipient Arab uprising and urged Great Britain to seize the Arab lands in the Middle East as vital to the British security arrangement from Gibraltar to Bombay. Kitchener saw southern Syria as particularly vulnerable and as a potential core, pro-British autonomous state.

From 1911 until the beginning of World War I, Kitchener's views in forming British relations toward the Arabs and the Turks began to eclipse those of the ambassador in Constantinople. In support of his views, it was Kitchener, for instance, who sent T. E. Lawrence and Leonard Woolley on a covert intelligence mission into southern Palestine in September 1913. It was Kitchener, more than any other British figure, who clearly saw the potential of the Hejaz and its Arab watchman of the Muslim holy places, Prince Hussein ibn Ali, toward fostering British advantage in a clash against Germany through a process of "detaching the Arabs from the Turks." British success on the diplomatic front, however, eased tensions vis-à-vis Germany in the short run over issues in the Middle East. British foreign policy, directed by Sir Edward Grey, was reluctant to antagonize German interests by directly supporting an Arab insurgency in the region. But Kitchener continued to maintain an open line with the Arabs in the Hejaz. On February 5, 1914, Hussein's second son, Abdullah, visited Egypt. He met with Kitchener and wondered aloud if Britain would aid Hussein if the Turks were to remove him from power. After much winking and nodding, Kitchener declined to make a firm commitment.

The Germans themselves also received overtures from various Arab factions. Syrian Arabs in particular were sensitive to possible French incursions into the area and sought support from the Germans. For their part, the Germans were anxious to negotiate a favorable settlement with the British over the Baghdad railroad and more pressing concerns in Europe and so avoided any direct support to the Arabs. In April, Kitchener sent Ronald Storrs to visit Abdullah in an effort to maintain contact and reassure Hussein that British diplomatic efforts were pressuring the Young Turks against consolidating their control over the holy places and deposing him as guardian. Despite all the maneuvering, a diplomatic stalemate had emerged in the Middle East by the time the guns sounded the opening round of World War I.

WHEN THE WAR broke out in August, Lawrence was back at Oxford working in the Ashmolean Museum, assisting David Hogarth's archaeological efforts. He immediately tried to enlist and during the initial glut of recruitment was turned down. Perhaps at the suggestion of Hogarth himself, Lawrence went to see Colonel Coote Hedley, who ran the Geographical Section of the General Staff for intelligence in London. He immediately offered Lawrence a commission as second lieutenant of intelligence, where he worked until December completing the Sinai maps he and Woolley had compiled during their strategic reconnaissance of Jordan and southern Palestine. Hedley realized that competent and experienced intelligence officers would be required in the Middle East and recommended Lawrence's appointment to Cairo.

Meanwhile, by September Kitchener was now secretary of state for war. On September 24, he sent the fateful signal to Storrs in Cairo requesting him to determine whether or not Hussein's faction would stand with the British in the event of a war with Turkey. On November 5 the British declared war on Turkey, and on the same day Kitchener received a favorable reply from Hussein. Kitchener immediately replied the next day, stating the British declaration of war was meant in part to preserve Arab sovereignty in a common effort against a common enemy. Hussein, however, tried to maintain the illusion of loyalty to the Turkish regime. The central government in Constantinople was pressing Hussein to join the jihad declared in November against the Christian infidels. Hussein demurred, arguing the rationale for the jihad was absurd given the fact that Turkey was allied to a Christian Germany. Turkish offensive failures against the Suez Canal in the first part of January 1915 placed renewed pressure on Hussein to commit to the fight, as the Turks were now seeking Arab "volunteers" to enlist in the struggle. On March 26, Hussein sent his youngest son, Feisal, to Damascus to assess the tenor of the anti-Turkish Arab factions in the heart of the empire. And again fear of European intervention, especially on the part of the French in Syria, made the question of a united Arab consensus impossible to gauge. When Feisal returned, however, on June 20, 1915, he had confirmed reports of Turkish atrocities in Syria. Despite the urgency in Syria, Feisal advised caution, while Abdullah urged action. Hussein continued to weigh the arguments until the middle of July, when he sent a letter to the high commissioner in Egypt, Henry McMahon, suggesting "joint action" against the Turks in return for British recognition of an independent "Arab nation." The correspondence between the two would continue for several months, almost in parallel with the negotiations that would lead to the famous Sykes-Picot Agreement.

As the various political and strategic machinations unfolded, Lawrence began to settle into his role as intelligence officer in Cairo. Much of his time was devoted to writing detailed "intelligence summaries" for the Intelligence Office. These were wide-ranging assessments of the political and military state of affairs in the war against Turkey collected from numerous, mostly unclassified, sources. Initially he began working for Leonard Woolley, George Lloyd, and

Aubrey Herbert, all of whom worked for Lieutenant-Colonel S. F. Newcombe. Lawrence continued his work and soon gained special expertise and knowledge about the Turkish army that culminated in the publication of a detailed Turkish army handbook. Of the period, Ronald Storrs recalls: "As a colleague [Lawrence's] quickness and instantaneous grasp of essentials was astonishing. 'What does he want?' he would ask as we examined an Arab, or an Arabic document. For what he wanted usually proved to be something very different from the demand expressed." In May 1915, Lawrence was dealt a severe personal shock when he received news that his brother Frank was killed in action in France. And a mere four months later, he suffered the cruelest blow of all. In September his youngest brother, Will, was shot down over the western front. Of all his brothers, Lawrence was closest to Will, whom he virtually helped raise. During Lawrence's many road trips, there was often a lengthy letter for Will offering brotherly advice on the passage from boyhood into manhood. The depth of grief from the two losses can be gauged by how seldom Lawrence mentioned their deaths. Writing to his mother just after Frank was killed, he reminded her of the importance of Victorian stoicism in the face of tragedy: "In a time of such fearful stress in our country it is one's duty to watch very carefully lest one of the weaker ones be offended; and you know we were always stronger, and if they see you broken down they will all grow fearful about their ones at the front." The deaths of his two brothers was a devastating blow he would carry all his life.

The sudden loss of Frank and Will induced a kind of "survivor's guilt" in Lawrence that made him increasingly restless with his relative inactivity in a gilded headquarters and dissatisfied with the general policy toward the Arabs and their role in the war. He wrote home: "We do nothing here except sit and think out harassing schemes of Arabian policy. My hair is getting very thin and gray. . . . I'm going to be in Cairo till I die." He began to desire a more direct and influential role with the operations in the field when he received a mission from an unexpected quarter.

DURING THE SAME month Will was shot down, British forces under General Charles Townsend moved up from Basra toward Baghdad.

Townsend's troops defeated the Turks at Kut-el-Amara. As the forces slogged toward their ultimate objective, they received a serious check at Ctesiphon late in November 1915 and were forced all the way back to Kut. There the Turks began to lay siege to the exhausted British and Indian troops. By March 1916, Townsend's position had become desperate as the bloated and rotting bodies filled the marshes at Kut like a diseased cesspool. It became imperative for the British to negotiate Townsend's surrender to prevent further loss of life. At this point, the long arm of English military bureaucracy reached down and tugged Lawrence by his shoulder straps, sending him to Mesopotamia to help with the surrender. He was sent with a strong endorsement from Henry McMahon as being "one of the best of our very able intelligence staff here and has a thorough knowledge of the Arab question in all its bearings."

In the end, however, the negotiations failed. While the negotiations were under way, the British attempted to "detach" the Arab troops from the Turkish army. This bumbling move proved ineffectual owing to poor planning and failure to develop Arab contacts to the fullest. Furthermore, Arab dislike in the region was less violent than among the nationalists in the Hejaz and in Syria. These futile efforts simply infuriated the Turkish garrison commander so that by April 28, a ransom sum in excess of six million dollars was rejected. The starving British surrendered the following day.

Lawrence termed the disaster "a British disgrace from end to end." When he returned to Cairo the following month, he wrote a searing report condemning every facet of the failed campaign. The scathing document was subsequently lost in the bureaucracy to prevent criticism from falling on the head of General Archibald Murray and others. For Lawrence, the mission provided several crucial lessons in his development as an unconventional leader. In the first place, he learned the importance of unity of command. In the failure there was a political and military fissure between the governments in Egypt and India that produced divided command and action. Second, he discovered the reality that in modern war the civilian population will always suffer when a European power pursues its national interests without regard to the culture and political aspirations of the native populace. In the end, Lawrence saw firsthand the consequences of an arrogance of power wedded to an ignorance of culture. These lessons would help him formulate a truly effective people's war against the Turks.

By the time Lawrence returned to Cairo, much had changed. His boss, Gilbert Clayton, had gone off in February 1916 to start the Arab Bureau in an attempt to develop a strategic intelligence capability working directly for the Foreign Office. The political intrigue continued between the British and Hussein as they tried to craft an understanding that would finally lead to an Arab revolt. On June 10, the revolt began at Mecca when Hussein's ill-armed guerrillas seized the small Turkish garrison after three days of fierce combat. Now the die was cast and only the British knew it was loaded; and Lawrence would soon discover the true nature of the game.

LAWRENCE WAS MORE or less aware that from the very beginning of negotiations with Hussein, the British were pursuing a two-track diplomatic strategy vis-à-vis the Arabs. As mentioned earlier, in 1915 Henry McMahon opened up a correspondence with Hussein almost simultaneously with the broader Sykes-Picot understandings—a series of arrangements between the British and French regarding the political fate of the Middle East following the Great War. The two sets of agreements were congruent on some issues, but on key principles of national interests they were mutually incompatible. McMahon's negotiating position was from a military perspective that viewed Arab support for the war as a more short-term opportunity that might benefit British strategic interests that were also congruent with Arab national aspirations. We can thus speak of a "military" position and a "Foreign Office" stance. The view of Sykes and Picot arose through a lens of realpolitik, where national and colonial interest held sway above all else. These talks were carried out at the highest levels in the European capitals of London, Paris, and St. Petersburg.

Both positions affirmed Arab independence but diverged on matters of implementation. A key difference was the active role France would play in securing its own sphere of influence under the Sykes-Picot accords. McMahon was unclear about the future status of Palestine, whereas Sykes-Picot promised an international mandate and access to ports at Gaza and Haifa. The British would still control the area of Iraq around Basra—and its oil. Although there was much jockeying going on for strategic advantage, in the end the Allies did deliver the Arabs from their Ottoman oppressors, though not in the manner the Arabs had anticipated. Naturally, a sense of betrayal of "what's right" lingers to this day. For Lawrence, the betrayal was real because he had to lie on behalf of British imperial interests; the political betrayal that he was of necessity a party to meant for him also a personal betrayal of his own character, something that would seethe within him until the very end of his life and have profound psychological implications as leader.

Hussein, meanwhile, was in negotiations with the Turks all the time he was bartering with the British. In the end, simple horse sense demanded that he back the Allied cause as the most likely to deliver Arab freedom. Hussein's broad ambition as Hashemite hegemon of a grand coalition of Arabia and Syria drove those around him to high hopes and aspirations. Though he dealt directly with McMahon, Hussein had no input or knowledge of the Sykes-Picot Agreement, which was signed in May 1916 even before the Arab Revolt began. McMahon himself was unaware of the agreement until a year later. Clearly, each side was betting on the other to fulfill the better part of the promises secured. By 1916, after British defeats at Gallipoli and Kut and the Arab failure to revolt up to that point, mere promises were all the negotiating sides could manage to wager. Only the dice of war could determine whether the bet had been a calculated risk or a dangerous gamble. In the end, both partners won—sort of.

BY THE TIME the revolt began, Lawrence was back from Mesopotamia to the mundane matters of intelligence work in Cairo. He suggested that the weekly intelligence summaries should be published with actual documents in a classified version that became known as *The Arab Bulletin*. Lawrence himself contributed several pieces to the journal, which was edited by David Hogarth until the end of the war. The *Bulletin* also provided a fairly accurate account of the war in the Hejaz desert.

After its initial blush of success, the revolt began to stagnate into a stalemate through the summer and into the fall of 1916. Lawrence looked on with a mixture of anxiety and frustration. At the same time, his position in Cairo intelligence became more and more untenable as Lawrence's strategic views and interests clashed with the more myopic outlook of tacticians such as G. W. V. Holdich, new head of military intelligence. Holdich's views toward the Arabs were a reflection of those of his military chief in Egypt, Sir Archibald Murray, who saw little military advantage in supporting the seemingly unreliable Arabs. What Holdich confronted was in fact a kind of pro-Arab cabal of officers—based mainly in Cairo intelligence—who began "to see that a new factor was needed in the [Middle] East, some power or race which would outweigh the Turks in numbers, in output, and in mental activity." Lawrence was one of the key leaders among this group of intelligence officers. He wrote, "Some of us judged that there was latent power enough and to spare in the Arabic peoples . . . , a prolific Semitic agglomeration, great in religious thought, reasonably industrious, mercantile, politic, yet solvent rather than dominant in character." After five hundred years under the Turkish yoke, they burned for freedom and independence. The war with Turkey now offered the Arabs the chance to seize liberty with their own hands.

Of all his contemporaries, Eric Kennington, the sculptor and artist, captured best the visage of T. E. Lawrence during this period in its timeless essence, immutable to place and circumstance: "He moved little, using bodily presence just sufficiently to make brain contact. I had never seen so little employment or wastage of physical energy. The wide mouth smiled often, with humor and pleasure, sometimes extending to an unusual upward curve at the corners, a curious menacing curve, warning of danger. . . . The face was almost lineless, and removed from me as a picture or a sculpture. However gracious its attitude, it remained distant." Almost Buddha-like, someone once said: serene, placid yet keenly aware. "The eyes roamed around, above, and might rest on mine or rather travel through mine, but never shared my thoughts, though noting them all. He stayed higher on another plane of life. It was easy to become his slave." The Arab insurgents would soon be under the thrall of his "crystal eyes" gazing with a kind of primitive, almost animal presence, "yet with a complete understanding. And at moments of thought, when he would ignore the presence of others, retiring into himself, they would diverge slightly. Then, he was alone, and as inscrutable as a lion or a snake. He would return, and graciously attend to one with limitless patience, dealing with our slower brains and limited understanding, our hesitations and fears, apparently never exasperated by our insufficiency."

Another observer said, "He always seemed to be looking from under a tent." Looking with those magnetic blue eyes that poet Robert Graves thought were maternal. Lawrence recounts a story of meeting an old Arab woman during his early travels through the Levant. She stares into his eyes with a mixture of fear and awe; she says his eyes remind her of the blue desert sky. With a flash of hesitation she adds: a blue sky seen through the eye sockets of a skull.

The eyes were set in the face of a boxer: that was Kennington's assessment. Perhaps reflective of Lawrence's Irish roots: "Though not broad he was weighty from shoulders to neck, which jutted, giving a forward placing of the head, and a thrust to the heavy chin." Thus the contrast: sensitive yet fearless eyes shielded by a pugilist's bones. "It was the face of a heavyweight boxer, and in all circumstances, dynamic. Above and around and behind this fighting machine was a full development of brain, deep from back to front, and more high than broad." Kennington "was puzzled how the head could be at once so strong and so sensitive." Lawrence stood up and the sculptor thought: "Boxer's face, and tightrope athlete's body." Foreshadowing the fighter Muhammad Ali, Kennington observed: "He stands as if floating—like a fish." Or perhaps a butterfly?

In October 1916, Lawrence learned that Storrs was going to the Hejaz to confer with Hussein and applied for ten days' leave to tag along. Clayton approved. On October 12, Lawrence wrote with characteristic understatement: "I am going off tomorrow for a few days. I hope to be back in about a fortnight or less." And so began Lawrence's adventure of a lifetime.

WHEN THE ARAB REVOLT erupted in June 1916, the Turks had one clear, key end in mind: For political and especially religious reasons, Mecca, as the navel of the Muslim world, had to be held at all costs. The sultan of Ottoman Turkey was also, as caliph, the spiritual leader of Islam—a role unique in the political leadership of the day. When Sherif Hussein's irregular forces seized Mecca on June 13, the Turks were quick to respond. This response was, however, shaped and influenced by several geographic considerations that Lawrence would soon exploit.

The railroad system of the region, conceived of as a large "T," formed the chessboard that would define the operations throughout the theater. The horizontal rail line ran from Baghdad westward through Mosul and Aleppo to Istanbul; sections of the twelve-hundred-mile line were in various stages of completion, so the line was not totally continuous along the east-west axis. (See map.) The thousand-mile vertical line ran south from Aleppo through Damascus, Deraa, and Maan, culminating in the holy city of Medina. Mecca lay 250 miles farther to the south across fairly rugged terrain without any rail connection.

The Arab forces initially tried the same methods at Medina that had eventually proved successful at Mecca. They had not considered, however, the signal advantage the railroad gave the Turkish army, which quickly reinforced the Medina garrison. With these reinforcements, the Turks pushed the Arabs fifty miles to the southwest into the hills, where they took up defensive positions astride the main road into Mecca. Here, mutually exhausted, both sides dug in as the Turks contemplated their next move.

Within a few short months, the railroad gave the Turkish army under Fakhri Pasha the means to establish a large expeditionary corps of about ten thousand men at Medina. Another twenty-five hundred secured the railway running to the north, and twelve hundred men garrisoned the Red Sea port of Wejh. By October, Hussein's Arab forces had coalesced into three main operational groupings under his sons: five thousand under Ali stationed at the key harbor of Rabegh; nearly four thousand under Abdullah at Mecca; and seven thousand under Feisal at the port of Yenbo, aimed to strike at the long rail line off to the east. On October 19, when the Turks renewed their advance, it was clear to all that the tiny port of Rabegh had become the linchpin to the defense of Mecca.

British logistical blood flowed from Egypt and something even more precious: gold. Two English pounds sterling bought a man and a rifle, four more bought a camel. Here it is important to point out that—contrary to Hollywood depictions—90 percent of the Arab forces fought on foot. The port at Rabegh had to be held at all costs.

Furthermore, it was the most defensible piece of terrain north of Mecca, where the flat bowling-ball landscape invited a direct Turkish attack. Finally, the road down from Medina went through Rabegh, becoming a natural line of communications for the Turks' advance to Mecca.

Lawrence and Storrs arrived at Jidda aboard the *Lama* on October 16, three days before the Turks launched their long-awaited offensive. The most memorable recollection of Lawrence's arrival was the heat: "Then the heat of Arabia came out like a drawn sword and struck us speechless."[1] The streets of Jidda were a shimmering dazzle of black shadow and white light. Walking through the town market, they watched as clouds of flies sortied back and forth between the meat and the dates. Lawrence idly noticed that Storrs's white uniform had been stained red where he had sat in the old leather armchair aboard the *Lama*. Now he appeared like a rhesus monkey in search of jungle shade.

The pair at length reached the local consulate and were greeted by Lieutenant-Colonel C. E. Wilson, lately dispatched by General Charles Wingate from the Red Sea Province of the Sudan. Wilson had arranged the meeting with Abdullah that was about to take place. The Arabs regarded Abdullah as a visionary statesman and a shrewd politician, the intellectual father of the Arab Revolt. In truth, he had initiated the revolt only so his family could control it and gain the fruits of its success. Abdullah arrived on a white mare with a covey of heavily armed slaves, full of himself after his recent victory at Taif. Although Lawrence had never laid eyes on him before, Abdullah readily treated Storrs as the old friend he had become. Lawrence immediately saw through the garrulous facade and the affective wrappings of feigned cheerfulness, wondering if this could be the true leader of the revolt: "The Sherif's rebellion had been unsatisfactory for the last few months: standing still, which, with an irregular war, was the prelude to disaster: and my suspicion was that its lack was leadership: not intellect, nor judgment, nor political wisdom, but the flame of enthusiasm, that would set the desert on fire. My visit was mainly to find the yet unknown master-spirit of the affair, and measure his capacity to carry the revolt to the goal I had conceived for it."[2] Lawrence's assessment was that Abdullah had been the immediate source of ignition, but he was too politic, too at ease with himself with the work he had already done, to become the true and enduring flame of the rebellion. His role would be important but not crucial. That leader had yet to be identified.

FOLLOWING THE FORMALITIES of introduction, discussion turned to matters of civil administration of which Abdullah and his Bedouin were wholly innocent. The populace in Medina and Mecca were cosmopolitan and urbane, mostly Egyptians, Indians, Africans, and other foreigners unsympathetic to the Arab cause. The commercial townsmen had always seen the Bedouin as an economic threat encountered only along the dark byways of the desert. Now they were ensconced in the heart of the city as liberators and tax collectors dispensing the newly found largesse to the countryside. Civil law became another matter of contention when Abdullah abolished the secular Turkish code and replaced it with sharia religious law, which benefited the Bedouins over the townsmen.

After further discourse, the topic of conversation turned to military affairs. Abdullah wondered what the two men thought of the idea of readying a British brigade of Muslims to reinforce, on call, the Arab position at Rabegh. Lawrence presented the military complications of such a requirement. First, there were no Muslim units in the British Army; second, naval shipping was rare, and empty hulls could not be held indefinitely back in Egypt. Besides, the alternative, a British brigade, was a clumsy tactical unit for the kind of guerrilla war being fought against the Turks; it would take too long to embark and disembark to be agile at the moment of crisis. The position at Rabegh was too large for a lonely brigade to defend in any case. At best the infantry would be able to defend a stretch of beach under the guns of its naval force. Abdullah replied that the allocation need only be temporary, as Arab strength was rapidly being mobilized. Lawrence made a further argument that British troops were immediately needed for the defense of the canal. Moreover, the use of Christian troops to support an Arab, though Muslim, cause might raise some questions among the Islamic world. In any case, Lawrence would present Abdullah's views fairly to general headquarters back in Egypt.

Then there was a brief pause: Lawrence wondered aloud if his arguments would be stronger if he could see the Arab situation himself, meet with Feisal—Abdullah's youngest brother—and report back with firsthand knowledge of the revolt. An imperceptible shadow of suspicion crossed the prince's bearded visage. He was about to nix the idea when Storrs suddenly jumped into the conversation with his full support of the notion. He told Abdullah the importance of getting full and timely information back to Murray as soon as possible. And for Murray to detail one of his best staff officers in the person of Lawrence would also signal to the Arabs the seriousness of British support for the whole effort. Abdullah, at last convinced, phoned his father, Hussein, for permission to send Lawrence up to Rabegh and Feisal's camp in Jebel Subh. Hussein had grave misgivings over the offer. At length, Abdullah handed the phone to Storrs, and here he proved his value a hundred times over. His natural charm and deep understanding of Arab culture transformed the old sherif so thoroughly that by the end of the conversation, Hussein presented the idea back to Abdullah as his own. The next morning, Lawrence left by boat for Rabegh.

LAWRENCE ARRIVED ABOARD the *Northbrook*. Hussein's eldest son, Ali, was not pleased to see him, but his father's orders were explicit: Help Lawrence get to Feisal by all means. Ali would have protested, but the only method of wireless communication was through the *Northbrook*. Since Ali could not bear to share openly a familial grievance with a foreigner, he complied. Lawrence found Ali more convivial than his middle brother, Abdullah. Ali "was of middle height, thin, and looking already more than his thirty-seven years. He stooped a little. His skin was sallow, his eyes large and deep and brown, his nose thin and rather hooked, his mouth sad and drooping. He had a spare black beard and very delicate hands. His manner was dignified and admirable, but direct; and he struck me as a pleasant gentleman, conscientious, without great force of character, nervous, and rather tired." He was also afflicted with tuberculosis. "His physical weakness . . . made him subject to quick fits of shaking passion, preceded and followed by long moods of infirm obstinacy. He was bookish, learned in law and religion, and pious almost to fanaticism."[3] Lawrence deemed him too detached and with too much integrity to be ambitious. He was therefore prone to manipulation in an effort to be all things to all men. At all events, if Feisal proved less the leader than Lawrence hoped, the revolt would be better served with Ali at its head than Abdullah. Ali was assisted by his half-brother, Zeid, who was only nineteen. His mother was Turkish, and he had been brought up in the harem with little love for the Arab cause. Though Zeid was even less a leader than Abdullah, Lawrence saw potential that could be exploited later as the boy matured under the proper tutelage of a real commander.

Ali kept Lawrence's departure a secret lest any of his followers see him leave. He left in the evening with two guides named Tafas and Abdullah. They traveled at a leisurely pace through the cool desert air. During the journey, Tafas pointed out three watering sites. Tactically this meant that the Turks could safely bypass Rabegh altogether simply by using the three wells in easy stages. Moreover, it meant that the requested British brigade would have had to extend its tactical reach twenty miles inland to block the maneuver.

The long ride was taxing to Lawrence, who had been deskbound for over two years in Cairo, "thinking hard in a little overcrowded office full of distracting noises, with a hundred rushing things to say, but no bodily need except to come and go each day between office and hotel. In consequence the novelty of this change was severe, since time had not been given me gradually to accustom myself to the pestilent beating of the Arabian sun, and the long monotony of camel pacing."[4] After more riding, the group finally reached Hamra and Feisal's headquarters in Wadi Safra.

Lawrence was brought immediately in to see Feisal, the younger of the sherif of Mecca's three Arab sons, after Ali and Abdullah. Lawrence "felt at first glance that this was the man I had come to Arabia to seek—the leader who would bring the Arab Revolt to full glory. Feisal looked very tall and pillar-like, very slender, in his white silk robes and his brown head-cloth bound with a brilliant scarlet and gold cord. His eyelids were dropped; and his black beard and colorless face were like a mask against the strange, still watchfulness of his body. His hands were crossed in front of him on his dagger." Lawrence greeted the leader and sat down on Feisal's carpet close to the door. Feisal seemed a bit diffident, gently caressing his dagger. At last he asked Lawrence of his journey. He mentioned the heat and the intensity of the pace. More silence.

"And do you like our place here in Wadi Safra?" Feisal asked finally.

"Well; but it is far from Damascus." Lawrence's reply was a veiled challenge to Feisal and his retainers. The word *Damascus* "had fallen like a sword in their midst." The word created a shiver among them, for Damascus was the great ancient seat of Arab power. "Then everybody present stiffened where he sat, and held his breath for a silent minute. Some, perhaps, were dreaming of far off success: others may have thought it a reflection on their late defeat."

At length Feisal raised his eyes and smiled at Lawrence, saying, "Praise be to Allah, there are Turks nearer us than that."[5] Feisal had deftly turned Lawrence's barb.

THE NEXT FEW days Lawrence spent with Feisal reviewing the state of the Arab Revolt since its inception. The first heady days of success at Medina were stanched by the raging realities of Turkish artillery. Demoralization ensued as the Turks began to play the cards of total war, trumping the rebellion with village massacres, rapine, and butchery. This brutal game, which had violated every rule of war known to the Arabs, had sent a powerful shock through them. Their first principle held that women were sacred; second, that children and those unable to protect themselves were inviolable; finally, booty impossible to carry away should be left untouched. All these were violated by the Turks. The turning point was at Awali, a quiet suburb of Medina where all the Turkish savagery was released to the fullest. Awali created the blood feud of all blood feuds against the Turks.

Lieutenant-Colonel C. E. Wilson brought money and reinforcements, but these were only the splinters of a cracking British defense: Egyptian gunners from Sudan with outmoded mountain guns that were unable to range the more powerful German-supplied pieces that the Turks fielded. By August, the whole fight had fallen upon Feisal as Abdullah demurred in Mecca and Ali and Zeid delayed at Rabegh. To preserve the remnants of his force, Feisal withdrew to Hamra, leaving a few detachments to harry the enemy supply lines. The Arabs were unwilling to advance under the Turkish guns, and the Turks were unable to advance beyond their encampments. The fight had degenerated into a duel of the vilest of epithets: the Turks calling the Arabs "English" and the Arabs calling the Turks "German."

In the midst of the discussions, Lawrence asked Feisal for his assessment. It was his considered judgment that the Turks under Fakhri Pasha at Medina would try to seize Mecca over two hundred miles to the south. As long as the Turks held Medina, they could drive on Mecca by way of several routes and so would hold the initiative. Feisal would thus be forced to dance at the end of a long Turkish string. Fakhri had now reorganized the bulk of his troops into a mobile center of gravity, a maneuver force that could advance on Rabegh by several avenues. The only Arab advantage was the certainty that the impending Turkish movement would have to advance near Rabegh because that land held the vital source of water.

From these considerations emerged Feisal's campaign design that was preemptive in its essence. He would withdraw even farther west from Hamra to Yenbo near the heart of the mighty Juheina tribe. With fresh reinforcements from the tribe, he would strike at the rail line supplying Medina. Abdullah would attack Medina from the east; Ali would strike from Rabegh in close cooperation with Zeid moving into Wadi Safra. The two would fix the large Turkish force at Bir Abbas. The three-sided assault would preempt the impending enemy advance toward Mecca and give the Arabs near that city time to strengthen their defenses.

The detailed and lengthy discussions of operational art and tactics seemed to offer Feisal renewed hope. The talks with Lawrence brought things to the surface, where he could see new potential, possibilities, and opportunities. Where Feisal had appeared exhausted when Lawrence first arrived, he now appeared merely "dead-tired. He looked years older than thirty-three; and his dark, appealing eyes, set a little sloping in his face, were bloodshot, and his hollow cheeks deeply lined and puckered with reflection. His nature grudged thinking, for it crippled his speed in action; the labor of it shriveled his features into swift lines of pain. In appearance he was tall, graceful and vigorous, with the most beautiful gait, and a royal dignity of head and shoulders. Of course he knew it, and a great part of his public expression was by sign and gesture."

Lawrence perceived many levels of Feisal's complex style of leadership: the political chief, the operational commander, the tactical leader. The complexity seemed rooted to a kind of duality of character: fiery yet sensitive, apparently frail yet courageous, proud yet humble, imprudent yet tolerant, self-absorbed yet empathetic. "He was a careful judge of men. If he had the strength to realize his dreams he would go far, for he was wrapped up in his work and lived for nothing else; but the fear was that he would wear himself out by trying to seem to aim always a little higher than the truth, or that he would die of too much action." Perhaps Lawrence could become the governor to that action and modulate it, ease the burden of command, sharpen the focus of thought. It thus seemed to Lawrence, at the long end of his journey, that he had found "a prophet who, if veiled, would give cogent form to the idea behind the activity of the Arab revolt. It was all and more than we had hoped for, much more than our halting course deserved. The aim of my trip was fulfilled."[6]

BY THE FALL of 1916, Great Britain and its allies were reaching strategic collapse. The Germans had embarked on a strategy of exhaustion, hoping to bleed its enemies white through a bombing assault meant to terrorize civilians, a relentless U-boat campaign, and a grinding war on land. Zeppelins began bombing London in January that year; the attacks would continue throughout the war. The U-boat campaign was initially successful, but poor world opinion forced the Germans to end the sinkings by the middle of the year. British and French ground losses in France were horrific: the battle of the Somme and the meat grinder at Verdun had destroyed the best troops the Allies had. Britain was forced to conscription, and the French army was on the verge of mutiny. In Russia, General Alexei A. Brusilov's offensive would run out of steam by September 20. Meanwhile, unrest in Ireland was moving toward open insurrection. Hordes of Senussi guerrillas were making incursions from Libya into western Egypt. In the Middle East, the British were still recovering from the twin debacles at Gallipoli and Kut. Now the Arabs were requesting a brigade of infantry at the worst possible moment: the strategic cupboard was bare.

At the same time, there was a larger division of geostrategic views toward the entire war in the Middle East. The "Westerners" included

General Murray himself, along with Major-General Sir Arthur Lynden-Bell, Murray's chief of staff and his chief intelligence officer, Lieutenant-Colonel G. W. V. Holdich. Their views reflected the views of the War Office, which believed that the world war could be decided only on the western front in the meat grinder of France. Their position was supported by the India Office, which saw meddling in Muslim affairs in the Middle East as likely to have a serious backlash among the millions of Muslims who lived in India, the "crown jewel" of the British Empire. Their world outlook was conservative, narrow, and opportunistic. The "Easterners" included Lawrence, Sir Henry McMahon, Storrs, Clayton, Wingate, Wilson, in time Admiral Wemyss, the Foreign Office, and a resurgent David Lloyd George, the new prime minister: all believed that since Turkey was the weakest of the enemy powers, its collapse would create a dominolike effect and produce the eventual overthrow of Germany and Austria-Hungary. Their larger collective worldview could be best described as "messianic imperialism," which saw as Great Britain's holy mission the assumption of the "white man's burden," civilizing and Christianizing the pagan world.

The larger strategic considerations had little effect on Lawrence as he sought to find the mainspring of the Arab Revolt. He continued to reside in Feisal's camp, gauging the measure of the man who now seemed to be emerging as the leader he had been seeking. Lawrence engaged Feisal in innumerable conversations, watching him chain-smoke through lengthy discussions, with the logic of his arguments stacking up at the same regularity as the piles of his cigarette ends. He was a master of the oral tradition, and this seemed to be the source of his thrall over the people. His mastery over his followers was natural and unaffected, and he seemed little concerned whether or not they followed him. He was a born leader and led out of love rather than through the power of physical strength or force of personality.

Lawrence also studied Feisal's method of leadership in defeat. He was most accessible to his troops in defeat when their spirits were darkest. He gave of himself in ways that encouraged his men. In this he displayed the utmost patience and understanding that seemed to make no battlefield sense. But Lawrence soon realized that Feisal was not only leading an army, he was leading an entire community, and his leadership therefore required the most inclusive and embracing form. As a community leader, he was able to demonstrate extreme self-control, personal abnegation, and humility. Lawrence recalled that "Feisal, in speaking, had a rich musical voice, and used it carefully upon his men. To them he talked in tribal dialect, but with a curious, hesitant manner, as though faltering painfully among the phrases, looking inward for the just word. His thought, perhaps, moved only by a little in front of his speech, for the phrases at last chosen were usually the simplest, which gave an effect emotional and sincere. It seemed possible, so thin was the screen of words, to see the pure and the very brave spirit shining out. At other times he was full of humor—that invariable magnet of Arab goodwill."[7]

Feisal's camp reflected his simple yet effective style of leadership. Near daybreak the army chaplain, the imam, would rise to a nearby hill and offer his call to prayer as a kind of reveille. Feisal's five slaves would attend their master with sweetened coffee. However, these were slaves in name only. He had freed them long ago, but out of respect for Feisal they had remained in his service. An hour or so after he had risen, his tent flap was thrown open as an invitation to his household staff to begin the morning routine, which opened with breakfast and news of the day. After breakfast, sweetened tea was offered between rounds of unsweetened coffee. Feisal usually spent the morning dictating letters to his personal secretaries. Occasionally the routine was interrupted by a private audience. By nine in the morning, Feisal would strap on his ceremonial dagger and repair to the reception tent, where he would greet the waiting supplicants who bore this or that grievance for judgment. At noon, Feisal took a light lunch. His heavy cigarette smoking no doubt contributed to his slim appetite. Many of his heavier acquaintances often ate before having lunch with him, knowing his meals would be quick and sparse. After lunch, his visitors would spend some time in idle conversation, sipping glasses full of a syrupy green tea. Feisal would then go into seclusion for an hour or so to sleep, read, pray, or attend to personal matters. By midafternoon, he would return to the reception tent and finish his audience.

After a second audience, if time permitted, Feisal would stroll with his friends to discuss the events of the day and other mundane matters. Sunset prayer was generally a public affair, and although he wasn't particularly religious, Feisal was a deeply spiritual man who saw the divine reflected in all things. It was only after the evening prayer that he would turn to military matters, since most reconnaissance took place after dark. While in the field, of course, his schedule was much different, with time spent on community issues in inverse proportion to the routine when he was in camp. The evening meal was more of a lunch, again reflecting his spartan existence and fondness for cigarettes. The meal, around eight or nine o'clock, completed the day, with time spent in relaxation and perhaps idle diversions like storytelling or chess. Feisal was an excellent chess player and seldom beaten. His tactical acumen at the game board was well reflected in the field of operations.

It was during one of these early visits with Feisal that Lawrence decided to don Arab dress. It was at the request of Feisal himself, who felt that Lawrence would be less obtrusive in camp if he dressed as a native. Only the Turks wore khaki, and Feisal was getting tired of explaining Lawrence's presence to all and sundry day after day. Lawrence was happy to comply and found the garb much more comfortable and practical in the hot desert atop a galloping camel. He was given a brilliant white-and-gold embroidered silk wedding gown, a bequest from Feisal's great-aunt. Feisal also gave him a splendid bay camel for his travels around the battlefields. From a distance, Lawrence was now taking on the guise of a real Arab fighter.

WHILE LAWRENCE WAS thus engaged with Feisal, pressure was also being placed upon British strategic interests by the French. France had large numbers of Muslims in its empire and saw Hussein's success as a way to reopen the pilgrimage to Mecca for French Muslim subjects, not to mention the opportunity it offered to meddle in British affairs to serve France's own aims. To that end, Lieutenant-Colonel Eduard Brémond, an accomplished Arab scholar, was put in charge of a military mission. The mission reached Alexandria on September 1 and soon arrived at Jidda. With the French came pilgrims and money, over 1.25 million gold francs, as well as offers for military support. The pilgrims headed for Mecca, where they were warmly received by their Arab co-religionists. However, Hussein was wary of their political influence, especially the French presence in Syria, where he had aspirations of his own. It was clear to Brémond and others that these differences could never be easily reconciled. In the short term, the British were willing to turn the French presence in the region to their advantage by requesting immediate French assistance. The French, however, were completely unprepared to send any significant troops to the Hejaz, at least until November, but to compensate for their own unpreparedness they too clamored for a British brigade at Rabegh.

When Lawrence landed at Jidda in October, the Turks had still not moved against Mecca, but as each day wore on, they were growing stronger. The Turks under Fakhri Pasha had more than made up for their early losses. At Medina they still had ten thousand troops, with a further twelve hundred guarding the northern railway and twelve hundred occupying the port at Wejh. Arab forces were still deployed in three main groupings: a force of five thousand raiders under Ali near Rabegh, four thousand men with Abdullah hard by Mecca, and the largest segment under Feisal raiding the railway out of Yenbo. Three days after Lawrence and Storrs landed, Feisal was driven back from Bir Abbas to Hamra, where Lawrence eventually joined him and conducted his assessment.

By November 1, Lawrence was ready to return to Cairo to report to Clayton. He traveled by camel as far as Yenbo and then received passage to Jidda, where he linked up with Admiral Wemyss. The two of them took a detour across the Red Sea to Port Sudan and then to Khartoum, where they both offered Wingate their appreciation of the situation. In Lawrence's view, British troops were unnecessary because he believed the Arabs under Feisal's leadership could hold off the Turks with British naval support. Whereas Murray and Robertson had little faith in the success of the revolt and therefore viewed the expenditure of British troops a waste of good men, Lawrence saw great opportunity. He also saw bringing British units into the region as an unnecessary complication on religious and political grounds, given increasing French interest.

Upon his return to Cairo, Lawrence made the same recommendation opposing the deployment of British troops to Rabegh that he had at Khartoum in conversations with Wingate. What the Arabs needed was strong artillery reinforcements, for their effect on Arab morale was as great as their tactical contribution. For months, Feisal had been asking for guns, but to no avail. Lawrence believed that Feisal's army could defend itself in the hilly terrain between Medina and Mecca as long as they had sufficient artillery and machine guns. British troops, on the other hand, would have been greeted with deep suspicion and bias, undermining any solidarity that might exist between the two allies. Tactically, the British troops were too cumbersome for mobile operations in desert terrain. Lawrence was all the more adamant when he discovered Brémond—who saw Hussein's reliance on Allied troops as a way to leverage the Arabs into greater subservience—urging the dispatch of troops. The essential consideration as far as Lawrence was concerned was that the Arabs had to be seen in their struggle for liberty as succeeding through their own independent efforts, cohesion, and strength of will. Nothing less could guarantee the achievement or its recognition before the whole world.

MEANTIME, THE TURKS began to intensify their information campaign. Back in August, they had stripped Hussein of his title as emir of Mecca and bestowed it on Ali Haidar. The intention was to bring Haidar with the Turkish advance from Medina and install him once Mecca was seized. The move was also meant to delegitimize Hussein and the entire Arab cause. By December, Turkish propaganda leaflets spoke of the impending arrival of whole Turkish divisions from Europe sent to recapture the holy city, and with Ali Haidar, the Arabs would be brought back to the path of righteousness.

In early December, Lawrence returned from Cairo to the Hejaz with official sanction to cooperate with the Arabs. He appeared unexpectedly at Yenbo, where new operational developments began to unfold. For the past six weeks, the Turks had been unable to break through the Arab hill defenses to the southwest of Medina. Hussein began to consider a strategy that would break the deadlock and allow the Arabs to seize the initiative through offensive action. A plan was developed that would extend military operations 180 miles north to the small port of Wejh in the Turkish rear. The port was also within raiding range of the Hejaz rail line. Severing the line would cut off

Medina from Syria and force the Turks to dispatch more troops from the Medina front to secure the now vulnerable railway.

The plan started off well but soon collapsed after the initial moves out of Yenbo were outflanked by advancing Turkish troops. Lawrence joined Feisal at Nakhl Mubarak and remained there for a few nights until he began to realize the potential threat to Yenbo. The Turks resumed their attack shortly after Lawrence left and routed Feisal's entire force, which fled to Yenbo, arriving there on December 9. The collapse of the Arab advance now had the makings of a complete disaster. On his own initiative, Lawrence began to organize defenses at Yenbo for a Turkish attack he was certain would come. In his efforts to organize the defenses, he received considerable aid from naval captain W. H. D. "Ginger" Boyle aboard the HMS *Suva,* which, along with four other warships, had just landed a convoy of supplies to help support the new offensive and to enlarge the port into a more effective base of operations. By December 10, Boyle and Lawrence had managed to deploy the ships in such dominating positions that the Turks called off the impending attack.

THE CRISIS AT Yenbo raised yet again the question concerning the need for British reinforcements, perhaps a brigade. For a brief time, even Lawrence and Feisal believed the day had finally arrived for the employment of British troops. As the crisis swiftly passed, they changed their minds for good. In a final definitive argument, Lawrence asserted that in the first place, even if troops were available— which was not likely under the circumstances then prevailing in Egypt—they would not reach Rabegh in time to matter. Second, even if a brigade was at hand, it was unclear the force could hold out against a determined corps-sized Turkish assault. Third, there was always the possibility that the enemy could simply bypass the entire position and make a dash directly for Mecca. Finally, and for Lawrence the most decisive argument, there was the potential presence of British troops in the theater. To the Arab rebels, the intervention of British forces—or any foreign units, for that matter—would mean a sellout of the whole revolt and the possible abandonment of the Arab cause. But against this volatile strategic backdrop, Wingate, largely on behalf of the Foreign Office, finally agreed to issue Hussein an ultimatum requesting that he decide definitively on use of the troops. While Hussein was thus considering his alternatives, the situation changed dramatically again.

On December 16, the Turks began a general evacuation from Yenbo; two days later, they withdrew from Nakhl Mubarak. These movements were swiftly followed up by Feisal's reorganized forces. Apparently, the Turks believed that Ali, who had left Rabegh some days earlier, was attempting an envelopment near Bir Abbas and threatening their lines of communications with Medina. The operation collapsed, however, when Ali for unknown reasons decided to return to Rabegh. By December 22, it was clear that Fakhri Pasha was reorganizing his forces. The signal question was whether he was reorganizing for a withdrawal or redeploying for another attempt at Rabegh.

While the Arab camps seethed with rumor and as they waited for the operational situation to clarify, the maneuver to Wejh was reconsidered, now as a way to spread the revolt to the northern Hejaz. Under the original formulation, Feisal had not intended to move north with his main body until the defenses southwest of Medina had been completely solidified. But time was slipping away: the Arabs had to act before the Turks. At this moment of decision, Lawrence reconsidered his options. He found it curious that the Turks had hesitated to rush the Arab positions at Rabegh after the enemy had made such successful gains against the port in late October. Why did the Turks waver? It occurred to Lawrence "that perhaps the virtue of irregulars lay in depth, not in face, and that it had been the threat of the attack by them upon the Turkish northern flank which had made the enemy hesitate so long. The actual Turkish flank ran from their front line [at Rabegh, their 'face' in Lawrence's words] to Medina, a distance of some fifty miles: but, if we moved towards the Hejaz railway behind Medina, we might stretch our threat (and, accordingly, their flank) as far, potentially, as Damascus, eight hundred miles away to the north. Such a move would force the Turks to the defensive, and we might regain the initiative."

Under the revised plan for the attack on Wejh, Lawrence also found a new way to disrupt the Hejaz railway closer to Medina. Up until that time, Abdullah had been located northeast of Medina, a position poorly chosen because the Turks found the line readily defensible from that direction. Lawrence expressed his dissatisfaction to Feisal, who recalled the existence of an old wadi north of Yenbo that directly bisected the railway like a dagger from the sea. This was Wadi Ais, where Abdullah was now charged to move and set up a new base. The wadi easily covered all movement against the track. Under the plan, the two Arab armies would now be able to dominate two hundred miles of the Hejaz railway.

On January 2, 1917, Lawrence conducted his first combat mission riding out with a patrol, scouting the location of the withdrawing Turkish forces. The raid was generally uneventful but auspicious, as the party captured two Turkish prisoners. On his return to camp, Lawrence reflected on the transformation of Feisal's men since he'd first met them three months earlier. "They were quiet but confident. Some who had been serving with Feisal for six months or more, had lost that pristine heat of eagerness which had so much thrilled me at Hamra; but they had gained experience in compensation; and staying-power in the ideal was fatter and more important for us than an early fierceness." At the same time, Lawrence noticed another change: "Their patriotism was now conscious; and their attendance grew more regular as the distance from their homes increased. . . . When the Sherif came near they fell into a ragged line, and together made the bow and sweep of the arm to the lips, which was the official salute. They did not oil their guns: they said lest the sand clog them; also they had no oil . . . but the guns were decently kept, and some of the owners could shoot at long range."

Tactically, the units were also gaining effectiveness as they gained experience. Lawrence mused, "In mass they were not formidable, since they had no corporate spirit, nor discipline nor mutual confidence. The smaller the unit the better its performance. A thousand were a mob, ineffective against a company of trained Turks: but three or four Arabs in the hills would stop a dozen Turks. . . . We were yet too breathless to turn our hasty practice into principle: our tactics were empirical snatchings of the first means to escape difficulty. But we were learning like our men."[8]

If Lawrence was learning, he was also teaching. A key attribute of his great leadership was his ability to be a powerful teacher. He had humility and tolerance as a leader, but as a great teacher he had empathy: he could sense the ignorance and even the stupidity of his pupils as if it were his own and then share in the joy of mutual illumination, as if seeing the world with new eyes in childlike wonderment.

And Lawrence continued his education in the leadership arts. He learned that the customary Western military style of leadership did not and could not work among the Arabs. The traditional cleavage between officer and enlisted man made no sense in a tribal culture and warrior tradition. "To have privacy . . . was ten thousand times more restful than the open life, but the work suffered by the creation of such a bar between the leaders and men. Among the Arabs there were no distinctions, traditional or natural, except the unconscious power given a famous sheikh by virtue of his accomplishment; and they taught me that no man could be their leader except he ate the ranks' food, wore their clothes, lived level with them and yet appeared better in himself."[9]

AND SO IT came to pass that in the middle of January 1917, the bulk of the Arab army prepared to slip away from Rabegh and steal by stages behind the coastal hills to Bir Waheidi, halfway to the port of Wejh still a hundred distant miles to the north. The army also had to reorganize itself to better cooperate with the British Royal Navy. Feisal's force now included some fifty-one hundred camelry and fifty-three hundred infantry: a large force to cover two hundred miles of desert. It was necessary that the Royal Navy transport the baggage and, especially, water along the sea flank of the Arab land march. Even with the additional sea beasts of burden, Feisal needed 380 camels to haul his baggage and other "ash and trash."

On January 18, all was readied. Lawrence recounts the march-out of the insurgent army: "After lunch the tent was struck. We went to our camels, where they crouched in a circle, saddled and loaded, each held short by the slave standing on its doubled fore-leg. The kettle-drummer, waiting beside 'Ibn Dakhil, who commanded the bodyguard, rolled his drum seven or eight times, and everything became still. We watched Feisal. He got up from his rug . . . caught the saddle-pommels in his hands, put his knee on the side and shouted: '*Make Allah your agent!*' The slave released the camel, which sprang up. . . . As his camel moved we had jumped for ours, and the whole mob rose together."

By most accounts, the seizure of Wejh on January 24, 1917, was the turning point of the Arab Revolt. It struck a severe blow against Turkish morale, not just in the desert, but across the whole Ottoman Empire, even shaking Germany's Triple Alliance. At the same time, the victory at Wejh reinvigorated Arab morale with renewed belief in the righteousness of their cause. It also consolidated the gains of the previous months into a viable base for success and demonstrated to the world that the revolt was a serious effort worthy of support.

After the victory, Lawrence wrote an after-action report to British military headquarters in Cairo, citing the words of Feisal, leader of the assaulting Arab army: "Yes, we are no longer Arabs, but a nation." Lawrence continued, "He was proud, for the advance on Wejh by the Juheina [tribe] was the biggest moral achievement of the new Hejaz government. For the first time the entire manhood of a tribe, complete with its transport and food for a 200-mile march, has left its own divan, and proceeded (without plunder or the stimulus of inter-tribal feuds) into the territory of another tribe with a detached military aim."

Lawrence was also concerned with what he saw as the needless loss of life that ensued in the capture of Wejh and saw every death in battle as a challenge to the leader's personal authority and legitimacy, for it called into question the sacred contract between the leader and his men. In a tribal culture, the contract was more tenuous and less formal: "To me an unnecessary action, or shot, or casualty, was not only waste but sin. I was unable to take the professional view that all successful actions were gains. Our rebels were not materials, like soldiers, but friends of ours, trusting our leadership. We were not in command nationally, but by invitation; and our men were volunteers, individuals, local men, relatives, so that a death was a personal sorrow to many in the army."[10] Lawrence was reminded again about the essential difference between leading in the military mess and leading in the tribal community.

The success at Wejh only raised the obvious question: With the possession of the port, what was to be done with it? The initial plan was to use the base as a *means* to strike at the Turkish rail lifeline fifty miles to the east—but to what strategic *end*? The adventurous idea of destroying a few miles of rail line and a couple of locomotives appealed to all. The high councils of war demonstrated that there was still no strategic coherence between the Arab Revolt and the British operations in Egypt. Four months later, the same condition persisted. The British had yet to weave their operations into a seamless strategic pattern. In two months, Lawrence would have to ponder deeply this enigma and offer a completely novel and revolutionary solution.

CHAPTER THREE

A Flash of Genius

In my case, the effort for these years to live in the dress of Arabs, and to imitate their mental foundation, quitted me of my English self, and let me look at the West and its conventions with new eyes: they destroyed it all for me. At the same time I could not sincerely take on the Arab skin: it was an affectation only. . . . Sometimes these selves would converse in the void; and then madness was very near, as I believe it would be near the man who could see things through the veils at once of two customs, two educations, two environments.

—T. E. LAWRENCE, *Seven Pillars of Wisdom*

The story is told that shortly after the capture of Aqaba in July 1917, a British colonel from Cairo general headquarters (GHQ) came to visit Lawrence, who was none too fond of rear echelon visitors and disdained interruptions to his normal routine. Upon arrival, the colonel eventually found Major Lawrence feeding his camels near the shoreline. The colonel sidled up to Lawrence to better observe the feeding. At length he asked, "I say, Lawrence, what *do* you give these beasts for lunch?" Without entirely acknowledging his intrusive guest, yet with exquisite timing, Lawrence thought a moment and said, "Half an hour, same as the donkeys." Whether or not the unnamed colonel realized he had been the brunt of one of Lawrence's many jokes is unrecorded. We can see, however, that different assumptions, presumptions, and perspectives can lead to humor and irony as well as serious misunderstanding. This idea of hidden assumptions, beliefs, and habits of mind—like cultural perceptions of time—is exactly what came to constitute the core notion underpinning historian of science Thomas S. Kuhn's idea of a *paradigm*. Lawrence not only had to overcome Arab social culture, he also had to overturn the predominant military culture of the day.

Thomas Kuhn sought to emphasize the personal significance and magnitude of a paradigm shift. He wrote, "The transfer of allegiance from one paradigm to another is a *conversion experience* that cannot be forced" [my emphasis]. Kuhn's epiphany was precisely the same sort of "transformation" that Lawrence would undergo in his tent in Wadi Ais during March 1917: a profound intellectual experience unique in the annals of war.

Of course, in a broader sense scientists are like any other community of practitioners. Lawrence himself was one such practitioner within a military community and operating inside a distinctive paradigm generally based on conventional military operations. He would struggle mightily to overturn the conventional paradigm and lead a new revolution in military art: the conduct of irregular warfare under modern industrial conditions.

A DOZEN OR SO years after the death of Lawrence, Sir Karl Popper wrote, "Institutions are like fortresses. They must be well designed *and* properly manned." Lawrence would have added, "They must be properly led as well." At this stage of the Arab Revolt, native leaders were beginning to emerge who would eventually lead—but lead what? The Arabs had no military institutions, no state institutions to speak of. They were still a nation of tribes. The institutional blocks would have to be hewn slowly with Lawrence's razor-edged mind, slab by slab, brick by brick, and integrated into a coherent whole, cemented by leadership. By the end of January 1917, Lawrence's masonry was still operating at the level of straw-made bricks. The straws of tactical leadership were readily at hand to mix with tribal clay. The kiln of combat had hardened them, but they still needed to be set together with strategic form and operational function. Fortunately, Feisal ignored his father's desires: the Arab army would have its mason.

As fast as Lawrence and Feisal sought to build up their fragile revolutionary edifice, others were ready to smash it down. French colonel Eduard Brémond, an artilleryman by profession and wrecker by trade, began to undermine the Arab efforts. At all costs he had to prevent the Arabs from ever reaching Damascus and laying claim to territory that would compromise French interests. Since the Arabs were desperate for artillery, his first sapping efforts were to prevent French artillery from reaching the Arab army, even though the guns were sitting idle at Suez. For a whole year, the Arabs would be denied these assets. His other political aim, at the direction of the French government, was to ensure British troops became sidetracked in the Arabian Peninsula, where they would have less influence on French designs in Syria. To this end, he struggled greatly to get English troops committed to the defense of Rabegh.

Soon after the capture of Wejh, Colonel Brémond came to Lawrence to cast a spell of deception. "Monsieur Lawrence, I have a proposal of the utmost strategic importance for you: the port of Aqaba is now ripe for the plucking. A combined Anglo-French brigade with naval support could easily seize it and of course you're well aware of its importance: it is now the only Turkish port left on the Red Sea, the nearest to the Suez Canal, the nearest to the Hejaz Railway, the nearest to the flank of the British Army. We could easily take the port and drive up Wadi Itm and crush Ma'an."

Of course Lawrence knew the area quite well from before the war and realized the concept was militarily infeasible. "We could take the beach of the gulf; but our forces there, as unfavorably placed as on a Gallipoli beach, would be under observation and gun-fire from the coastal hills; and these granite hills, thousands of feet high, are impracticable for heavy troops: the passes through them being formidable defiles, very costly to assault or to cover. In my opinion, Aqaba, whose importance is all and more than you say, would best be taken by Arab irregulars descending from the interior without naval help."[2]

Lawrence knew the real political reasons behind the proposal—and he knew that Brémond knew he knew. The Frenchman concluded the discussion with a thinly veiled warning that he would take his case to Feisal himself. Of course Feisal was unaware of this intrigue, assuming, perhaps naively, that the French and British were acting in complete concert as true allies. After Brémond left, Lawrence rushed to Wejh by boat, arriving two days later to warn Feisal, who now began to understand the duplicitous game of the French. When Brémond appeared ten days later, Feisal was ready, with Lawrence silent and Polonius-like at his side. The colonel's opening gambit was to offer six Hotchkiss machine guns. Feisal replied that the "noble gift" would be better appreciated if it came with a battery of quick-firing mountain guns. The Frenchman decried the use of guns in the desert, saying it would be much better "if Feisal made his men climb about the country like goats and tear up the railway." Ignoring Lawrence's stifled guffaw—from the shadows—at the colonel's cultural gaffe about goats, Feisal angrily wondered if Brémond's fat ass would allow him to "goat" around hills as easily. Oblivious to the insult, the wrecker pressed his argument, only to have Feisal replay a variant of Lawrence's original rejoinder.

For now, Brémond's sapping efforts had been countermined, though Lawrence knew he would try again. In the meantime, he would spend a week in Cairo offering Sir Archibald Murray a new appreciation of the situation.

TURKISH COMMANDER FAKHRI Pasha held a defensive position by Medina that dangled at the end of an extended rail line. Newcombe in the northeast and Major H. G. Garland southeast had gone off to blow bridges and rails along the length of the entire line. Like a long line of ants, the Turks spread themselves out trying to secure water points and other key installations. Meanwhile, the Arabs began to take Feisal's successes seriously and offer military service. The Billi and the Moahib tribes were the first of the new enlistees, whose enrollment gave Feisal control of Arabia from the railway west to the Red Sea. He directed the Juheina to reinforce his brother Abdullah at Wadi Ais.

At present, neither Lawrence nor Feisal made a distinction in their strategic outlook between combat and persuasion. Intuitively, Feisal saw the need to use his leadership powers of argument to enlarge the enrollment of tribes. He already had the coastal Howeitat under his suasion and looked toward the northeast to the Beni Atiyeh and their chief, Asi ibn Atiyeh, who swore fealty to Feisal. Lawrence did not expect active participation from Asi, who was motivated through jealousy of his brothers, but he did expect a source of equal value: freedom of maneuver throughout the tribal lands. Farther afield lay the many tribes owing allegiance to Nuri Shaalan, the grand emir of the Ruwalla and fourth in stature after Hussein, ibn Saud, and ibn Rashid.

To ensure the well-being of his tribes, however, Nuri maintained close contact with the Turks, who still held Damascus and Baghdad, the focus of his tribal markets. Without this loose collaboration, the enemy could have shut down the trade and starved his tribes in less than three months. Lawrence and Feisal knew, though, that when the crunch came, they would be able to rely on Nuri and his men.

Strategically, Nuri's tacit support would open up the entire Sirhan passage, an important axis of advance that offered campsites and water holes in a chain of linked depressions that would give cover during movement behind Aqaba. The passage through the Sirhan would further provide access to the eastern Howeitat under Auda abu Tayi, the fiercest fighter in all of northern Arabia. Only with the tactical leadership of Auda could Lawrence hope to wield the various tribes as a single weapon and strike at Aqaba from the rear. Thus it was on February 17, 1917, that Auda sent his cousin and chief retainer, ibn Zaal, to Feisal's tent. As Lawrence recalls: "He kissed Feisal's hand once for Auda and then once for himself, and, sitting back, declared that he came from Auda to present his salutations and to ask for orders. Feisal, with policy, controlled his outward joy, and introduced him gravely to his blood enemies, the Jazi Howeitat. Ibn Zaal acknowledged them distantly." After several hours of intense but friendly negotiations, ibn Zaal offered the formal oath to Feisal on behalf of Auda, vowing "to wait while he [Feisal] waited, march when he marched, to yield obedience to no Turk, to deal kindly with all who spoke Arabic (whether Baghdadi, Aleppine, Syrian, or pure-blooded), to put independence above life, family, and goods."

Finally, Feisal addressed the long-standing blood feuds among all those present. Feisal played the role of Solomon, wise judge in adjudicating and redressing the internecine hatred of decades, often paying his own money to achieve agreement and resolution. In all these efforts, Feisal rose from a tribal head to the true head of an Arab nation. For two years, Feisal would struggle mightily to put together the jigsaw puzzle of Arab society into one coherent vision for the defeat of the Ottoman Empire and freedom for his people. In the end, no blood feud existed anywhere in western Arabia. Of Feisal's leadership, Lawrence would recall: "He never gave a partial decision, nor a decision so impracticably just that it must lead to disorder. No Arab ever impugned his judgments, or questioned his wisdom and competence in tribal business. By patiently sifting out right and wrong, by his tact, his wonderful memory, he gained authority over the nomads from Medina to Damascus and beyond. He was recognized as a force transcending tribe, superseding blood chiefs, greater than jealousies."[3] Feisal's leadership would soon turn the revolt from a limp hand into a heavy fist.

FEISAL CONTINUED HIS diplomatic efforts toward the enlargement of the Arab Revolt for the next several weeks. Sometime around March 10, a wireless telegram was intercepted by British intelligence in Cairo under Brigadier Gilbert Clayton. The partially decoded intercept from Jemal Pasha, the Turkish commander in Syria, ordered Fakhri Pasha at Medina to begin the entire evacuation of his position around the town. The concept had been concocted by the German staff in Istanbul, supporting the nominal Turkish commander in chief, Enver Pasha. The message ordered the march of the Turks northward astride the railway, with the bulk of the rail transport chugging along in the center of the massed troops. Clayton feared that the bulk of the Medina force, perhaps as many as twenty-five thousand men, would now end up in the main theater facing the British at Beersheba. It was imperative, therefore, that this redeployment be halted at all costs. Clayton sent an order to Lieutenant-Colonel S. F. Newcombe to plan an attack, but the colonel was away operating against the railway farther north. Lawrence, on his own initiative, seized the mission and urged Feisal to take immediate action. On very short notice, Lawrence helped Feisal cobble together four loose detachments that were sent out to operate against the Turks out of a chain of forward-operating bases. Then Lawrence himself went out to see Abdullah at Wadi Ais and challenge him for not taking any serious action against the enemy for the past two months and to urge him that concerted action would now be necessary if the Turks moved north.

Lawrence headed out the next day, already ill with coastal dysentery. His companions turned out to be a rather ragtag lot traveling on ill-fed camels, which meant the journey would be long. Four Rifaa and one Merawi Juheina acted as his guides; Arslan, a Syrian, acted as his aide; four Ageyli, a Moor, and an Ateibi, Suleiman, acted as guard detachment. The journey took the party across the shattered granite approaches of two sugar loaves of low hills, the Sakhara and the Sukhur. The ravine between the brown rocks was rough and made slick under a gentle winter rain that began to break. The peak of the gorge was thin and sharp; the weak and laden camels had difficulty crossing at the knife of the pass. On the downslope, the passage was partially blocked by a huge granite boulder containing the ganglike graffiti of generations of travelers who had hacked their tribal signatures into the stone along the way. Here the path opened onto a jumble of jagged chips of flint. As the riders continued, the rain washed down the shards to reveal a foot-polished and rain-slicked goat path dangerous in the drizzle. The path soon trickled into a trail, and the men had to dismount and lead their beasts on foot.

BY THE SECOND day, the party found a suitable place to camp. Lawrence's dysentery had grown worse, and he now began to suffer from a severe case of boils that had erupted on his back. The infection induced an enervating fever and hammering headaches that also caused brief fainting spells. Exhausted, he threw himself under the shadow of a shale cliff. All day long his comrades had been fighting among themselves, something he was finally able to ignore by slipping into a stupefied slumber. After some remote time, he was roused by a gunshot. Thinking that his unruly companions were plinking at the abundant rabbits and fowl in the area, he tried to return to a torpid sleep. As if in a drugged dream, Suleiman came to awaken him, begging Lawrence to follow him across the canyoned valley to the other side. The waking dream became a nightmare when Suleiman led him to a dead man lying among the rocks with a bullet through his forehead. As he looked down upon the hapless Ageyl, Lawrence reeled from the sight, catching himself on one knee and nearly falling upon the corpse.

Salem, one of the four Ageyli, had been shot at close range, judging
by the telltale powder burns near the temple. The other Ageyli were
running about in rage and grief. Lawrence regained his footing and
lunged at the nearest, catching Ali by the hem of his cloak. Hamed
the Moor was the murderer, he said. Lawrence ordered Ali and the
others to find the guilty Hamed, while he sought the pile of baggage
that was now graced by the shadow of the rock-braced canyon. As he
lay there, Lawrence's pained mind sank back into a vigilant sleep.

The waking dream resumed with a raspy whisper of dry leaves: it
was Hamed at the baggage, gathering his kit and readying his escape.
When he set aside his rifle, the unnoticed Lawrence drew his Webley
and ordered Hamed to stop. When the others returned, a field tribu-
nal was held and Hamed confessed, ending the trial. The storied law
of the empty desert, not the civilized courtroom, would mete out the
punishment: tooth for tooth, eye for eye. Salem's kinsmen demanded
Hamed's death for his crime. Lawrence pleaded with Ali, the most
reasonable of the Ageyli, but it was to no avail: Western reason stood
eloquently mute before the dock of tribal justice.

Just then, the leader within Lawrence stirred and awoke from the
waking dream. The implications of a dead Moor, murdered at the
hands of Ageyli tribesmen, were stark and foreboding. The Moroc-
cans among the Arab army would rise up in vengeance. The punishment would have to be dealt to Hamed by Lawrence himself. Now
Lawrence became in their eyes the outsider, the kinless stranger in the
strange land: his bloodied hands would set him ironically above the
blood feud.

The judgment was announced, and Hamed was led away by Lawrence: "I made him enter the narrow gully of the spur, a dank twilight
place overgrown with weeds. Its sandy bed had been pitted by trickles
of water down the cliffs in the light rain. At the end it shrank to a
crack a few inches wide. The walls were vertical. I stood in the entrance and gave him a few moments' delay which he spent crying on
the ground. Then I made him rise and shot him through the chest."[4]
Lawrence botched the execution: Hamed fell screaming to the ground,
thrashing and shrieking about in the narrow gulch. He fired again,
and his shaking shot pierced Hamed through the wrist. After some
minutes, the dying Hamed finally rolled before Lawrence's wet feet

and stony gaze. Aiming carefully, he shot Hamed under the jaw. Satisfied, the Ageyli buried Hamed where he died.

Lawrence staggered off to his bedroll, no longer the man he once knew. The old Lawrence of the days of innocence seeped into the sand with Hamed's blood, and once again the ancient desert had become the blood blotter of history.

THE NEXT MORNING they carried Lawrence, exhausted, to his camel and departed the life-stealing Wadi Kitan, crossing into the tributaries of Wadi Reimi and Wadi Amk. Midday brought them into the furnace of Wadi Marrakh. The heat engulfed the riders in heavy waves. "The puffs of feverish wind pressed like scorching hands against our faces, burning our eyes," Lawrence recalled. "My pain made me breathe in gasps through the mouth; the wind cracked my lips and seared my throat till I was too dry to talk, and drinking became sore; yet I always needed to drink, as my thirst would not let me lie still and get the peace I longed for. The flies were a plague."[5]

The valley floor was strewn with powdery quartz and a fine sparkling sand that thrust dazzling daggers into the travelers' eyes. Here patches of dry white grass shimmered in the fiery light, offering an illusion that the riders were marching atop sun-dogged clouds. The camels found the grass "clouds" especially tasty, and here the men stopped to rest. Lawrence was laid to the side of the grazing beasts in the shade of some thorn trees. The camels engorged their many-chambered stomachs in a belching, regurgitating, chomping orgy. A green slobber dripped down the sides of their working mouths and chins to fall into the sand with a quiet *slap*. Lawrence idly watched the feast through leadened, fevered eyelids. Close behind him, a camel pissed heavily upon a gray rock, spraying a fine ammoniated mist in his direction. The outriders had killed a gazelle that was now roasting over a fire that seemed flameless against the fiery sun.

After the men had eaten, the ride resumed up a multiterraced lava field strewn with rusty clinkered rocks. Here, Wadi Gara flowed toward the retreating horizon between two deep, irregular ditches of stagnant rainwater. The camels trod gingerly among the clinkers, trying to avoid the jagged edges. By five in the afternoon, the valley had turned into a floor of black winnowed ash, as though sifted through a colander. The powder turned a silvery gray under each of the camels' footfalls. Farther on, the riders encountered a Bedouin campsite where Sheikh Fahad el Hansha ruled his clan. The sheikh was one of the earliest supporters of Hussein and the revolt. Now he refused to let Lawrence sleep outside the hospitable embrace of his tent and urged his guest to sit beside him. Here he regaled Lawrence with a litany of questions: What is Europe? What is your home tribe? What is the nature of the English camel pasturages? Who is winning the revolt? Who is winning the war in Europe, in Egypt? How is Feisal? Why do you seek Abdullah? And "by what perversity do you remain Christian, when our hearts and hands wait to welcome you to the Faith?" Lawrence sought to answer these and other questions between sips of warm camel milk. At ten in the evening, the guest sheep was ceremoniously slaughtered and baked over a bed of buttered rice. Lawrence ate heartily as desert etiquette demanded and, after further conversation had ended, fell into a dream-filled stupor: he dreamed that he and his party sizzled across the desert like an egg on a grill, chased by the ghost of Hamed.

Lawrence awoke the next morning barely refreshed enough to walk to his camel and mount her unaided. The ride to Abdullah's camp continued until well into the morning, when the party at last reached Abu Markha in Wadi Ais. At Wadi Ais, Lawrence's fever still lingered, and the thought of a tribal cure was dreadful to him. The prescribed treatment was always the same: burn holes in the affected part. In the case of fever, that meant a wholesale torching. Better to suffer the disease than submit to the cure.

At length, Lawrence found Abdullah's tent and delivered the documents from Feisal and recounted the situation at Medina: Abdullah's forces were required to strike at the railway to the north of the town in order to block the escaping Turks. The sheikh received the news calmly. By now Lawrence was veritably tottering over with fever, fatigue, and exhaustion and asked to excuse himself. Abdullah offered to erect a tent for his guest, who was too weak to refuse the gesture. Within the hour, Lawrence collapsed.

THE SICK MAN lay facedown on a stinking cot in a stinking tent in a stinking desert. A humid, cloying breeze blew in from the west, from the Red Sea. Lawrence awoke sick as ever with dysentery and infected boils that would eventually lead to a dangerous blood poisoning. The long desert rides and lack of sanitation had created the serious condition. The ensuing fever racked Lawrence's body, but an unreasonable, looming sense of failure now assaulted his mind.

Lawrence, a rank amateur, was leading an entire nation of desert Arabs in an all-or-nothing revolt against their Turkish oppressors, and so far he—and they—had largely failed despite the success at Wejh. Through the oppressive haze of illness and depression, Lawrence saw no solution, no hope, for his dilemma. In every direct encounter with the Turks, the Arabs had been beaten and beaten badly. Even the most enthusiastic of the Arabs, the most motivated, were beginning to lose heart. Through the long dark nights of the soul that would follow, Lawrence would meet a personal crisis. Would he be forced to pack up his tent and steal away in defeat with the Arabs, or would he stand against the Turks and the very weight of history? The answer revolved around a riddle, a riddle of war as old as conflict itself. But it could not be solved in one day or with a fever-leadened brain: Lawrence would need to rest, to sleep.

To a fever-addled mind, time means nothing. All sense of it is lost; there is no temporal duration, only an unendurable pounding in the temporal lobes. Dream's nighttime domain and reason's daylight abode trespass each other. Both dance together in an awkward, heated embrace where human reason succumbs to a siren's dream of past images and rememberings. All cast up in a silent fog of ambivalence, hope, and regret: the Lawrence family secret of his bastard birth, the Arab uprising, the death of two beloved brothers in combat on the western front—and more. For several days, the fevered ballet in Lawrence's head continued, mere shadows cast by a real struggle in his febrile body.

At last the infection was driven from the field, defeated for now, and a slow recovery ensued. The mind cleared and reason returned once again to find in its midst the same riddle that had eluded Lawrence since the Arab Revolt had sparked. Even its very articulation had eluded him in the beginning. Now it presented itself before his mind's eye: a four-sided pyramid. Gazing but unseeing at the early morning sun, he pondered what his mind had imagined.

. . .

THE ART OF war had always been a dynamic resolution of a four-sided conundrum of *ends, ways, means,* and *risk.* Even a mere private could understand and appreciate the relationship, but as Lawrence was beginning to discover, understanding did not necessarily lead to effective action: and action against a fierce enemy changed everything in the dynamic calculus. Actually, the relationship included a fifth element, the *enemy,* but the commander had no control over him.

In every war, the commander had to consider first the *ends* or aim he had to achieve in his military operation. Second, he had to consider his own *means* available to accomplish those *ends,* recognizing at the same time that he had to overcome the enemy's *means* opposed to him. Ideally, the friendly *means* should be proportional to the *ends* plus the *means* opposed. In reality, this was seldom the case. Where *means* were lacking—soldiers, bullets, units, morale, will—the *ends* could be adjusted to create a balanced proportionality once again. But what if this latitude was foreclosed to the commander, as Lawrence was beginning to realize? The mismatch would create an *ends-means* imbalance or deficit. Within this deficit or gap roamed the elements of *risk* and chance, the third part of the relationship. A commander thus had to assume the burden of *risk* in every operation where his *ends* and *means* were out of whack. Yet the situation need not be hopeless, especially for a gifted commander like Lawrence—for embedded within the riddle lay its very solution: the *ways.*

The fourth aspect of military art, the *ways,* is the most creative factor, as well as the most elusive. The imaginative strategies, tactics, maneuvers, gambits, moves—all bring the static calculation among *ends, means,* and *risk* into dynamic tension when placed before an active enemy where anything becomes possible. A small army can defeat a larger force; a technologically inferior force can overwhelm a technologically advanced opponent. Lawrence would have to reinvent a *way* to defeat an old opponent. In doing so, he would embark on a path of military heresy into the pages of history.

LAWRENCE'S INSIGHT, RECOUNTED in *Seven Pillars of Wisdom,* is one of the most astonishing and creative revelations in the entire history of the art of war.[6] Yet it is seldom mentioned in accounts of

Lawrence. B. H. Liddell Hart, the British military historian, recognizing its historical significance in his biography of Lawrence, spends a
chapter discussing its implications, though missing the theoretical
import of its meaning. Most writers dismiss Lawrence's revelation as
the incoherent ramblings of a pyrexic mind. Lawrence's powers of
physical recovery were legendary, and he seemed able to transform
mental energy into physical force. As he continued his slow, tent-
bound convalescence, Lawrence extended his four-way assessment to
focus more closely on the *ways*. Up until this time, he had spent several months fighting beside the Arab Bedouin against the Ottoman
Turk. From this experience he derived two theorems governing the
ways and methods of guerrilla warfare. These two principles provided a point of departure for the development of his new theory of
irregular warfare. Lawrence asserted first that irregular troops like
the Arabs were unable to defend a position against conventional
forces; and, similarly, irregular troops were incapable of effectively
attacking a conventionally defended position. If these theorems were
correct, as he surmised, then of what value were his irregulars in the
first place? Essentially, Lawrence was suggesting to himself that his
means were not only insufficient and inadequate for the task at hand,
they were also unsuitable.

Reflecting inward on his own education and study, Lawrence
understood that his attitude toward war, like that of any officer
schooled in Western military thought and tradition, was dominated
by the dogma of *annihilation*: an obsession that "the ethic of modern
war is to seek the enemy's army, his center of power, and destroy it in
battle." The centrality of the decisive battle formed the conceptual
lens through which every military professional viewed his world, the
relevant problems that existed in that world, and the set of solutions
that would solve those problems. In terms made famous by Thomas
S. Kuhn, the paradigm of annihilation held sway over the officer
corps of every major army for most of World War I. Lawrence pro-
posed, instead, a lens-smashing alternative: a view heretical in the
extreme. It occurred to him that in fact no decisive battle of annihilation had yet taken place; the Arabs were not winning, but neither
were they losing. *How could this be?*

On his sickbed, the military implications of the victory at Wejh became more apparent and took on new significance: "As I thought about it, it dawned on me that we had won the Hejaz war. We were in occupation of 99 percent of the Hejaz. The Turks were welcome to the other fraction till peace or doomsday showed them the futility of clinging to our window pane. This part of the war was over, so why bother with Medina? It was not a base for us, like Rabegh; no threat to the Turks, like Wejh: just a blind alley for both. The Turks sat in it on the defensive—immobile, eating for food the transport animals which were to have moved them to Mecca, but for which there was no pasture in their now-restricted lines. They were harmless sitting there; if we took them prisoners, they would cost us food and guards in Egypt: if we drove them out northward into Syria, they would join the main army in blocking us. . . . On all counts they were best where they were, and they valued Medina and wanted to keep it. Let them!"

Lawrence wondered, then, if there were no other wars, different in kind from the wars of annihilation that French generals like Ferdinand Foch and others advocated and wrote of so enthusiastically in their efforts to emulate the great master annihilator, Napoleon Bonaparte. He concluded, following a recollection of his study of Carl von Clausewitz, that there was indeed more than one kind of war, that the determining factors again boiled down to the relationship among *ends, ways* ("strategies"), *means,* and *risk.*

It was simply not within the compass of Arab interests (*ends*), or even within their capability (*means*), to annihilate the Turks. Rather, the Arab *ends* could change and become geographic: to occupy as much of the desert theater of operations as possible.

Now if the aim of the Arabs was one of geographic interest and focus rather than the destruction of the enemy forces, it put the *ways* and *means* of irregular warfare in a different light. Given the validity of the facts that Arab irregulars could neither defend nor attack against a strong conventional force, what *way* or strategy was left open to them? Clausewitz had considered a second possible strategy, a strategy of *exhaustion.*

LAWRENCE WAS ONE of the few modern commanders to understand the value of military theory. *Theory is a conceptual device that allows us to visualize what we cannot see.* The developers of the atomic bomb, for example, were unable to *see* the atom, but through their theories of nuclear physics they were able to *visualize* it. In the same fashion, an explorer is able to *visualize* by means of a map the underlying terrain that he does not *see*. Thus Lawrence used theory to help him visualize the war he was fighting and imagine its future outcome.

To explore the theoretical questions, Lawrence began the inquiry from his perspective as commander and "began to unravel command and analyze it, both from the view of strategy . . . and from the view called tactics. . . . In each I found the same elements: one algebraical, one biological, a third psychological." This became his simple conceptual framework: a kind of mental pegboard on which to hang key concepts or ideas in relation to one another, yet with sufficient structure to analyze and think of the ideas altogether in a coherent whole. Lawrence's "pegboard" thus had three conceptual "hooks": the algebraical, the biological, and the psychological.

By algebraical, Lawrence meant those factors subject to mathematical calculation, fixed in time and place, and generative of military power: the *means* of war. Thus he began to calculate the size of the area that the rebellious Arabs would have to conquer and how many Turks it would take to defend it. Assuming a fortified post with twenty men, staged at four-mile intervals, he calculated it would require a Turkish army of six hundred thousand men to defend adequately the whole Arabian Peninsula. Yet he knew the enemy possessed only one hundred thousand men, and most of these were concentrated around Medina or defending the long rail lifeline. Lawrence further recognized that the Turks, with their mental baggage stuffed with ideas about climactic decisive battles, would approach the insurgency from the perspective of a strategy of annihilation. But this would be a mistake, because making "war upon a rebellion is messy and slow, *like eating soup with a knife.*"

The second element in his framework was the biological, a term he later refers to as "bionomics," a reference to the wear and tear and friction within a military system. Lawrence concluded that rather than destroy the Turkish army, the Arabs merely needed to *wear* it down. A strategy of *exhaustion,* not destruction, was the *way* that would bring this about indirectly through tactical attacks on the enemy's matériel: "The death of a Turkish bridge or rail, machine or gun, or high explosive was more profitable to us than the death of a Turk." Thus, the weakness of the irregular—his inability to stand toe-to-toe with the regular in battle—could be rendered moot provided the Arab attacked the enemy's readily accessible matériel. But the key to such a strategy was the possession of nearly perfect intelligence—both timely and accurate. Lawrence, himself a practiced intelligence officer, argued that knowledge of the enemy had to be "faultless, leaving no room for chance. We took more pains in this service than any other staff I saw."

A war driven by a strategy of exhaustion meant to the Arabs "a war of detachment: we were to contain the enemy by silent threat of a vast unknown desert, not disclosing ourselves til the moment of attack. This attack need be only nominal, directed not against his men, but against his materials: so it should not seek for his main strength or his weaknesses. . . . In railway cutting this would be usually an empty stretch of rail. That was a tactical success. We might turn the average into a rule . . . and at length we developed an unconscious habit of never engaging the enemy at all. This chimed with the numerical plea of never giving the enemy's soldier a target. Many Turks on our front had no chance all the war to fire a shot at us, and correspondingly we were never on the defensive, except by rare accident."

The final factor of analysis was the psychological. Lawrence understood that in an insurgency, the real battle resided within the minds of the opponents. To be successful, the Arabs had "to arrange their [own] minds in order of battle, just as formally as other officers arrayed their bodies." This also meant that moral support among the populace had to be mobilized for the rebellion. In their amateurish ignorance and naïveté, Lawrence and the Arabs saw the revolt as a conflict of infinite possibility and opportunity. Nothing was dismissed from useful consideration that a serving regular officer might reject out of hand. This was especially true with regard to the supporting role of the media during the uprising. "The printing press is the greatest weapon in the armory of the modern commander. . . . The regular officer has the tradition of forty generations of serving soldiers behind him, and to him the old weapons are the most honored. We had seldom to concern ourselves with what our men did, but much with what they thought, and to us the [psychological] was more than half [of] command. In Europe it was a little aside and entrusted to men outside the General Staff. In Asia we were so weak physically that we could not let the metaphysical weapon rust unused. We had won a province when we had taught the civilians in it to die for our ideal of freedom: the presence or absence of the enemy was a secondary matter." Freedom was the motivating spark that turned the tinder of discontent into a raging flame of revolution. Lawrence had written that "conviction needed shooting to be cured." Every Arab fortified with a conviction of freedom had the heart of a soldier and was thus a menace to every Turk.

In light of his analysis, Lawrence developed a basic war plan that he adhered to until virtually the end of the conflict in the desert. It rested upon a foundation of a realistic reframing of the Arab irregular and his Turkish adversary. The object was to impose upon the Turks the burden of a long, protracted defense that would eventually exhaust them. The method of accomplishing this was through the employment of small, highly skilled and motivated mobile raiding units.

FOUR DAYS INTO his desert reverie, Lawrence suffered a further physical setback. Around March 21, "a great complication of boils developed out, to conceal my lessened fever, and to chain me down yet longer in impotence upon my face in the stinking tent." Even during this period of relapse, Lawrence never stopped his revolutionary thinking. Strategy had to be brought into existence through tactical action. He recognized that the problem of conventional and unconventional warfare reflected two great streams of military culture. The conventional soldier embodied the long tradition of the yeoman warrior, fighting for hearth and home. The insurgent rebel espoused an ethos of the homeless raider, fighting to seize the labored fruits of a sedentary civilized foe. The raider from his temporary base fought only for a thief's booty and a pirate's fellowship. The yeoman was always shackled with an urban chain to a common good. The raider had to move to survive; for the yeoman, movement meant displacement, loss, and defeat. To Lawrence, the raiding culture perfectly described the Arab nomad and made him the ideal instrument for his raiding strategy of exhaustion.

The two primary strategies—the *ways*—of war had been one of annihilation, the other of exhaustion. Lawrence rendered a third, a hybrid of exhaustion bent to the unique raiding style of the Arab guerrilla nomad. Accordingly, his assessment demonstrated "that the idea of assaulting Medina, or even starving it quickly into surrender was not in accord with our best strategy. We wanted the enemy to stay in Medina, and in every other nameless place, in the largest numbers. The factor of food would eventually confine him to the railways, but he was welcome to the Hejaz railway [and to the other major] railways for the duration of the war, so long as he gave us the nine hundred and ninety-nine thousandths of the Arab world. . . . Our ideal was to keep his railway just working."

The strategy of exhaustion and the implementing tactics of raiding were not about the direct concentration of solid mechanical *force*, but rather about the application of a kind of diffused gaseous *pressure*. The distribution of his desert corsairs in the "empty space" led Lawrence to consider that the ratio of troops to space would determine the ultimate nature of the war: "The ratio between number and area determined the character of the war, and by having five times the mobility of the Turks we could be on [equal] terms with them with one-fifth their number." Thus Lawrence began to view desert warfare, in some sense, as more akin to naval warfare. He cites approvingly Sir Francis Bacon to that effect: "He who commands the sea is at great liberty, and may take as much and as little of the war as he will."

For Lawrence, the camel was indeed the ship of the desert. It gave the desert guerrilla an incredible operational reach. In fact, the camel gave him and his Arab forces great operational *mobility*. With it, troops were able to carry a ration lasting six weeks. Even under the hottest conditions, camels could travel three days without water. According to Lawrence's estimation, this meant that the animals could cover nearly 250 miles between watering at a remarkable sustained rate of march of 3.5 miles an hour. It also meant that the Arab irregular had the operational reach of more than a thousand miles, sufficient to cast a threatening net over the entire Arabian Peninsula and beyond.

Having rejected the necessity to defeat the Turk through decisive battles, Lawrence was able to dispense with the need for organizing and maintaining dense, vulnerable field formations that characterized the force structure of conventional armies. The primary maneuver formation that he employed almost exclusively was the raiding party for the reasons previously mentioned. The Turks, however, used the unwieldy field division. Lawrence's operational aim was to achieve "maximum articulation" of the Arab forces. If this purpose was to expand mistlike into the vast reaches of the Hejaz desert, then it only made sense that he employ clouds of raiders to occupy that vast territory. This approach, of course, exploited the innate independence of the Arab raider, and no one understood this better than Lawrence.

The Arab guerrilla was an independent force unto himself. Lawrence noted: "The Arab was simple and *individual*. Every enrolled man served in the line of battle and was self-contained. We had no lines of communications or labor troops. The efficiency of each man was his personal efficiency. We thought that in our condition of warfare the sum yielded by single men would be at least equal to the product of the compound system. . . . In irregular warfare if two men are together one is being wasted."

TOWARD THE END of March 1917, Lawrence had recovered his strength and health—more or less. He strolled into Abdullah's tent to share with him the practical implications of his revolutionary reframing of the Arab Revolt. He urged his host to strike against the Hejaz railway, but Abdullah was more interested in hearing about the gossip among the royal families of Europe, the slaughter that became known as the battle of the Somme: anything that would distract him from the boredom of his own small war.

At Abdullah's side, though, was one who grew more and more interested in Lawrence's recast strategy. The leader most prominent in Abdullah's entourage was Sherif Shakir. He was the emir's cousin and second in command, as well as head of the Ateiba. Without his support, Lawrence's initial foray against the Turks would never have occurred. Shakir was an unusual Arab. His mother and grandmother were both Circassians, considered the "purest of white person." The Circassians had been deported from the Caucasus Mountains by the Russians in the 1860s and 1870s to various parts of the Ottoman

Empire, especially the Levant area. He was now twenty-nine and had been companion to Hussein's sons, including Feisal and Abdullah. His fair face was sandblasted with smallpox, giving him an unnerving countenance: diminished eyelashes and eyebrows, large and penetrating eyes. Slim, tall, and athletic, he exuded authority and confidence; his voice had a calm and decisive tone about it. His facile wit came from the same source as his keen intellect. Though he had little book learning, he was worldly, knowledgeable, and even cunning, often being sent on key diplomatic missions by Hussein. He dressed simply yet elegantly. He would rather play backgammon than read the Koran; though devout, he disliked Mecca. As a warrior, he excelled above all else, and this most endeared him to the Bedouin. He wore his hair in long tresses down the sides of his pocked face. He washed his hair often in camel urine and set it to a high sheen with butter. Infected with the Englishman's enthusiasm, he offered to lead his tribe with Lawrence against the Turks. The target chosen was the train station at Aba el Naam.

By March 26, Lawrence had all in readiness. An Algerian officer named Raho from Brémond's detachment also offered his services. At eighteen, Mohammed el Kadhi was their guide. He had led the Turks down to Yenbo the previous December, but now he worked for the revolution. Twenty Ateiba and six Juheina freebooters formed their escort under Sherif Fauzan el Harith, the conqueror of Eshref. They left the Wadi Ais in the morning. Yet even the short three-hour ride was too much for the convalescent Lawrence, who stopped the party under the cloaking shade of a jujube tree. Spring was upon the valley, with white butterflies chasing one another through the sweet-scented wildflowers.

The ride continued early the next morning around the flanks of the rising Jebel Serd, zigzagging through Wadi Turaa and Wadi Yenbo. Another tree was found near a Juheina campsite that their guide visited. Along with the others, Lawrence slept on the ground and was awakened in the night by a nasty scorpion sting to his left hand, which by morning had swollen up, its venom causing a stiff and aching arm.

The party broke camp early in the morning, making the final leg to their objective at Aba el Naam across a wide, wavy landscape called the Jurf. The station lay behind a high hill, screening their new camp from sight. After a brief rest, Lawrence climbed the six-hundred-foot hill in careful stages, resting along the way. Finally, at the crest of the hill he could see the railway nearly three miles off in the distance. The station itself was on the near side of the railway, perhaps a half mile closer to their position. They could see a pair of two-storied basalt blockhouses looming large and darkly ominous near a round water tower, huts, bell tents, and other outbuildings. At least three hundred infantry manned lines of trenches.

Turkish tactical doctrine, inherited from their German advisers, ensured that the area would be actively patrolled at night. However, doctrine is only as good as the motivation and skill of the troops executing it, and as usual, the Turks were found wanting. At night, Lawrence sent two pair of skirmishers near the blockhouses and ordered them to open fire at dark. The ragged shooting spooked the enemy into thinking a large-scale attack was imminent, so they stood to in their trenches the whole night. In the windy morning, they found an empty desert under a gray sky. Beyond the ridge, the Arab party was still fast asleep. They soon roused themselves and crept back up the hill to observe their edgy foe as he began his reveille ritual: bugles were called, and men rushed about, transforming themselves into serried blocks of khaki flesh; more calls, and the blocks slowly dissolved around smoking breakfast fires. Just then the now distant bugle calls were answered by the sharp, shrill whistle of a locomotive steaming slowly toward the station. As the puffing train creaked to a halt over a rickety bridge, a sharp cry was heard from behind the party's location. Lawrence looked back and saw a herd of sheep and goats leading a tattered little boy up the hill toward the Arabs. He immediately realized that the shepherd and his flock could unmask their concealed position. Two of the Juheina grabbed the youth, who began screaming and crying in fear at the sudden sight of the raiders. More terrifying to the boy, though, was the risk of losing his flock while seized by the men. It took all the powers of Sherif Fauzan to calm the lad and coax him to offer information about the Turkish defenses.

At dusk, the raiders left their hilltop position to return to the main camp with their shepherd captive. Shakir had arrived with the main body during light and had begun to roast some of the boy's flock. Now inconsolable, the boy refused to eat. The men tried to comfort him with the thought that tomorrow the railway station of his Turk-ish masters would lie in rubble. Finally, they forced bread and rice into him under threat of death and tied him to a tree.

Meanwhile, Lawrence, Shakir, and Fauzan discussed the tactical situation. It had suddenly changed once Lawrence realized that Sha-kir had brought only three hundred men instead of the promised eight hundred to nine hundred tribesmen. The whole plan had to be recast. It was now impossible to seize the station. Instead the party would fix the Turks in their defensive position with the one artillery piece they possessed and with concentrated small-arms fire. Two smaller detachments would strike the rail line north and south of the station with explosives and sever the line. Lawrence would lead the southern group guided by Mohammed el Kadhi, who led them to a deserted part of the rail near midnight. This would be Lawrence's first combat mission as leader. For the first time in the war he would lead offensive action against the enemy, and he was thrilled at the thought as he laid twenty pounds of explosives under the line. The painstaking work took nearly an hour. A portion of the party set up a machine-gun position about four hundred yards from the mine in hopes of covering the train after it was derailed. Lawrence took the rest of the party up the line to cut the telegraph wire, hoping the isola-tion would induce panic among the garrison. After an hour of riding, they found an isolated telegraph pole. Unfortunately, the four re-maining Juheina, being warriors of the desert, lacked the skill of shin-nying up a tree, much less a telegraph pole. Despite his recent illness, Lawrence tried his hand. After he'd climbed up the sixteen-foot pole and cut the third wire, the loosened pole suddenly began to gyrate erratically, causing him to lose his grip and fall. Fortunately, Moham-med, catlike, ran forward to break Lawrence's heavy fall. After a quick breather, the group found its way back to camp.

The entire mine-laying effort took four hours longer than ex-pected. Lawrence realized that the delay meant the demolition party would either have to go out with the main body without rest or let it advance without them. After he consulted with Shakir, it was decided to stay behind and rest. Lawrence fell into a deep, exhausted sleep. An hour later, just when night and day in dreamlike struggle create the dawn, Mohammed crept over to the Englishman to awaken him by crying out the morning prayer in his ear. Lawrence pleaded for more sleep, but Mohammed was afraid of missing out on the one battle of his life. So Lawrence rolled over on his black-and-blue body and pushed himself into the new day, leaving the shepherd to tend his few remaining sheep.

After following Shakir's winding trail, they arrived at the battle of Aba el Naam just as the mountain howitzer opened up with a dull crump. The Egyptian gunners were immediately successful in knocking out the station's pump room and holing the water tower. Another lucky shot hit one of the train's boxcars, setting a furious blaze. This hit shook up the train crew, who immediately uncoupled the locomotive and tried to slink away to the south. At that move, Lawrence winked knowingly at Mohammed and they both strained to see it depart. A short time later, they heard a muffled explosion in the distance and saw a ragged plume of smoke rise into the air. When the engineers leapt off the train to assess the damage, Lawrence expected them to be mown down by the concealed machine-gun crew. As it transpired, the machine gunners had suffered pangs of loneliness and ran off at the first sounds of the attack. The train somehow managed to recover some clanking mobility and trundled off to the south.

By now, smoke was pouring out of the station. Under cover of the bombardment, the tribesmen were able to seize one outpost and destroy another. The enemy withdrew to the center ring of his defensive trenches and prepared for the worst. At this point, the fight reached its crisis: the smoke from burning tents, wood, and boxcars made it impossible to shoot accurately. The decision was made to break off the attack. In Lawrence's first battle, he could reasonably claim a draw. His forces had captured thirty prisoners, a mare, two camels, and more sheep. They had killed or wounded seventy of the garrison, with the loss of only one man, slightly wounded. Perhaps of even greater importance, the line was shut down for three days and offered proof that Lawrence's revolutionary raiding strategy could be successful.

AFTER LEAVING TWO detachments to observe the station, Lawrence returned with the main body to Abdullah's camp at Ateiba on April 1. The camp greeted the warriors with a huge celebration, with Shakir taking center stage as the primary celebrant, performing an ancient tribal dance before hundreds of cheering Ateiba tribesmen.

The next day, Lawrence formed another group to return and test a new automatic detonator for the explosive mine. The action had seemed to operate improperly at Aba el Naam. The trek was uneventful, but as the day passed the heat became a cloying, oppressive mugginess. All morning there had been crackles of thunder over the low hills. The two distant peaks of Serd and Jasim were shrouded in gaseous clouds, blackish blue and jaundiced. Like a golden column of papier-mâché, the towering cloud over Serd advanced down toward the riders, throwing up an escort of dust devils in its wake. The escorts now coalesced into two guardian columns on either side of the wall cloud. Dakhil-Allah, hereditary law-giver of the Juheina tribe, looked right and left for shelter, then looked at Lawrence and warned him that the storm cloud would lay a heavy hand upon them. As it closed in, the once hot, fetid air now blew chilly and wet into their backs with a hissing wind that seemed to snuff and blow out the sun itself. The gale raged for eighteen minutes, smothering them in an ocherous wet pigment. They backed their camels into the storm, but the swirling wind spun them this way and that; shards of desert pelted them, driven hard by ropes of rain. Grit and flying debris blinded their ragged advance.

At last, when the front passed them by, a strong, cold, numbing wind blew down from the north. By midafternoon, they reached the top of the escarpment that paralleled the rail line, but the howling storm swept them off the wet, greasy ridge. Lawrence tried to observe the valley below, but observation was impossible. As the group retreated from the gale, the trusty Ateibi servant of Sultan el Abbud, one of the chiefs of the Ateiba, slipped and fell to his death forty feet below. At this time, the slower, explosive-laden camels caught up with Lawrence and his advance party. The wind now carried with it the Turkish bugle call to supper, and the party then realized they were near the small station of Madahrij. With the encroaching night plunging them into darkness, they decided to camp at a random location near kilometer marker 1121, ironically—and mockingly—the distance to Damascus. The storm made any campfire impossible, so they chose to work instead.

The charge Lawrence set was an intricate mine with a central detonator primed to fire simultaneous charges placed thirty yards apart. This would catch a train, going either north or south, in the wake of its blast. The placement of the charges took four long hours because the pounding rain had hardened the desert into a caked concrete. The activity created telltale signs of their presence, so it became necessary to trample the camels repeatedly across their path. After nearly a mile of trampling, the evidence was obliterated and the party slunk off, shivering and chattering, to find shelter from the gripping cold.

At sunrise, the storm was well past. Dakhil-Allah now took tactical control of the mission and led the party in ones and twos back up the hill to observe the railway. The sun soon rose higher and began to dry the storm-soaked clothes of the raiders. They observed a small work party on a handcar pass across the mine without exploding it—as designed. An hour and a half later, a detachment of sixty men stormed out of the station and seemed to head for their concealed position. At the last instant, they veered off down the line to replace five telegraph poles that had been knocked over in the storm. As they continued their work, a section wandered near kilometer 1121 and began to scrutinize the track bed and the disturbed, trampled ground around it. Poking and prodding the area, they found no evidence of the mine and soon went on to other tasks. But just then, farther to the south, Lawrence spied a heavily laden train puffing toward Madahrij. Nine of the boxcars were crammed with women and children and household baggage being deported from Medina to Syria. As the train approached the mine, the Juheina crowded around the top of the ridge, finally visible to the garrison below. The train soon passed over the mine—with no result. In an instant, Lawrence was overwhelmed with decidedly mixed emotions: "As artist I was furious; as commander deeply relieved: women and children were not proper spoil."7

Two hundred Turks below began a ragged fire at the onlooking Arabs up on the ridge, and Lawrence was certain the outpost at Hedia, six miles distant, would soon rouse its eleven hundred men as well. A quick council of war was in order. The party relied on its tactical mobility for its survival. The captured German Maxim machine gun was sled-drawn by an overworked and underfed mule. The crew itself were either on foot or on the slower mules. It was decided, therefore, that the camelry would allow the gun crew a long head start back to Wadi Ais and cover their retreat. The detachment of the slower gun crew allowed Lawrence's party to regain its mobility and offered the opportunity to return to the scene later in the afternoon.

As they approached the garrison once more hours later, the party drew fire. When they reached the railway, the sun was setting upon them. At that moment Dakhil-Allah, as imam, called the party to sunset prayer. They made their camels kneel down between the tracks and prayed quietly. At the sight of the sunset prayer service, the bewildered Turks stopped firing and looked on with some embarrassment. It was probably the first time the Juheina warriors had prayed in over a year. More momentous was the fact that, as Lawrence recalls, it was the first and last time he ever prayed in Arabia as a Muslim.

After the service, it was still too light for any further action. Eventually, Lawrence tried to find the location of the mine and dig it up to perform a postmortem of its failure. The other party members eagerly offered to help him in his efforts. To Lawrence's horror, they began to thrust bayonets and daggers into the ground as though, quite improbably, on an Easter egg hunt. Lawrence knew that the hair-triggered mine would blow a seventy-foot section of the rail to hell and gone, and he would much rather see his efforts spent on a legitimate target. At last he found the mine himself. The postmortem revealed that the previous night's rain had caused the mine to settle a tiny sixteenth of an inch, enough to disable sure contact of the pressure plate as the train passed over the mine. Lawrence quickly relaid the mine. The party then tore up other parts of the line to spoof their real intentions.

After more mischief, the raiders cantered for three hours under a dull moon until they overtook their detached gun crew. The crew spotted them and, thinking they were attacking Turkish sympathizers, opened up with the Maxim. No real damage ensued after the gun jammed halfway through a belt of ammo. After a joyful reunion, all apologies were accepted and the men slept well into the morning. A casual march took them to breakfast at the first well in Wadi Ais. Just then, as the men smoked and joked after the leisurely brunch, they heard the rolling force of a distant explosion near the rail line. Two scouts had been left behind to hover over the mine and report its effects. The party resumed its advance at a slow pace to allow the scouts to catch up and report the news of the explosion. In any case, the still-wet mud made the march a slog along the flooded Wadi Ais. At dusk, as the party prepared its camp, the scouts lolled into view and were quick to report. The mine was a success, destroying a vital repair train and sending its parts and pieces across the desert like a hammered pocketwatch.

The tactical importance of the mission was significant: it demonstrated that a carefully laid and concealed mine could become the stealth weapon of choice in the Arab Revolt. Its furtive quality would offer another nail in the coffin of Turkish morale.

LAWRENCE HAD TRAVELED to the Hejaz to evaluate the leadership qualities of the Arabs to lead their own revolt; that was his chief and essential mission. His own leadership abilities, though latent and still evolving, made his role key in that assessment. Over time, of course, he would himself take on a more central leadership and command role among the Arabs. In his own words he wrote: "I combined their loose showers of sparks into a firm flame: transformed their series of unrelated incidents into a conscious operation."[8]

In Lawrence's eyes, Abdullah was found wanting as a leader. There was a certain *Animal House* or frat house ambience in Abdullah's camp. Most important, Abdullah was never fully committed to the revolt in word and deed, even though the revolt had been his brainchild. Though Lawrence continued to find the emir kind and generous, his initial favorable impression of Abdullah thus changed rapidly.

Now that the crisis of a Turkish evacuation of Medina had receded—indeed, had been shown to be a false alarm—Lawrence decided that it would be best to return to Feisal. Here he would be close to the true center of gravity of the Arab Revolt and be able to influence it accordingly. On the morning of April 10, Lawrence left Wadi Ais with his party and returned to Wejh armed with the renewed confidence that he had at last grasped the intellectual nettle of the uprising and found its solution. All that remained was to find a true Arab tactical leader who would put Lawrence and Feisal's strategic vision into effect.

When Lawrence went off to war, along with virtually every other serving officer, he believed that the war would be short, swift, and decisive; after all, the dead hand of Napoleon and the paradigm of conventional operations had so promised. Four years later, it was evident that the promise had betrayed everyone, though only a few rare and gifted individuals like Lawrence would eventually see beyond Napoleon's influence and recognize that a revolution in the art of war had truly occurred.

LAWRENCE'S DESERT EPIPHANY was an extraordinary intellectual and theoretical achievement, generally and historically. Insofar as the accomplishment itself is concerned, it is important to understand that he did not invent guerrilla warfare; guerrillas had long operated throughout military history. Instead, Lawrence was the first theorist and practitioner to revolutionize the guerrilla within the broader context of modern industrialized warfare. The reimagination and reframing of guerrilla warfare was a heresy that few initially grasped. Those who did would follow Lawrence through the halls of legend: Mao Tse-tung, Ho Chi Minh, Vo Nguyen Giap.

Reduced to its essence, Lawrence's heresy consisted of seven Luther-like theses of guerrilla warfare. First, a modern reconceptualization of guerrilla warfare meant that under most circumstances, an irregular force could actually operate hand in glove with a conventional army. Lawrence was able to demonstrate this to the British commander in chief, General Edmund Allenby. This thesis was to become the hardest to prove and the last to be realized. The difficulty concerned the problem of synchronization and coordination between the conventional force and its guerrilla counterpart. Guerrilla forces simply do not possess the command, control, and staff overhead necessary for tight coordination and integration. Lawrence, however, largely overcame these deficiencies thanks to the crucial role of modern wireless communications, as well as his own extraordinary efforts and ingenuity as a one-man commander and general staff.

Second, a successful guerrilla movement had to have an unassailable base: a base secure not only from direct physical assault, but from attacks in other forms as well, especially psychological attack. A secure base meant that a sanctuary existed where the insurgents *in extremis* could always escape to and reconstitute their force. Psychological security was just as important in Lawrence's heresy. The fortress of the mind meant that the irregular was secure in his cause because his commitment was total and without reservation; he was a true believer in final victory. Yet for the individual, victory was sometimes beyond his personal horizon and less significant than the length and duration of the struggle itself. The guerrilla, often dominated by a culture of fatalism, would rejoice in the struggle—for victory or defeat was ultimately in the hands of the gods.

Third, the guerrilla must have a technologically sophisticated enemy. This technological sophistication meant an exploitable vulnerability. In the case of the Turks, the reliance on railroad technology offered a peculiar weakness that Lawrence was able decisively to exploit. The railroad also meant telegraph technology and a further command, control, and communications susceptibility. For the guerrilla, the often primitive nature of his communications meant further security and strength. The massive decentralized cellular structure of the irregular, united by a single idea and motive, created a redundant, "borglike" coherence that was extremely difficult to disrupt.

Fourth, the guerrilla's foe must be sufficiently weak in number to prevent him from occupying or influencing the disputed territory through some direct means of control. Adequate troop strength is always relative to the size of the country, the nature of the terrain, the disaffection of the populace, and especially the determination of the guerrilla. Even if the weak Turkish forces could have found a way to occupy or otherwise control every square mile of desert, there was no known system of logistics that could have sustained them all. Thus there was always enough "white space" on the chessboard where the insurgent could flourish.

Fifth, the guerrilla must possess at least the passive support of the populace, if not its full involvement. By Lawrence's calculation, "Rebellions can be made by 2 percent active in striking force and 98 percent passively sympathetic." As this condition persisted throughout most of the revolt, the rebels had a completely secure rear and worried only about the enemy to their front. A passive populace meant a secure active contingent that had little to fear from overt betrayal. The active force could rely on some element of sympathy that could be converted into direct logistical support, aid, and comfort. A passive populace also meant a potential source of recruitment. With a passive populace, the insurgent could move invisibly through a region. From the Turkish perspective, the passive populace was another opaque impediment to victory, as well as a source of deception and surprise. For the guerrilla, the populace was a continuous and invaluable source of accurate and timely information.

Sixth, the irregular must have the fundamental qualities of speed, endurance, presence, and logistical independence: he had to present the effect that he was everywhere, every time, all the time. If the Turk stood to fight under the heavy desert sun, the insurgent would be his dark shadow: ubiquitous, oppressive, and deadly. Whether imagined or real, the guerrilla specter sapped the morale and will of the Turk, limiting his combat potential and operational reach to the range of his own barracks. The 24/7 endurance of the outnumbered irregular meant a tactical tempo of operations that could only exhaust his stunned and immobilized opponent.

Finally, the irregular must be sufficiently armed with modern weaponry to be able to hit at the enemy's logistics and communications vulnerabilities. It was less necessary to kill the demoralized Turk than to kill his matériel. Lawrence and his men needed more dynamite than bullets. A dead Turk was a man who could no longer eat and remain a logistical burden; a dead Turk was a man who could no longer fear and spread the virus of terror among his living comrades. Lawrence wanted a living demoralized mob, not an army of dead heroes, for heroism is a powerful inoculation against fear that makes demoralized armies well and willing to fight.

In summarizing the practicality of his heresy, Lawrence offered the following theoretical bottom line: "Granted mobility, security (in the form of denying targets to the enemy), time and doctrine (the idea to convert every subject to friendliness), victory will rest with the insurgents, for the algebraical factors are in the end decisive, and against them perfections of means and spirit struggle quite in vain."

LAWRENCE'S SEVEN HERETICAL theses had to be put into action if they were to have any military or political value at all. The refinement took time to develop in the laboratory of the Hejaz desert, where the

Turkish army would act as his unwilling guinea pig. He pieced together several experimental hypotheses that would have to be tested in practice.

First, wherever possible when operating with a conventional army, that force would do the dying by *fixing* in place and distracting the main Turkish army. Lawrence's rebels would harass and pick the bones of the exhausted enemy: Allenby would hammer the Turks senseless; Lawrence and his raiders would simply knock them over.

Second, since the media in its many manifestations is a weapon of the insurgent, it is his to manipulate; and if he manipulates it, he owns it. The passive populace was vulnerable to Lawrence's leaflets— and he knew it. He knew he could blow up a minor skirmish into a huge victorious battle. The news would scream across the taut telegraph lines throughout the Arab world and generate more support, more recruits, and less passivity.

Third, for the insurgent, warfare had to be offensive, never defensive; always protracted, swift but endless; a risk but never a gamble; determined but never obstinate. For the Turks, there was no horizon of time: instead, he would bleed time as much as blood.

Fourth, in the experiments the guerrillas always had to organize into the smallest possible—and most lethal—formations; this was the key to survival in the first place. All units were units of action; there was no hierarchy, no wiring diagram, for this ultimately flat organization. Hierarchy meant hesitation, hesitation meant habituation, habituation meant anticipation by the enemy.

Fifth, as Lawrence understood, the ratio of troops to space determined the essential character of military operations in the desert. The simple field-and-bench physics of his desert laboratory made the conventional regular force a mechanical solid under constant *pressure* from the corrosive, erosive mist of the raiders. The irregulars simply leaked into the mechanical gears of the Turkish army to leach and desiccate the iron out of its will and existence.

Sixth, because the guerrilla controls precision information regarding the location, organization, and status of his enemy, all offensive actions become precision strikes. There are no misses, no near misses; maximum effectiveness leads to maximum efficiency. Nothing is wasted, nothing is gambled. Where risk arises, it is simply the residue of bad planning, just as Branch Rickey had said.

Last, where the insurgent had the physical quality of a corrosive mist or fog, it had the organic character of a hive: a complex network of chaotic social nets cast broadly throughout the desert. Here the primitive clan and tribe structure proved invaluable. The insurgent hive is perhaps the most evolved of human networks. It could never become completely disorganized, because it thrived on its own and the enemy's chaos; it could never *be* organized because it was in a constant state of *be*-coming. Lawrence never wholly controlled the rebellion any more than he commanded the wind; he could only influence it by the breathing presence of his leadership and will.

In the end, Lawrence's experiment rested most heavily on his leadership skills, abilities, and personal character. This also became the insurgents' greatest vulnerability: take away the leader and you have rendered the revolt impotent, ineffective, and incoherent. Lawrence was the tight fist that held close the rebellious bird shot; without his steady hand, all would have fallen away into the desert dust. His subversive leadership style, dominated as it was by his heretical genius, became a rare combination in a guerrilla leader that was unique in at least two ways. First, Lawrence combined wisdom, integrity, humanity, courage, and discipline with *empathy*: the ability to identify emotionally with all ranks. In an insurgency, empathy plays an especially crucial role; it places the leader inside the hearts and minds of his own men. He knows immediately and intuitively the physical and psychological limits of his troops. In guerrilla warfare, the insurgent must always operate at the limits of normal human endurance—and often beyond—to maintain a physical and moral advantage over his more powerful foe. Empathy also places the insurgent leader in the mind of his superior, a superior like Allenby. Often operating out of communications and at vast distances from his higher headquarters, Lawrence had to operate *as if* Allenby were at his side; *as if* Lawrence were his own supreme headquarters.

Second, insurgent leaders like Lawrence are successful because they are *enablers*: they provide their men with the requisite motivation, training, and skills necessary to accomplish a mission they otherwise could not accomplish alone. A leader who is an enabler makes his troops *believe* in themselves; they believe they can achieve goals they had never before imagined possible. Enablers operate much like catalysts in a chemical reaction as a factor that induces or precipitates action and change. Lawrence accomplished this in three ways as mentor, designer, and steward.

First, as teacher and mentor he taught his guerrillas the basic tactical skills of attack and defense, while imparting to them his new revolutionary theory of guerrilla warfare in an industrial context. Second, as designer he crafted tactical plans and operational concepts that were skillfully implemented within the overall strategic guidance handed down by Allenby. Finally, as steward he conserved, preserved, and invigorated the combat power of his lethal yet fragile guerrillas. At the same time, he was steward of the great Arab vision of revolution and statehood.

GIVEN LAWRENCE'S REVOLUTIONARY heresy of modern guerrilla warfare outlined above, was there any possible counterstrategy that the Turks could have employed? Assuming a Turkish version of T. E. Lawrence, one can make the following argument recognizing that conventional forces have confronted insurgents throughout the history of warfare and these challenges have been met with success on occasion with patience, creativity, diligence, and sound judgment. In the first place, the Turkish force had to think like an insurgent. Every move, plan, concept, and action had to be seen through the eyes of Lawrence. This demanded a level of imagination that the Turks apparently did not possess. Second, the Turkish army had to act with speed, shock, endurance, and initiative. And by endurance I mean especially *moral* endurance characterized by strength of will and *logistical* endurance as operations conducted independent of a continuous line of supply. Instead, time after time the Turks responded to Lawrence's moves with torpor and malaise. Third, the Turkish commander had to cast an unblinking eye upon the irregular through constant surveillance and precise intelligence. Instead, he was confused and befuddled by Lawrence. Fourth, the Turks had to present the insurgent with no obvious pattern, shape, or structure. This was impossible for the Turks, who were shackled to the railroad and the

Muslim holy places: their appearance was as apparent as muscle stretched over bone. Fifth, the only *active* strategy for the Turks to pursue was a strategy of *inoculation*: organizing Turkish conventional forces into small, cellular offensive "antibody" units that could "vaccinate" the local tribes against Lawrence and his guerrillas. Yet this had to fail simply because it demanded highly skilled and competent junior leadership, which the Turks, as a mass conscript army, never possessed. Sixth, the nature of Lawrence's theory of guerrilla warfare required that the enemy isolate Lawrence and his irregulars physically, cybernetically, and psychologically from their bases of support and from any means of communication. Of course, this meant taking risk and decisive offensive action that increasingly became impossible. Seventh, the Turks could have simply bought off the rebellious tribes with gold. Of all the counteractions taken by the Turks, this had some measure of success; in the end, however, the bankrupt Ottoman Empire never possessed near as much gold as the British. Eighth, the Turks sought, though rather ineptly, to destroy the Arab uprising by destroying its leadership: despite numerous close calls, Lawrence was able to survive. Finally, the most decisive strategic act the Turks could deliver in defeating Lawrence and the Arab insurrection was to defeat Allenby's main conventional army in Palestine; had these forces been defeated, it is almost certain that the fulminating revolt would have flickered out. Allied disasters on the western front would greatly weaken Allenby's forces, but in the end the Turks were unable to exploit these weaknesses strategically or operationally. British forces eventually grew strong enough to triumph at Damascus.

Of course, the final outcome was not necessarily foreordained or predetermined. Certainly Lawrence had no such vision from his sickbed in the Arabian desert. Victory was still two years away, beyond a horizon obscured by doubt and uncertainty. Only by dint of imagination, determination, genius, and optimism could Lawrence glimpse shadows of triumph amid the fog of war. Intellectually, this meant the kind of commitment to the future usually reserved for the heretic, and this heresy would lead Lawrence to his triumph at Aqaba.

CHAPTER FOUR

Aqaba!

The same problem, two different value systems; therefore, two different criteria, different decisions, and different solutions. This is the *problem of problems,* the subjective element of problem solving and decision making. Man's value system, his priorities, guide his behavior as manifested in problem solving and decision making. Two people, using the same rational tools of problem solving, may arrive at different solutions because they operate from different frames of values and, therefore, their behavior is different. When society faces problems, consensus must be formed to establish a societal value system. The subject of values and value theory is indeed the problem of problems. . . .

—MOSHE F. RUBINSTEIN, *Patterns of Problem Solving*

The large tent was dark, save for a small brazier warming the pots of coffee and tea. A few lanterns flickered, casting dim silhouettes upon the sooted canvas walls. Around the brazier two men sat, cross-legged, speaking in low voices. The light and shadow danced in unison with their softly spoken words: brightening and darkening, rising and falling.

It was the end of April 1917. Lawrence and Feisal were discussing the new hit-and-run strategy Lawrence had devised on his sickbed in Wadi Ais the previous month. But now the conversation turned to leadership. Lawrence frankly admitted to Feisal that he was a reluctant leader: more of an Odysseus than an Achilles, more of a

Xenophon than an Alexander, maybe even more a Saladin than a Richard the Lion-Hearted. He continued to describe the heavy burdens of leadership and responsibility. Feisal listened quietly and nodded in knowing sympathy.

Suddenly, the entrance of the tent flew open and lancing shafts of light stabbed the dazzled eyes of Lawrence and Feisal. At the threshold stood a dark figure, yet luminous in the radiant, blinding sunlight. "Ho, Feisal!" it called out in a powerful voice. Feisal knew the voice immediately. Auda, of the abu Tayi—the great eastern Howeitat tribe—had come to pay homage and help raise the intensity of the Arab Revolt to a new level.

This was the first time Lawrence had ever laid eyes on Auda abu Tayi. He saw a strong, tall, impressive figure with a haggard visage, at once passionate and compassionate, sad yet hopeful. He was dressed plainly in the northern manner of white cotton with a red Mosul head scarf. His age was an enigma; he might be at least fifty, with black hair trying to hide its gray. He was well built, straight like a ramrod: lithe and supple, with the energy of a much younger man. His face evoked tales of an epic life, rich in shadow and light and most recently etched in sorrow with the death of his beloved son, Annad. Auda's eyes were black and shiny like marbles; they could flash and glitter in anger. They were set beneath a broad and sloping forehead and above a sharp-beaked hook of a nose. His mouth was perpetually locked in a determined grimace that also carried a haughty whiff of disdain. A beard and mustache were clipped and trimmed to a point in Howeitat fashion and offered an exclamation to Auda's whole face.

Centuries earlier the Howeitat arrived from the Hejaz, and now their clans prided themselves on being true nomads in the Bedouin manner. Auda was the tribal archetype: a heroic leader and warrior in the tradition of Cochise, Geronimo, Crazy Horse, Sitting Bull. His generosity made him poor as his growing legend made him ever richer in reputation. He had taken twenty-eight wives during his adult life; his body bore the scars of thirteen wounds; he had seen most of his relations slain in countless raids. Auda had slain seventy-five Arabs with his own hand. How many Turks? Auda did not tally them: they simply didn't count. His retinue comprised the fiercest men of the tribe, fighting beside Auda with a relentless courage. He had known them all since boyhood, when they numbered twelve hundred, but now only five hundred fighters remained; the rest lay scattered across thirty years and many more miles of desert.

Auda was a robber baron, a desert pirate: no need to put a fine point on the fact. His corsairs raided from Aleppo, Wejh, Wadi Gawasir, and even as far east as Basra and Baghdad. There was scarce a tribe in the desert that did not fear and even despise Auda, which was fine with him: fewer friends meant all the more to steal. He leavened his hot passion with an unusual calculated cunning. His recklessness was only a facade that covered many days of planning and rational consideration. He had the stalking patience of a jaguar, and when Auda was ready to act, his strike was just as swift and deadly. He took counsel of no one but himself: he was autonomous, autarkic. In his tactical craft he was without equal. Who could give Auda advice? Who else had thirty years of constant raiding experience? Who had the temerity to give advice to a legend?

As a cultural artifact, Auda was also a latter-day Homer who saw his life as a long epic struggle. Yet this heroic conceit only reflected his powerful imagination. He could conjure poems of himself in epic Homeric fashion: saga-sung in his own deep, stentorian voice. At each rendition the story changed in subtle refinement, always a work in progress, like his own life. He even referred to himself in the detached third person. He loved his own self-made legend more than his real self. At a personal level, he was able to detach himself from his mind-forged epics to remain a humble, modest, and charismatic leader. To those close to him, he more often hurt with his sharp tongue than with his well-honed sword: he was direct, honest, and warmhearted.

Auda was just the tactical leader Lawrence required to help implement his new strategy of exhaustion that would grind down the Turks into powder. And Lawrence himself was leader enough to recognize that he would need Auda in the long months ahead. He knew the Bedouin tribesmen would rather follow an animated legend like Auda than some sublime cause—or pale Englishman.

After the ritual dinner with Feisal, Auda, and the other guests, Lawrence carefully laid out his strategy. He began with an admission that his initial assessment of the campaign was wrong. First, he said, since the Arab irregulars were incapable of attacking places and defending fixed positions, they must change their strategy to one of maneuver. Second, since they were incapable of conventional attack or defense, they could not impose a decision on the Turks. Yet a tactical decision was unnecessary. As long as they did not lose, they were winning, even if it meant never fighting another battle. Finally, their real strength resided in their ability to strike deep into the enemy's territory and into his rear.

Lawrence rose from his discarded meal and continued, padding softly on the outstretched rug: "This Arab war is geographical, and the Turkish Army an accident. We must seek the enemy's weakest material link and bear only on that till the rest is moved and dislocated. Our largest resources, the Bedouin on whom our war must be built, are unused to conventional operations. But"—he paused in midstride on the colorful carpet—"they have the assets of mobility, toughness, self-assurance, knowledge of the country, intelligent courage. With them dispersal will be our strength. Thus it seems we must extend our front to its maximum, to impose on the Turks the longest possible passive defense, which is to them the costliest form of war."

To Feisal, Lawrence's new strategy was becoming clearer; he nodded toward Lawrence to continue. "My lord Feisal, we must remember that our duty is to achieve our end with greatest economy of life, since life is more precious to us than money or even time. But think of it: in relative terms we are stronger than the Turks in transport, machine guns, cars and high explosives—*at the decisive point*. We can deploy a highly mobile, lightly equipped striking force of the smallest size, and use it successively at distributed points along the Turkish line, to force them to strengthen their posts beyond the usual twenty men. This will be our shortcut to success."

Lawrence now stopped his peripatetic monologue in front of Auda. He looked up at the Englishman with a curious twinkle in his black eyes that slowly softened to a dark velvet: yes, Auda understood, too. Still, Feisal was not completely convinced. All the plans had been made—the troops deployed, the supplies prepared—to support operations toward Medina in the south. Why change now? Wasn't it too late? Lawrence turned to Feisal: "We must not take Medina. The Turks are harmless there. If we imprisoned them all—say, in Egypt—they would cost us in food, water and guards. We want them right where they are, at Medina and at every other distant place in the largest numbers. Our goal must be to keep the railroad working, but just barely while inflicting maximum loss and discomfort on the Turks. That simple factor and water will confine him to the railways; and let him have them all: the Hejaz Railway, the Trans-Jordan and the Palestine and Syrian lines. He can have them for the whole war, while we take the rest of the Arab world. His stupidity will be our ally, for he believes that his success depends on holding as many of the older provinces as possible. This pride in his imperial heritage will keep him in his present absurd position: all flanks and no front."

Feisal nodded, almost imperceptibly falling slightly toward Lawrence, seeming to understand fully at last. Yet the fact remained that plans were afoot, troops in motion. And of course Lawrence was cognizant of all this. He had had his fair hearing with Feisal and his advisers and had at least made a strong case that a possible raid on Aqaba could be a useful diversion to aid Feisal's designs against the Turkish supply lines. At length, Feisal gave his consent to the raid on the port.

Lawrence next turned to Auda: "We should be able to march to the Howeitat in their spring pastures in the Syrian desert. From there we can raise a mobile camel force and rush Aqaba from the north into their naked back where they have neither guns nor machine guns." The whole landward side of the Turkish defenses at Aqaba was unguarded. Auda's considered response was plain and direct: "All things are possible with dynamite and English gold; the smaller clans of the Howeitat will join us, definitely."

Auda looked at the curious Englishman, seemingly for the first time. Truly there was a touch of genius upon this smallish man. At that instant, Auda realized here was a man who would help his legend grow even greater.

Lawrence turned away from Auda and brushed close to Feisal and in a low voice said: "You know, I have no official sanction to conduct this operation. This is completely on my own."

Feisal looked at Lawrence, now painfully aware of his youth, all the more distinct beside the grizzled Auda. The prince said almost inaudibly, "Then you must succeed."

Just then Auda suddenly leapt to his feet, crying out: "God forbid!" and quickly ran from the tent. Lawrence and the rest stared at one another in disbelief. Had Auda finally gone mad? They soon heard a pounding sound from outside; at that they all rushed out to investigate the clamor and Auda's odd behavior. Once outside, they saw him hammering his false teeth into smithereens with a large rock. Halting his demolition, Auda looked up at the puzzled group and said casually, "Oh, I had forgotten; Jemal Pasha gave me these. I was eating my lord Feisal's bread with Turkish teeth!" After a moment of stunned silence, the onlookers erupted in laughter, dancing around Auda and clapping him on the back.

Off to one side, Lawrence was enjoying the spectacle, taking everything in. Clearly Auda was like a knight-errant—like the ones he had studied and read about at Oxford. Indeed, he thought, this man Auda abu Tayi is the Prophet's sword. He must now be unsheathed.

BY MAY 9, all was ready. Lawrence and his small band rode out from Feisal's camp with his blessing—and four hundred pounds of gold. They were also joined by Sherif Nasir, a veteran raider like Auda and proven leader of forlorn hopes. He was a leading emir in his own right, from Medina; a trusted confidant of Feisal and one of the few leaders who understood fully the Arab cause and the idea of national freedom. Now the strain of the struggle was beginning to weigh upon Nasir. For months, he had led the advance guard of Feisal's rebel army and been at the forefront of every skirmish and battle. The dangerous mission clearly was grinding down on his nerves. As with Lawrence, his relative youth was starting to slip ever faster through his life's fingers, and it seemed as if his spirit were dying quicker than his mortal body. If only both would last long enough to complete the revolt.

The first leg of the journey was to the northeast, to the old fort at Sebeil where Egyptian pilgrims used to rest and water by a great brick cistern set in the shade of the dusty fortress. The first leg was a shake-out march, as more warriors joined the caravan. Auda, the tactical leader of the group, led with his retainers; Feisal's political emissary to the Syrians, Nesib el Bekri from Damascus, rode with Lawrence. Nesib's political acumen was unique among the Arabs: a desert cosmopolitan who wore his urban sophistication with ease, not as a badge. He was also good-natured, fond of risk, tough, and a true patriot of a promised nation. His eloquence and persuasion would be crucial in the weeks to come. Along with Nesib rode Zeki, a former Syrian officer and trusted aide.

Thirty-five Ageyli tribesmen under the watchful and brooding ibn Dgheithir commanded the escort. Sheikh Yussuf was the expedition's stingy quartermaster, doling out half a bag of flour to each rider. The forty-five-pound sack was expected to last each man six weeks and represented a prisoner's ration of soft bread and water: perhaps a boon to the unfortunate Auda, whose lingering snaggleteeth would have to await replacement by an Allied dentist.

The gold was distributed among the riders for safekeeping and to reduce its risk of catastrophic loss or capture. At present, the baggage camels were overloaded, but two weeks of eating would soon ease their burden. There was little room for spare ammo. Extra rifles were carried as special blandishments during Nesib's negotiations with the tribes. Six of the camels bore a load of special dynamite packs for the anticipated encounters with rails, trains, and bridges. Nasir brought an elaborate tent in which to host Nesib's visitors and a camel load of rice for their gratitude. In the end, however, the desert riders, in moments of hungered weakness, would eat it themselves and express immense gratitude.

Lawrence's personal bodyguard had increased as well. The dour Merjan, the hapless Ali, and the jocular Murkheymer were joined by the paunchy Mohammed. The renegade Gasim also enrolled. He was on the run for killing a Turkish bureaucrat over a cattle-tax dispute. The crime gave Gasim a certain cachet among the men since they all hated the taxman.

After a long repast at Sebeil, Lawrence and the men mounted up and rode into the midnight desert toward the oasis of El Kurr. During the ride, Auda continually rode up and down the column of riders like a sheepdog, keeping the formation close and tight. His concern was in losing men in the night march, but there was also another fear: the riders might overtake the mange-ridden pack animals and lose the sorry beasts in the dark. The riders groused at the slow pace, but Auda merely raised his whip hand and the bitching ceased.

Nasir was out in the lead, guiding the caravan under a bright desert moon. After a while, Lawrence sidled up to the desert ranger.

They rode in silence for a long time. "I was thinking," Nasir said at length, rocking easy in the saddle. "I was thinking about my home in Medina: the stone-paved house with sunken walls and vaulted ceilings standing against the summer sun. The gardens are beautiful, like Eden with every imaginable fruit tree offering shade from the sun and easy paths through their verdant depths. The well is quite large and serves a huge reservoir where my brother and I used to swim after lunch. I ask myself now why I gave this all up to become a rebel chasing about in the desert. The Turks came and seized my home, demolished my garden and chopped down my palm trees. Even the well, driven by oxen for over six hundred years, has become silent. The whole place is now cracked by the sun. I am wondering: for what?"

Lawrence was quiet, for he had no answer, though the question always lingered, lurking in the minds of all the riders, just at the edge of awareness, waiting to rush in at moments of weakness and fatigue.

AFTER SEVERAL HOURS of night riding, the men had two hours of rest and were awakened by the sun. Auda rousted the raiders and drove them for six hours into the morning heat. The sun reflected off the white glittering sand and cast dazzling razor blades into the eyes of Lawrence and the others. The shimmering heat rose from the parched sand about them like ancient apparitions, clouding their aching minds. From a distance, the caravan appeared as insubstantial as the heat, like ghost raiders.

By eleven o'clock the men were wasted, and despite Auda's urgings, they rested until midafternoon. The ride resumed for several more hours over gentle terrain toward the face of a great valley that clutched the oasis of El Kurr with its pleasant gardens of dates and palms. After he arrived, Lawrence learned that the reinforcements led by Sherif Sharraf would not be at hand as planned. Sharraf was still off raiding and was not expected to return for a few more days. The news was greeted with elation by all, since it meant that Auda's furious pace would halt for the time being. This was especially beneficial to Lawrence, whose bout with boils and fever returned. The green oasis would soon work its soothing magic on all.

By the second night at El Kurr, the men were in much better fettle. From inside Abdullah's tent, Lawrence could hear the riders as they feasted on Nasir's rice and celebrated around the cooking fires. Nesib el Bekri had taken a manuscript of songs of the Turkish revolutionary Selim el Jezairi. Nesib had gathered the men around and they sang the songs in a fervent emotional chant, the words conjuring up the hope and passion that began to renew the moral strength of the riders. For a time, it seemed to Lawrence, Emir Nasir's question of personal doubt had been answered.

THANKS TO AUDA'S impatience, the idyll was shattered: the men mounted up and at two in the morning left the oasis. Auda took the lead, this time singing an old Howeitat marching song that seemed to Lawrence to consist of nothing more than an interminable "ho, ho, ho" chanted in bass notes up and down the musical scale and sometimes even sideways. The purpose of the melody was to maintain coherence and direction of the advance by riding to the sound of Auda's booming voice. At times the chant ricocheted off the flanking black cliffs, adding yet more monotony to the sound—a sound that could have been sung in any language.

On the ride, Lawrence was able to use the time to help perfect his Arabic, a crucial capability for a leader operating in another culture. Without a common language, military or any other kind of social action is impossible. During the long journey, Lawrence spent the saddle time improving his Arabic, thanks to the patience of Nasir and Auda's sour-pussed cousin Mohammed el Dheilan. They drilled Lawrence in the classical Medina dialect and variants of the desert Arab slang. The education broadened Lawrence's Middle Euphrates brogue, which he had picked up while digging at Carchemish, though at a short-term price: initially every conversation became an adventure in the vernacular. For a time Lawrence seemed illiterate or sun-addled, even retarded. The constant practice, however, soon led to improvement and broadened the scope of Lawrence's leadership.

The ride continued until dawn with an unmemorable break till late afternoon with the men dozing beneath stinging flies and under makeshift blanket lean-tos. After supper, Nasir replaced Auda in the lead of the formation. During the ride, Lawrence pondered the seemingly dysfunctional style of Arab leadership. Nasir, Auda, and Nesib were leaders in their own right, yet it was apparent the competition over the right to lead was growing. At the moment, Nasir held the hand of command by virtue of the fact that Lawrence was his guest. All three had to consult together on even the minutest and most trivial detail, lest one of the others be slighted. The competition wore especially heavily on Auda, who had never followed anyone in his entire life. Yet the key to success at Aqaba would be the utmost cooperation, something the Arabs had yet fully to master.

As Lawrence reflected on the matter, he thought, "Such people demand a war-cry and banner outside to combine them, and a stranger to lead them, one whose supremacy should be based on an idea: illogical, undeniable, discriminate: which instinct might accept and reason find no rational basis to reject or oppose." Lawrence imagined Auda as the "war-cry" and Feisal as the "banner." If Lawrence was the "stranger," did that make him the leader? At least as far as this move on Aqaba, it did. Out of necessity, then, Lawrence began to slowly, almost imperceptibly, impose a unity of command and control on the expedition.

THE RIDERS CONTINUED over ever-changing terrain. The track soon became little better than a goat path: crooked and steep, little more than a seam edging near a precipice. Halfway up the climb, it became impossible to urge the camels forward as they slipped dangerously over loose rocks. Auda then decided that the animals had to be repacked to better distribute the loads of food and dynamite. This eased the climb a bit, but two of the mangy beasts broke down in the pass. Here, the Howeitat killed them with swift precision where they fell, striking an artery deep in the camels' necks. Under their last, selfless exertions, blood spewed forth in a mist, seemingly turning to rust in the desiccating air. They were then quickly sliced up in silence and shared out among the raiders as the creatures' final bequest.

At last the pass was traversed, and the riders came upon a broad plateau known as the Shefa crest, sloping more easily to the east and becoming a white-shingled valley that held the water hole of Abu Saad. Vegetation grew around the well that promised shade, comfort, and rest. The air in this high desert was cooler as it wafted across a great black lava field, hemmed in by red and striped sandstone pillars and precipices. Here Nasir ordered a halt, to the relief of Lawrence, whose boil-induced fever continued to burn.

The following morning, the men breakfasted on the fresh camel meat; then, refreshed, they marched out and down into a deep gorge called the Wadi Jizil. The gouge in the earth was at least two hundred feet wide. The dank, musty smell evoked a memory of water that had recently coursed through this gutter. The cliffs soaring above them cast fantastic silhouettes in the dancing light. The high-walled gorge was filled with sweet tamarisk and sand dunes, some twenty feet high. The walls bore the same multicolored striations as the high desert cliffs. Here the pinks and vermilions seemed more subdued out of direct sunlight. By evening, the sun had crept into the full length of the wadi, flashing an intense and vibrant red. Slowly the sun moved along, leaving a purple pall in its wake through the gorge and alerting Nasir that it was time to stop.

The camp was set up in a cleft of the wadi out of the sun's reach, where sand and other detritus had gathered from the earlier rains. The camels seemed to enjoy the novelty of weeds and brackish water. Off in the distance, Sharraf's raiding contingent could be seen encamped near a large thicket of oleander. Still, Sharraf had not completed his mission, so Lawrence's men lounged about in grateful leisure. Lawrence's fever had finally broken, and he wandered about the camp taking stock of the morale of the riders.

On the second morning, as the caravan continued to wait for Sharraf, two outcasts straggled in from his camp seeking refuge from Sharraf's wrath. Daud and Farraj had burned down one of the tents in a prank that had gone awry. The two pleaded their case throughout Lawrence's encampment and found no mercy until they came to the Englishman himself. He took pity on them and with Nasir's blessing allowed them to stay. The rest of the day witnessed a bored Nasir, flicking flickering matches at a dozing Lawrence.

SHARRAF FINALLY ARRIVED in camp on the third day, his entrance heralded with a rattle of rifle fire. He and his raiders had captured several prisoners, destroyed a portion of the rail line, and blown up an important culvert. He also brought the good news that the Wadi

Diraa was full of fresh rainwater and would shorten the waterless march to Fejr by fifty miles. The news brought special relief to Auda and Nasir. It meant the ration of twenty gallons of water for fifty men could be increased to a more tolerable margin of risk.

The next day, the riders left the dank Abu Raga campsite. Auda led the caravan up a branch valley, which soon opened up into the sandy flat plain of the windy Shegg. The valley transformed into a maze of ice-cream-cone pinnacles of red limestone that seemed impossible to navigate without getting lost. The dry wind blew through the formations with an eerie, whistling cry. Only the veteran Auda seemed unfazed as he swept through the tangle of blind alleys without any hesitation: all the more remarkable since there were no footprints left on the ground to follow. The sandblasting wind had brushed everything over with its stippling breath. All that remained were a few camel droppings, blown about like tan golf balls. But the remnants provided Auda with the thread of his assurance and confidence through the labyrinth. The riders marveled at Auda's pathfinding skills, as much as they were astonished by the wind-chiseled terrain.

By May 19, every one of the raiders' camels was sick with mange. Nasir began to worry that the whole expedition might collapse in the long ride ahead and leave them all ditched in the desert. None of the riders had medicine for the crippling disease. But then Auda hit on the field expedient of dressing the sickest animals with butter. The trick seemed to work, but Lawrence wondered how long the butter would last. The concern seemed irrelevant, however, for now the horizon of worry had shrunk to the next ridgeline.

THE RIDE TOWARD Fejr took them across the main rail line and offered an opportunity to strike at the Turks that could not be lost. Lawrence and three or four others crawled up a high dune to observe the line and found this stretch abandoned, save for a weed-ridden blockhouse. All seemed quiet: Lawrence urged the raiders to move across to the far side of the track. While the move was in motion, he and several Ageyli set dynamite charges at various places along the line. The men set off the explosives in a special set progression to get maximum effect from the blasts. Auda had never before seen the power of dynamite and took a childlike pleasure in its force. As an afterthought, some of the Ageyli cut three telegraph lines. For no discernible purpose, they attached the lengthy wire to the saddles of six of the riding camels and twanged across the rails into the dusk, sounding like a badly tuned guitar. After some hours of riding and much laughter, they released the wires from the nervous camels.

Auda had the riders up at four the next morning, moving uphill until a broad plain opened wide to the east. The Bedouin called the place El Houl, which meant "Desolation." It was aptly named, for the party now saw no signs of life. As Lawrence rode, he thought about the place in its growing vastness: "How tiny we must all feel in it: our urgent progress across its immensity is a stillness or immobility of futile effort. The only sounds we hear are the hollow echoes, like a shutting down of pavements over vaulted places, of rotten stone slab on stone slab tilting under our camels' feet."[1]

A breathless wind began to blow; it had the metallic taste of an open furnace, harbinger of a sandstorm—the deadly khamsin. As the day wore on, the sun fueled the wind, which blew great gulps of dust down from the anvil of the great Nefud desert, just beyond the khaki clouds rising to the east. At noon, the desiccating dust was blowing with a thirty-knot wind, sucking moisture from the mouths and eyes of the riders. The men rode on, bending into the thirsty wind, covering their faces as best they could from the invasive dust. The column was now virtually invisible amid the blowing powder. A choking talcum made breathing a gasping effort for both men and beasts as the grinding grit chafed mind as well as body.

The raiders plodded on through the blasting storm for almost fifty miles until encroaching dusk finally tamed the storm. The men rallied in camp and were as dry as the deadwood they gathered for the night fire. When it was time to torch the pile, no match could be found, save for the fiery glances cast at the match-flinging Nasir.

AT NOON ON the following day, they finally reached the large well at Fejr. It was thirty feet deep, full of brackish but refreshing water. And around the well persisted a ragged but sufficient pasturage for the camels. Auda sent out hunters who returned with gazelle to replenish the party's meat stocks. The attentive Nasir and Nesib had carefully managed the endurance of the party by doling out meat, water, and rice when they sensed man and animal were breaking. This keen intuition, based on long experience, was one of the key lessons Lawrence learned since the long trek began exactly two weeks earlier. He would take the teaching to heart and to practice.

The next phase of the journey would take them to Arfaja in the Wadi Sirhan and hard by the great Nefud. Lawrence asked Auda for the opportunity to cross a small portion of the desert, just as all the famous desert explorers had done. At this Auda merely sneered: "What? Only fools and raiders cross the Anvil, and only raiders out of necessity. And I, Auda abu Tayi, would never raid on this mangy tottering animal."[2]

Auda's wise leadership had the caravan riding over the less risky, though more monotonous terrain of glittering sand and gleaming mud called *Giaan*. In the distance, the ground looked black and polished like onyx and reflected the sun with a mirror's intensity. The sun beat down upon the riders from above, doing double duty in its rebounding reflection from the stone below. By now, Lawrence and the men had developed the ability to ride in a near trancelike state to cope with the heat and exhaustion. Only the camels—and Auda— seemed to maintain sensory vigilance.

After a brief halt, Auda decided to change course and follow a tiptoe route through the plain of Biseita and avoid the flint daggers.

BY MAY 24, many of the men were walking their camels for fear the animals would be dead by nightfall. The column was now straggling badly, with Auda and Nasir doing their best to maintain a manageable pace through the remnants of the sandstorm. Lawrence was in the rear, trying to rally the stragglers, when he noticed that Gasim was missing. After riding forward to the main body, he found Gasim's riderless camel bearing only saddlebags and rifle: Gasim appeared to be missing and probably lost. In the mirage and shroud of the desert heat, it was impossible to see clearly beyond a distance of a mile. If Gasim was beyond that range, he would see nothing but shimmering desert.

Lawrence at once sought out Mohammed, Gasim's kinsman, to have him track down his wayward fellow. But it became immediately evident to Lawrence that Mohammed's own camel was shot and would barely make the night's encampment. Lawrence hesitated: "If I send him, it would be murder. This shifts the difficulty to my shoulders. The Howeitat would help me, but they are away somewhere in the mirage aiding Auda's path-finding. Ibn Dgheithir's Ageyl are so clannish that they would not put themselves out except for one another. Besides Gasim had become one of my men and upon me lay the responsibility of him."

Lawrence glanced at the men straggling past, wondering briefly if he could send one of them out instead: "My shirking the duty would be understood, because I'm a foreigner—but that's precisely the plea I dare not set up. How can I, if I'm here to help these Arabs in their own revolt? It's hard anyway for a strange leader to influence another people's national movement, and doubly hard for a Christian, and an amateur at that, to sway Moslem nomads. I'd simply make it impossible in my own mind, if I claimed the privileges of both societies."[3]

At that last thought, Lawrence turned his bleating camel around and without a word headed through the mirage. His mind filled with the regret of letting a ne'er-do-well like Gasim join his bodyguard. Throughout the trek, he had demonstrated his worthlessness to the cause. In the irony, Lawrence wondered at the thought that the revolt might now lose his own contribution over a single skulking malingerer like Gasim.

In twenty minutes, the straggling caravan was out of sight, consumed by the wall of shimmering heat. The desert now seemed more desolate than ever: the glimpse of every passing hoof- and footprint mocked Lawrence's decision to rescue Gasim. The wind slowly brushed away his own tracks, so Lawrence was forced to leave his trail by riding through patches of *samh,* a desert wildflower. The sun was now mercifully at his back.

After riding for over an hour, Lawrence saw a black object through sand-encrusted eyes. Was it a bush? A man? A mirage? The shimmering heat obscured size and distance, though the object appeared to be moving at a tangent to the caravan's path. Lawrence urged his camel on, and at last the mirage parted to reveal the lost Gasim, nearly mad with thirst and blind from the pounding sun. He stood before Lawrence in a pathetic stance: arms outstretched, mouth agape, tears streaming. Lawrence handed him his water skin—the last of the water among the Ageyli. Gasim spilled the water insanely over his seared face and chest in eagerness to quench his thirst. After finally regaining his senses, he regaled his rescuer with a tale of woes.

Without a word, Lawrence grabbed the unfortunate man and tossed him on the rump of the life-preserving camel and set an azimuth with his compass in the direction of the caravan. As the two set out, the camel seemed to sense some great achievement, for she carried the men in an easy shuffle into the sun. The beast's renewed spirit sparked joy in Lawrence's own heart, so he ignored the ragged moaning of Gasim. Yet the farther the pair went, the louder he became, bouncing down hard on the camel and causing Lawrence to fear that Gasim's recoil would induce the animal to founder. At this danger, Lawrence reached behind and cracked Gasim over the shoulder and back with his riding crop. After a final pathetic whimper, Gasim settled down, clamping a life-and-death grip on the saddle.

A half an hour or more into the rescue, Lawrence saw another black blob dancing and shimmering amid the mirage ahead. The dark amoeba split into three gobbets, and Lawrence wondered if these were the desperate raiders Auda had warned of, coming out of the fiery Nefud. A few moments later, the bubbled images dissolved to reveal the toothless grin of Auda with two of Nasir's riders. Lawrence, to hide his great relief, mocked Auda for leaving a comrade to die alone in the desert. Auda pointed to the miserable figure of Gasim and said, "For that thing? He's not worth a camel price." At that, he struck Gasim over the head for emphasis.

After a hard ride, the five rejoined the column, to be greeted by a vexed Nesib. He chided Lawrence for endangering the mission for a man of dubious quality and imperiling Auda and the others. Auda, though, enjoyed the opportunity to demonstrate the difference between the town Arab and the desert Arab. He said to Nesib, "But here we have the collective responsibility and group brotherhood of the desert; while you townsmen with your cutthroat existence live in isolation."[4]

The caravan at last reached Arfaja in the pleasant Sirhan valley. All the riders marched in exhausted; and to his exhaustion Lawrence melded his sense of exultation at being alive and at meeting the challenge of leadership: some might question Lawrence's choice over the age-old dilemma of whether the mission came before the men. In Western militaries, the mission always superseded the man. In his mind, the question was knocked in a cocked hat. In the desert culture, men came first; let the effete stand with the mission, for in the end, without the soldier, what does the mission matter?

ARRIVAL AT ARFAJA meant at last meeting the eastern Howeitat and the beginning of recruitment for the final push on Aqaba. After a long night of fasting, for the men had no water with which to eat and cook, they spent the day in a state of happy recovery. The wells around Arfaja were at least eighteen feet deep, containing the strong brackish desert water. Abundant grazing was at hand for the exhausted camels, too.

Enemy riders encountered the camp the next morning but seemed passive and rode off. The afternoon lulled everyone into a lazy, detached stupor. Coffee was brewed at the campfire, and Lawrence spent the time with Mohammed el Dheilan. After Auda, Mohammed was second in influence among the abu Tayi clan and had even more followers than Auda himself. Mohammed was the true brain behind the clan, the political and strategic counterpoint to Auda the tactician. Lawrence was fond of Mohammed's serious and critical outlook on military matters and sought to use him as an effective mouthpiece for his own ideas at the forthcoming tribal councils.

The perilous journey had now created a powerful cohesive force among the raiders. The men were thus musing as the coffeemaker strained the brew through a palm fiber mat when shots suddenly rang out from behind the dark dunes to the east. Assaf, the Ageyli fighter, screamed and pitched forward into the fire, spewing fire and ash all around. He was stone dead.

Mohammed was the first to react, leaping up and dragging a heavy foot through the sand into the sputtering fire to extinguish it. The caravan's outriders immediately returned fire. Auda's cousin Zaal ran out on cat's feet to assess the enemy's strength. Half an hour later, he returned and reported casually that the enemy had been defeated and left.

After passing a sleepless night, the men rose before dawn to bury

Assaf, the party's first casualty, according to Muslim tradition. Lawrence peered at the white-shrouded body and realized the dying had begun and wondered how long it would continue.

Auda led the group a day's journey farther north into the heart of the Sirhan. It was clear to the leaders that if they hung around the contested wells at Arfaja, they would end up killing more fellow Arabs than the hated Turks. At midday on May 27, dark riders from the east pounded hard for the caravan. The sharp-eyed Zaal dismissed the moment of drama by calling out, "Howeitat!" The men had at last arrived at the core of the Howeitat encampment, stretching from Isawiya to Nebk. The first part of their strategic mission had been accomplished. The caravan moved fast to Isawiya and the tent of Ali abu Fitna, one of Auda's chiefs. Ali was old and seemed to have a chronic allergy, a rare malady in the desert. His nose dripped like a leaky faucet into his beard, and despite the heavy watering, his beard remained scraggly. With every word he sniffled and snuffled, dripped and dropped, making the riders suddenly thirsty.

Ali had prepared a great homecoming feast in the Bedouin tradition that would take hours to prepare. While waiting, the command group—Lawrence, Auda, Nasir, and Nesib—met to discuss a matter of some political delicacy: how much money to give Nuri Shaalan, the emir of the region. Lawrence recalled that Nuri was the fourth most powerful leader among the desert Arabs, after Hussein, ibn Saud, and ibn Rashid. Nuri was the leader of the powerful Ruwalla and also a good friend of Auda's. It was therefore decided that Auda should carry the gift of six thousand British pounds to the emir on the morrow.

The huge dinner found the men the most relaxed and at ease they had been in over two weeks. Much had been accomplished: the raiders had cohered into a cohesive fighting force with a common motivation and understanding of the mission; they had developed an esprit and genuine fondness for one another. Yet the whole process was more of luck than by design. The desert march was a true test of that luck, but an even greater test was still to come.

Lawrence considered all this as he looked across at the happy Auda—though hapless at being toothless—as he gummed the roast mutton into submission. Perhaps, Lawrence thought, the good troops make their own luck. With men like Auda and Nasir, at least, the dice were cocked.

Auda went off to Nuri with six sacks of gold heavy in his saddle-bags. As he rode, Auda painstakingly went over in his mind the passage from Wejh to the Howeitat encampment. The details were necessary in order to extend and refine the legend he had been weaving all his life. His mind's epic would now have to be recounted anew for his host, Nuri. In distilled form, the story of the passage had taken the caravan on an eighteen-day journey through Abu Raga, Diraa, across the Hejaz railway, the Desolation, and the western flank of the great Nefud, Fejr, and finally to Arfaja, the gateway into Wadi Sirhan and the great Howeitat encampment.

On a map, though, the journey seemed oddly conceived. If the objective was Aqaba, why take such an eccentric route? Where Auda now rode, he was still two hundred miles from his goal. Of course, the answer revolved around the necessity to mobilize and recruit Auda's clans in order to generate additional combat power for the final strike on Aqaba. To Auda's mind, these strategic and operational essentials were mere cumbersome details that distracted from the central narrative of Auda's life epic, its recrafting and its retelling.

While Auda was on his mission to Nuri, the rest of the caravan enjoyed a desert cornucopia of three days of feasting. Twice a day, the riders were treated to the limitless beneficence of Bedouin hospitality.

On May 30, Ali abu Fitna's entire camp suddenly detached itself from the earth and began to move. As one mind, the clan embarked in complete unison, losing all its manifest chaos. Like a perambulating flea market, the untented nomads gathered everything and withdrew with a silent renewed sense of purpose. Lawrence and his riders blended in readily with the desert migration. The move was an easy march to a more central campsite better designed to facilitate the arrival of Auda with his recruits. The redeployment took them farther along a north-westerly line deeper into the Sirhan valley to Abu Tarfeiyat.

To Lawrence, the displacement would become a memorable encounter with terror. For some unknown reason—perhaps because of an overabundance of seasonal rain—the wadi was utterly infested with every known variety of desert snake: horned viper, puff adder, cobra, and lizard. Movement by night was especially perilous, and the party had to beat the brush as they warily trod about with bare feet. The infestation was particularly dense around the watering areas, where the reptiles naturally stalked their thirsty prey. In the heat of the day, the snakes became especially bold, wandering into the circle of men huddled around the brewing coffee and tea. The riders killed forty snakes by the end of the two days, losing three men to the deadly strikes. The nightmare was made all the worse for Lawrence thanks to the pranks of Daud and Farraj, who found creative ways to adorn the Englishman's sleeping form with the colorful snakes, both dead and alive. The two paid for their impudence by serving daily kitchen duty with the women.

The caravan also had to endure the prolonged culinary assault to their digestive tracts: the long trek across the desert had essentially shut down all normal gastric reflexes. In a week, the fifty men had consumed as many sheep. Now they were all paying a heavy price in fast trots through the knots of snakes to seek relief.

The easy march continued through Ghutti to Ageila, where Auda, who had received the blessings of Nuri to proceed, waited with the rest of the Howeitat contingent. Auda was in his huge tribal tent. Lawrence and Nasir settled in and immediately began receiving pledges of allegiance from the tribesmen. As sheikh and Feisal's formal representative, Nasir received the oaths on Feisal's behalf. The ceremony would take several more days, as the visitors queued through the tent to find carefully brewed coffee as a token of thanks for their oaths of allegiance.

The enrollment of the eastern Howeitat clans under Auda meant a significant expansion of the Arab Revolt, for it opened up a whole new front against the eastern flank of the Turkish forces in Jordan and Syria. What had been just a political hope for Lawrence and Feisal had now become a strategic reality. The question yet to be answered was, how best to unsheathe and strike with this new weapon?

DURING THE NEXT few days, Auda and Nasir continued the enrollment of the various clans at the more central location of Nebk. The area had fewer snakes and was also better watered, holding the Blaidat, or "salt hamlets." Meanwhile, Lawrence spent his time with Nesib and Zeki, Feisal's two Syrian political advisers. The long traveling adven-

ture of men and earth that had brought a measure of fragile coherence to the caravan soon came under challenge during the period of
leisure and recovery. Nesib began to express his personal agenda,
which in Lawrence's view was purely delusional—and dangerous.

Nesib started to concoct a plan whereby the group would strike
out, not against Aqaba as planned, but at the far glittering prize of
Damascus. Nesib argued that he could enroll the Syrian tribes of the
Shaalans, the Druzes, and others. As for the Turks, they would be
completely unprepared for such a gambit: "We must seize Damascus!" The eagerness and force of Nesib's argument disturbed Lawrence, who rejoined: "My dear Nesib, truly you must be mad: Feisal
is still in Wejh, of no help to us or Damascus; the British are on the
wrong side of Gaza and the Turks are amassing a new army at
Aleppo." Nesib, perhaps now seeing himself more as a Syrian liberator
and less as an Arab revolutionary, rejected Lawrence's arguments.
Still, Lawrence persisted with Nesib and Zeki. "If we seize Damascus,
it would be impossible to hold it for more than six weeks at the
utmost. There is no way General Murray could organize an offensive
against the Turks on such short notice. Nor would he be able to have
the necessary amphibious transport to land a force at Beirut to link
up with us in Damascus. And when we lose Damascus—for surely we
will—we will lose all the support and momentum for the revolt that
we have so painstakingly built up." Nesib dismissed Lawrence's concerns as irrelevant, saying that he knew the Syrians best and what
they might accomplish.

At length, Lawrence withdrew from the conversation. It was clear
that Nesib's mind was made up and he was determined to pursue his
harebrained scheme aimed at Damascus. Lawrence had by now detected a delusional component to Nesib's character but at first had
imagined it simply as an aspect of his Syrian nature. Now he began to
wonder if Nesib's euphoria had some deeper psychological root. In
any case, the argument was far from over; he would have to seek out
Auda and Nasir and apprise them of the situation.

He quickly briefed the two on the new internal challenge to the
Aqaba mission. Both immediately scoffed at Nesib's impertinence.
Lawrence, however, insisted that the issue be confronted directly with
a strong cogent argument based on fundamental strategic principles.

He reiterated his views on Aqaba, now from a strictly Arab perspective, which consisted of two key propositions. First, the revolt needed Aqaba to broaden, in time and space, the military front against the Turks. Second, this meant in turn the opportunity of linking up with the British in Palestine. Securing Aqaba implied securing the Sinai and would be viewed by Sir Archibald Murray with gratitude as a positive contribution by the irregular force and the Arab Revolt as a whole. If the Arab army was in direct physical contact with the British right wing, that would facilitate immensely operational coordination and cooperation between the two forces. This further meant direct aid in food, gold, guns, and advisers. At the mention of gold, Auda's eyes glowed bright with anticipation. Nasir nodded as he grasped the tenor of Lawrence's argument.

But now Lawrence clinched his position with an even stronger reason: "I want contact with the British as their right wing and the right wing of the Allies. This gives us the fundamental right as Arabs to make the claim that we had fought with the main fight against the Turks for freedom—and with our own hands and blood. If we are not part of the main fight, we will simply remain a side-show of a side-show—and reap rewards accordingly."[5] Lawrence had convinced them both.

After reaffirming the Aqaba principle, the three confronted Nesib and Zeki. Auda and Nasir reiterated Lawrence's case, but Nesib remained unconvinced. To prevent a complete rupture in the unity that had brought the raiders so far, Auda and Lawrence arranged a compromise. The two Syrians would go off on their own half-baked scheme with the idea of fomenting a revolt among their fellow Syrians. However, there was a proviso. If Nesib would hand over two of the bags of gold Feisal had shared out at the beginning of the mission, Lawrence promised abundant English money, as long as Nesib could deliver Damascus. Without hesitation, the optimistic Nesib agreed and handed over the treasure, knowing anyhow the three leaders would refuse to let him leave without it.

THE WHOLE UNHAPPY episode brought Lawrence face-to-face with his own essential duplicity in the imperial scam directed against the Arabs, reminding him of the betrayal of "what's right": "The Arab

Revolt had begun on false pretenses. To gain the Sherif Hussein's help our Cabinet had offered, through Sir Henry McMahon, to support the establishment of native governments in parts of Syria and Mesopotamia, 'saving the interests of our ally, France.' This last modest clause concealed a treaty—kept secret, till too late, even from McMahon, and therefore from the Sherif—by which France, England and Russia agreed to annex some of these promised areas, and to establish their respective spheres of influence over all the rest."

Of course, rumors of the "fraud" had been running rampant throughout the Middle East for months. Lawrence himself was asked repeatedly about them and, to his own acknowledged and bitter shame, simply lied and reaffirmed British good intentions. At the same time, though, Lawrence began to recognize that if the Aqaba operation was successful, his role as adviser would be greatly enhanced—with the Syrians and, especially because of the potential for direct cooperation, with the British Army in Gaza. At the same time, Hussein and his sherifs would be in a weaker position in their ability to influence political and strategic events so far from their base of power. Lawrence reveled in the irony of the situation. The new circumstances, if Aqaba fell, offered him a more direct opportunity to become the main deliverer of the Arab Revolt to the British. If he played his hand correctly, Lawrence could make the British pay a heavy price for securing his moral duplicity. In poetic revenge, he vowed to himself: "I will make the Arab Revolt the engine of its own success, as well as the handmaid of Murray's Egyptian campaign: and vow to lead it so madly in the final victory that expediency should counsel the Powers a fair settlement of the Arabs' moral and political claims. This presumes my surviving the war, to win the later battle at the Council Chamber. . . ." The irony and its hope were extraordinary, breathtaking, presumptuous—all these adjectives and more. Lawrence would lead and unleash the energy and chaos of the revolt and by his success would turn his duplicity on its head. The revolt would be more successful than the imperial frauds ever imagined, and Lawrence would gain moral redemption through victory at Damascus.

The happy thought was delicious to Lawrence's ironic palate, and in the savoring moment another bold plan emerged: Nesib's mad scheme held within its core a fleeting opportunity of real strategic value. Clearly the liberation of Syria was part of the essential logic and design of the Arab Revolt, but only *after* Aqaba. By now, the Turks were aware of the noisy move of Lawrence and his men from Wejh into the Sirhan. They were also aware of the natural vulnerability of Aqaba. Yet Aqaba wasn't the only point of danger; Deraa and especially Damascus were also sensitive. By clever deception, the Turks could be made to believe that the force was really intended to strike at Damascus. It now appeared like a masterstroke of military genius to let the bumbling Nesib and Zeki loudly proclaim the approach of the revolt to Damascus; they would provide the deception effort Lawrence would need.

Syria had a further attraction for Lawrence: as the land of the Crusades, it beckoned and bestirred his memory.

AROUND JUNE 2, 1917, Lawrence left the Arab camp at Nebk to begin a major strategic reconnaisance alone. He traveled to Azrak, where he donned the appropriate mufti and continued on to the train junction at Deraa. Part of the mission also reinforced the deception effect of the unknowing and unwitting Nesib. Lawrence began with a dangerous sea voyage from Haifa to Beirut, moving inland to the teeming Damascus metropolis. Here he tested his disguise, ever conscious of his shaky linguistic skills, and was able to gain important information, more from his keen powers of observation than from casual dialogue with the locals. When he did chat with the natives, it was to drop hints of an impending raid on the city by an Arab army. He was able to discover that the immediate concerns of the Turkish military were toward the region south of Beersheba and the threatening posture of Murray's army. Military rail activity was especially heavy from Damascus to Deraa, following the rail line west and south toward Nablus and Jaffa as the Turks concentrated for the defense of Jerusalem and land to the south. As far as Lawrence could determine, there was no special concern over Aqaba.

Lawrence next rode the rails from Damascus to dusty Amman to gather intelligence and spread rumor among the locals, plying them with pieces of British gold. Here he was surprised to discover strong pockets of Turkish loyalty among the town-dwelling Arabs, making a mental note to avoid the area in future operations. At this stage of the recon, Lawrence began to reconsider his leave from the caravan, thinking perhaps it was time to return. But he hesitated: by now he had amassed a significant amount of intelligence that would be invaluable to Murray and his staff as they planned for the offensive to retake Jerusalem. Furthermore, there was an opportunity to strike at the great Yarmuk Valley bridges that supported Turkish rail traffic west into Palestine.

He had left the camp on merely his own authority, a perilous journey over hundreds of miles of enemy territory. The risks were enormous, though the gains in intelligence and the destruction of the bridges on the face of it might seem worth the gamble. But what of the revolt? Would the possible loss of Lawrence mean the loss of the Arab cause? Was any one man that valuable? Lawrence smiled to himself: he would take the risk—and he would fail at Yarmuk, just narrowly escaping with his life.

LAWRENCE ARRIVED BACK at Auda's camp on June 16. During his absence, Auda and Nasir had played on each other's nerves and a rift had developed between the two. Although the tension was easily remedied, it caused Lawrence to appreciate anew the constancy of Nasir's and especially Auda's leadership. And realize that he would have to rely on the two even more during the next phase of the operation. In Lawrence's mind, the three leaders had become a kind of trinity: Lawrence offered direction; Nasir provided purpose; and Auda gave motivation to the whole endeavor.

The strike against Aqaba had arrived at a crucial turning point. Now five weeks out of Wejh, Lawrence had spent nearly all the gold; his men had consumed all the Bedouin sheep; and all the wasted camels had at last been replaced. The deprivations of the long march had been largely forgotten, and the raiders looked forward to the last ride into Aqaba. Caught up in the new euphoria, Auda offered a final farewell feast for the newly expanded army. The display of Auda's boundless largesse offered Lawrence a natural setting to see the true scope of Auda's native leadership. Auda's authority sprang from his powerful unaffected charisma. When he entered a tent, all would rise out of fondness as much as respect—and this was an honor rarely accorded even the highest-ranking sheikhs. It was evident that Auda was the clan's father-leader.

After the great feast was consumed, Lawrence wandered about the camp to find Mohammed el Dheilan and thank him for the fine gift of a she-camel. Soon Lawrence came upon Auda and mentioned the missing Mohammed: he had looked several times in his tent, always to find it empty. As if on cue, Auda pointed to a dejected Mohammed sitting across the way, unobserved in the shadows of the campfire. After a moment, Auda exclaimed in a loud voice, "Ha! Shall I tell you why Mohammed for fifteen days has not slept in his tent?" Auda's exclamation was a call for all to hear one of his inimitable stories. The whole camp now gathered around their leader to listen. Auda began by claiming that while in Wejh, Mohammed had bought a fine set of pearls, yet while he had been in camp lo these many days, he had not seen fit to give it to any of his wives. Auda's claim, of course, was a pure fabrication, but it was presented in the great nomadic oral tradition to maintain tribal cohesion. After some further elaboration from Auda, the unhappy Mohammed, who had endured the same story at least a dozen times, turned to Lawrence to bear witness against Auda's falsehood. At this Lawrence ceremoniously stood up and gravely cleared his throat, getting a rise from the crowd. Auda quieted the spectators and asked him to confirm the truth of the incident.

Lawrence began his tale with a formal introduction to a story: "In the name of Allah the merciful, the loving-kind. We were six at Wejh. There were Auda, and Mohammed, and Zaal, Kasim el Kimt, Muffadhi and a poor man—myself; and one night just before dawn, Auda said, 'Let us raid against the market.' And we said, 'in the name of Allah.' And we went; Auda in a white robe and a red head-cloth, and Kasim sandals of pieced leather, Mohammed in a silken tunic of 'seven kings' and barefoot; Zaal . . . I forget Zaal. Kasim wore cotton, and Muffadhi was in silk with blue stripes with an embroidered head-cloth. Your servant was as your servant." The listeners were amazed as Lawrence continued his parody of Auda's epic style in the oral tradition: the same precise intonation, elocution, and emphasis as Auda. Lawrence described meaningless detail after detail: the tents, the names of the tents, every horse and camel they encountered, every village, virtually every stone and blade of grass—for the sake not only of entertainment, but also for information.

After a while, Lawrence resumed the story with the march from Wejh and described for all how the land was "all bare of grazing, by Allah that country was barren. And we marched: and after we had marched the time of a smoked cigarette, we heard something, and Auda stopped and said, 'Lads, I hear something.' And Mohammed stopped and said, 'Boys, I hear something.' And Zaal, 'By Allah you are right.' And we stopped to listen and there was nothing, and, I, humble man, said, 'By Allah, I hear nothing.' And Zaal said, 'By Allah, I hear nothing.' And Mohammed said, 'By Allah, I hear nothing.' And Auda said, 'By Allah, you are right.'

"And we marched: and beyond the whatchamacallit there was what-there-is as far from hither to thither, and thereafter a ridge; and we came to the ridge, and went up that ridge: it was barren, all that land was barren: and as we came up that ridge, and were by the head of that ridge, and came to the end of the head of that ridge, by Allah, by my Allah, by very Allah, the sun rose upon us."[6]

The end of the tale found the spectators in the throes of riotous laughter, with Auda laughing the loudest, both at the story and at the parody of himself. The story had finally wound in upon itself after several hours of verbal turning, tightening into a mirthful knot of pointlessness. With the laughter dying away, Auda stood up and embraced Mohammed, admitting to all that the pearl necklace story was sheer fantasy. In gratitude, Mohammed invited the riders to his reclaimed tent for a parting breakfast before tomorrow's long march.

Lawrence, walking back to his tent alone, had witnessed another dimension of nomadic leadership: the role of the leader as central storyteller and mythmaker. The story was a way to bind the listeners together in a common physical presence and within a common literary narrative and cultural tradition. Among the nomads, the warrior-leader was also a *heroic* leader, one who was the object of story and legend. Furthermore, the leader himself had to tell the story as his own. It meant that the hero had to wield the word with the same skill as the sword. Auda's skill was matchless in his ability to thrust and parry using a narrative foil. With the leader as the center of the story, his character and competence became reaffirmed among his followers. For their part, his companions vied and competed among themselves for inclusion and honor in the narrative. In this way, they would achieve their immortality. That alone, Lawrence thought, was a powerful motivating force for the raiders, who knew they would help write the next chapter in Auda's epic.

THE RAIDERS STARTED out before noon, Nasir on his new camel, Ghazala, Lawrence riding Naama, and Auda on Ageila. The raiders had increased tenfold since they'd left Wejh, now numbering over five hundred fierce Howeitat warriors—the equivalent of a conventional light cavalry regiment of the day. They left Sirhan after climbing a sixty-foot ridge, Ard el Suwan. The column was headed for a group of wells at Bair, thirty-five miles east of the Hejaz railway and some sixty miles distant. Here the caravan would camp for a few days, replenishing their food stocks from the villages near the Dead Sea. Nasir would make it a special "rice night" to celebrate the first leg of the journey.

In the morning, the party made the last few miles into Bair proper. Auda asked Lawrence to accompany him alone as the two rode off ahead of the rest. They rode fast for a couple of miles until Auda suddenly stopped by a small hill. Just over the hill were the grave sites of Auda's family, including his dead son, Annad. Annad had been murdered by five of his Motalga cousins. They sought revenge after Annad had killed their boss, Abtan, in a hand-to-hand fight. Auda continued the story, telling Lawrence how his son had charged into his killers without fear before meeting a bloody death. Now Auda, in a demonstration of his great fondness and respect for Lawrence, grieved and wept openly—not only for his tragic loss, but for fear that only his little son, Mohammed, stood between him and childlessness.

Off in the distance, beyond the graves, the two men were astonished to notice for the first time smoke rising. Cautiously they approached the ancient ruins surrounding the wells at Wadi Bair. The ground was ripped and darkened by some heavy demolition. Looking down one of the wells, Lawrence found that the steyning was severely cracked and he could smell the acrid taint of dynamite. The well was choked with debris from a recent explosion.

Auda ran to another well and found it too was jagged about its head and fouled with blackened blocks of stone. "This is Jazi work," he said solemnly. They walked cautiously over to a third well, one used by the Beni Sakhr. It too was a black pit of rubble. Zaal arrived at last and surveyed the grim scene. He sniffed the air, studied the ground; the ranger's keen sense grasped the danger. "There were at least a hundred horse here," he said with some urgency. They then wandered over to a fourth well, just north of the ruins, detached from the other three, hoping against hope that it had survived. To their relief it was untouched, but the fact reinforced Auda's belief: the undisturbed well belonged to the Jazi, a Howeitat clan who cooperated closely with the Turks from time to time. It was by now clear that the enemy was aware of their maneuver and had anticipated the march to a certain degree. The serious consideration next arose that perhaps even the wells farther on at El Jefer might also be destroyed. Such a situation would be perilous. El Jefer was to be the final staging place for the strike on Aqaba. Without the waters of El Jefer, the entire mission would be hopelessly compromised.

The immediate concern, however, was the destruction at Bair. The single well simply could not water five hundred thirsty men and camels, that much was obvious. It became crucial, therefore, to repair at least one of the other wells. Some of the Ageyli outriders found an empty case of explosives, apparently used by the Jazi. By now Nasir had come up with the main body of riders. He went with Lawrence, Auda, and Zaal to reassess the damage. Peering down one of the wells, Lawrence could see demolition wires dangling some twenty feet below the opening. The explosives had been improperly wired and set, the charges poorly tamped. Closer inspection revealed that only the first charge had exploded; the second had hung fired. Lawrence quickly unrolled ropes from the water buckets and slowly lowered himself into the well. He saw that the explosives were less than three pounds each, jury-rigged with unreliable telephone cable. After clearing the dynamite, he scrambled out of the shaft. Now they had a second operational well.

It was then decided that the caravan would remain at Bair for at least a week and carefully reconnoiter the surrounding area. Zaal would head out for El Jefer to recon the important wells there. A small group led by Nasir would prepare an innocent caravan of obscure Howeitat clans and travel west to Tafileh to buy flour and gather intelligence, especially from the clans along the road into Aqaba. It was imperative that they remain neutral during the maneuver south. If Nasir's diplomatic skills were up to the task, several of the clans might even join the enterprise.

The next evening around the campfire among the darkened ruins of Bair, Lawrence, Auda, and Nasir went over the details of the final strike on Aqaba. This would be the last gathering that the three would have time together to scrutinize every last detail and examine every eventuality. The plan of attack called for a sudden advance south from El Jefer, crossing the rail track and quickly moving through the great pass at El Shtar. The defile opened up from the Maan plateau into the ruddy Guweira plain. To hold open the route, the raiders would have to capture the spring at Aba el Lissan, sixteen miles from the large Turkish garrison up at Maan. The enemy forces at Aba el Lissan were believed to be small, and the place could be seized in stride with the main attack. An initial success here, Lawrence believed, would rally the local clans and all would converge on Aqaba.

The outcome to the entire operation hung on the likely reaction of the Turkish forces at Maan. Lawrence believed the garrison, about the strength of a reinforced battalion, would hesitate, waiting for further orders and reinforcements. His assessment of the reaction was reinforced by his careful knowledge gained from years of studying the Turks. They *never* made any move based on local initiative or without receiving higher authority first. If only the raiders could reach Aqaba swiftly, they could secure their rear through the pass with a stout defense of the deep gorge at nearby Itm. By then if Aqaba was seized, their "rear" would become their "front," facing the sea and British and French naval support. The garrison at Maan thus had to be lulled into distraction by a careful deception plan.

Zaal returned the next morning from his scouting mission and confirmed their worst fears: the seven wells at Jefer were indeed destroyed. It was apparent that the Turks were alert to some impending, though unspecified, threat. Along with Zaal's arrival, the Ageyli scouts came in with new information. Evidently, the Turks were focusing their concerns to the north, toward Deraa and Damascus. The rail junction at Deraa was pivotal to the whole Turkish defense. Its loss would mean a pell-mell withdrawal from Palestine and the Hejaz to new positions just south of Damascus. In Lawrence's mind, the helter-skelter work of Nesib's mad scheme and his own covert operation through the region a few days earlier had stirred up a hornets' nest of concern for the Turks. The uncertainty facing them was compounded by the fact that Newcombe, back at Wejh, contrived to plant false plans of a major attack against Aleppo and Damascus with Lawrence and his raiders as the vanguard. The discovery of Nasir, Feisal's masterful outrider, with the caravan reinforced the ruse's validity. At the same time, Nuri Shaalan, while maintaining a guise of friendship with the Turks, warned them of the column's movements—to the *north*. To Lawrence's thinking, everything now revolved around the stupidity of the Turks themselves. His study of them encouraged his belief that the deception plan might just work.

THE FOLLOWING MORNING, a war council gathered around the ashes of the previous night's cook fire. Although the plans for Aqaba had been finalized the previous night, the question of the deception scheme had yet to be addressed. Lawrence sat cross-legged in the sand and with his riding crop drew a long gray line, running from north to south, through the burned remnants of the fire. "Here is Deraa," he said, pointing to the northern end of the line. "And here is Aqaba"— tapping the southern point—"a stretch of more than 250 miles." Then he drew two sides, first one from the southern tip and a second one from the northern tip, extending them to the east to form the apex of a triangle. Indicating the eastern point with a gesture, he said, "And here we are at Bair, roughly equidistant between Deraa and Aqaba. Now"—he paused, patting his stick midway along the Deraa-Bair side—"here is Azrak. We must make the Turks believe we are *here*"—the ashes flying—"while we make our strike *here*," more silver and black dust, now flying at Aqaba. The essential geometry of Lawrence's design was grasped immediately by Nasir and Auda, who were standing directly behind him, looking down from above.

After some further elaboration, a basic tactical deception plan was put into execution: Nasir would ride with the small merchant caravan and journey the sixty miles to Tafileh, as previously planned. In addition to his logistics and intelligence mission, he would spread rumor and misinformation. Next, Auda ordered the formation of a small detachment of a hundred men under the command of Lawrence and Zaal. The raiders would attack the rail line near Deraa, giving the impression all the while that they had debauched recently at Azrak after a long march through the Sirhan. They would return within a week to coincide with Nasir's arrival from Tafileh.

Lawrence's detachment left shortly before noon, riding hard day and night for six hours at a time, stopping briefly for one- or two-hour breaks in order to cover swiftly the 175 miles to Deraa. By the second afternoon, they had ranged over a hundred miles and reached the Circassian village of Zerga, just north of Amman. Here they watered their camels among the ancient cisterns below the ruins of an old Roman village. They waited until dark, fully aware of the local hatred of the Circassians toward most Arabs. Nearby was the heavy bridge at Dhuleil. Zaal and Lawrence scouted the bridge and discovered it was in the process of being rebuilt and at the moment was inoperative. Cursing their luck, the pair ordered the column to the small village of Minifir farther north at a vulnerable rail line. Lawrence explained to Zaal that blowing the track would have greater strategic—and therefore greater "deceptive"—effect than blowing the bridge anyhow, and besides, the town was on a direct route from Azrak, some fifty miles to the southeast.

The party rode until dawn and found a suitable place to lay a mine under the tracks. The men then waited on a height above the site, looking down at the few unsuspecting guards dozing in the heat. The mining would have to wait until evening and cover of darkness; so the raiders rested, watched, and waited. Suddenly, about mid-morning, a troop of cavalry appeared out of nowhere, riding hard, straight for their position on the hill. Perhaps the local Belga shepherds had reported them. Left with no other choice, Lawrence and his men quickly scampered off to the east to seek cover among the shepherd hills, where they waited in ambush. The Turkish cavalry, however, was totally ignorant of the Arab location, since they had no native scouts. Instead, they seemed out and about on a morning joyride.

After the threat passed, the raiders made a circuitous move to attack another portion of the rail line. This time they sent out scouts to reassure the Belga that they weren't robbers after all, but in fact the advance guard of Feisal's army of liberation riding up from Azrak. They camped by a nearby Belga village for the evening, feasting on bartered Belga bread, a fine respite from the usual fare of bleached raw corn. After the meal, Lawrence and Zaal crept down from their location to plant a Garland mine in a culvert underneath the adjacent rail track. The device was set with a pressure fuse that would detonate under the weight of the unsuspecting train. The pair retreated back to the encampment to reap the fruits of their labors. But when dawn broke, the mine still had not been triggered. After investigation, Lawrence found that the triggering device was defective and had to be replaced, and the interminable waiting resumed. Then shots were heard off in the distance, in the dead space under the hill. After several minutes, a ragtag pair of deserters from the harassing Turkish cavalry appeared, urged on by their captors. Both men were wounded, one severely, the other shot through the foot. The first died of his mortal wounds in the late afternoon. His death was particularly unmanly, thought Lawrence, who had seen most dying men accept death stoically: this Turk died hard in misery. The other trooper was weak and exhausted, as much from the wound as from generous doses of Turkish discipline that had left its telltale purple marks on his frail body. As his condition worsened, he was forced to lie in a facedown position to ease the pain. Lawrence's men offered him the last of their bread and the soldierly comfort that always seemed universally to transcend the enmity of strife.

Another scare intruded later in the afternoon when a large Turkish force mounted on mules approached their position out of the west. Zaal and Lawrence were immediately confronted with a tactical decision. Should they attack the unsuspecting cavalry or let them ride away unscathed? Zaal argued that his heavier camels with their downhill momentum would have the advantage of raw physical force and surprise on their side. He pressed Lawrence: "No Turk can withstand the collision nor endure a running fight with my raiders." The decision had to be swift, the threat was imminent, and Zaal's men were already mounting for action. Quickly Lawrence posed a question that was also a threat: "How many men will we lose?" "Five or six," was Zaal's guess. Lawrence assessed the situation in a flash: all along his eye had been on Aqaba; at the moment, his detachment was part of a larger deception operation. If any of his men were captured in the charge, interrogation would give away the whole game. Besides, his five or six dead men would be five or six fewer rifles at the decisive point in Aqaba. Lawrence said quietly but firmly, "No, let them pass." For a moment Zaal was stunned, frozen midstride as he was about to mount his camel; he started to speak. Then he stopped with a foot caught in the stirrup and turned oddly sideways toward Lawrence. A cunning grin flashed across his face. In that instant, Zaal became a true leader as his struggling mind overcame the irrational urge to seize short-term personal gain for the sake of strategic profit. He threw up his arms and waved off the attack, beating back a deluge of insults and outrage. Zaal and Lawrence both knew that only three things mattered to the raiding culture: arms, mounts, and clothes; money itself was of little use in the desert. The pair also reckoned that if the raiders triumphed in the charge, they would all ride off victoriously with their two hundred captured mules back to their tents and to their women as heroes, never to be seen again. They also knew that Nasir would hardly welcome two hundred new prisoners: they would have to be shot out of hand. Yet only by the force of Zaal's leadership was Lawrence able to restrain the raiders from reacting naturally to thousands of years of bandit culture. And for this Lawrence was exceedingly grateful; he would later write in his diary: "We sat there and gnashed our teeth at them and let them pass: a severe ordeal, from which we only just emerged with honor. Zaal did it. He was on his best behavior, expecting gratitude from me later; and glad, meanwhile, to show his authority over the Bedouin. They respected him as Auda's deputy and as a famous fighter, and in one or two little mutinies among the men he had shown a self-conscious mastery."[7]

Yet the danger was far from over. As the Turks passed unaware, not more than three hundred yards to their front, Hubsi, one of Auda's cousins, impulsively leapt off his camel and ran toward the mules, yelling and waving his arms. Zaal reacted in an instant with a furious body tackle that left Hubsi in a muffled heap, defending himself against Zaal's savage blows. With Zaal's sudden display of tough discipline, the man's outrage abruptly vanished and he regained composure and self-control. One by one the men stood down, now willing to embrace the command of reason. As the enemy rode off in the distance, Lawrence tallied another stroke of luck to the credit side of his gambling ledger, hoping fate's audit would be long deferred.

By evening, still no train had passed, and the camels by now needed watering. Zaal and Lawrence decided to plant thirty charges of dynamite along the rail track and create a lasting footprint of their presence. The blasts were successful, severing the rail link between Damascus and Deraa for three days.

In the morning, Zaal's detachment prepared for the three-day journey back to Bair. They left behind the lone wounded soldier after leaving a sign attached to a downed telegraph pole. The pole was tumbled onto the track with a note in French and German giving the location of the prisoner. As the column headed off, Lawrence glanced back at the Turk and wondered if he would ever be found alive.

SLIPPING INTO THE night, the force continued along the route but soon became lost in the dark among the rocky ridges along the Dhuleil Valley. At dawn, after some more floundering, they finally located a previous watering place near ancient Khau. The camels would need extra food and water to make the eighty-mile-per-day sprint back to Bair. Only the low hills provided reasonable cover for the raiders under a rising sun. Within a few hours, the camels were ready to carry the men on the ride home. Along the way, they passed a small railway station at Atwi lying low beneath some limestone cliffs. Two stone blockhouses were in easy reach of attack, one lined up behind the other. Turkish soldiers could be heard from within singing some obscure provincial melody. Behind the stone houses a lone soldier could be seen urging a flock of sheep to higher pasture. The sheep made a mouthwatering sight to the famished riders, who had eaten no meat for days. Zaal slowly counted out loud the number of animals in the flock, the men's hunger all the while increasing with each tally. He stopped at twenty-seven, enough sheep to feed the entire detachment at one sitting. He then decided that as recompense for the dismissed opportunity of the previous day, the men should at least feast amid their sorrow. Zaal crept down the rough slope with a file of picked men until they faced the station across an open grassy meadow. Lawrence remained, reluctantly, on the heights with the others to provide cover fire if needed. Some officers had by now emerged in front of the nearest blockhouse to drink their coffee and prepare for the daily troop harassment they understood as training. The officers sat in the shade nearest the ticket window. One particularly fat officer leaned heavily in his chair against the stone building. As it happened, Zaal had a special loathing for obese Turks. He crouched and rested the muzzle of his rifle atop a tall anthill, taking precise aim at his well-fed target. He squeezed the trigger and a bullet ripped into the man's large chest, knocking him over; his hobnailed boots crashed into the table as he toppled. The other officers stood up in disbelief, and only then did they appear to hear the report of the rifle. And as they rose, their reflex seemed to act as a signal to unleash a lethal volley from the heights above. Immediately, steel shutters clanged open and the unseen Turks inside the building returned a ragged fire. The exchange lasted a few minutes until both sides realized neither had the advantage. Though the Turks were outgunned, seemingly they had the advantage of an impregnable defense. During the stalemate, several of the raiders snuck behind the fight and captured the wayward sheep, now frightened and dispersed after their cowardly shepherd had run off at the first shot. A contingent of Sherarat clansmen herded the lost sheep skillfully back to the camels to the rear of the firing.

Meanwhile, Zaal used the standoff to turn his attention toward a second, unguarded building and led his squad into the stone house. Here the men began to plunder the place at their leisure. Unbeknownst to everyone, a rail handcar operated by four Turkish engineers came casually down the track. A detachment of Ruwalla tribesmen spotted the innocent quartet and crept under a large culvert, waiting in ambush for the trolley to pass overhead. At that moment, Zaal and the rest of his looters crossed the track in front of the rail workers, who saw them with horror and attempted to jump off the car. They were greeted with such a vicious volley of fire from the Ruwalla that they were dead before they touched the dirt. The trolley then continued on down the line, in slow motion, the hand pump seemingly animated by the ghosts of its former operators. Soon a Ruwalla jumped aboard to ransack its load of copper wire, rail, and telegraph tools.

Some of the former sheepherders returned with petrol to crown the raid by setting off a plume of fire in the gasoline-drenched block-house. Zaal considered a similar fate for the occupied position, but a stout defense held him off. The guts of the empty house were now burning furiously, sending forth telltale tongues of flame and pillars of smoke high into the air. The culvert was blown at the same time, causing great consternation among the tired sheep and knee-haltered camels. As if by design, a final loud blast signaled the end of the skirmish. All the raiders quickly rallied near the animals and rode off a few miles to the east. Here a hasty field slaughter was set up to render the sheep. The men soon discovered they were short of knives and had to set up an assembly line to carve up the animals, supplementing their shortage of cold steel with hot flint.

With the meat quickly loaded, the column rode off toward Azrak, leaving as much offal in their wake as possible. Near nightfall, the raiders camped to partake of their victory feast. The victors consumed all the sheep in one sitting. The leftovers were given to the hardy camels, which had long been trained to appreciate well-cooked meat. Then on June 27, the deception force arrived back at Bair, where a week earlier 110 men had ridden out and now 110 men had returned.

LAWRENCE, AUDA, AND Nasir spent the next morning in consultation, reevaluating the final plan. On its face the concept appeared fairly simple, but when considered in its broader context, the strike against Aqaba was exceedingly complex. Each objective could be seen as one block in a long row of dominoes: Lawrence had placed the first at Wejh and strung them all the way to Aqaba, and each one had to fall precisely and correctly to affect the next link in the chain of action. The failure of one coupling could affect all the rest and, therefore, the whole operation. The mission had now reached its final and most critical stage. Here and now at Bair, an apparent starburst of eccentric domino chains was extending outward in complicated configurations—chains that could shackle the Turks if they all toppled as planned or manacle the entire endeavor if they failed to fall properly.

Fortunately, the part of the logistics nexus had been resolved by the steady work of Nasir. He had returned from Tafileh with his little caravan and a week's worth of flour; whether or not Aqaba was successful, now at least the men would have food. Nasir had also applied his diplomatic skills brilliantly, securing three of the region's key Howeitat clans: the Dhumaniyeh, the Darausha, and the Dhiabat. These alliances were crucial because they effectively controlled the critical pass at Nagb el Shtar along the Aqaba-Maan corridor. The clans also offered Nasir their help in a decisive blow at Aba el Lissan. Meanwhile, Nuri Shaalan continued to contribute to the deception scheme. He now sent a dispatch by fast courier to inform Auda of a new and clever ruse. The Turks had just ordered Nuri to provide one of his scouts to guide four hundred Turkish cavalry sent to track down Lawrence's raiding party that had caused such mischief around Deraa. The Turks now believed the raiders were in the vicinity of Azrak at the mouth of the Wadi Sirhan. Nuri would send his nephew Trad as hostage-guide to lead the hapless squadron on an Alice-in-Wonderland ride through the canyon. The lost squadron would thus be unable to report the status and whereabouts of Lawrence's detachment for some time. This lack of information would only serve to reconfirm the existing Turkish bias of expectation: that Lawrence was indeed in the Sirhan.

At the time, the more troubling "domino" that appeared to hang fire was the water situation at El Jefer, where the King's Well had been blasted to rubble. But again, Bedouin ingenuity helped set the plan back on track. Dhaif-Allah, chief of the Jazi Howeitat, was able to repair the key well by the time the raiders redeployed from Bair two days later. For his efforts, Dhaif-Allah and his diggers received a choice carcass of camel meat.

When they arrived at the repaired wells at El Jefer, the caravan spent the whole day of June 29 watering the animals, and by June 30 all was ready to initiate the tactical actions that would carry them to Aqaba. The first fight would be against the blockhouse at Fuweilah, a cork in the bottle of the Aba el Lissan pass. A detachment of raiders under Zaal linked up with some of the Dhumaniyeh to stage the assault. The plan was to launch the attack two days before the scheduled arrival of the weekly supply column coming down from Maan. In case the house couldn't be stormed, then perhaps the garrison could be starved into submission. While the attack was being executed, Lawrence was with Auda and the others, waiting for news from Zaal and continuing with preparations for the final maneuver on Aqaba. Later in the morning, they received full details concerning the Fuweilah affair.

The assault, after making some initial progress to the main line of breastworks, was driven off by a strong Turkish defense. Zaal's detachment then withdrew to lick its wounds and decide on a reframed course of action. Meanwhile, the Turks, wholly ignorant that they had just been victims of the opening moves of a major offensive operation, believed the action was simply the usual manifestation of local Arab discontent. The Turks, therefore, responded in the usual manner: they sent out a punitive sortie against the nearest Dhumaniyeh encampment. The site they chose was virtually abandoned, save for one old man, six women, and seven children. The Turks began to trash the camp and, outraged at not finding any worthwhile targets, proceeded to slit the throats of the fourteen innocents. Only after they rode off did Zaal's forces in the hills realize that the atrocity had taken place. They immediately became enraged and pursued their murderers back to Fuweilah, where they were caught and cut down to the last man. With the garrison now seriously depleted, Zaal and his forces stormed into the place and seized it, adding to the scorecard of revenge by taking no prisoners.

The eventual success at Fuweilah tripped the next domino. On July 1, the entire attack force under Lawrence, Auda, and Nasir mounted up and headed toward Ghadin el Haj, the first railroad station south of Maan and directly on the road to the pass at Aba el Lissan. At the same time, another domino was tipped in the direction of Maan: here a small column was sent north of the town to create a diversion there. The mission was to harass the herds of wounded camels on the Shobek plain. The beasts had been brought down from the Palestine front to recuperate for further action and were especially dear to the Turks, whose chronic shortage of camels would impede their operations throughout the war.

Now, since all the actions of war take place in a fog of misinformation, disinformation, and missing information, certain assumptions must be made. Lawrence made a key assumption that it would take the Turks at least one entire day to react to their defeat at Fuweilah. Unfortunately, Lawrence's assumption was little more than a hope and would soon be dashed. While the Turks continued to bask in their ignorance, the main Arab force attacked at Ghadin el Haj and was successful. However, knowing the garrison would have notified its higher headquarters at Maan, Lawrence expected a relief force would not arrive until the following night. A night march would also expose the reinforcements to ambush. With that case in mind, Lawrence with a few others worked feverishly to set explosive devices along the approach route of the relief column. After the engineer work was complete, the raiders moved a bit to the west to cover the road and await the Turks, who were expected to arrive the following evening.

At their new location, the men began to bake bread and relax under the setting sun. The mood was suddenly upset when three scouts rode furiously into camp with vital news: Lawrence's assumption had been proved wrong. Instead, it turned out that a newly arrived motorized column was already *in* Maan when the news of Fuweilah was received. Since the column had just arrived at Maan, it was ready for immediate action. The garrison commander merely added a battery of pack artillery and sent the men south. And since the force was motorized it took a route by road, but it was the route by rail that Lawrence had anticipated. What the scouts reported next disturbed the whole command group. Not only had the relief force already arrived, it had retaken Fuweilah, without firing a shot, from Zaal's disorganized detachment. Now the pass was lost and in the hands of a fresh garrison with artillery. To Lawrence, it now seemed that the Turks had unexpectedly just untipped one of his critical dominoes.

THE LOSS OF the pass at Aba el Lissan was a shock to the leadership and a potential blow to the entire operation. Yet despite the Turkish thunderbolt now thrown in their direction, Lawrence, Auda, and Nasir recovered and demonstrated the most important attribute of all great leaders: *presence of mind*. Their force of character, their determination, and their native intellect prevented a spiral into despair and defeat. Instead they refused to take council of their fears and quickly began to reframe the new situation. Immediately they assessed the nature of the emerging threat from Maan and discovered that the relief column was in no mood to take part in any kind of active op-

erations against the Arab force. Rather, they formed a defensive pe-
rimeter around the watering places nearby, placing themselves out of
direct tactical reach of the pass itself. It was clear that the Turks were
still unaware of the magnitude of the fight they had on their hands,
still imagining that they had to contend with a few disgruntled tribesmen. The tactical maldeployment was quickly recognized by Lawrence and offered a possible solution to his problem.

The raiders quietly vanished into the night, slipping off to the east
toward Batra. The mood was upbeat during the move, with Auda
leading the men in song. Soon the whole column became animated
with the tune and carried a renewed sense of success. When they
reached Batra, Gasim abu Dumeik, leader of the Dhumaniyeh, was
anxiously waiting their arrival with the rest of his clan. The inactivity
of the Turks continued, a few miles off to the west. There was no
question but that the Turkish column would have to be dislodged or
somehow neutralized if the drive on Aqaba was to succeed. The leadership all agreed that the Turks were sitting ducks where they were,
so in small squads the Bedouin crept back toward the Turkish position and began a sniping action that lasted the whole day. As the day
passed, shooting soon became as intense as the hot sun, with more
men collapsing from heat exhaustion than from enemy fire. The rifles
became so hot that they cooked off rounds in the ammunition chambers of the weapons. What was worse was the fact that no uncommit-
ted men were free to return to Batra for water: every man was required
in the firing line.

As bad as it was for the raiders, the Turkish situation was infinitely worse. The unit was newly arrived in the theater from the cool
Caucasus far to the north and was poorly acclimated to the heat.
They fired wildly in all directions. Their mountain howitzers were
useless and ineffective: all the shooting was arcing well over their opponents' heads.

At noon, the battle reached a crisis. Lawrence, who himself was
on the verge of heatstroke, crawled off the field in search of water and
found a puddle of mud to quench his thirst. Nasir joined him, his
lips bleeding, cracked, and parched from the blazing sun. Then Auda
suddenly appeared, an apparition seemingly materialized from the
ground, striding toward them, his eyes bloodshot and transfixed on a

point that seemed to pass beyond the two men; his face was knotted up in berserker exhilaration and anticipation. His mouth cracked into a sneer and he said in a mocking tone, looking at Lawrence, "Well, boys, how are we doing? All talk and no work?" Since the very beginning of the operation when the caravan left Wejh, there had been developing an underlying unspoken tension between Lawrence and Auda over the capabilities of the Bedouin to stand and fight against the Turks in a conventional action. Now, under the stress of combat, this pressure erupted to the surface. Lawrence detected a veiled challenge in Auda's query and replied angrily, "By God, indeed, they shoot a lot and hit a little." In the heat of battle, Auda took the reply as an insult. He impetuously ripped off his head cloth in a fiery rage and threw it in a pile beside Lawrence. Without a further word, he turned on his heel and ran up to higher ground, calling all his troop leaders together. Nasir and Lawrence looked at each other in horror and growing dismay, watching Auda give unheard orders to his men. Then the pair struggled up the hill, exhausted. Auda ignored their arrival and stood—hand on hips—glaring at the Turks. Then finally he turned to the breathless Lawrence and said, "You—get your camel if you want to see the old man's work." At that Auda seemed to disappear into a mirage of heat. Lawrence and Nasir lurched off to find their camels and came upon the rest of the army, now mounted and huddled behind a protective knoll. Nasir asked Shimt, one of Auda's bodyguards, where Auda was. "Over there with the horsemen," he said, pointing to the far side of the Turkish position. Auda had somehow managed to maneuver a hundred men, mounted on horseback, around to the rear of the enemy, using the hilly terrain as cover. The Turks had gradually migrated from their initial position to huddle beneath a limestone cliff, out of reach of the hot fire raining down from above. All at once, Auda came thundering up the hill into the exposed rear of the Turkish defense. In the initial rush, several of the horsemen immediately fell dead from their saddles as the Turks realized their mortal danger. As the charge crested the hill, it began to gain momentum and began slowly to dislodge the Turks fighting beneath the limestone wall. The Turks, however, continued to maintain some cohesion, fighting and retreating slowly toward the north.

From higher ground, Lawrence gazed down with awe and fascination as Auda unleashed his mad charge. Suddenly, Nasir screamed beside him, "C'mon!" Blood flecking from his torn mouth, Nasir realized that the Turks had been pushed beyond the cover of the cliffs and were now open to a charge from their front. At that moment, the other four hundred tribesmen mounted on their camels surged forth to add weight to Auda's blow from a new direction. The sheer physics of a camel thundering downhill at thirty miles an hour was virtually unstoppable under the circumstances. Lawrence followed Nasir, racing downhill on Naama, his Sherari racer, who was running faster than she had ever run in her life. The Turks were now disintegrating fast, and Lawrence was soon in their midst. He threw away his clumsy rifle and began a heavy destruction with his Webley revolver. All of a sudden his great racer went down in a great heap, as if poleaxed by some unseen leviathan. Lawrence flew from the saddle in a high arc and landed hard, stunned and breathless. He lay there, calmly, waiting for the Turks to finish him off, reciting some long-lost poem, now half-forgotten: "For Lord I was of all Thy flowers, but I chose the world's sad roses; And that is why my feet are torn and mine eyes are blind with sweat." In another part of his mind, instead of fearing an angry Turkish bullet or bayonet, Lawrence was anxious about being crushed under a rampaging camel.

After many minutes and many verses, the battle swirled away from him. He soon regained his senses and leaned up on one arm, surveying the dust-laden destruction. Then he saw his gentle Naama, lying beside a rock: staring up sightlessly, without reproach or blame, at Lawrence, who had shot her through the head during the frenzied charge; her forelegs, outstretched in midstride, were still striving to trample some hated Turk, now unseen.

While he was recovering from the tragic accident and his fall, little Mohammed—Auda's son—brought up Lawrence's spare camel, Obeyd. Nasir rode past with the wounded Turkish commander in tow, rescued from the vengeance of Mohammed el Dheilan. For the wrathful Howeitat, yesterday's slaughter of innocent women and children at the encampment revealed to them a whole new side to the horrors of war. When the battle was over, it became clear that the Reaper had exacted a heavy toll on the Turkish battalion, virtually destroying it: 300 dead and dying were strewn across the plain and another 160 were prisoners, mostly wounded, now in the hands of the victors.

The vengeful Mohammed el Dheilan continued to pursue the remnants of the battalion for another three miles beyond the battlefield, chasing the mounted officers and lucky artillerymen whose distant perspective off the field permitted them a view of the unfolding disaster even before it happened. The fleeing Turks ran pell-mell to Mreigha with Mohammed's rude insults biting at their heels. The fugitive Turks would soon infect the small garrison there with the virus of defeat and weaken the post's ability to defend.

Lawrence began to repack Obeyd when Auda suddenly materialized again, silently from behind. He began to speak incoherently: "Work . . . work . . . where are the words . . . work . . . bullets . . . abu Tayi. . . ."[8] His babbling continued. Lawrence turned to him as he listened and was utterly stunned by what he saw: Auda, standing there like a veritable Bedouin god of war, his eyes glassy, red, and wild; his lips cratering into his toothless mouth at every heaving breath; his face dirty, dusty, a sepulchered white. His binoculars had been shot to pieces; bits were hanging from his neck on a strap, like some amulet of war; his holster and scabbard now hung tattered about him like strange ribbons of rank. His robes had been pierced and eviscerated by many bullets. At the very moment of culmination when his furious charge struck the cowering Turks with its greatest impact, his beloved mare had been shot from under him.

Slowly, Lawrence was able to calm Auda and lead him back to his senses. Auda then reached under his robes and brought forth a small talisman of the Koran. He held it reverently in both hands and told Lawrence how it had saved him from death many times. Lawrence recognized the tiny book as a cheap Glasgow knockoff selling for 18 pence. Auda revealed in confidence that he had paid 120 pounds for it, and in his eyes the original was the counterfeit. Auda was ecstatic in his triumph, most of all because he had seemingly repudiated Lawrence's thesis that Arab irregulars could not fight toe-to-toe, hand-to-gland, against a conventional Turkish force. Instead, Auda appeared to demonstrate how the force of inspired leadership could impart a transcendent, transformative power to this kind of war.

Both did agree, though, that the Reaper had been kind to them on this day: only two men were lost, one Rueili, the other Sherari. Mohammed el Dheilan, however, was vexed at Auda and especially at Lawrence—at Auda for initiating the mad charge and at Lawrence for insulting Auda in the first place. But time was now too short for vexations and recriminations. There was much more fighting to do.

Lawrence went to the prisoners, who were virtually all incoherent, psychologically shattered by the crushing defeat. At length he was forced to be stern with one of the prisoners, an officer, who began to regain some of his former composure. Yes, the relief battalion was the only one in the area, and a reserve unit at that; there were only two weak companies left at Maan, and they would have difficulty defending their own wire, let alone attempting to sally out to reinforce the southern posts. The discovered vulnerability at Maan quickly created its own leadership crisis: the jubilant Howeitat now wanted to drive immediately against Maan and seize its rumored wealth. But again Lawrence and Nasir had to stay the Arabs' recklessness and maintain focus on the objective at Aqaba. They argued: "We have no supports, no regulars, no guns, no base nearer than Wejh, no communications, no money even, for our gold is exhausted, and we've had to issue our own scrip, with promises to pay 'when Aqaba is taken,' for daily expenses. Besides, a strategic scheme must not be changed to follow up a tactical success. We must push on to the coast, and reopen sea-contact with Suez."

At the same time, pressure still had to be maintained at Maan. Paralysis, not destruction or capture, was all that was required. By the evening of the battle, shocks from all sides struck the Turkish headquarters at Maan: two small posts, one at Mreigha and the other at Waheida, were stormed by Howeitat mounted detachments; the camels at Shobek were lost; local tribes were in full riot; and an entire motorized battalion was destroyed. The news caused a panic in Maan, where planning commenced to consider evacuation of the entire place. On the strategic game board it appeared to Lawrence that perhaps, at last, the final dominoes were beginning to topple.

THE ARABS CONTINUED to plunder the Turkish dead until well into the evening. Lawrence relaxed and tried to enjoy the cool west breeze blowing up at Aba el Lissan, four thousand feet above the Red Sea.

He was near the quenching stream that now ran silver under the desert moon. Soon Auda came by, seemingly renewed since the fight. He told Lawrence that the raiders must move from the position. After some heated discussion with Nasir joining in, Auda's order made sense. First, he and the men were superstitious about camping through the night among all the dead. Auda was also concerned that now that the fight was over, some of the Howeitat clans who were still his blood enemies would turn against him in his sleep. His decision quickly stirred the men into action. They had to dress out some twenty-odd camels that had been killed in the fighting. They also had to prepare the prisoners for movement. Twenty or so were wounded and had to be left by the silver stream so as not to die of thirst. Nasir sought blankets for these few who were half-naked by now from the continuous plundering. Lawrence sought clothing from the dead still remaining on the battlefield. As a matter of raider honor, all the dead had been stripped naked. In the Bedouin culture, the victor was entitled to wear the uniform of the vanquished.

Later, reflecting on the moonlit battlefield, Lawrence would write in his diary: "The dead men were wonderfully beautiful. The night was shining gently down, softening them into new ivory. . . . Close round them lapped the dark wormwood, now heavy with dew, in which the ends of the moonbeams sparkled like sea-spray. The corpses seemed flung so pitifully on the ground, huddled anyhow in low heaps. Surely if straightened they would be comfortable at last. So I put them all in order, one by one, very wearied myself, and longing to be of these quiet ones, not of the restless, noisy aching mob up the valley, quarreling over the plunder, boasting of their speed and strength to endure God knew how many toils and pains of this sort; with death, whether we won or lost, waiting to end the history."

The raiders finally began their slow departure from the field of strife. There were still three more garrisons between them and Aqaba: Guweira, Kethera, and Khacra. Lawrence found a Turkish officer and induced him to write letters of surrender that were dictated by Nasir. He promised them good treatment and a safe journey to Egypt; otherwise a vicious death would carry them all to Paradise. In the morning, Auda began leading the column to the top of the zigzag Shtar pass. From here the men could see the Guweira plain several hundred feet below, its pink sands and sparkling limestone holding the tiny garrison in its grip. The raiders rode fifteen miles down to the plain, greatly impeded by the slow prisoners. Auda was about to decide whether or not they should all be killed. At that moment, Sheikh ibn Jad rode up with news that he had accepted the surrender of the Guweira garrison, so all the prisoners were turned over to the sheikh for safekeeping in the garrison. The rest of the day was spent in confining the prisoners to their makeshift jail.

The following day was July 4, and two more obstacles still remained at the back door to Aqaba. Kethera happened to be the next post, and it doggedly refused to surrender. The clans then drew lots to see who would have the difficult task of seizing the garrison by direct assault. Ibn Jad drew the lucky straw but demurred, saying he could not possibly attack under the bright full moon. But as luck would have it, Lawrence had made a previous note in his diary indicating that a partial eclipse would occur on that very night. When the eclipse happened as predicted, the forecast heartened ibn Jad's men and they seized the post without loss. There they found the superstitious Turks in a state of high excitement, clanging pots and pans to scare off the moon-devouring spirits.

The success at Kethera unlocked the way into the Itm gorge the next morning. The gorge was like the pass at Thermopylae, so narrow that a determined platoon with several machine guns could have held the defile against several divisions. Here the garrison at Khadra stoppered the defense. By now, the defenders at Aqaba were aware of the advance into their rear. As a consequence, they had reinforced Khadra with three hundred infantrymen. As soon as the new troops arrived from Aqaba, a local clan surrounded Khadra and reported the situation to Nasir, who immediately sent demands for its surrender. The Turkish commander vowed to give up the place if he had not received reinforcements from Maan within the next two days. Nasir then asked to speak to the officer's deputy. He reminded the Turk that resistance was futile and would only lead to their complete massacre. After more discussions, the Turks at last yielded, promising to surrender the very next morning.

During the night, however, news of the Bedouin success began to spread throughout the region, and soon more clansmen descended on the area to join the fight and share in the spoils of war. Several of the latecomers, unaware of the surrender arrangement, began to attack the garrison on their own. Heavy fighting immediately broke out at first light. Nasir marched out with a detachment of his retainers, careful to ride between the two sparring parties. After more negotiations, the shooting ceased and the Turks at last realized the hopelessness of their position and surrendered. The newcomers quickly swarmed over Khadra in search of loot. At that moment, Lawrence and Auda decided to rush past the confusion and chaos with the rest of the force and strike directly at Aqaba. By now the entire defense was depleted of its forces, drawn off to cover positions to their rear. Under cover of a brief sandstorm, Lawrence and his raiders sprinted the last four miles and stormed into Aqaba, reaching the shores of the Red Sea to find British and French naval forces waiting for them offshore.

The date was July 6, almost two months to the day since Lawrence had departed from Wejh with his raiders. During that time, Lawrence, Auda, and Nasir had demonstrated decisively that an active native contingent, provided it was well led, could achieve significant military results against a conventional enemy. For Lawrence, the triumph seemed anticlimactic. He had seized Aqaba but still had no idea what to do with it. He wrote in his diary: "In the blank light of victory we could scarcely identify ourselves. We spoke with surprise, sat emptily, fingered upon our white robes; doubtful if we could understand or learn whom we were. Others' noise was a dreamlike unreality, a singing in ears drowned in deep water. Against the astonishment of this unasked-for continued life we did not know how to turn our gift to account."[9]

Lawrence had reached the moment of personal catharsis, the washing away of success and triumph by the onrushing waters of loss, grief, and tragedy. These springs had slowly deepened over the past two months, drop by drop, until the final days when the fury and passion at Aba el Lissan burst into a rising tide of raw emotion. How well Lawrence stood against this moral and emotional torrent would be his next great test as a leader.

CHAPTER FIVE

Lawrence in LEGO-land

The beginning and ending of the secret of leading Arabs is unremitting study of them. Keep always on your guard; never say an inconsidered thing, or do an unnecessary thing: watch yourself and your companions all the time: hear all that passes, search out what is going on beneath the surface, read their characters, discover their tastes and their weaknesses and keep everything you find out to yourself. Bury yourself in Arab circles, have no interests and no ideas except the work in hand, so that your brain shall be saturated with one thing only, and you realize your part deeply enough to avoid the little slips that would undo the work of weeks. Your success will be just proportional to the amount of mental effort you devote to it.

—T. E. LAWRENCE, "Twenty-seven Articles"

At Aqaba, Lawrence was finally driven from the lassitude of his success by the encroaching pangs of hunger. He had not eaten for two days, and the final assault on the port had sapped his full store of energy. Now he was strapped with seven thousand prisoners as well as his own troops. The twenty-five hundred Arab victors were essentially immobile with inadequate forage, while unripe dates swayed overhead, their funky taste yet concealed by an appealing green attraction. Cooking could do little to the green dates other than delay the inevitable gastric flagellation.

By evening, tactical matters had displaced the taste of unrequited gluttony. Forty-two Turkish officers had to be cared for immediately, but beyond the logistics of imprisonment Aqaba had to be secured militarily. The security of the port, it was decided, would be formed upon four stout defensive pillars. Auda would take his men to Guweira and protect the sandy Shtar gorge. A second outlying position would be established twenty miles farther up the valley at Petra. Auda would also send troops to a third location at Delagha. The final defensive linchpin would be at Batra. The four small forts were mutually reinforcing but independent: one post had to be taken before the next, and each assault would likely take the Turks weeks.

With the defensive plans complete and after a frugal supper, Lawrence realized that news of the desert triumph had yet to reach Suez. He decided to carry information of the victory to headquarters himself, leading a party of eight Howeitat warriors and riding the best camels in the army. The journey of some 150 miles was immediately essential, not only to bring vital information about the success, but also to dispatch a greatly needed supply ship to Aqaba. On the evening of July 6, the messenger set out, covering fifty miles a day, now totally at the limits of endurance. By the second night, a crisis was reached when one of the camels collapsed and had to be sent back. Only a mechanical resolution seemed to drive the party forward, passing through a silver-shadowed moonlight: the gray light shone on the sand and glittered, cold, like speckles of ice. Above the riders, silvered clouds spilled through the night sky like great beads of mercury blown before a powerful wind. On the final day, they came to a field of melons: like the dates, they lay unripened in an unripened desert land. Finally, forty-nine hours after leaving Aqaba, Lawrence, the herald, reached the Suez Canal. He had a real story to tell, but with Murray gone, who would listen?

Lawrence and his Arabs had achieved the ultimate strategic trifecta: they were able to seize Mecca the previous summer, opening the Arab Revolt; they captured the port of Wejh in January 1917; and now the important harbor at Aqaba was theirs. The great victory at Aqaba would introduce a number of important changes to the whole conduct of the war in the Middle East. One of the most important changes was the arrival of a new visionary commander who would replace the ponderous General Murray. The incoming leader would also bring a completely new relationship among Lawrence and the Arabs and offer a reimagined vision of British strategy and victory. The new dynamic broadened the entire strategic canvas for Lawrence that would create unique leadership opportunities and offer full scope to his theories of guerrilla warfare.

EARLIER IN MARCH, as Lawrence lay on his sickbed in Wadi Ais contemplating his new theory of guerrilla warfare, the War Committee in London convened a thorough review of imperial strategy generated by cataclysmic events in Russia and British successes in Mesopotamia. On March 9, the Russian Revolution erupted, and two days later an army under General Sir F. S. Maude seized Baghdad. With the initial reports from Gaza arriving in a positive light, the committee saw an opportunity to press the advantage against the Turks throughout the Middle East. The events in Russia were at first viewed with hope. Alexander Kerensky vowed to continue the fight, and many saw a revitalized Russian army springing from the new regime. Strategically, this meant that a potential Russian offensive south toward Mosul could link up with Maude's planned advance north from Baghdad. Murray's apparent success at Gaza could be exploited into an opportunity to pluck Jerusalem from the reeling Turks. As more information flowed into Murray's headquarters, it was apparent that the first battle of Gaza was an unmitigated defeat. This reality, however, was slow to reach London, which pressed Murray to continue the attack. Reluctantly, he prepared for another offensive, and on April 17 he launched the attack. The Turks had used the time to prepare heavily fortified positions, and this made the second battle of Gaza very different from the first. In its outcome, though, the result was the same. The defeat was a severe blow to the morale of the British Army and offered a tremendous boost to the disheartened Turks, who had just delivered two major defeats to their opponent in less than a month.

The Turkish success encouraged the reinforcement of more troops to southern Palestine, including more German and Austrian contingents. Both sides now settled down into a trench-style posture reminiscent of the western front. The second defeat also led to another, more sober assessment of the strategic realities in Palestine. In May, the failure of the major offensive in Champagne, France, led to a fundamental confrontation in Whitehall between the "Westerners" under William Robert Robertson and the "Easterners" led by David Lloyd George. Perhaps not since the war leadership of Abraham Lincoln had the leader of a democracy recognized the fundamental changes wrought by the Industrial Revolution in strategy and the conduct of war. Much as Lawrence had reconsidered the conduct of modern campaigns during his March epiphany two months earlier, Lloyd George realized that in an industrialized protracted war, psychological mobilization of the civilian populace was at least as important as the fighting morale of the troops in the field. As Lincoln understood during the American Civil War, a war leader had to sustain the morale of his civilian forces on the assembly line as much as the soldiers on the battle line. According to the new industrial paradigm, Lloyd George had to secure military triumphs wherever and whenever he could, even if that meant fighting for victories in places as far away from France as Palestine. The prime minister's argument fundamentally changed the entire conduct of the war from the British strategic perspective. From now on, sideshow or not, if the operations brought victory and boosted the morale of the civilian population, then he would support the fight. From a grand strategic point of view, decision makers began to consider the relationship of Palestine and the Middle East critical to the economic stability and strategic integrity of the entire British Empire. Palestine would act as a buffer to Egypt and the Suez Canal and ensure a tight link to the eastern reaches of the empire. It also provided an entrée to the oil-laden regions of the Middle East that were beginning to have huge implications as naval and transportation technology advanced beyond the coal-burning stage.

A strategic reevaluation was occurring on the Turkish side as well. In Germany, General Erich von Falkenhayn was replaced as chief of the General Staff. His strategy of exhaustion had failed to yield the promised fruits of victory. Instead, it was Germany that was now near the brink of exhaustion. But Falkenhayn's reputation as a field commander was outstanding, so on May 7 he was sent to Constantinople to determine the feasibility of recapturing Baghdad. His assessment suggested that Baghdad could indeed be retaken if a strong force could be marshaled at Aleppo. Such a deployment, however, could succeed only if the Turks held the southern gateway into Palestine. There was also concern that the British incursion across the Turco-Egyptian frontier posed a serious threat to Jerusalem, one of the holiest sites of Islam.

While the Germans and their Turkish allies began to implement their new strategy, General Murray's fate was being weighed in Whitehall. Even after the first Gaza battle, questions were raised concerning his competence. The second defeat at Gaza sealed his fate. Murray was not so much incompetent as a victim of the changing paradigm of warfare. Like most generals of his day, he was guided by the dead hand of Napoleon and the idea of the central battle. Gaza demonstrated that modern battle would always be distributed— widely dispersed and spread out—without the privileged view of a Napoleon mounted on horseback surveying the whole field of battle. Those days were gone for good.

REFLECTING ON THE recent setbacks in the Middle East, Lloyd George remarked, "In Palestine and Mesopotamia nothing and nobody could have saved the Turk from complete collapse in 1915 and 1916 except our General Staff." But he not did relieve the General Staff; instead, the responsibility for defeat fell upon the head of the leader, Sir Archibald Murray. On June 11, 1917, Murray received his walking papers from Lord Kitchener. His replacement would be a relatively unknown, unremarkable (some might say mediocre) cavalryman by the name of Lieutenant-General Sir Edmund Henry Hynman Allenby. He was nicknamed "the Bull" for his imposing size and predilection to tempestuous outbursts. As history would show, he would emerge as "the Hedgehog" to Lawrence's "Fox."

Allenby was not Lloyd George's first choice to replace Murray. For political reasons, he had wanted the South African Jan Christian Smuts, but when he refused, Robertson suggested Allenby. Allenby was no political officer, but he had the confidence of Sir John French, though that support in some sense was negated by Sir Douglas Haig's general dislike of the cavalryman. Allenby had commanded the Third Army under Haig, commander in chief of the British Expeditionary Force. In the end it was Allenby's low-key style of leadership that seemed to attract the interest of Whitehall. He believed in the inextricable bond between the Victorian virtues of loyalty and discipline that he learned at the knee of his mother. He saw that loyalty extended down the chain of command as well as up. He was not a theoretically minded general. He took each problem as it came along and studied it intensely and deeply as a unique challenge without the preconceived bias of any past experience. He listened carefully to his subordinates, constantly trying to learn from them. When he made a decision, he gave them his full support, relying on the judgment of the local commanders on the scene. He was not a micromanager; instead, he was continually trying to maintain a balanced and synoptic view of the development of the campaign as a whole system. He was incessantly seeking to anticipate the next phase of the operations, rather than focusing on the tactics at the immediate front. It was perhaps the opportunity to command in an independent theater that gave him the scope to develop his own style and confidence as an operational commander. Few campaign commanders in World War I developed in four years as much as Allenby did in two. Although he is most remembered for his momentous dash toward Damascus in the latter months of the war, perhaps his greatest victory was the taking of the holy city of Jerusalem in December 1917.

After Allenby assumed command on June 28, he spent most of his time getting familiar with the troops under his command. His tireless activity had a profound effect on the men in the theater. They saw him as a moral tonic that had been sorely lacking under Murray's diffident manner of leadership. He took the men into his confidence, carefully explaining what had to be done and, more important, why it had to be done. As one officer wrote: "Everybody is in a great state of delight at getting a move on at last and, specially, as we know beforehand the general outline of the scheme. Why does no other commander realize that the men are capable of taking intelligent interest in things, and that if they know what is going on, are much more likely to hit on the right solution when things don't go exactly to plan? Thank goodness, Allenby has some common sense. And understands his Tommy Atkins." Major Richard Meinertzhagen, an intelligence colleague of Lawrence's and recently arrived to the theater, remarked in his diary: "[I] was introduced to Allenby, to whom I talked on intelligence matters for a while. My word, he is a different man to Murray. His face is strong and almost boyish. His manner is brusque almost to the point of rudeness, but I prefer it to the oil and butter of the society soldier. Allenby breathes success and the greatest pessimist cannot fail to have confidence in him. . . . The Egyptian Expeditionary Force is already awaking from its lethargic sleep under Murray, and I am happy to say GHQ will shortly move into Palestine and be near troops instead of wallowing in the fleshpots of Cairo."

Allenby's interest in the practical side of military science was also noted as "insatiable. Whether it was a fly expert from the British Museum, a railway engineer, an expert on town planning or a naturalist who could tell him something about the flora or fauna of the country, he had them all up and sucked their brains of anything they could tell him." This last predilection of Allenby's was what would most endear Lawrence to him: Lawrence's agile mind, heretical outlook, and encyclopedic mastery of the Arab and his culture. The two men would meet within a week of Allenby's appointment to his command.

LAWRENCE HAD JUST arrived, bearing news of the victory of Aqaba. He was still in his Arab garb when Allenby sent for him. He flip-flopped into the general's office, unsure of what to expect after just hearing the news that Murray had been sent down. He recalled: "It was a comic interview, for Allenby was physically large and confident, and morally so great that the comprehension of our littleness came slow to him. He sat in his chair looking at me—not straight, as his custom was, but sideways, puzzled. He was newly from France, where for years he had been a tooth of the great machine grinding the enemy. He was full of Western ideas of gun power and weight—the worst training for our war—but, as a cavalryman, was already half persuaded to throw up the new school, in this different world of Asia, and accompany [us] along the worn road of maneuver and movement; yet he was hardly prepared for anything so odd as myself—a little bare-faced silk-skirted man offering to hobble the enemy by preaching if given stores and arms and a fund of two hundred thousand [gold] sovereigns."

But the two men needed each other: that was the fundamental basis of their kinship, and they both recognized it immediately. "Allenby could not make out how much [of me] was genuine performer and how much charlatan. . . . He did not ask many questions, nor talk much, but studied the map and listened to the unfolding of Eastern Syria and its inhabitants. At the end he put up his chin and said quite directly, 'Well, I will do for you what I can,' and that ended it. I was not sure how far I had caught him; but we learned gradually that he meant exactly what he said; and that what General Allenby could do was enough for [me] his very greediest servant."[1]

Lawrence's next stop was to visit Brigadier-General Gilbert Clayton and apprise him of the details of the Aqaba operation and the manner of its military exploitation. The first question was who would command at Aqaba. Clayton suggested Major Pierce C. Joyce. Joyce had done yeoman work building the bases at Rabegh and Wejh, a necessary skill at Aqaba.

There were a number of strategic issues that had to be discussed as well. Lawrence believed that the Yenbo-Medina sector had become a dead letter. Operations here were winding down and the center of gravity of effort was shifting north. He advised Clayton that the Rabegh and Wejh bases should be consolidated and moved to Aqaba. In this he received half a loaf from Allenby: Wejh was moved, but Rabegh would remain active in support of the Medina siege. The second issue concerned the command relationship accorded Feisal. Hitherto Feisal had been under the command of his father, King Hussein. Lawrence argued that with Aqaba now the right flank of Allenby's army, Feisal should come under his command. The decision would have to rest with General Wingate, who was now high commissioner in Egypt. Wingate presented no difficulty, but still there was the suspicious Hussein himself.

Lawrence would speak with Hussein, but he would require the help of Colonel Wilson, who had become Hussein's most trusted foreign adviser. After traveling to Jidda, Lawrence arranged a meeting at which the king readily agreed—for his own unknown reasons. Lawrence recalled: "In foreign politics he betrayed a mind as narrow as it had been broad in unworldly things; with much of that destructive tendency of little men to deny the honesty of opponents. I grasped something of the fixed jealousy which made the modern Feisal suspect in his father's court; and realized how easily mischief-makers could corrode the King." While they were thus engaged, telegrams arrived stating that trouble was brewing among the Howeitat and somehow Auda seemed to be the instigator. By taking passage aboard the HMS *Hardinge,* Lawrence returned to Aqaba by the third afternoon.

Lawrence found Auda, Zaal, and Mohammed el Dheilan in a tent at Guweira. By the time he arrived, Lawrence had determined the mischief Auda and Mohammed had been up to. Both were upset by the British failure immediately to recognize the great victory at Aqaba and, like Moses's children, had sought comfort in a lesser god. Mohammed had made overtures to the Turkish governor at Maan. The Turks were willing to offer certain emoluments for his services. At the agreed-upon time, he went to Maan to receive his gifts. Meanwhile, Auda had learned of the double-dealing and had ambushed Mohammed, robbing him "to his skin." At first Lawrence feigned ignorance of the double-dealing; then, in the quiet manner of Arab diplomacy, he made Auda coldly aware that he knew of his transgressions.

Lawrence then explained the new strategic situation, pointing out that now Feisal's entire army would be coming north to join them, with camels heavily burdened with the king's appreciation for their great triumph. Lawrence then offered the two a monetary advance for their continued trust and loyalty. By Auda's reckoning, it was more profitable to work the alliance than sell his services cheaply to the Turks, for the Turks would always be there to be fleeced by Auda and his wolves at any time.

Afterward Lawrence contacted Cairo, saying the treachery was a mere misunderstanding. This seemed to satisfy GHQ and the matter was ended, though it was a lesson to Lawrence, who saw the force of his leadership was still based on a slender reed of tribal greed. But no matter. Greed was a powerful source of motivation, and after all, leadership was all about motivation, whether the pecuniary kind or the patriotic kind.

LAWRENCE NOW TOOK time to address certain planning shortcomings he had had to deal with ever since his arrival to the Hejaz desert. Through him, the rational tradition of the West came into contact with the oral or narrative tradition of the Bedouin. The former was steeped in the culture of military science and strict attention to detail, the latter to a prophet's narrative of a future unfolding in the palm of a deity's hand. Lawrence was able to create a workable synthesis between the two cultures. Following the seizure of the port of Aqaba on July 6, 1917, he offered the following assessment: "So far our war had had but one studied operation—the march on Aqaba. Such haphazard playing with men and movements of which we had assumed the leadership, disgraced our minds. I vowed to know henceforward, before I moved, where I was going and by what roads." The problem was to be able to link means to ends through some reliable method of execution. The Bedouin, so poor in means and unschooled in establishing elaborate goals, would have to reinvent himself: "Aims and ideas must be translated into tangibility by material expression. The desert men were too detached [rationally] to express the one; too poor in goods, too remote from complexity, to carry the other."

For the leader and his staff, it is one thing to recognize that future expectation, in the modern sense, is a question of minimizing uncertainty through control, but it is another matter to implement a design for the future. Perhaps the one thing that distinguishes the narrative prophet from a true agent of change like Lawrence is that the prophet has no plan—only a vision. Knowledge and understanding of the substance of planning and design are what give the agent of change influence over the future. The emphasis on substance is meant to get beyond the fetish of the planning process and move toward issues of structure and content, for it is this dimension that Lawrence fundamentally brought to the desert revolt. The leader's will becomes the prime mover—the engine—of all action and movement into the future. In the military realm, a tactical plan is thus the "crystallization" of the leader's will in his struggle to control and dominate events moving toward the future. The motive force of the leader's will, in its crystalline form, is cut and polished by his planning staff. The plan—sharp and diamond hard—cuts through the glaze of the present and into the future. A flawed plan, like a flawed diamond, will shatter as it cuts into the rock-hard reality of uncertainty. Branch Rickey recognized the same thing in playing and managing baseball. "Luck," said Rickey, "is the residue of good planning." The debris from a shattered plan can cover our expectations with a fine, abrasive dust of chance and ambiguity. The light powder of risk can so completely blanket an army that its friction grinds away its ability to function. The broken plan itself can thus compound the uncertainty and danger already inherent in war.

BY JULY 17, Lawrence was at an impasse, waiting for Joyce and Feisal to come up with the Arab army and formally occupy Aqaba. As he formalized his planning methodology, Lawrence conducted an after-action review of the operation, and this much was clear: "At Wejh the Hejaz war was won: after Aqaba it was ended."[2] The movement to Aqaba and out of the Hejaz was a movement into Syria, and the entire milieu of the revolt would soon change. The Hejaz was the land of desert and the raider; in Syria, the cultivated country belonged to the peasant farmer. If the revolt was to succeed, it would have to transform itself and embrace the villagers; otherwise the struggle would lose its essential legitimacy. Syria was a complex warren of factions that had to be considered and assessed independently of the whole. The natural geography had created regional "neighborhoods" that had social and ethnic differences as diverse as any political jigsaw puzzle.

Six major towns reflected the complexity of Syria. Foremost was Jerusalem, holiest city to all believers of a single God. It had grown into a kind of squalid backwater during the Turkish occupation. It was also the most eclectic, with the citizens as "characterless as hotel servants." It was the city that had special meaning at the moment for the British and for Lloyd George, who fancied it an ideal Christmas present for his Christian people. Beirut was the newest and most cosmopolitan town, heavily stained with French influence that was rather modulated by a Greek and American presence in the harbor and the university. Beirut was the commercial gateway into Syria and in later years would become the Paris of the Middle East for a few shining moments. The city was abuzz with radical ideas and articulate intellectuals who could express those ideas. It resembled Paris in the salon-packed days of the French Revolution. As Lawrence recognized, Beirut "was to be reckoned with."

The four remaining cities formed a jeweled necklace of ancient Syrian cultural heritage that bedecked the Western-cultivated region of Syria: Damascus, Homs, Hama, and Aleppo, with Damascus the glittering crown jewel. Here lay the capital of the region and seat of government and Turkish military headquarters. In the secular midst stood a dynamic religious center that rivaled Mecca in importance. In religious thought and dialogue, it perhaps even exceeded Mecca. The revolt, if it was to be successful, would have to hang its banner on the beetling ramparts of that historic capital. Homs and Hama were the Manichean, yin and yang "twins" of Syrian civilization. The prosaic wool and cotton of Homs competed against the finer fabric of Haman silk. The tension was parochial and local, spurred on by the belief that the true ancestral soul of Syria was cloaked in Manichean brocade. As for Aleppo, in some sense that city stood out from all the others: it was the commercial heart of Syria and Palestine; it had the greatest social diversity and therefore the most cooperative and cosmopolitan spirit of all the urban areas in the region.

Despite all this diversity, the "master key" of the Syrians was their common language. This was what Lawrence hoped to exploit in the next campaign; this was what he had tried to explain to Allenby during their first meeting, and it seemed he grasped intuitively the military implications of a linguistic common denominator. Upon all this complexity, the Turks attempted to overlay a Potemkin veneer of political unity, all the while seeking to exploit the many petty jealousies among the competing groups. The idea of an Arab nation would have to be imposed, at least initially. Lawrence believed, though, that an Arab outsider, a Sunni Muslim like Feisal with outstanding religious credentials, might weld a coalition that would carry the Syrians against their Ottoman masters. The coalition, spurred on by victory, might last long enough to secure victory and the stability of peace when "everything material and moral might be pawned."

The campaign in Syria would have to be much like the maneuver from Wejh to Aqaba: a movement across tribal areas as though across a magic carpet or stepping-stones or, in Lawrence's evocative metaphor, by means of a "ladder of tribes." The rungs of the ladder from Aqaba to Damascus would consist of the Howeitat, Beni Sakhr, Sherarat, Ruwalla, and Serahin, and Lawrence would "climb" the three hundred miles to Azrak, the nearest oasis to Hauran and the Jebel Druze. The nature of the operations would be like "naval war, in mobility, ubiquity, independence of bases and communications, ignoring of ground features, of strategic areas, of fixed directions, of fixed points." Lawrence would "command the desert. Camel raiding parties, self-contained like ships, might cruise confidently along the enemy's cultivation-frontier, sure of an unhindered retreat into their desert-element which the Turks could not explore."[3]

The operational design that Lawrence had worked out in theory during his epiphany at Wadi Ais in March had already been tested in practice during the Aqaba campaign. Now it would be duly refined. The camel and the desert rider's frugality would be their firepower. They could operate independently for six weeks with a forty-five-pound bag of flour and a pint of water. Deficits would be made up at the wells, which were rarely a hundred miles apart. The six-week reserve of food gave the raiders an operating range of nearly two thousand miles, a thousand out and a thousand back—a ride from Kansas City, Missouri, to Savannah, Georgia, and back. A ride of fifteen hundred miles could easily be made in a month. Starvation was seldom a factor, for each man rode two hundred pounds of grade-A meat. Any rider rendered camel-less would simply piggyback with a comrade.

On the face of it, Lawrence's desert force was a primitive army—except in one key department: light machine guns. His men carried Lewis and Hotchkiss guns that outclassed anything the Turks had. The men were clueless as to their mechanics but were made expert in their operation. If they jammed, broke a firing pin, or overheated, they were simply tossed aside. Nothing was allowed to slow the tempo of tactical action and the "eighteen miles an hour" fight. In maneuver warfare, Lawrence believed, "one long-range gun outweighed ninety-nine short." Along with the heavy use of machine guns, Lawrence developed a highly crafted skill in the employment of explosives. By war's end, he and his men could destroy any length of track, any segment of bridge, with precision, efficiency, and care.

The organization of his raiding parties evolved rapidly based on the Aqaba experience. Because of long-standing feuds and jealousies, it became virtually impossible to integrate or amalgamate the various tribes; nor could one antithetic tribe operate in the territory of another. To overcome this organizational constraint, Lawrence operated in the greatest dispersion possible, which contributed greatly to his agility, fluidity, and mobility.

Maximum disorganization created maximum articulation: as with a box of LEGOs, Lawrence could create any organization and function as unique as the new task at hand, for each mission was unlike any other and had to be considered afresh. The LEGO-like articulation meant that the enemy response could never develop a classic order of battle, for there *was* no order, only disorder; his system was unsystematic.

The ordinary rank and file—if that is the proper term for the massively articulated character of the Arab army—were bound together by the common ideal of the revolt. They were all volunteers; some may have hoped for wealth, but this idea distracted their tribal leaders more than the private soldier, who was always at liberty to leave the ranks "without penalty whenever the conviction failed him: the only contract was honor." The conventional army was held together by a common denominator of discipline, which ensured control. In Lawrence's LEGO army, control was less important than the diversity of quality and the redundancy of action. There were no common denominators here because nothing was common about the nature of insurgent warfare; and where one man failed to act, one of his mates would rise to stand in his stead. The conventional force was always willing to reduce risk through control: "By this substitution of a sure job for a possible masterpiece, military science made a deliberate sacrifice of a capacity in order to reduce the uncertain element, the bionomic factor, in enlisted humanity. Discipline's necessary accompaniment was compound or social war—that form in which the fighting man was the product of the multiplied exertions of a long hierarchy, from workshop to supply unit, kept him active in the field." The diverse quality of a single guerrilla, in Lawrence's mind, would equal the composite strength of a conventional squad, for every man was a killer, whereas the soldier fought with one hand tied to his logistical rear.

In practice, it was more important that the guerrilla threaten his foe at all times than engage him actively in a fight, for the threat of the raiding specter continually haunted the regular soldier, draining from him initiative, courage, and hope. The success at Aqaba had demonstrated one thing for all to judge: "Irregular war was far more intellectual than a bayonet charge, far more exhausting than service in the comfortable imitative obedience of an ordered army. Guerillas must be allowed liberal work room: in irregular war, of two men together, one was being wasted. Our ideal should be to make our battle a series of single combats, our ranks a happy alliance of agile commanders-in-chief."[4]

DURING THE REST of July and into August, Lawrence continued to refine his theory of guerrilla warfare that he had first spun back in March. Lawrence's theoretical reveries were finally disturbed on August 23, when Feisal arrived with four hundred Arabs and a small force of Egyptians. Admiral Wemyss was sailing about in his flagship HMS *Eurylaus,* protecting the small harbor as it began to stretch and grow to accommodate its new role as base of operations for the revolt. A new pier was built while Lawrence waited for the arrival of the promised armored cars and aircraft.

Meanwhile, the Turks began preparation for a counterattack from Maan with six thousand men and sixteen artillery pieces. Later in September, a cavalry regiment was sent from the Palestine front to reinforce the push on Aqaba. The Turks began by sending forth a detachment of two thousand infantry to Aba el Lissan, several miles short of Aqaba to the southwest. To counter this move, Lawrence began to worry the eastern flank of the Turks with a series of small raids. Simultaneously, air strikes were sent from El Arish in Palestine. The Turks were further troubled by the constant pinprick attacks to their railway. Lawrence took charge of the rail demolitions himself, making the operation part of a training exercise for his Arabs. He brought along an Englishman nicknamed "Stokes," who instructed the men on the employment of the Stokes mortar, and an Australian labeled "Lewis," who trained the raiders on the Lewis machine gun.

The first objective of the raiding party lay seventy miles south of Maan at Mudowwara station. The plan was to destroy the well that had fed the steaming locomotives that plied the nearby track. The column reached Guweira several miles north of Aqaba on the morning of September 9, where they met Auda, who had somehow drawn the wages for the Howeitat. He was using his new role as paymaster to coerce various clans of the great tribe to his leadership. The tribal majority, including three southern clans whose participation in the next phase of the revolt had been counted on, resented this challenge and threatened to break away immediately. Feisal had sent Sherif Mastur to negotiate a solution to the impasse. After long hours of talking in the unwelcome heat had sapped all patience, the three clans were ready to return home. Upon hearing the news, Lawrence lost his temper and rushed into Auda's tent to prevent his continued meddling. Here he found the troublemaker in the arms of his new wife. As Lawrence recounts the story: "To gain ground with him, I began to jeer at the old man for being so old and yet so foolish like the rest of his race, who regarded our reproductive processes not as unhygienic pleasure, but as a main business of life. Auda retorted with his desire for heirs. I asked if he had found life good enough to thank his haphazard parents for bringing him into it, or selfishly to confer the doubtful gift upon an unborn spirit?"

Auda, maintaining his cool, replied, "Indeed, I am Auda and you know Auda. My father—to whom Allah be merciful—was master, greater than Auda; and he would praise my grandfather. The world is greater as we go back [in time]."

"But, Auda," replied Lawrence, "we say honor our sons and daughters, the heirs of our accumulated worth, fulfillers of our broken wisdom. With each generation the earth is older, mankind more removed from its childhood. . . ."

The sudden separation from his wife's embrace was not placing Auda in a humorous mood. He squinted his eyes at Lawrence and gestured toward his youngest son. Outside the tent, he was trying to ride a camel like a racehorse, striking its neck with a stick to move it along. Flicking his chin at the boy, Auda said to Lawrence, "Oh world's imp, if Allah please he has inherited my worth, but thank Allah not yet my strength; and if I find fault with him I will redden his tail." After a long pause, he said very slowly with irony, "But no doubt you are very wise." Lawrence's take on the brief discussion was that he "should go off to a clean spot, to await events."

AFTER WAITING OUT several more Turkish air strikes, Lawrence and his escort turned east toward the Valley of Rumm, watering area of the Beni Atiyeh. The place was a Grand Canyon of breathtaking beauty—three hundred yards wide in some places—reminiscent of the outback country of southern Utah, where jagged gorges splinter into fiery embers under a setting sun. It became Lawrence's favorite place of all.

They reached a watering place shared by the disaffected clans angry with Auda. The nominal leader of the party, Sherif Aid, had gone sun-blind and was unable effectively to lead the negotiations. Lawrence attempted in his stead but seemed only to raise their ire all the more. On the next morning, September 12, the situation had changed little, though the crusty Zaal arrived and was seen merely as the main henchman of Auda. Hot words were exchanged, the men shuffled about, glared, clicked prayer beads, and otherwise grew restless. Sensing a crisis brewing, Lawrence decided to return quickly to Aqaba to inform Feisal of the high drama simmering at Rumm. He hoped a word from the emir would cool the hotheads. After meeting with Lawrence, Feisal promised to send his best negotiator, Abdullah el Feir. Abdullah and Lawrence returned the following afternoon, and the negotiator began to work his magic with the malcontents: "He began to smooth over their griefs with the ready persuasiveness which was the birthmark of an Arab leader, and which all experience served to whet."

While Feisal's "fixer" soothed over the tense situation, Lawrence wandered off to explore the exquisite beauty of Rumm. He climbed one of the citadel-like ledges to reach a splashing waterfall the Arabs called El Shellala. Here he decided to take a refreshing shower to wash away the frustration and tension of the past few days. Lawrence had laid his clothes in the hot sun to drive away the infestations of lice and destroy the agglomeration of nits he had collected over the many days of travel. As he was enjoying his cool cleansing, a desert beggar—seemingly from nowhere—shuffled up a path and sat himself nonchalantly on Lawrence's baking clothes. He was a "gray-bearded, ragged man, with a hewn face of great power and weariness. . . . He heard me and leaned forward, peering with rheumy eyes. . . . After a long stare he seemed content, and closed his eyes, groaning, 'The love is from Allah; and of Allah; and towards Allah.'" The words of the holy man stunned Lawrence, for it was the first time he had heard an Arab rejoice in simple human love: "The old man of Rumm loomed portentous in his brief, single sentence and seemed to overturn my theories of the Arab nature."

Lawrence coaxed the desert apparition down from the rocky bastion to the camp in hopes of finding the source of this ancient's wisdom. Mohammed brewed the coffee, and they fed the man. He was familiar to the Howeitat, known to them as a wandering ascetic, exclaiming mysterious pronouncements among the sheep and goats. He never seemed to require shelter or nourishment along his doddering journeys. Lawrence continued to probe his disconnected utterings late into the night, until "he rose painfully to his feet and tottered deafly into the night, taking his beliefs, if any, with him."[5] He listened as the old man—an Arab "Leibowitz"—pattered off, bone white under the waning moonlight and bone thin under his cloak of rags, into the desert darkness, proclaiming his canticle of love.

THE NEXT MORNING, the rebellious clans had been brought to heel thanks to the efforts of Abdullah the "fixer." Although calm returned, an underlying resentment lingered so that Lawrence had only a third of the men he had planned for the mission. His biggest challenge, however, was a leadership concern. Sherif Aid's blindness rendered him *hors de combat*. Zaal was the natural leader, but he was too closely aligned with the rapacious Auda to carry the proper authority and legitimacy with the men.

So on September 16 the party rode out of camp "like a broken necklace." There were four tribal "jewels" in the necklace: the Zuweida, the Darausha, the Togatga, and the Zelebani. Another group soon joined them: the Dhumaniyeh, out of embarrassment for whiling away their time with the women instead of raiding. None of the groups would ride or mingle with the others; no words were exchanged. Lawrence rode among the groups trying to generate some cohesion and found it impossible. The only point of common agreement was that they trusted Zaal no farther than they could throw him. In the end, Lawrence assumed the role of leader himself.

The next day they arrived at the Mudowwara well, two or three miles west of the station. The well was a broad pond covered with an icing of emerald slime. Islets of pink scum floated dead in the water. These turned out to be the rotting remnants of perished camels the

Turks had thrown in to pollute the pool. Fortunately, the passage of time had rendered this form of biological warfare ineffectual. With no other choice, the men reluctantly filled their water skins. The disturbed water sent a yellow, cloying haze into the still air that lingered, perhaps the common spirit of the dead animals.

At dusk Lawrence, Zaal, and some others crept toward the station under a new moon, trying to move to within the three-hundred-yard range of the Stokes mortar. Lawrence and Zaal moved closer, leaving the rest of the raiders with the mortar. A brief reconnaissance revealed an enemy strength of at least two hundred rifles and a machine gun. Lawrence had 116 disunited irregulars and perhaps the shock of surprise. After a quick consultation with Zaal, he decided against an attack. The men were waved off and returned to camp.

The following morning, they headed south along the railway hidden in some dead ground, idly following the tracks of a leopard. The group followed the line until they came to a place where the tracks crossed over a culvert, an ideal location to set a heavy charge. A rocky ledge to the rear of the target offered a stable firing platform for the mortar and machine guns. After securing the camels, Lawrence hefted his fifty pounds of explosives, wire, tools, and firing magneto into position. Burying the gelatine was extremely difficult, because the site dipped off into a steep slope. The watercourse also had to be carefully camouflaged to disguise any signs of tampering under the culvert. Lawrence dug and prepped the site for a full five hours before the charge was finally set. All the while the sun-baked gelatine leaked from its sandbag and mingled with his sweat, creating a cocktail of acrid stench. When the task had been completed, Feisal's favorite slave, Salem, asked for the honor of firing the mine at the appropriate time.

Leaving a guard to watch the track below for any signs of a train, Lawrence returned to camp to find his men crouching on a steep ridge, highlighted against the setting sun like crows on a telephone line, visible for all to see. The Turks saw them and opened a heavy, though inaccurate, fire in their direction. Night quickly descended to hide them from the enemy and their own tactical embarrassment—and Lawrence's anger.

The men were awakened the next morning around nine o'clock

with an alarm from the night sentinels: a platoon of forty Turks was advancing on their position from Hallat Ammar, a train station to the south. Lawrence immediately ordered a patrol to feign a retreat to the east. The ruse worked, drawing off the enemy into the hills, while the engineering party continued its vigil for any unsuspecting train that was sure to come. At noon, another warning was raised when one of the local rail repair detachments wandered down the line but completely missed seeing the carefully hidden mine and Lawrence's hideout. Just as the repair party trudged south, Lawrence spotted another serious threat from the direction of Mudowwara. Through his captured Zeiss binoculars, Lawrence saw a hundred Turkish soldiers approaching. Though moving at a snail's pace, the company would be upon them in less than three hours. This would place his raiders between two fires: the party of a hundred men advancing from the north and the forty men who had been taken on a wild goose chase into the hills. He had to make a swift decision, and in a moment he decided to retreat, leaving the mine in place with the hope of returning later at a more auspicious time.

Just as he was about to issue the order, another cry of alarm was raised. One of the sentinels excitedly brought news that the train they had been waiting for was finally approaching from Hallat Ammar. The news immediately halted all thoughts of retreat. Lawrence quickly gave orders for the Arabs to man their firing positions and fire. Stokes and Lewis, battling dysentery from the slime pool, soon forgot their ailments and hurtled into position. Salem, the designated triggerman, rushed to the exploder, muttering an echo of prayers to Allah granting him beneficent success.

The train was big: two locomotives pulling ten heavily laden boxcars bristling with rifle fire. Atop the roof, sandbagged rifle nests poured forth a hot but inaccurate fire. Lawrence had not expected two engines and quickly made an assessment that he would blow the mine under the second locomotive. The train continued to chug toward its unsuspecting doom when, just at the precise moment, Lawrence chopped down his arm in signal to Salem. He squeezed the charger, and after three heartbeats Allah blessed Salem with a tremendous, deafening roar. The concussion of the blast knocked him out of his dancing jubilation. Then everything went black. . . .

. . .

"OUT OF THE darkness came shattering crashes and long, loud metallic clangings of ripped steel, with many lumps of iron and plate; while one entire wheel of a locomotive whirled up suddenly black out of the cloud against the sky, and sailed musically over our heads to fall slowly and heavily into the desert behind. Except for the flight of these, there succeeded a deathly silence, with no cry of men or rifle-shot, as the now gray mist of the explosion drifted from the line towards us and over our ridge until it was lost in the hills." The silence was suddenly shattered by the chatter of machine guns firing from atop the ridge into the gray cloud. Salem picked up his rifle and charged into the mist, where he was enveloped and seemingly spirited away. The bullets struck heavily against the rifle nests on top of the boxcars. The Stokes mortar then opened up, seeking the Turks who were hidden farther down the line. The second burst scored a direct hit and scattered bodies along the track like old rags. The train began to empty its human cargo, which ran across the desert toward the station at Mudowwara, sweeping away the oncoming patrol. The gunners now reaped a bloody harvest amid the panic, while Lawrence rushed to the crushed culvert to assess the damage. The front boxcar, filled with sick and wounded, had fallen into the mine's crater. Peering into the unbelievable carnage, he saw three or four dazed survivors. One cried out, "Typhus!" Lawrence quickly backed away and looked farther down the track: "Succeeding wagons were derailed and smashed: some had frames irreparably buckled. The second engine was a blanched pile of smoking iron. Its driving wheels had been blown upward, taking away the side of the fire-box. Cab and tender were twisted into strips, among the piled stones of the bridge abutment." The first engine was in better shape and possibly salvageable. Lawrence dragged a box of gun cotton over to the boiler and lit a thirty-second fuse: enough time for him to drive off the horde of plunderers from the devastating explosion.

In Lawrence's recollection, the valley had become a surreal, brightly colored apocalyptic scene: "The Arabs, gone raving mad, were rushing about at top speed bareheaded and half-naked, screaming, shooting into the air, clawing one another nail and fist, while they burst open trucks and staggered back and forward with immense bales, which they ripped [open] by the rail-side and tossed through, smashing what they did not want." The train was full of civilians, mostly refugees and the sick, as well as the wives and children of Turkish officers returning to Damascus. "There were scores of carpets spread about; dozens of mattresses and flowered quilts; blankets in heaps, clothes for men and women in full variety; clocks, cooking-pots, food, ornaments and weapons."[6]

A group of women charged at Lawrence, begging protection, but their husbands threw them aside to grasp Lawrence's feet and beg for mercy. He kicked them off with his bare feet and ran over to a group of Austro-German troops—instructors of the new Skoda mountain guns about to be deployed in the theater. They asked for quarter, but a dispute broke out with the marauding Arabs and all but a handful were killed before Lawrence could intervene again.

When the Goyan scene was over, the audit of battle was reckoned: seventy dead Turks, just teeth and smoking boots; ninety captured; and apparently not one Arab casualty. In the hysteria, Lawrence had to defend himself at least three times from his own men. The Arabs suddenly dispersed with their loot without a word of leave. Lawrence was alone at the wreck with Lewis and Stokes when suddenly Zaal galloped up with a comrade to find their lost leader. The five men found enough straying camels to load their weapons and engineering equipment for the trek back to Rumm.

The journey to Rumm was uneventful. There Lawrence learned that one man was killed and three lightly wounded, but Salem was missing. Lewis had seen him lying near one of the shattered engines severely wounded but in the excitement had forgotten to give notice. Lawrence became angry when he discovered that half the party knew the same information but had said nothing. Salem had been placed in the personal charge of Lawrence by Feisal: it was his responsibility to recover Salem—or his body. Lawrence immediately asked for volunteers to go back with him and rescue Salem. After a few moments, Zaal volunteered with twelve of his outriders.

The party raced back to the wreck and came atop the ridge overlooking the disaster. Below, they could see almost two hundred Turks crawling over the scene like ants. The prospect of finding Salem alive now seemed hopeless: the Turks always mutilated and killed any

Arab they might capture. After recovering more of their gear under Turkish fire, the rescue party reluctantly returned to Rumm. At the camp, the Arabs had reorganized themselves in Lawrence's absence. They looked like a band of gypsies. He looked over the image and reflected: "Victory always undid an Arab force, so we were no longer a raiding party, but a stumbling baggage caravan, loaded to the breaking with enough household goods to make rich an Arab tribe for years."

Lawrence stood at the side of the "caravan" as it moved past him, and to his utter astonishment he saw Salem strapped to the crupper of the saddle of one of Feisal's slaves. After his first rush into the explosive torrent, Salem had been shot. Again Allah smiled upon him: though he'd been shot through his back, the slug narrowly missed his spine. Salem recovered, but Lawrence felt that he always bore him a small grudge for being left behind. Salem had taught him another lesson in leadership: "I had failed in staunchness. My habit of hiding behind a Sherif was to avoid measuring myself against the pitiless Arab standard, with its no-mercy for foreigners who wore its clothes, and aped its manners. Not often was I caught with so poor a shield as blind Sherif Aid."[7]

LAWRENCE'S ROLE IN the desert meant a direct intellectual engagement with the form and substance of planning for future military operations set within a fundamentally different social and military culture. Controlling the future of the desert revolt began as an act of thought sustained by Lawrence's will and shaped by his leadership. The disembodied will crystallized into the form of a design. The crystal of planning provided a laserlike focus for all action in a manner that was efficient and surgically precise. Lawrence's leadership provided five essential elements of direction and regulation to the Arab planning effort, especially with respect to time.

First, planning became more than simply a mechanical checklist that, when followed, automatically led to the fulfillment of set goals. A plan became a blueprint for the future, imposed on the future. When Lawrence spoke of an "end state," he was able to translate that into a narrative vision of the Arab future. Second, Lawrence was able to integrate thoroughly British planning staff and procedures into the Arab cause. Third, he was able to provide an element of flexibility in all his plans and operations. Fourth, Lawrence was able to create ad hoc Arab units organized for the immediate task at hand. Finally, Lawrence and his staff were able to address one of the central problems of warfare in the desert: the visualization of the theater of operations in all its many dimensions. The days of the omniscient, omnipresent commander leading on his horse while surveying the battlefield were gone when Lawrence arrived in the desert. Even the proverbial "glance at the map" provided him with much less information than it did during preindustrial times. Not only had the theater of war exploded in scale, it had also expanded in scope. Beginning with the American Civil War and certainly by 1917, the military dimensions of space, time, energy, and mass began to embrace the social, economic, cultural, and political dimensions of mass industrialized warfare. Lawrence had to fuse and synthesize all this complex information into a coherent whole. He was able to fill in the mosaic of missing information with synthetic leaps of intuition. From a cognitive standpoint, it clearly demonstrated strength of mind and strength of will.

CHAPTER SIX

To Whom the Gods Pray

The rare man who attains wisdom is, by the very clearness of his sight, a better guide in solving practical problems than those, more commonly the leaders of men, whose eyes are misted and minds warped by ambition for success. But to give such guidance he must for the moment cease straining after the Infinite and become, in a relative sense, shortsighted. Lawrence seems hitherto to have made this adjustment. But now, one feels, he had for some months so strained himself, in conquest of his physical being, that his power of practical guidance may have been affected. Here, to some degree, if still more in the adverse conditions of the problem, may lie the explanation of what followed.

—B. H. LIDDELL HART, *T. E. Lawrence*

Soon after the successful raid, Lawrence returned to Aqaba sometime around September 21. His party was greeted as heroes. Lewis and Stokes were sent off to Cairo having been sorely missed by their headquarters. Allenby was pleased to throw in a medal for each to assuage their dysentery. Meanwhile, the general continued his preparations for a renewed attack against the Turkish positions around Gaza and Beersheba. The preparations had continued through the long and terribly hot summer. The scorching khamsin blew sand, dust, and flies through the camps on both sides of the line. The Turks endured more suffering because of a severe food shortage and heavy artillery bombardments from the British guns. Sandfly fever was the common, most hated scourge of all. The fever was an influenzalike disease, usually lasting three days, that laid up the patient with malaise, fever, headache, eye pain, and dehydration; the recovery period, owing to the dehydration, was often longer. The military effect was to delay and disrupt training and exercise schedules. The Turks were also impeded by the slow movement of reinforcements to the front. The raiding of Lawrence and others induced a paranoiac fear among the Ottomans as they constantly looked behind them at their vulnerable logistics rear. Two infantry divisions finally arrived in September, but these were not battle ready or battle hardened, having arrived from the temperate Caucasus front. Their German advisers, meanwhile, introduced the Turks to new techniques of fieldcraft brought with them from the western front.

Except for the heat and disease, the British had a relatively easier time of it, being able to withdraw men from the front and place them in special training camps near the cooler Mediterranean Sea. Acclimatization was an important consideration for troops arriving from the northern climes of Europe. This process could take several months and continue until well into October. British supply arrangements sought to establish certain planning norms to support the kind of mobile operations Allenby's campaign design envisaged. Practically, this meant that his army had to find a way to operate up to a week at a time at long distances from its main base of operations. Great emphasis was therefore placed on establishing extensive storage facilities immediately behind the lines. Since the poor and nearly nonexistent roads ruled out motorized transport, Allenby had to rely heavily on water pipelines, Holt caterpillar tractors, and an old standby, the camel. Much of the logistical success was the result of the improvement of Qantara as the major supply port.

Operationally, the greatly improved logistical situation meant that Allenby's force could attack across a much broader front and would also generate enough combat power to drive a wedge deep into the enemy's defenses. If a decisive penetration could be achieved, a rapid cavalry exploitation could lead to the complete dislocation of the Turkish front in Palestine. The labored process of assembling such a large support base, however, meant that Allenby's initial offensive schedule would be thrown off by several weeks. His original design had contemplated an attack in mid-September, when the weather would offer the most reasonable conditions for his troops. The complex preparations had now imposed a D-Day of sometime toward the end of October.

Allenby informed Robertson of the delay and also noted that twenty divisions would be necessary to guarantee success. Although the War Committee accepted Allenby's decision, they were optimistic that if he could seize Jerusalem, Turkey would be knocked out of the war by Christmas. While the committee was willing to dispense optimism without accepting a commensurate measure of responsibility, it rejected his plea for fourteen additional divisions: he would have to make do with what he had. Robertson did agree to resurrect the Alexandretta operation as a deception project that would bleed forces from the front opposite Allenby. Demonstrations were made at Cyprus, but limited shipping due to U-boat losses and an active Turkish air reconnaissance effort gave the lie to the ruse.

By the end of September, the Turkish operational situation continued its downward spiral toward ruin and collapse. Initial optimism over possible operations to retake Baghdad gave way to the practical realities looming on the Palestine front as Allenby's forces began preparations for a major offensive. A dispute arose over who would control the German troops that had just arrived in the theater. Originally, the German Asia Corps was designated the spearhead in Mesopotamia, but now the crisis facing Palestine led to a redeployment of forces. As part of the deliberations, General Falkenhayn toured the Palestine front in early September. It was his assessment that, despite reinforcement, the British were vulnerable to a spoiling attack against their eastern flank. Based on Falkenhayn's appreciation, the Turkish high command agreed to reorganize their forces for such a strike. A serious debate arose, however, over the command of these forces. The Turks were fearful of a German seizure of strategic direction and resisted a unified commander. These debates lingered into October and were further frustrated when a huge supply base at Haidar Pasha station was sabotaged, destroying most of the ammunition for the forces reinforcing Palestine. The failure to arrive at a unified command subverted unity of effort in the face of the pending British offensive at Gaza as well as the ongoing operations north of Aqaba. A command arrangement was finally established whereby one headquarters would control forces west of the Dead Sea and south of Jerusalem and another headquarters would control troops in Syria and the Hejaz. Of course, this arrangement created a natural—and vulnerable—seam between the two commands, one that Lawrence and Allenby would soon exploit.

WHILE ALLENBY FORGED ahead with his designs on Gaza, Lawrence used the time to train raiding parties for the purpose of maintaining effective pressure on the Turks north of Aqaba. One of Lawrence's first pupils was Captain Rosario Pisani. The artillery captain, a sometime French Lothario sent by Brémond to spy on Lawrence, quickly fell under the spell of Lawrence's leadership. For variety's sake, the two men took a demolition party north of Maan. They rode up out of the desert heat of Arabia into the high cold plains of the Trans-Jordan. Operating near kilometer 475, the men laid a mine consisting of a new, more powerful form of lyddite. Lyddite, named after the area in the southern United Kingdom where it was manufactured, was the common explosive used by the British since the Boer War. It was made into a molded form of picric acid and used in artillery shells as well. Struggling through the night, the party managed to lay the mine by dawn and waited. . . .

Lawrence waited for a long time: it took six days for a train to roll by, driven by the twice shy Turks. The empty time led to a minor leadership crisis for Lawrence: "These decisions were arrived at despite my imperfect knowledge of Arabic. The fraudulence of my business stung me. Here were more fruits, bitter fruits, of my decision, in front of Aqaba, to become a principal of the Revolt. I was raising Arabs on false pretenses, and exercising a false authority over my dupes, on little more evidence than their faces, as visible to my eyes weakly watering and stinging after a year's exposure to the throb, throb of sunlight. . . . After a night it would give way to that unattractive, and not honorable, internal ache which in itself provoked thought and left its victim yet weaker to endure. In such conditions the war seemed as great a folly as my sham leadership a crime; and, sending for our sheikhs, I was about to resign myself and my pretensions into their puzzled hands. . . ."[1] As Lawrence was struggling with the relentless burden of leader's grief, a nearby scout finally heralded an oncoming train.

It was a water train coming down from Maan, chugging across the mine, which failed to explode. The Arabs rejoiced, for there was no honor and little booty in such a priceless cargo. The second day, enemy patrols scuttled up and down the line like khaki beetles, though the heat of day reduced their numbers and activity, even at eight o'clock in the morning. Another victim rolled out of Maan, proclaiming its death wish with towering plumes of smoke and billowing hisses of steam. A foot patrol shepherded the iron creature at a foot's pace, its twelve boxcars burdened with loot, the engine huffing and puffing up a steep incline. As it rolled over the bridge the mine was executed, lifting the black beast to its death amid a choking cloud of yellow ash and green suffocation. Pisani led the Arabs in a furious assault, leaving twenty Turks dead in the initial charge. The explosion knocked out the topmost arch of the bridge, and the engine was ripped open like a sardine can, the oil soaking slowly, staining the desert sand. Lawrence was examining the contents of the cargo and found the train heavily laden with seventy tons of food and sweetmeats. While he was assessing the loot, a Turkish colonel took a potshot at him, grazing Lawrence in the hip. Despite the wound, he felt great satisfaction with the success of his mission and the conduct of his men. There were no casualties, and Pisani conducted himself in an exemplary manner, showing great promise for the future. Moreover, an effective program of training was beginning to emerge. A whole entourage of dynamiters trained in the "lurens" method gained notoriety among the tribes.

Over the next four months, Lawrence's desert sappers would destroy seventeen locomotives. The whole railroad was vulnerable: terror would travel down the rail line like lightning down a wire. His audacious raiders had boldly posted a notice on the Town Hall door in Damascus, warning that everyone traveling by rail would do so at their own peril. Because all the rolling stock was under centralized control, any losses on the Trans-Jordan front would affect the operations in Palestine. The continuous, formless raids against the terrified and disorganized Turks made Aqaba virtually invulnerable, suggesting again that an offense is the best defense. When Lawrence returned to Aqaba on October 8, he was almost immediately whisked off to Cairo to explain how the railroad operations would fit into Allenby's grander campaign design.

A NUMBER OF new personalities graced Allenby's growing staff. At the top reigned Allenby himself, whose "calm drive and human understanding . . . was the man the men worked for, the image we worshipped." The competent Lynden-Bell had been replaced by the staunch Louis Bols, Allenby's chief of staff when he was with the Third Army in France. Guy Dawnay came over as well. A former banker, Dawnay had studied Greek history, becoming an autodidact as strategist. He planned the battle of Suvla Bay and the two battles for Gaza. He quickly became attuned to Allenby's needs, and the two worked together as one mind: he would deliver Jerusalem for Allenby.

Dawnay's assessment of the situation was contrary to Allenby's initial inclination to continue the massing of forces opposite Gaza and push scrumlike into the Turkish line. Dawnay had a different plan. He would draw the Turks into a defense in depth in front of Gaza and swing the main British strength, under the cloak of deception, around toward Beersheba, thirty-five miles to the southwest. Beersheba, along with Gaza, was one of the historical avenues into Palestine and gateway to Jerusalem. In the end, Allenby's thrusting cavalry soul overcame his tendency to continue with the western front's nonstrategy of attrition. But to pull off the ruse, Allenby needed to add another actor to his cast.

In Dawnay's stable of impresarios was an ornithologist named Richard Meinertzhagen. In addition to professional bird-watching interests, he was an intelligence officer. Meinertzhagen was the joker in the pack, willing to employ deceit as readily as destruction. A man of agile and subtle intellect, he made war seem a grand game. This detached view also made him the perfect strategist. "Meiner" created a packet of forged operational maps and documents and carried them into no-man's-land on a feigned reconnaissance mission. When he was spotted by curious pickets, he raced off toward his own lines, dropping the satchel with the fake deployments and designs and thus setting the trap. A Turkish noncom rescued the wayward pouch and brought it to headquarters for examination.

Now that Allenby had his planning team constituted at last, he wanted to better mesh Lawrence's activities with his own. It was beginning to dawn on Lawrence that success on Allenby's front would create great opportunity in front of the Arabs. As he examined the map, his eyes were drawn to Deraa, "the navel" of the Turkish forces in Syria. Here lay the junction of the Jerusalem-Haifa-Damascus-Medina railways. A coincident strike by Lawrence's Arabs when Allenby's hammer fell would have tremendous consequences for the destruction of the Turks and their German allies. Perhaps even Damascus could be grabbed in the same reach. Such an operation would be decisive only if the British could carry through, but Lawrence reckoned that British past failures in the theater and Allenby's inexperience in the desert would count against them. The army was still in the mind-set of the western front: ponderous, oversynchronized, fearful of chaos. It tried to impose order where none was possible, failing to recognize opportunity amid disorder. In the end, it seemed better to delay the gamble until next year if it became necessary. A failed British attack would clearly leave Feisal out on a limb and vulnerable.

The necessity of weighing the consequences of the success of two masters was becoming troublesome to Lawrence. He had a duty to Allenby as an officer in His Majesty's service, and he had a duty to Feisal and the Arabs as the leader and mainspring of the Arab Revolt. He was like a movie director having to satisfy the producers and studio moguls with an Oscar-winning production while meeting the needs of flighty rock stars heavily indulged by their union. His role was thus a synthetic and mediating one, where the circle of disagreement and disunion had to be squared. It meant he had to maintain a promontory perspective, taking in the views of both sides and balancing them on the scales of strategic merit and justice. But in the end, Lawrence recognized that Allenby, as producer, was paying the bills: "The Arab Movement lived on Allenby's good pleasure, so it was needful to undertake some operation, less than a general revolt, in the enemy rear: an operation which could be achieved by a raiding party without involving the settled peoples; and yet one which would please him by being of material help to the British pursuit of the enemy. These conditions and qualifications pointed, upon consideration, to an attempted cutting of one of the great bridges in the Yarmuk Valley."

THE TWO PLANS were synchronized: Allenby's attack would begin on October 31; Lawrence would strike on November 5. The Yarmuk Valley was a very deep gorge that followed the Yarmuk River on its way to marry with the Jordan River just south of the Sea of Galilee near the town of Samakh. The railway from Palestine left Samakh and serpentined eastward toward Deraa across several bridges. The westernmost and easternmost bridges would be the most difficult to repair or rebuild, and if the strike was successful, it would isolate the entire Turkish army facing Allenby for at least two weeks. The raid would entail a 420-mile maneuver through Azrak, 50 miles due east of Amman. If everything went according to plan—always an unlikely scenario—the Turks would be trapped east of Deraa for two weeks and the Arabs might have a free ride into Damascus.

From the Arab side, the plan needed a political component if it could induce the Beni Sakhr to join in the "pickup game" approach to strategy. Sherif Nasir of Medina was momentarily out of the picture; however, Sherif Ali ibn Hussein of the Harith was available. He had a great relationship with Feisal and had developed a tactical stature that was now priceless, having led several successful train raids near El Ala. He was an incomparable desert fighter, nearly the equal of Auda himself. Ali would deliver the Harith: Lawrence could count on it. The strongest players in the game, though, were the Ruwalla, who were currently in winter quarters and inaccessible for the time being.

The plan was fairly simple: Assemble a raiding party of about fifty men on Azrak and in two long but swift marches pounce on the westernmost Yarmuk bridge at Um Keis. The challenge was in the complexity of the demolition required to drop the rail bridges. The sapper team would consist of Lawrence; Zaal abu Tayi with a handful of Howeitat; Captain C. E. Wood, base engineer at Aqaba and recovering from a severe head shot suffered in France; and a platoon of Indian machine gunners. George Lloyd (not to be confused with the prime minister, David Lloyd George) of the Arab Bureau would tag along and offer his scintillating conversation as far as Jefer. At the last

minute they were introduced to Emir Abd el Kader, who was grandson of the leader who had repulsed the French in Algeria some fifty
years earlier. The grandfather had been sent into exile with his followers to the exact region of Yarmuk that Lawrence intended to
strike. Abd el Kader was returning from a visit with Hussein in Mecca
and was now offering the help of the exiled villagers at Yarmuk.

While Lawrence was pondering the offer, Brémond sent down a
telegram warning Lawrence that Abd el Kader was a spy. After ob-
serving him carefully, Lawrence decided there was no evidence to
support the charge. Feisal told Lawrence, "I know he is mad. I think
he is honest. Guard your heads and use him." Lawrence would soon
come to a more realistic assessment: "As a matter of fact, he was an
Islamic fanatic, half-insane with religious enthusiasm and a most violent belief in himself. His Muslim susceptibilities were outraged by
my undisguised Christianity." In the end, though, Abd el Kader would
become a chief nemesis to Lawrence and dog him all the way to Damascus—not out of willfulness, but out of sheer "bullet-headed" stupidity, wounded pride, and obstinacy. He was also nearly stone-deaf.

The mission departed Aqaba on October 24, traveling through
Rumm toward Jefer, where Auda ruled. Lawrence reconstituted his
bodyguard with six motley men. He had to bail Farraj and Daud out
of trouble for painting up Sheikh Yusuf's prized camel like a circus
clown. The party straggled badly, with Wood becoming separated
and lost in Wadi Itm. When Lawrence arrived at Rumm, Wood was
already there, sick from exhaustion and his nagging head wound. Ali
and Abd el Kader arrived the next day, in a bitter argument over
tribal precedence. The Indians recovered their stray camels and the
march continued the next day, with Ali and the emir continuing their
strife from the rear of the column.

On October 28 they reached Auda's camp, where they found him
still squabbling with the minor sheikhs over wages. They ate in Mohammed el Dheilan's tent; ever gracious, he greeted Lawrence with
generosity and respect. After dinner Lawrence went out in search of
Zaal, "one of the finest raiders alive." Lawrence found him much
changed since the raid on Aqaba and the summer that followed. The
Zaal of Aqaba was not the Zaal of the present. He was losing his
nerve and offered Lawrence his help only if asked directly, as a point

of personal honor. Of course, Lawrence would never burden the warrior, or challenge their honor and friendship, with such a request, though he could seek Zaal's advice. As he was presenting him with his plan, the "most competent to judge my half-formed scheme," a camel boy rushed up in terror to announce that a "dust-cloud" of riders was approaching fast from Maan. The fear was that a large part of the Turkish garrison force, consisting of a cavalry regiment and a dragoon regiment mounted on mules, would soon overrun the camp. Lawrence had thirty rifles and Auda's five able-bodied men—the rest of the tribe had gone to greener pastures. He quickly formed a firing line among the alkali bushes and terrain depressions, while Auda tore down the few remaining tents. The machine guns found dominating fields of fire, and the entire force commanded a fire sack eight hundred yards deep. As the "dust-cloud" crested the bank, to everyone's relief, Sherif Ali ibn el Hussein el Harith and Abd el Kader miraculously materialized. The "odd couple" had diverted their ride in the night to shoot up a portion of the railway, losing two men and a horse in the venture.

After the excitement, George Lloyd left the party on a diplomatic effort for the long journey to Versailles. His genial personality and his moral contribution to the mission would soon be sorely missed. At night around the tribal campfire, Lawrence chose to resolve the issue of Auda's quarreling with the lesser chiefs over money and wages. By midnight, he appeared to be gaining ground in the matter through the force of his leadership and his argument, when suddenly Auda raised his riding crop for silence. The men tensed at the apparent danger: "After a while we felt a creeping reverberation, a cadence of blows too dull, too wide, too slow easily to find response in our ears. It was like the mutter of a distant, very lowly thunderstorm. Auda raised his haggard eyes towards the west, and said, 'The English guns.'"

ALLENBY HAD JUST launched the second bombardment of the offensive with this firestorm directed at Beersheba. Although he had issued orders for the attack on October 22, the redeployment of a rifle corps and the Desert Mounted Corps turned into an extremely intricate maneuver that had to be carried out at the last moment. Darkness and a full moon facilitated the complex move, however. A sudden encounter with the Turks by one of the redeploying units on October 27 almost wrecked the whole plan, but the initial barrage on Gaza turned the enemy's attention in that direction. The movement was completed flawlessly by October 30, and thanks to a preponderance of manpower, the British could afford to split their forces in half, leaving a sizable and therefore credible force behind at Gaza. At Beersheba, the British outweighed the Turks two to one in infantry, eight to one in cavalry, and three to two in artillery. The advantage was necessary in order to achieve maximum shock and momentum. It was crucial that the nearby waterworks be captured swiftly and intact.

The attack was launched on the early morning of October 31 and was initially successful. By early afternoon, most key objectives surrounding the town had been reached, but heavy machine-gun fire from the town proper began to slow the advance. The capture of Beersheba before nightfall appeared doubtful, when General Harry Chauvel ordered his Aussies to mount an all-out attack. Led by the Fourth Australian Light Horse Brigade, and supported by the other brigades of the Australian Mounted Division, the unit led a pell-mell charge across nearly three miles of shell and fire into Beersheba. The shock of the attack was the tipping point that led to the cascading disintegration of the defense.

After the battle, it was clear that the scale of the British deception had led the senior Turkish leaders to expect the main blow to fall at Gaza. The Turkish high command was also critical of German commander Kress von Kressenstein for nailing them to the cross of a static defense. They claimed he had denied them the mobility to fight an active defense. In this they were correct, and Falkenhayn agreed with them, for within a few days Kress was relieved of his duties. The Turks suffered nearly five thousand casualties. Their immediate fear was the perceived threat toward Jerusalem. This energized the Turks sufficiently to heed the potential danger. Meanwhile, the British were in the midst of an operational pause as they reconsolidated their strength for the next phase of the operation, which was to roll up the entire Turkish line all the way to the Mediterranean Sea. This was planned to occur around November 4. In order to fix the Turks at Gaza, a diversionary attack was ordered for November 1, with the bombardment of October 27 as part of the diversion. The artillery prep also included naval gunfire and was the most intense barrage outside the western front, with fifteen thousand shells fired in one day alone. The attack was successful in that it forced the commitment of the only Turkish reserve in the area and so prevented its redeployment to Beersheba.

While the Gaza attack continued, events unfolded around Beersheba. Lieutenant-Colonel S. F. Newcombe, old friend and colleague of Lawrence's, had led a hundred-man raiding party deep around and behind the town with the intention of attacking from the east. This small force, though ultimately destroyed and Newcombe temporarily captured, caused sufficient confusion to keep the Turks and their German advisers off balance. But now the Turks were beginning to rally along the heights about ten miles north of Beersheba. With reports coming in from the front, Allenby was beginning to sense that an opportunity was slipping away. As he glanced at the map toward Yarmuk, he wondered, *Where was Lawrence?*

LAWRENCE WAS PREPARING to leave Auda's encampment on the morning of October 31 after spending the night listening to the far-off British artillery barrage. Auda was in an especially good mood, having reconciled himself to Lawrence's demands over the issue of sub-chiefs and booty. As Lawrence was about to mount his camel, Auda embraced him and whispered in his ear: "Beware of Abd el Kader." With so many others about, Auda could say no more.

The party moved off at a slow pace, dictated mainly by the Indians and their poor riding skill. For Lawrence, the thirty-five-mile-a-day pace was a comfortable walk in the park. They had camped for their noon meal when suddenly the alarm was raised: riders were swiftly bearing down upon the camp from north and west. By now, the Indian machine gunners had been drilled into readiness by such alarms. Their four machine guns formed the anchor of the position, located in a shallow fold of ground. Sherif Ali urged the men to hold fire as Lawrence expressed a nodding pride at the professional manner of their tactical deployment, when all of a sudden Awad, a Sherari camel boy, jumped up and ran off in seeming recognition toward the attackers. After some shooting and confusion, the "attackers" turned out to be a clan of the Beni Sakhr. Once greetings were exchanged, the clan welcomed the raiding party with a celebratory show of horsemanship around the wells of Bair.

Ali had some other business to attend to: it was at Bair that Lawrence and Nasir had encountered the dynamited wells on their way to Aqaba in the summer. Mifleh, clan-chief of the Beni Sakhr, had asked Feisal for some masons and well drillers to reline the wells, so a team of masons was sent from Bisha to do the repair. But now months later the work was still unfinished, and Feisal had sent Lawrence and Ali to investigate the costly delay on their way to Yarmuk. It turned out that the men had been lounging about, forcing the local Arabs to feed them in luxurious style while they delayed in their well repair. Ali unleashed his servants, who meted out the appropriate tribal justice, and after they received promises of rapid progress, all was forgiven and the entire party prepared for Mifleh's great feast.

Where the Howeitat used butter in abundance, the Beni Sakhr feasts were awash in the goo. Lawrence's party fairly dripped in the stuff, their mouths and faces reflecting a gluttonous, buttery sheen. All were enjoying the generous meal when Abd el Kader committed one of his many faux pas by suddenly rising from the feast before the host and the others had finished and moving off to the far wall of the tent. The rest looked at one another in astonishment, then at Ali, who seemed to shrug and muttered into his mutton chop, "Asshole." After several more helpings, the dogs were drawn in to their share of the banquet at the mouth of the pavilion. They chomped and shattered bones in feral delight, the noise a counterpoint to the more docile chewing of the satiated raiders. Abd el Kader contributed to the spectacle with a solo rhapsody of grunting, spitting, flatulating, and belching. The immensity of his grossness was meant to impress the clan with his grandeur. But instead he only boasted his ignorance in failing to understand the Bedouin culture with respect to proper table manners.

When the celebration finally abated, the rumble of British artillery could be heard again off in the distance. Lawrence took the opportunity to vaguely inform Mifleh of their intended raid on Deraa. At this his eyes lit up with greed, and Lawrence pressed the moment and asked him for his leadership and fifteen men. Mifleh eagerly agreed and offered to bring along his son, Turki. In gratitude, Lawrence gave the son one of his fine silk robes after the dinner was formerly ended.

The next day was November 1. The reinforced party moved out at dawn, with Lawrence riding with the Beni Sakhr contingent, trying to learn as much of the new dialect as possible and so extend the compass of his leadership. In the oral tradition of the desert, it was crucial that men knew the great tribal narratives that defined and bound the tribes into a coherent and definable social force. "To have fallen short in such knowledge would have meant being branded either as ill-bred, or as a stranger; and strangers were not admitted to familiar intercourse or councils or confidences. There was nothing so wearing, yet nothing so important for success of my purpose, as this constant mental gymnastic of apparent omniscience at each time meeting a new tribe." Between the Arabs—especially the desert dwellers—and the Turks it was much more complex. There was personal identity at work here, but there was also a corporate aspect in the mix. "There were Englishmen whom, individually, the Arabs preferred to any Turk, or foreigner; but, on the strength of this, to have generalized and called the Arabs pro-English would have been folly. Each stranger made his own poor bed among them." The corporate attraction between Arab and Turk was part religious but seemed mostly cultural. "The Arab respected force a little: he respected craft more, and often had it in enviable degree: but most of all he respected blunt sincerity of utterance, nearly the sole weapon God had excluded from his armament. The Turk was all things by turn, and so commended himself to the Arabs for such while as he was not corporately feared."

As the sound of English guns thrummed and ricocheted off the Dead Sea, Lawrence heard the Arabs whisper, "They are nearer; the English are advancing; Allah deliver the men under that rain." Thus, even at a distance Arab commiseration and solidarity with the Turks could be strong: "They were thinking compassionately of the passing Turks, so long their weak oppressors; whom, for their weakness, though oppressors, they loved more than the strong foreigner with his blind indiscriminate justice."[2]

The following day, they approached Azrak. While Lawrence's Ageyli bodyguards were combing their hair with butter to suffocate the feasting lice, a scout spotted a covey of riders approaching through the dense tamarisk. They were men of the Serahin tribe, on their way to offer fealty to Feisal. After a wild greeting, the two parties tented together for the evening at Ain el Beidha. In the early morning, Lawrence was roused from his slumber by the fierce hunger of the local fleas, lice, and ticks. Finding sleep now impossible, he sought out Sheikh Mteir, headman of the tribe, and discussed his mission with him.

After he heard Lawrence's intentions, the sheikh's jaw fairly dropped: the western Yarmuk bridge was out of the question. The Turks had just brought up scores of wood choppers in the area, heavily armed and alert, making it impossible for a raiding party to sneak through to the west. Mteir's greatest concern, however, was the one shared by the rest of his tribe: an overwhelming mistrust of Abd el Kader and his recently emigrated Moorish villagers, who had become the tribe's diehard foes. Any attack against even the closer bridge at Tell el Shehab would leave vulnerable the tribe's rear to an attack from the villagers. Furthermore, if it rained, the tribe would be cut off by the subsequent morass across the Remthe plain.

Lawrence was now in a serious bind. The Serahin was the last tribe along the route to the bridges with sufficient manpower to support the raid. If they refused to aid the effort, the entire mission would have to be scrubbed, an eventuality that would mean failing Allenby and his operations in Palestine. It was now up to Lawrence to persuade the tribe and overcome their natural resistance and fear. Accordingly, he gathered together around the campfire his own picked men—Ali, Mifleh, and Fahad and Adhub, who were the chief war leaders of the Zebn clan—and the more courageous of the Serahin. Then he began to speak to the tribe—slowly at first, demonstrating a common solidarity against the Turks. Lawrence began to play out a thread of motivation, carefully spinning it around the tribesmen: "We put it to them . . . how life in mass was sensual only, to be lived and loved in its extremity. There could be no rest-houses for revolt, no dividend of joy paid out. Its spirit was accretive, to endure as far as the senses would endure, and to use each such advance as base for further adventure, deeper privation, sharper pain. Sense could not reach back or forward. A felt emotion was a conquered emotion, an experience gone dead, which we buried by expressing it." He challenged their pride by stoking their defiance: they would defy death because it was in their honor to defy it; it was an essential exercise of their desert freedom. There was a balance in life and death, body and soul, leisure and hardship. The two ran in parallel tracks played out through the flowing desert sands of time; the wise man was he who could bring both streams to a simultaneous conclusion through action.

True: the fight for the bridges would be dangerous, with no guarantee of success; men would be killed and maimed. Yet it was the greater man who acted in defiance of the long odds; who threw down the gauntlet to fate, daring it to exert himself even in the face of human frailty. It was the greater man who found joy in the defiance of fate and rejoiced in the struggle against Destiny: "There could be no honor in a sure success, but much might be wrested from a sure defeat. . . . To the clear-sighted, failure was the only goal. We must believe, through and through, that there was no victory, except to go down into death fighting and crying for failure itself, calling in excess of despair to Omnipotence to strike harder, that by His very striking He might temper our tortured selves into the weapon of His own ruin."[3] The speech was as much about Lawrence's self-motivation as it was about persuading the tribe. For almost a year he had struggled against his own fear to the point of despair. And now, driven by the courage of despair, he would drive others into battle under the same lash. In this realization, he discovered the fundamental métier of the desert warrior and the true source of his thrall over them: fearlessness through despair, defiance against death. All these things Lawrence had harbored for a long time within his own psychology—his leader's grief.

AFTER THE LONG oration, Lawrence sank into an exhausted sleep. Early in the morning, he was awakened by the tribesmen, eager to pass in review in tribute to his persuasive oratory. They made a poor showing: ragged, full of bluster, mediocre riders; but it was all Lawrence had. Mteir was too decrepit to offer any real leadership. His protégé, ibn Bani, was too immature and political to be his real successor. At length, the review sputtered to a weary halt as the tribesmen prepared their noon meal.

On November 4, Lawrence's reinforced party moved off for the fort and oasis of Azrak. Azrak carried the same haunting qualities as Rumm. It had been home to long-dead Roman legionnaires, caretaker to the bones of kings and sages; Azrak had borne witness to the march of history through its silent blue stone. The men rejoiced among the shaded springs and palm gardens, for few of them had ever seen Azrak. After the celebrations ended, Lawrence noticed that Abd el Kader and his entourage were missing. An intense search revealed that he had left for the Jebel Druze, a mountainous region of Syria. With Abd el Kader's sudden departure, Lawrence wisely assumed the worst and considered the entire plan compromised. This meant that under the worst possible circumstances the Turks would be waiting for the raiders at the westernmost bridge at Yarmuk. Lawrence decided that under the extreme circumstances only the eastern bridge at Tell el Shehab was worth the risk; the new objective also meant a more dangerous trek across open terrain between Remthe and Deraa.

The raiders marched out the next day in great haste, crossing into Wadi el Harith, bearing the namesake of Sherif Ali. A halt was made at lunch, and several of Lawrence's bodyguards went off in search of gazelle. The party was successful, but the success quickly turned deadly when a feud broke out between Ahmed and Awad. Awad blew off Ahmed's head rope with a stray shot, while Ahmed tattooed Awad's cloak with an eight-millimeter "needle." Lawrence threatened the men with mutilation of the right thumb and index finger, which immediately caused Ahmed and Awad to throw themselves at his mercy and publicly repent and reconcile their blood feud. Sherif Ali ibn el Hussein el Harith meted out the ritual Bedouin punishment by striking several blows to their heads with the blunt edge of a heavy dagger, causing blood to gush forth as the true sign of tribal justice.

After driving on a few miles farther, the party found the perfect base for their bridge raid: a long trough of clear rainwater that had just been scouted out by a troop of Circassian cavalry. The next morning, they filled their water bags and pushed into the foothills below Deraa. Here they waited for night's cloaking embrace, fully cognizant of the fact that they would have no more water until they accomplished their mission and returned. In the darkness, Lawrence and Fahad scouted the two-hour stretch to the bridge. Here they found a hollow full of thick vegetation at Ghadir el Abyadh, the perfect place to rest until dawn. As the sky turned pink, the two crept from hiding to look directly at the bridge below, less than a rifle shot away. The Turkish guards appeared to be in an amiable mood, evidence that Abd el Kader had ridden by without revealing any sinister intent toward the bridge, or at least the usual Turkish incompetence kept hidden its own secrets.

The rest of the party slowly infiltrated the gardenlike depression at Abyadh. Lawrence and Ali went over the plan one last time. They would first have to wait through the heat of the day until nightfall to conduct the demolition. If the feat could be accomplished, the real challenge lay ahead in having to ride eighty miles in thirteen hours to get east of the rail line by morning. The Indians were beyond such a task: their animals were already spent, despite the light march Lawrence had imposed on them. Lawrence decided, therefore, to pick the six best riders and give them the six best camels under their best leader, Hassan Shah. They would take just one Vickers machine gun, dramatically reducing their firepower. The rest of the machine-gun company would remain behind.

The bridge itself would have to be assaulted on foot. The Beni Sakhr under Ali would lead the charge, while the distrusted Serahin would watch the camels and hump the explosives. The blasting material had to be repacked into more manageable thirty-pound units and placed in easily recognizable and more visible white bags for the night attack. Engineer Wood repacked the gelatine, shrugging off the annoying nitrous-induced headaches with ease. The final task left Lawrence to rearrange his bodyguard so that each man was buddied up with one of the Serahin. The final organization of the striking force consisted of seven Indians, Sherif Ali ibn el Hussein el Harith and six of his servants, twenty Beni Sakhr, forty Serahin, and Lawrence's bodyguard. Two of Lawrence's men had a sudden attack of jitters and were immediately relieved of all duties. The remaining men were instructed to retreat to Abu Sawana at nightfall to await eventualities.

AT DUSK, LAWRENCE led his raiders west, scuttling down a steep ridge, when all of a sudden the lead detachment charged ahead of the main body: they had stumbled upon a frightened raisin peddler leading his two wives on a pair of donkeys. The situation proved awkward, since the merchant was heading to the nearby railroad station at Mafrak. Lawrence quickly decided to have the three encamp under the supervision of one of the Serahin. Lawrence regrouped to follow the track of an old pilgrim trail: "It was the same road along which the Arabs had ridden with me on my first night in Arabia out by Rabegh. Since then in twelve months we had fought up it for some twelve hundred kilometers, past Medina and Hedia, Dizad, Mudowwara and Maan. . . . But we were apprehensive of tonight: our nerves had been shaken by the flight of Abd el Kader, the solitary traitor of our experience. Had we calculated fairly we should have known that we had a chance in spite of him: yet dispassionate judgment lay not in our mood, and we thought half-despairingly how the Arab Revolt would never perform its last stage, but would remain one more example of the caravans which started ardently for a cloud-goal, and died man by man in the wilderness without the tarnish of achievement."[4]

The party trudged onward, only to be plinked at by some careless shepherd boy firing an antique rifle, wildly missing Lawrence's army. Mifleh el Gomaan, who piloted the caravan over the rough terrain, seemed to find every possible impediment along the way: a barking dog, arcing flares, a screaming mad gypsy woman, twinkling tracers. The dark night melded with the heavy smell of black ashes as they came upon a deep leafy depression. The raiders creaked along to the other side and halted. Just off to the north was Deraa station, emitting an eerie glow as a presentiment of the future. They crested the lip of the hollow and plunged down a narrow valley leading to the plain of Remthe. Here the ground was half plowed and sticky to the camels' tread, slowing the advance to a shambling crawl. Lawrence turned around on his red camel and went down the ragged line, urging the men forward. The Indians were riding their camels like horses, exhausting both to man and beast; the others stuttered manfully through the furrowed clods of mud. Lawrence decided to maintain his position in the rear, while Ali took the lead with his superb racing camel.

By nine o'clock, the riders left the muck of the plowed field and the pace increased. But just as the party started to regain its momentum, a light rain began making the furrowed fields greasy and slick.

Several of the camels slipped, throwing their riders and pitching the column into a jumble of camel flesh and cursing men. The drizzle soon stopped and the raiders quickened their stride, this time with greater determination. Up ahead, Mifleh suddenly reached up high in the air and cracked the darkness with his riding crop: a taut *twang* revealed the overhead telegraph line running up to Mezerib. The plucking noise of the wires faded into the empty night to give way to another, more subtle sound: a hushing, breathless whisper off in the gray distance, which finally uncovered the great cataract beneath Tell el Shehab, feeding the wide maw of the Yarmuk gorge.

A short ride later, Mifleh halted the column. They were now just above the sixty-foot bridge that lay off to their right, a steely gray skeleton under the rising moon. Lawrence quickly organized the raiders for the impending raid, doling out the precious gelatine among fifteen of the Serahin sappers. Adhub led the Beni Sakhr as the advance guard to recon a safe way to the bridge. The brief drizzle had rendered the steep ridge wet and slippery. Some of the men were fearful that the explosives would blow them to Allah in a fall. "When we were in the stiffest part, where rocks cropped out brokenly from the face," Lawrence recalled, "a new noise was added to the roaring water as a train clanked slowly up from Galilee, the flanges of its wheels screaming on the curves and the steam of its engine panting out of the hidden depths of the ravine in white ghostly breaths. The Serahin hung back. Wood drove them after us. Fahad and I leaped to the right, and in the light of the furnace-flame saw open trucks in which were men in khaki, perhaps prisoners going up to Asia Minor." Engineer Wood took command of the Indians, deploying the lone machine gun to cover both the guard tent and Lawrence's raiding party as it crept silently along the old abandoned construction trail to the closest abutment. The dirty ragged raiders shaded perfectly into the shadowed limestone walls, becoming all but invisible. As Lawrence touched the cold steel of the bridge, he saw a guard on the other side casually pissing into the wild stream below. "I lay staring at him fascinated, as if painless and helpless, while Fahad shuffled back by the abutment wall where it sprang clear of the hill-side. [But] this was no good, for I wanted to attack the girders themselves; so I crept away to bring the gelatine bearers. Before I reached them there was a loud clatter of a dropped rifle and a scrambling fall from up the bank. The sentry started and stared up at the noise. He saw, high up, in the zone of light with which the rising moon slowly made beautiful the gorge, the machine gunners climbing down to a new position in the receding shadow. He challenged loudly, then lifted his rifle and fired, while yelling the guard out."[5]

Suddenly, all hell broke loose. The Beni Sakhr flattened, firing away at the lucky sentry. The rest of the guard mount spilled into a nearby trench and blazed away at the Arab muzzle flashes. The Indian machine gunners were maldeployed and could not get the Vickers into action in time to rake the guard tent. Bullets ricocheted and echoed off the canyon wall in shrieking reverberations. Almost immediately, the Serahin bomb bearers came under direct and intense raking fire. In their limited engineering training, they learned well the lesson that if gelatine is struck by a bullet, they could kiss their callused arses goodbye. Holding that thought uppermost in their minds, they tossed the deadly cargo over the abutment into the raging water below and fled for their lives.

At that tipping point, success, quantumlike, turned into disaster: it was now every man for himself. The raiders scattered and ran back up the hill. In the melee, Lawrence took one last longing look at the bridge and ran. Along the way, he and Ali stumbled into Wood and the Indians, aghast, and told them "it was all over." The mad dash continued back to the camels, where the Serahin were already mounting the beasts and fleeing, while the Turks continued to blaze away in the darkness below. With the plan now in shambles, the retreat was turning into a frenzied rout. The ashen rags of cloud began a race with the gray light of dawn, both trying to catch the panic-stricken raiders. The tumult and noise started to awaken the neighboring villages; the closest was Turra. The other homesteads on the plain twinkled alive in the wake of the routing mass of riders. As the men crested the plain, they overran a group of peasants on their way from Deraa. The Serahin now became desperadoes in fact as well as appearance as they began, in a frustrated rage, to waylay the peasants and rob them blind. The victims ran screaming across the plain, spreading the ululating Arab alarm: now every village in Remthe for miles around was alerted. Sharpshooters appeared on rooftops firing at shadows, friend and foe. The bullets cracked and whistled sharply overhead.

The robbers were left in the distance heavily laden with their ill-gotten loot, while the raiders pressed on in glum silence and despair. Lawrence's "trained men did marvelous service helping those who fell, or mounting behind them those whose camels got too hurt to canter on. The ground was still muddy, and the ploughed strips more laborious than ever; but behind us was the riot, spurring us and our camels to exertion, like a pack hunting us into the refuge of the hills. . . . Gradually the noise behind us died away, and the last stragglers fell into place, driven together, as on the advance, by the flail of Ali ibn el Hussein and myself in the rear."

They reached the telegraph line at dawn and began to cut it seemingly for no purpose but general principle. The irony struck Lawrence immediately: "We had crossed the line the night before to blow up the bridge at Tell el Shehab, and so cut Palestine off from Damascus, and we were actually cutting the telegraph to Medina after all our pains and risks! Allenby's guns, still shaking the air away there on our right, were bitter recorders of the failure we had been. . . . We were fools, all of us equal fools, and so our rage was aimless. . . . Our minds were sick with failure, and our bodies tired after nearly a hundred strained miles over bad country in bad conditions, between sunset and sunset, without halt or food."[6]

THE RAIN BEGAN again and added more darkness to an already black mood. The rations would give out in the evening. The question of food soon broke the reflective silence, but the talk quickly passed from concern for restoring empty bellies to the need for restoring personal honor. The Beni Sakhr hungered especially, while the disgraced Serahin sought salvation. Ali, now become a true believer in the revolt, said to Lawrence, "Let's blow up a train." There was a great shout of approval, and all eyes flashed upon Lawrence the dynamiter. In anticipation, a heavy stillness fell like a shroud.

Lawrence was overwhelmed: the selfless acclamation of the follower toward his leader is a rare expression of love few leaders experience and seldom savor. For Lawrence, this was a validating moment of his trial of leadership; it was an act of forgiveness proffered the leader by the follower, who knows intuitively that the leader must always bear the ultimate responsibility for failure. Even though the follower may be the cause of ultimate disaster, he is instantly absolved through the absolution of leadership. His sins become the sins of the leader; yet, paradoxically, his triumphs are his own. The men wanted another chance, and Lawrence could not deny his children.

He still had a spare bag of gelatine: thirty pounds, and just enough to do the job. There was still the problem of food, however. Though the Arabs would happily eat their camels in a pinch, the Indians, also Muslim, found the thought abhorrent. Of course, this meant detaching the Indians and leaving no machine-gun support. Ali immediately stood up and vowed that his Arabs would double their efforts to make up for the loss of the machine gunners. Lawrence still mulled over the idea in his head. There was a strong possibility that the train they might encounter would be a logistics train armed with incapable reservists; there was just adequate explosives, no margin for error; they would be without the Indian machine guns. In the balance, he decided to take the risk for the sake of leadership. The men were in a dismal psychological state. If they didn't gain a success, they would never find redemption. He announced his decision and the men rejoiced again. Their uplifted hearts made the evening meal taste doubly good.

On the next morning, November 9, the Arabs bade farewell to the stalwart but disconsolate machine gunners. Lawrence sent Engineer Wood with the Indians "to soften the blow with honor." Wood was also showing signs of the early stages of pneumonia, and the weather would only make his symptoms worse. The column was now reduced to fewer than sixty men. None of the men knew the area. Lawrence was familiar with the region because of his operations with Zaal in the spring. He took them to the old crime scene at Minifir, an ideal site for their mischief. At twilight, they crept down to the rebuilt culvert at point 172. As they were laying the mine, a train suddenly appeared out of the darkening mist, sending them fleeing for cover under the masonry arch. As the train rolled over them, Lawrence inspected the target. The span was over sixteen feet long, running across a gully that had been chiseled deeply by the recent rains. The cut was at least four feet deep, creating a winding path of cover a hundred yards beyond the rail line. Lawrence embedded the charge painstakingly under the crown of the arch, though this effort took longer than usual because of the muddy condition of the gulch. The demolition wires were carefully paid out into the concealment of the ravine. Unfortunately, logistical problems arising all the way back in Egypt left them with a length of wire only sixty yards long. Apparently, a shortage in insulated wire had not been made good by the time the party left Aqaba. Because of the dampness, the detonator could not be left connected to the charge in the normal fashion. Lawrence would have to make a last-minute connection and then run down to the exploder to fire off the charge. This left little time for preparation, forcing Lawrence to spend a miserably cold night under the wind- and rain-blasted arch. Unable to sleep, he spent most of the time covering over the evidence of the mining.

Dawn was interrupted by a patrol of Turks on their routine guard tour. Lawrence raced out of hiding and up the gully to huddle with the others. Just then a lookout alerted him that another train was approaching the culvert, but yet again the short notice left them unprepared to deal with the mist-enshrouded train. By now frustration was beginning to settle over the raiders with the same gloomy effect as the damp mist and clammy chill. Ali began to curse the fate of the entire mission, wondering if any good at all could come of it. Lawrence took quick notice of this despair: perhaps an indication of an evil eye. He tried to divert attention from this general mood of hopelessness by giving the men something to do. He ordered them to redeploy their lookouts and then make a game of being hungry by pretending not to be. They clustered together for warmth, their backs up against the steaming camels. Thoughts of a failed mission surrounded the party like the swirling damp wind. Gnawing hunger seemed a mocking reminder, as though from Allenby, of their incompetence.

JUST AS LAWRENCE was fleeing from the Tell el Shehab bridge, Allenby was finally beginning to make progress across his whole front, especially at Gaza. Despite German efforts to stiffen the Turkish defense, the enemy was pushed slowly north and northeastward. Allenby also was hopeful that Chauvel's Desert Mounted Corps would be able to drive northwest and cut in behind the retreating Turks in front of Gaza. But again, lack of water slowed progress more than enemy bullets. The Royal Navy tried to ease the situation by off-loading supplies along the coast, but this had limited effect owing to the lack of motorized transport with which to distribute the maté-riel among the advancing troops. Though Lawrence had worried about the weather on Allenby's front, in fact it was hot, dry, and windy, unlike the cold shower the Arabs were experiencing across the Jordan.

By November 10, just as Lawrence was huddling with his mates among the camels, it was becoming clear to Allenby and Dawnay that the Turks fleeing from Gaza had escaped the cavalry trap they had set for them. From a broader strategic—or, more precisely, operational—perspective, both sides demonstrated Larry Addington's old adage from military history that "railroads are the bones of strategy." Like the great sweep of a pendulum, the momentum of the British advance was approaching the high arc of culmination. The Turkish Eighth Army was beginning to rally along the Nahr Sukhereir. The purpose was to defend the lines of communication that flowed along the rail network in Palestine. The establishment of a new front here meant that the Turks could protect the important rail nexus at Junction sta-tion, which fed into Jerusalem. Loss of this decisive point at Junction station would cut off Jerusalem from the integrity of the entire defen-sive scheme in Palestine and cut the Turks in two, isolating the Sev-enth Army in the Judean Hills. As long as the line held, Jerusalem would be safe. It was therefore a singular operational achievement that the Turks were able to establish a new front along the Nahr, tying it in with Wadi Surar and the numerous villages that afforded good defensive positions atop the hills. Allenby recognized the ur-gency of the situation. The more he delayed, the stronger the Turkish position would become; it was imperative, therefore, that he strike immediately.

WHILE ALLENBY WAS thus considering his options, Lawrence waited under the cloud of rain at kilometer 172. Finally, at noon on Novem-ber 10, the weather broke sufficiently to provide the scouts with sev-eral hundred yards of good visibility. They quickly spotted a train, but its progress was slow. Like virtually all of the wood-burning lo-comotives Lawrence encountered, this one was defective. It took nearly an hour to crawl over the culvert where Lawrence waited with the exploder. The first ten open cars were jammed with troops, and when the engine was directly over the mine, he jacked the plunger: nothing. Again: nothing. Two more times, and still no result. Crouch-ing behind a foot-high bush, Lawrence suddenly realized his "fig leaf" nakedness: a train full of troops was just fifty yards away. He could make a run for it, but movement would probably reveal his existence. He decided to play the rabbit and just sit motionless. As he sat there, he counted the cars slowly rolling by: eighteen open cars, three boxcars, and three officers' carriages. No one took notice until one of the officers pointed curiously in his direction. Several of his companions stood up and waved at Lawrence, who waved back rather furtively. The train looked as if it would break down at any moment as it labored under its heavy cargo. Finally, after struggling five hundred yards beyond the mine, it shuddered to a halt. At that instant, Lawrence leapt up, quickly covered over the demolition wires, and ran up the creek to safety. Soon a party of officers sniffed around the culvert, looking for the out-of-place Arab dressed in his fine Meccan garb. Then a whistle blew and the Turks disappeared.

By now the raiders were inconsolable. The Serahin complained that "bad luck is with us." Lawrence rejoined that perhaps they much preferred "to sit on camel-guard" rather than do any real fighting, as they had demonstrated that night at the bridge. This insult brought immediate outrage from the Serahin. The Beni Sakhr rose in unison to defend Lawrence, when Ali, hearing the uproar, came running to intervene. Ali insisted that as an ancestor of the Prophet, he had the "sight" and ordained that their luck was about to turn. Since no one was in the mood for a real fight, they accepted his vision, and calm eventually prevailed. Lawrence then began fidgeting with the ex-ploder. He managed to jimmy it open with his prized ornamental dagger and to remove the moisture and grit from the firing mecha-nism inside. Confident that it was now operational, Lawrence re-turned to the mine and another night of cold and hungry waiting.

In the dawn, they chipped some of the gelatine to start a small cooking fire and with their entrenching tools chopped to pieces one of the camels for breakfast. Just as they were separating the gore from the good, a scout yelled, "Train!" Everyone immediately dashed to their positions. The train was magnificent: two engines and a dozen passenger carriages, probably a corps headquarters. Lawrence quickly fell to his knees and connected the exploder to the explosive wires. In an instant he jammed hard the plunger: "The explosion was terrific. The ground spouted blackly into my face, and I was sent spinning, to sit up with shirt torn to my shoulder and the blood dripping from long, ragged scratches on my left arm. Between my knees lay the exploder, crushed under a twisted sheet of sooty iron. In front of me was the scalded and smoking upper half of a man. When I peered through the dust and steam of the explosion the whole boiler of the first engine seemed to be missing."[7] In addition to his lacerations, Lawrence suffered a broken toe, making it difficult and painful to move. As he tried to move, the stupor in his head gave way to a terrific headache. He began to stagger off to the Arab position, where heavy firing was now directed at the mass of stunned troops on the train. As he shambled off in his muddy robe, headdress askew, Lawrence muttered to himself again and again: "Oh, I wish this hadn't happened."

Meanwhile, the Turks had recovered from the blast and began to return a misdirected volley at the Arabs hidden among the rocks in the ravine. Lawrence was now caught in a crossfire and tripped over his broken toe, falling heavily to the ground. Ali thought he had been severely hit and rushed to his aid along with twenty or more of the Beni Sakhr. The Turks caught the rescuers in a beaten zone of deadly fire and nailed seven of them instantly. The rest half dragged and half carried Lawrence to safety, while the other raiders maintained a heavy and accurate covering fire. Under cover, Lawrence did a quick damage assessment and found that in addition to the broken toe and slashed arm, he had taken five bullet creases that had shot his fine Meccan garb to shreds.

The damage to the Turks, however, was infinitely greater. Both locomotives were shattered beyond repair, and at least three coaches were crushed into one another like a telescope. The rest of the train was badly derailed, the cars strewn around the track like jackstraws. The insignias on the coaches indicated the staff of the VIII Army

Corps, under the command of Jemal Pasha the Younger, which was coming up from Amman to reinforce the Turkish army in Palestine against Allenby. The initial rush against the train was made by Mifleh on his horse. He charged a group of officers who had spilled out of the saloon coach, but in his berserker frenzy he forgot to shoot them, so they were able to run away. The Beni Sakhr followed him through the breach, but the Serahin stopped to loot bags and pick up precious rifles along the way. Fahad, sheikh of the Beni Sakhr, had made his own dash immediately after the explosion and was swallowed up in a black cloud of debris. From Lawrence's position, it was now apparent that the loss of the machine guns would make it impossible for the party to capture the train. Had the Indians been present, most likely not a single man would have escaped. There were at least four hundred Turkish soldiers who increasingly were gaining their tactical coherence and responding with heavy fusillades of fire.

As Lawrence was assessing the situation, Mifleh and Adhub returned and asked about Fahad. The Serahin said he went down hard after his initial rush; they had his combat gear to prove it. Suddenly Adhub leapt from cover and ran down toward the wreckage, while the Turks merely watched in astonishment. In a short moment, Adhub reappeared from behind a damaged boxcar, dragging a limp object out of the gully, while the others rushed breathlessly down to his aid. It was Fahad. Unconscious, he had been shot through the face; the bullet shattered four teeth and grazed his tongue. After he'd been moved to safety on Mifleh's mare, he regained consciousness enough to be placed on one of the camels.

While the rescue was going on, the Turks, under the watchful eye of their corps commander, slowly began to flank the raiders' exposed position. By now there were forty effective men left under Lawrence's command. They began to withdraw, and because of his hobbling wounds, Lawrence ended up as part of the rear guard. Ali admonished him for his dawdling, but Lawrence feigned a slow and studied curiosity of the Turks in action to hide the severity of his wounds. At length the Turkish envelopment was too sluggish to trap the swifter Arabs. Finally reaching the crest of the hill, they all leapt on their camels and scattered. After riding hard five miles to the east, they stopped and rallied. Here the wounded were treated with a dose of piss—human and otherwise—to quell any infection until they reached proper medical care. Lawrence dispensed largesse in the form of money for the captured rifles, emoluments for heroism, camel meat and a death bounty to the relatives of those killed. The captured rifles were a real boon, for now all the Serahin were armed, some with two Mausers apiece.

That night, the raiders feasted well on a meal of prime-cut camel. In the morning they marched off to Azrak, "having a great welcome, and boasting—God forgive us—that we were victors." Their role in Allenby's third battle of Gaza thus ended, though their work was far from over.

ALLENBY'S TEN-DAY pursuit of the shattered Turkish army through the plain of Philistia ended on November 16. The British had advanced an average of fifty miles, the quickest and most sustained advance in the region since the war began. The success, though, came at a high price, as the Allies suffered more than six thousand casualties. The Turkish ledger tallied even greater losses, including more than ten thousand prisoners, eighty artillery pieces, and over a hundred machine guns. The greatest blow to the Turks was their loss of operational advantage in the new configuration of forces that emerged on Allenby's map. The two Turkish armies, the Eighth Army along the coast on their right and the Seventh Army among the Judean Hills on the left, were completely separated by road and rail and could potentially be defeated in detail. The Seventh Army south of Jerusalem was especially vulnerable, as now it had lost direct access to the railroad with the capture of Junction station on November 14. All supplies would have to be brought forward by an unreliable motor transport system over bad and nonexistent roads. Allenby was now at a natural decision point: should he drive immediately for Jerusalem or announce an operational pause to refit and reconstitute for the next phase of the campaign?

Under his original campaign design, Allenby wanted to halt operations after his forces had reached Jaffa, which they seized on November 16, virtually outflanking the Turkish position beyond Junction station. Still, several of his infantry units, like the London Regiment, were nearly at half strength. Moreover, Lloyd George had hinted that some of his troops might have to be withdrawn to the western front to meet increasing manpower needs there. Where prudence might dictate a pause in operations, political and broader strategic considerations suggested to Allenby that he press the fight. The moral effect of seizing Jerusalem by Christmas was another major consideration. The more he delayed, the more time the Turks would have to prepare their next defensive position. Here the Seventh Army was most vulnerable and closest to Jerusalem. He decided, therefore, to press hard the attack. After only a one-day hiatus, Allenby began planning for the next operation.

A serious constraint in his planning was his desire to prevent any collateral damage to Jerusalem. This meant that a direct assault on the third holiest city in Islam had to be avoided at all costs; the alternative was to hand an easy propaganda coup to the Turks. Allenby therefore decided to secure his left flank solidly with two divisions on Nahr el Auja, a river four miles northeast of Jaffa. With his remaining force he would drive eastward, hoping to surround Jerusalem and starve the Turks into surrender. The offensive would move along three main axes: pressure up from Hebron and Bethlehem, a push east through the Vale of Ajalon, and finally a deep strike behind Jerusalem at Nablus to cut the last supply line from the north.

BACK AT AZRAK, Lawrence prepared himself for the long winter. It was essential that Azrak be held at all costs. It would offer a base from which to spread the message of revolt among the northern tribes, and it would also be a lookout post to keep an eye on Nuri Shaalan. Nuri had yet to declare himself for the revolt and was nominally supporting the Turkish cause. Lawrence's presence would ensure that Nuri's support would remain passive. He had great economic holdings in Syria that the Turks had essentially held hostage. Until the Allies made a concerted move in that direction, Nuri would be on a short tether.

The old fort at Azrak was quickly made livable by the occupants. The Indians especially took special care in weatherproofing their quarters in the southeastern part of the castle. Supply was regularized with the establishment of a caravan to the Jebel Druze. There were also medical issues to attend to. Engineer Wood overcame his bout with pneumonia only to have it replaced with dysentery. Lawrence decided to send Wood back to Aqaba and have him return to his normal duties as base engineer there. Most important, Azrak became Feisal's political center in the north. Here the little post hosted dozens of visitors on a daily basis with great pomp and circumstance in the Bedouin tradition—the Ruwalla, Sherarat, Serahin, Serdiyeh, and Beni Sakhr, along with their great headmen: ibn Zuhair, ibn Kaebir, and Rafa el Khoreisha. Azrak was fast becoming Feisal's commercial entrepôt in the north as well. Entrepreneurs and sellers from all around, especially from Damascus, brought the finest goods to the camp: candy, sesame, spices, caramel, apricot jam, nuts, silk clothing, embroidered cloaks, fancy head cloths, sheepskins, felt rugs, Persian carpets, and, most important of all, intelligence from Syria and Mesopotamia. In exchange, the residents at Azrak offered coffee, sugar, rice, white cotton cloth, rifles, and, of greatest benefit to the merchants, news of the war. The conflict in the Middle East would always have a great influence on the commercial markets, so any war news offered a competitive advantage.

At the center of this seething activity was Lawrence and especially Sherif Ali ibn el Hussein el Harith. Ali was Feisal's "greatest asset" and de facto ambassador to the local tribes, and his influence extended even into Syria and Damascus. As Lawrence described him in his new role: "The lunatic competitor of the wilder tribesmen in their wildest feats was now turning all his force to greater ends. The mixed natures in him made of his face and body powerful pleadings, carnal, perhaps, except in so far as they were transfused by character. . . . He dressed spotlessly, all in black or all in white; and he studies gesture. . . . Fortune had added physical perfection and unusual grace, but these qualities were only the just expression of his powers. They made obvious the pluck which never yielded, which would have let him be cut to pieces, holding on. His pride broke out in his war-cry, 'I am of the Harith,' the two-thousand-year-old clan of free-booters; while the huge eyes, white with large black pupils slowly turning in them, emphasized the frozen dignity which was his ideal carriage, and to which he was always striving to still himself."[8] As with Zaal abu Tayi, this long protracted war was beginning to suck the life spirit out of him. He seldom wished to be alone, constantly seeking material distraction from the emotional struggle kept weakly at bay in his mind. The more visitors that arrived the better, if only for engagement's sake. Whatever it was that disturbed him, he was betrayed by his own lack of articulation. Lawrence could only guess at the dark shadows that chased after his mood.

Just as Allenby was about to launch his offensive against Jerusalem, Lawrence left Azrak on a reconnaissance around Deraa. Any forthcoming military operation to the east of the Jordan would have to consider Deraa as the primary decisive point. Upon his return, he learned some disturbing intelligence about the Algerian Abd el Kader. Apparently, after going AWOL with his seven servants, he left immediately for his village and entered the place as though he had conquered all of Syria, going so far as to threaten the Turkish governor with beheading. By now the Druzes and everyone else realized that the old man was suffering from some form of megalomania or other desert madness. He was unceremoniously thrown out of town, whereupon, completely unchastened, he made another victorious village entry, this time at Deraa station. With his reputation preceding him, the Turks received the Algerian as the mad prophet he was. But when his vision—that Lawrence and the other raiders would attack the Yarmuk bridges—was revealed as true, he was taken prisoner immediately and sent to Damascus for the usual interrogation. Here he was persuaded to act as a Turkish agent provocateur, using his network of associates to counter the influence of Arab nationalism that was beginning to smolder throughout Syria.

Meanwhile, the weather in Azrak turned dismal, slashing the occupants with snow, sleet, and freezing rain, forcing Lawrence into a deep, self-reflective funk. The thought of inactivity for the next several months until the campaign season opened was depressing. It meant he would have to spend his time among the tribes trying to convince them of the righteousness of the Arab cause and the tantalizing reach of victory. Lawrence did not like the role of political salesman or missionary. The elevation of Lawrence to the exalted position of adviser and intermediary to Feisal also wore on him. He had no interest in the trappings of majesty. He had come to do his duty out of personal motivation that had long predated the present crisis. In this general mood of unease, Lawrence decided to return to Aqaba.

Around November 22, he turned over command of the forces at Azrak to Sherif Ali ibn el Hussein el Harith and rode south with Rahail, one of his retainers. They stopped to visit Auda for a new relay of camels, but he had none to spare. After eating a few dates, they moved on, and all the while Lawrence fell deeper under a cloud of gloom and depression. His low spirit slowed his usually fast riding pace, which further frustrated him, as he wanted to reach Wood's caravan before it left Aqaba on its return to Azrak. They rode until midnight, when, exhausted, they stopped and immediately fell asleep in the mud.

Dawn's light found a breeze blowing, which helped to dry out the track, but still the camels broke through the crusted layers of mud, making swift progress impossible. At noon the ground hardened sufficiently to improve their tempo, and the route took them up to higher ground. All of a sudden, several rifle shots just below them shattered a brief conversation. They saw four men riding madly toward them, their yelling quickly catching the wind. Lawrence and Rahail remained calm, bringing their camels to a leisurely halt. A conversation ensued while Lawrence kept the leader covered with his Webley concealed under his cloak. It quickly became clear that the riders were a band of highwaymen. Primarily through Lawrence's humorous insults, the astonished robbers became increasingly unsure of themselves and of whom they had waylaid. While the dense strangers sat looking at one another in bewilderment, Lawrence and Rahail managed to scurry off toward Aqaba. A hundred yards farther on, the cutthroats regained their composure and began shooting at the pair, but the rough terrain provided so much dead ground that the two cantered off safely. Though extricating themselves from a potentially deadly encounter, they became lost as they tried to lose their pursuers, which delayed them even further. Finally, around midnight on November 25, the two stumbled into Aqaba. Lawrence immediately asked after Allenby's progress in Palestine, for he knew full well there was still another year of war to fight.

As a leader, Lawrence had now learned to extend the range and scope of his leadership. Relying increasingly on outstanding local Arab leaders like Auda, Zaa., and Ali for their tactical leadership, he was free to migrate to the role of operational leader by empowering his subordinates to act under their own direction. Where the tactician leads through his sheer physical presence, as an operational leader Lawrence demonstrated the force of ideas as the key source in providing purpose, direction, and motivation. In this instance, the *idea* of the Arab Revolt was worth a hundred Napoleons on the battlefield. Lawrence was like a sweeper in the sport of curling, enabling the other players on the team to succeed through their own efforts. Still, Lawrence was beginning to doubt that the burning idea of the Arab Revolt could be nurtured through the long winter.

CHAPTER SEVEN

The Grief of Leaders

People surmount tragedy when they use themselves up fully, when they use what they have and what they are, whatever they are and wherever they find themselves, even if this requires them to ignore cultural prescription or to behave in innovating ways undefined by their roles. The tragic sense does not derive from the feeling that people must always be less than history and culture demand; it derives, rather, from the sense that they have been less than they could have been, that they needlessly betrayed themselves. . . .

—ALVIN GOULDNER, *The Coming Crisis in Western Sociology*

The renewal of the advance against Jerusalem began all across the front on November 18. Movement into the Judean Hills was stymied by the extremely heavy winter rains that descended upon the forces. The hills consisted of high ridges sometimes soaring to two thousand feet. The hills created deep valleys, which meant that the high ground had to be cleared before assaults could be made through the dale lands. The sudden change in weather affected the troops, as well, as they confronted the cold, damp winds instead of the dry desert heat. The muddy roads and tracks slowed movement to a crawl and gave the defenders a significant advantage. In some cases, the advantage was short-lived as thick blankets of fog obscured the advance of British infantry in the low-lying areas among the hills. By the second day of the attack, it was clear that the mastermind behind the Turkish defense, General von Falkenhayn, was conducting a delaying withdrawal to give the defenses about Jerusalem time to dig in. The key to the British offensive was predicated upon a quick seizure of the Nablus-Ramallah-Jerusalem road. Here the assault stalled after almost a week of heavy fighting. Allenby quickly realized that his tired men were in need of rest and reinforcement and that the one-day pause provided on November 17 was hardly sufficient for the troops to recover after three steady weeks of tough fighting. Reluctantly, he ordered a halt to the offensive on November 24.

In the ensuing lull, the weather improved considerably, allowing British engineers to solidify their supply lines. While the British were refitting, the Turks discovered a five-mile gap between Allenby's forces arrayed in the hills and the troops fighting along the coast. They attempted to exploit this opening and did so with limited success. By December 3, Turkish spoiling attacks had ceased as fresh English reinforcements were brought to the front. On December 7, British forces had completed a major redeployment of troops, which saw XX Corps swap its position along the coast with XXI Corps in the Judean Hills. This was completed with utmost secrecy and thoroughly confused the demoralized Turks, who despite their dogged resistance continued to suffer from the weather and the intense fighting.

During the hiatus, Allenby reconsidered his plan and changed it significantly. Instead of fighting to cut the Nablus road so far north of Jerusalem and into such rugged terrain, he decided to shorten his swing by attacking closer in to Jerusalem, through the suburbs around Jericho, and then around to the east side of the holy city. The initial attack kicked off during the night of December 7, followed by the main assault at first light. Again, poor weather played a role in diminishing the force of the attack. Heavy rain turned into a shroudlike mist that slowed the advance, but by now the usually tenacious Turks seemed more willing to give up ground than in the past. Although unbeknownst to the British at the time, several fortified positions had been lost by the Turks. The cumulative moral effect upon them, however, was largely out of proportion to the posts' real value. Nevertheless, the anxiety began to push the Turks toward a defensive crisis point. That point arrived when the British made another attempt to seal the Nablus road later in the day. On the evening of December 8, the Turks began a massive, almost panic-driven pullout from Jerusalem. The last official to leave was the Ottoman governor-general, riding in a purloined cart seized from a local American. Order was quickly restored as the mayor of the city handed over the holy keys to Major-General Sir John Shea. Although a sharp fight occurred at the Mount of Olives, the entire city was surrounded as darkness fell on December 9.

JUST AS JERUSALEM was about to fall, Lawrence was urgently recalled from Aqaba to Allenby's headquarters. He arrived in time to be the guest of Brigadier-General Gilbert Clayton at the official entry into the city. Lawrence had to scramble to get in proper uniform, and when the time came Allenby made the entry on foot through the Jaffa Gate. Allenby was quite conciliatory to the occupying Turks, noting the importance of Jerusalem to the faiths of Christianity, Islam, and Judaism. For Lawrence, the fall of the great city of the Crusades was "the supreme moment of the war." As the luncheon ceremony commenced afterward, Lawrence was able to hear the French representative, François Georges-Picot, say rather demurely to Allenby, "And tomorrow, my dear general, I will take the necessary steps to set up civil government in this town."

There was shock among the British officers unaware of the high-level British-French diplomatic arrangements. Lawrence recorded with heavy irony that this was "the bravest word on record; a silence followed, as when they opened the seventh seal in heaven. Salad, chicken mayonnaise and *foie gras* sandwiches hung in our mouths unmunched, while we turned to Allenby and gaped." The general was also momentarily at a loss for words. His entourage feared that perhaps its great idol might betray some hitherto unrevealed weakness. But just then "his face grew red: he swallowed, his chin coming forward (in the way we loved)." Allenby turned to Picot and said through clenched teeth, "In the military zone the only authority is that of the Commander-in-Chief—myself."

"But Sir Grey," the flustered Picot began, "Sir Edward Grey—"

Immediately Allenby cut him off with a chop of the hand: "Sir Edward Grey referred to the civil government which will be established when *I* judge that the military situation permits." At that there were schoolboy nudges under the table and stifled grins; lingering winks into the chicken salad. Allenby had triumphed over the politicians: the food now tasted so much better.

After lunch, Lawrence sped by car with Allenby and Dawnay to the general's headquarters to discuss strategy for the next phase of the campaign. Dawnay talked about the British triumph in Palestine. They had accomplished in five weeks what planners had expected to take six months. They had broken the Turkish army and seized territory that the Ottoman Empire had held for centuries. They had captured the holy city of Jerusalem as a Christmas present for the British people and their Christian allies. But for the supply and weather difficulties, the Allies could easily have overrun the fleeing enemy. Allenby—the Bull—had played a crucial role in the victory. His vision, commitment, and competence had energized the forces out of its desert malaise. A War Cabinet telegram captured the importance of the success: "The capture of Jerusalem . . . is an event of historic and worldwide significance and has given the greatest pleasure to the British and other Allied peoples."

On the Turkish side, the blow reverberated throughout the empire, redounding upon the Germans as well. The loss of Jerusalem was now added in the audit of war to the defeats at Mecca and Baghdad. The loss of Jerusalem decisively forced the Turks to redeploy forces from other regions to defend the vulnerable line in Palestine. This secured the British gains already made in Mesopotamia and entailed their continued advance from Baghdad. Turkish defeats would also weaken the empire's hold on its indigenous masses, especially the Arabs. The material losses were staggering and difficult to replace. The Turks lost 28,443 men among the dead and wounded as well as nearly 12,000 captured, whereas the British lost substantially fewer with 18,928 troops. Operationally, the Turkish army was cut in two. One wing held positions in the hills near Jaffa and Ramleh overlooking a flat plain. The other wing had dug in four miles north of the holy city in the rugged hill country. The problem for the Turks was that they had no lateral (east-west) lines of communication between them. The nearest was almost thirty miles to the north at the rail line between Nablus and Tul Keram.

As the exchange turned to operations in the desert, Lawrence was keen to discover the new mission for the Arabs. It made obvious military sense for Allenby to link up with the Arabs at the Dead Sea. Lawrence and Feisal had already anticipated this move, with Feisal beginning an advance on Tafileh to the southwest of Azrak. Allenby still had some adjustments to his own line to make. These were minor operations that would enable a secure base from which to launch the next phase of the campaign. The general expected he needed two months of preparation until February in order to launch the next offensive. Meantime, as the railway moved up to Jerusalem, supplies could be staged near Jericho and shipped across the Dead Sea to the Arab forces. If Allenby could maintain a flow of fifty tons a day, Lawrence's forces could abandon Aqaba and thus shorten their own lines of supply. The area east of the Dead Sea was also a significant economic resource to the Turks, providing grain for food and timber to feed the wood-eating steam engines. The Arab regular army was now at three thousand men and could be readily enlarged with this kind of logistical commitment. In fact, Feisal was now elevated to the equivalent British rank of lieutenant-general commanding the "Arab Northern Army." It was agreed, then, that by the end of March the British and Arab lines would join just north of the Dead Sea by the river Jordan. With the plan already in motion, Lawrence decided to take a busman's holiday in Cairo to learn and test new methods and types of explosives.

UPON LAWRENCE'S RETURN, he found that P. C. Joyce had procured some armored cars. They decided, with the extra time on their hands, to conduct a reconnaissance with the new toy. They left with eight cars, traveling from Guweira to Mudowwara, where they shot up the nearby train station. They learned, most significantly, that they could raid from Guweira virtually the entire length of the Hejaz railway south of Maan. As Lawrence saw it, "All the Turks in Arabia could not fight a single armored car in open country. Thereby the situation in Medina, already bad, became hopeless." The German leadership recognized this as well and had tried to convince the Turks to shorten their lines and abandon everything south of Maan, but Falkenhayn was overruled by the necessity of the caliphate, for the sake of its religious authority and legitimacy, to maintain control of the line down to Mecca.

There was also an odd blind spot from the British viewpoint. They continued to press for the capture of Medina despite the cost in blood and treasure. Of course, Allenby understood this point perfectly and seemed to feel that as long as the Turks were willing to defend a position, the Arabs should earn their pay and improve their fighting qualities if nothing else than by attacking it.

AFTER THE BRIEF tactical exercise and foray with armored cars, Lawrence returned to Aqaba and set about reorganizing his bodyguard. He argued that since the capture of Aqaba and the mining of Jemal Pasha's train near Yarmuk, the bounty on his head had risen to ten thousand pounds alive or twenty thousand pounds dead. Obviously, it seemed, a beefed-up bodyguard was in order. Lawrence had already gathered quite a motley crew of bandits and cutthroats, though there was a core of honest riders. At this point, however, he "needed hard riders and hard livers; men proud of themselves, and without family." His requirements read almost like an ad for the Pony Express: "WANTED. Young, skinny wiry fellows. Not over 18. Must be expert riders. Willing to risk death daily. Orphans preferred."

One of his first new recruits was Abdullah the Robber, a nickname, he insisted, acquired from his father. He came unannounced one day into Lawrence's tent and, without a word, dropped a luxurious saddlebag of finely crafted workmanship at Lawrence's feet and then quickly withdrew. The next day the Robber returned, this time with a camel saddle of exquisite beauty, graced with ancient Yemeni characters. Again, no word save a wave of the hand; then he vanished. On the third day he arrived without a gift, dressed plainly, almost shabbily, in a cheap cotton shirt. He threw himself at the feet of Lawrence, who took a closer look at his supplicant. He was slight, almost frail looking; he had a beardless face shriveled like a prune, the wreckage of smallpox. His eyes were concealed in a persistent squint, half-hidden by long, braided tresses; his lips twisted into a wry half-smile, almost cast with derision. In the ensuing conversation, Abdullah's life story emerged. He grew up in Boreida. A certain incident in a married woman's home forced him to leave in haste and seek employment with ibn Saud, the great emir of Nejd. Here his heavy cursing yielded constant beatings and jail time. He fled yet again, this time to Kuwait, and was imprisoned for being "amorous." After his confinement, he enrolled in the army of Emir ibn Rashid, where he got into trouble again with a superior officer. The Robber intensely disliked the man to the point of beating him in public with his riding crop. He now turned, in desperation, to manual labor. The building of the Hejaz railroad offered him an opportunity for employment, which he seized immediately. And as it happened, he found trouble again: his foreman docked the unfortunate Abdullah for sleeping during the noon break. The Robber retaliated, in Lawrence's words, "by docking the contractor of his head." By now the Turkish authorities had set upon him and imprisoned him at Medina, where he quickly slipped away through a small window. Fortune found him in Mecca at a time when few questions were asked. He began a new life based on his riding abilities and curious character: he was given the mail route between Mecca and Jidda. Here he thrived and was able to send for his parents, who set up a simple sundries shop.

After a year of prosperity, the Robber was robbed of his camel and post on one of the mail runs. In retribution, the police claimed his family's shop, but phoenixlike, he rose again and somehow managed to outfit himself as a constable in King Hussein's camel police. Slowly he advanced through the ranks, but he was continually stymied by his knife play and dirty mouth: "a maw of depravity which had eaten filth in the stews of every capital in Arabia." The last straw occurred when he knifed a troublesome Ateibi in court in front of a shocked Sherif Sharraf. Sharraf had Abdullah beaten to the point of death, but somehow Abdullah managed to cling to life. After a long recovery and displaying no hard feelings, he entered into the sherif's entourage. With the start of the war, the Robber became the orderly of ibn Dakhil, chief of Feisal's bodyguard. After Dakhil was appointed to an ambassadorship, he offered Abdullah a letter of recommendation to serve with Lawrence, who accepted his services and promoted him to the joint command of his bodyguard, a duty he shared with el Zaagi. In all the subsequent time serving Lawrence, the Robber's only infraction was to be arrested for sitting in Allenby's office, fully armed, waiting for his master.

Lawrence put his new applicant to work immediately, having him examine the most recent recruits. There was, however, some resentment toward Lawrence and his household "pets": "The British at Aqaba called them cut-throats; but they cut throats only to my order. Perhaps in others' eyes it was a fault that they would recognize no authority but mine." By now Lawrence had ninety men rallying to his colors, the nominal strength of a British cavalry troop. Over half, fifty of them, were Ageyli, the same Nejdi villagers who thronged to Feisal's bodyguard. They were expert "cameleers" who could spot their own mounts at three hundred paces and possessed a gift of the "camel whisperer." Paid mercenaries, they fought best under the heavy and glittering motivation of gold. But pride also drove them, and one of the greatest feats of reconnaissance during the whole Arab Revolt was conducted by an Ageyli who twice swam through the deep sewer system at Medina to offer Feisal key intelligence of the besieged town.

Lawrence paid his retinue six pounds each a month, the going rate for a man with a camel. However, he provided them with his own mounts, so they were making a ransom of a profit and also receiving a bounty for new recruits. Lawrence bought the best possible camels he could find, chosen for swiftness, power, and endurance. He even established a kind of camel clinic where his beasts could recover at ease from the long campaign beatings they took. The men were likewise cared for under the stern gaze of el Zaagi, whose harsh discipline held every man accountable for the welfare of his mount and the condition of his equipment. Lawrence was clearly proud of his men and they of him: "They fought like devils, when I wanted, and sometimes when I did not, especially with Turks or with outsiders. For one guardsman to strike another was the last offence. They expected extravagant reward and extravagant punishment. They made boast throughout the army of their pains and gains. By this unreason in each degree they were kept apt for any effort, any risk."

ALLENBY SECURED JERUSALEM by the end of December, constructing roads and forward supply bases, securing his right flank, and extending the rail line forward. For the Arabs, the nature of the war began imperceptibly to turn more and more conventional. Feisal had a new military leader by the name of Maulud el Mukhlus, in command of his regular forces. He was a former Turkish officer who had been taken prisoner on the drive to Baghdad. After the new year, an operation was designed to support more directly the campaign in Palestine. A fertile area between the Hejaz railway and the Dead Sea was considered an important economic region for the Turks. Rich in maize and corn, the belt contained four market towns. From south to north there was Shobek, near the old Crusader castle of Montreale, which lay twenty miles to the northwest of Maan; next came Tafileh, which paralleled the bottom end of the Dead Sea; next stood Kerak, site of another famous Crusader castle, Krak des Chevaliers; and finally, near the top of the Dead Sea lay Madeba. A regular Arab force had assaulted Shobek back in October, tearing up a light rail system used by the Turks to feed the main line with grain produce. A struggle for the town continued until January 7, 1918, when the Turks pulled back to Maan. The capture of Shobek now opened the door into the plain of Jefer and the grain belt, uncovering Tafileh to exploitation and attack. Sherif Nasir was put in charge of the attack, with a party of Beni Sakhr directly under him. Nuri Said led a detachment of three hundred Arab regulars with a light mountain gun and a few machine guns. The initial attack was directed against the nearby station of Jurf ed Derawish.

The force struck at dawn and immediately achieved success. The Turks were quickly driven from the field and fled into the station, where they surrendered, two hundred strong. The Arabs lost only two men. The Beni Sakhr also captured twenty-five mules and seven boxcars of delicacies bound for the officers in Medina, including a carload of tobacco, whose seizure rendered Medina a "smokeless" garrison. The plunder made the Bedouin rich beyond belief. Some of the wealth was divvied up among the regulars as well, including the tobacco. Lawrence points out that later, when the inveterate smoker Feisal learned of the tobacco seizure, the prince's empathy overwhelmed him and he sent camels full of cheap cigarettes (Camels?) under a flag of truce to the nicotine-starved Turkish garrison.

Soon news of the success quickly spread, and Auda abu Tayi

suddenly became interested, sending his scouts to inquire further. Meanwhile, the Turks sent a small detachment down from Maan to investigate the commotion. Nasir became aware of the move and offered Auda the opportunity to ambush the investigators, but to no avail, as the shy detachment hightailed it back home. Perhaps the real factor for the Turkish hesitation was the weather. The Jefer plain is a high desert plateau, a miniature of the Great Basin in the western United States, standing an average of four thousand feet above sea level. Winds began to blow and created blizzardlike conditions for the next three days in the high desert. British logistics had not accounted for such conditions, leaving the Arab regulars without proper winter gear.

The seizure of the Jurf station triggered the next phase of the plan. The Arab highlanders in the region under Sherif Abd el Mayin now came into play, driving the Turks out of the hills between Petra and Shobek and cutting them to ribbons. The hill men then seized the supplies in the town, where they settled in comfort as winter storms blew through. The Motalga horsemen under Sherif Mastur, archenemy of Auda and the abu Tayi Howeitat, rode up from the warm desert plains below to join Nasir. Once the weather cleared, Nasir invested Tafileh, which he knew well from his Aqaba mission. Meanwhile, the regular contingent under Nuri Said had trekked back to Guweira in search of warmer clothes. Unfazed and full of bluff, Nasir demanded that the Turks surrender. There were only 180 among the Turkish garrison, but they were reinforced by the local village peasantry of the Muhaisin clan. While Auda deployed his band along the ridgeline, the villagers began to tease the attackers with a desultory, ineffective fire. The resistance of the peasants, typically held in the highest contempt among the desert tribesmen, was a biting affront to Auda's heroic honor. Seething in anger and very much alone, he led his horse down to the eastern edge of the village. He dropped the reins and stood in the saddle, shaking his fist at the stunned townsmen. In a thundering voice, he said, "Dogs! Do you not know Auda?" In an instant it was over: "When they realized it was that implacable son of war their hearts failed them, and an hour later Sherif Nasir in the town-house was sipping tea with his guest the Turkish Governor, trying to console him for the sudden change of fortune."[1]

Mastur rode into Tafileh at night with his Motalga horsemen, blood enemies of Auda and his Howeitat. The Motalga had blood in their eyes as they jealously noticed how the Howeitat had taken all the best lodging in the place. And Nasir was in no position to negotiate, because he had become increasingly aligned with Auda as Mastur had become an associate of the Jazi Howeitat, equally hated by the abu Tayi Howeitat. The situation was made even more complicated by the fact that the Muhaisin villagers were struggling against two other anomalous factions: a party of Senussi strangers from North Africa and the unhappy remnants of deported Armenians, about a thousand strong. The villagers were in an ethnic melting pot stirred up by the war and feared for their lives. Typically, food was short and the peasants hid their grain in small caches as a hedge against the uncertain future. They drove away their pack animals into the hills and fate's safekeeping. The village provided a microscopic view of the Ottoman despotic form of government: it was predicated on a culture of local intimidation, inertia, and servitude. Throughout the empire, the numerical odds were everywhere stacked against the Turkish masters, if only someone with will and initiative would rise above the ignorance-induced malaise. Even now the Muhaisin outnumbered Nasir's little army and could have cut it to pieces with an energetic leader—but none existed.

Although Nasir led the small army in this push north, the overall command of the drive devolved upon Feisal's half-brother, Emir Zeid. Zeid was advised by Jaafar Pasha, whose force was hung up around Petra because of the weather. The two rode into Tafileh to assert Feisal's authority and found a vipers' nest seething with hatred. Auda began a campaign of condescension toward the villagers, projecting an image of himself as their pseudoliberator. This shameless patronizing was galling to the Motalga, who were left with the dregs of the self-image of occupiers. Two Motalga boys were especially insulted, sons of Abtan, whom Auda's elder son had murdered. Auda declared that he would personally beat them in the village square in front of the entire population if they didn't back down. This was another of Auda's wild boasts, since he was outnumbered two to one by Mastur's horsemen. By now the tension had reached a Wild West level of suspense. Weapons were locked and loaded; the townsmen were scuttling for cover; firing positions were prepared. Just then Zeid and Jaafar, along with Lawrence, intervened. They thanked Auda graciously for his help in capturing the town and gave him a pile of gold, then sent him on his way. Zeid continued to dispense largesse about the town, totally defusing the situation. His final civil act was to appoint a governor loyal to Feisal.

MEANWHILE, THE TURKS had not been idle. The threat against one of their chief economic regions had not gone unnoticed by the Turkish high command. The threat was serious enough to divert resources from the Palestine front in order to retake Tafileh. The Turkish Forty-eighth Division under Hamid Fakhri Pasha organized a task force in Amman consisting of three infantry battalion totaling nine hundred men, one hundred cavalry, two mountain guns, and twenty-seven machine guns. They rounded up some civilian officials who would take over the administration of the town once it fell. The force left Kerak on January 23 and on the following day struck a picket line at Wadi Hasa, a deep arroyo ten miles northeast of Tafileh. The Turks quickly blew through this defensive position in speed-bump fashion and advanced on the town itself.

The news of the attack 'astonished" Lawrence, who expected the Turks to play their usual defeatist game. In perhaps the only time during the whole war, Lawrence was genuinely surprised. The initial reaction was to implement Jaafar's plan and defend on the high ground south of the town, which offered stout defensive positions at nearly forty-six hundred feet of elevation. Lawrence disagreed with the plan, however, arguing that the steep ridge to the east offered dead ground for the attacker to move in a flanking maneuver out of sight. Moreover, abandonment of the town would be a serious political defeat. In the end, it was *sauve qui peut*: a wild panic ensued as the villagers saw the Arabs leaving them to their fate in a cowardly escape. As the main body of Arabs streamed from the village, Lawrence stayed behind with his retainers to assess the true mood of the townsmen. He soon realized that there was a willingness among the peasantry to defend themselves against the Turkish onslaught; the few days of freedom had sparked a sudden resolve and determination among them to fight for their newly gained liberty. All they required was a determined leader, and Lawrence was ready to provide that leadership.

Lawrence sent the sons of Abtan—Metaab and Annad, the Jazi tribesmen who sought revenge against Auda in the lingering blood feud—to bring reinforcements. The Motalga stamped around the outskirts of the village, firing down at the Turks on the road from Kerak. Lawrence then crunched through the thick ice and found Zeid redeployed on the hill as planned about a mile south of town. The emir was perched upon a rock: he seemed blasé, apathetic, and almost in a state of shock. He kept peering through large binoculars that appeared incongruous against his small head and odder still given that it was in the pitch of night. While Zeid was losing his presence of mind, Lawrence had found his in a rage at dawn: "The Turks should never, by the rules of sane generalship, have ventured back to Tafileh at all. It was simple greed, a dog-in-the-manger attitude unworthy of a serious enemy, just the sort of hopeless thing a Turk would do. How could they expect a proper war when they gave us no chance to honor them? Our morale was continually being ruined by their follies, for neither could our men respect their courage, nor our officers respect their brains. Also, it was an icy morning, and I had been up all night and was Teutonic enough to decide that they should pay for my changed mind and plan."

The real source of Lawrence's anger was the fact that the Turks had forced him into a loathsome, conventional fight. There was now little scope for him to fight in the irregular, guerrilla manner he personally favored. He would have to match them mano a mano in a regular death match: "I would rake up my memory of the half-forgotten maxims of the orthodox army textbooks, and parody them in action. This was villainous, for with arithmetic and geography for allies we might have spared the suffering factor of humanity; and to make a conscious joke of victory was wanton. We could have won by refusing battle, foxed them by maneuvering our center as on twenty such occasions before and since: yet bad temper and conceit united for this time to make me not content to know my power, but determined to give public advertisement of it to the enemy and to everyone."[2] But here Lawrence is a bit disingenuous. It was more than "bad temper and conceit" that led him to fight; the very fact that he decided to *fight for Tafileh* ensured that he would have to fight conventionally, for he was being nailed to a defense of his own choice. The very nature of guerrilla warfare implies the kind of freedom of maneuver that a defensive posture denies. The real reason was that he had no other choice: the Turks had outfoxed the fox.

The fact that the Turks advanced so swiftly and silently indicated to Lawrence that they were a small force. He used this assessment to motivate Zeid from his detached funk. Lawrence advised Zeid that Abdullah should take a detachment of Lawrence's bodyguard to test the strength of the Turkish force. The Robber advanced with his party and two machine guns. The sight of Abdullah engaging the enemy was motivation enough to rally the Motalga horsemen and the townsmen who joined him in driving the Turkish cavalry back toward Kerak. The cavalry had covered the Turkish main body as it rolled out of its nighttime bivouac for a daylight attack on Tafileh itself. Now it found itself crashing in upon the roused infantry, who pitched in to salvage their horsed brethren from Abdullah's early onslaught. Meanwhile, Lawrence urged Zeid to reinforce the initial attack with more troops, but he demurred and ignored the impulsive suggestion. With his conventional influence thus waning, Lawrence went back into the village, where he found his bodyguard, as if at a rummage sale, leisurely picking through the scattered goods left behind by the routing villagers. He quickly spurred them to action below the village.

Tafileh overlooked a small plain to its east that was shaped like an upside-down triangle. There was a series of small ridges running down from the town in stair-step fashion into the plain falling along the southwestern face of the triangle. Lawrence designated the highest step as his rally point and reserve base. The Turks were deployed upon the high ground along an angle formed by the northern base and the southeastern face of the triangle. The forces were separated by about a mile of terrain opening across the plain. As Lawrence glanced about his new position, he saw twenty of Zeid's Ageyli bodyguard milling around in a nearby hollow. He ordered them to the reserve redoubt with a mission to hold at all costs. He gave the leader his signet ring as authority to rally any stragglers to the position and walked northeastward to reconnoiter the fighting.

Along the way, he ran into Abdullah on his way to Zeid. He provided Lawrence with a brief situation report and was sent on to the prince. Lawrence found the Turkish shelling around him ineffective because of long fuses, which caused the shells to hit the southeastern ridge and bounce harmlessly beyond into the trees. Eventually, the Turks managed to extend their line along the northern base of the upside-down triangle to the west and get Lawrence's positions under direct observation. He also saw the Turks moving south along their side of the triangle toward its apex. Movement here threatened to outflank Lawrence's entire position. The battle was now reaching its crisis point; near midday, the fight had gone on for almost four hours.

Lawrence then moved down to the lower "stair steps" and found the remnants of two groups cowering in defeat along the southwestern face. The first group were townsmen, who told Lawrence they were out of ammo and it was all over. He disagreed: "I assured them it was just beginning and pointed to my populous reserve ridge, saying that all arms were there in support. I told them to hurry back, refill their belts and hold on to it for good. Meanwhile we would cover their retreat by sticking here the few minutes yet possible." Lawrence next went on to the other remnant, who were Motalga led by Metaab of the blood feud: "He was beating his hands together and crying hoarsely with baffled vexation, for he had meant to do so well in this, his first fight. My presence at the last moment, when the Turks were breaking through, was bitter; and he got angrier when I said that I only wanted to study the landscape. He thought it flippancy, and screamed something about a Christian going into battle unarmed. I retorted with a quip from [Carl von] Clausewitz, about a rearguard effecting its purpose more by being than by doing: but he was past laughter, and perhaps with justice, for the little flinty bank behind which we sheltered was crackling with fire."[3]

Nearby there was a stone barrier four feet high and fifty feet in length. It offered durable protection, but now the Turks opened up with as many as twenty machine guns on the position. The bullets twanged and ricocheted in a cacophonous, jackhammering dirge, sending flint chips everywhere, more deadly to blind than to kill. Metaab promised Lawrence he would hold the position for ten more minutes but no longer. Remarkably, as a true testament of Lawrence's leadership, the second side of one blood feud could fight just as hard for him as the first.

Lawrence ran to the rear to take charge of the reserve, which had grown considerably, when a calm fell over the battlefield. After settling his men, Lawrence took an hour's nap behind a large rock. Around three in the afternoon he was awakened by Zeid, Mastur, Rasim Bey—an Arab regular—and Abdullah the Robber. They had brought men from the original position south of Tafileh and had also scrounged up more villagers. The Turks noticed the reinforcement and began to shell the position. Their poor gunnery had no effect on the reorganization of the defense, which saw Lawrence begin a swift transition from the defense to the attack. He took all the mounted men, now numbering eighty, and placed them under the command of Rasim. He ordered him to attack into the rear of the Turks arrayed along the southeastern ridge. Meanwhile, Lawrence's reserve had now become the main line of resistance. His troops here made a demonstration to cover Rasim's maneuver. At the same time, the Turks reinforced the fight with an apparently endless chain of machine guns, deploying them as if on a parade ground. Lawrence had the range and quickly dispersed them with shrapnel from a lone mountain gun.

Just then, in the waning sunlight of a desert winter, a hundred angry villagers from the small town of Aima to the north struck the rear of the Turks at the northern base of the upside-down triangle. Simultaneously, but purely by accident, Rasim and his riders crashed into the flank and rear of the enemy on the southeastern side. The physical and psychological shock was instantaneous. The entire Turkish line visibly recoiled; a brief and eerie silence ensued; and all the while Lawrence and the men on the ridge observed the whole looming disaster. He immediately ordered the reserve to assault across the valley into the heart of the stunned enemy. Mohammed el Ghasib, the comptroller of Zeid's household, led the charge under the red banner of the Ageyli; banner and robes became unfurled as Zeid's master of the household rode the wind upon the shattered Turkish line. For Lawrence, the climax of the battle had arrived: "The day had been too long for me, and I was now only shaking with desire to see the end: Zeid beside me clapped his hands with joy at the beautiful order of our plan unrolling in the frosty redness of the setting sun. On the one hand Rasim's cavalry were sweeping the broken left wing into the pit beyond the ridge: on the other the men of Aima were bloodily cutting down fugitives. The enemy center was pouring back in disorder through the gap, with our men after them on foot, on horse, on camel. The Armenians, crouching behind us all day anxiously, now drew their knives and howled to one another in Turkish as they leaped forward." Lawrence imagined it would be a slaughter from this point to the end. The berserker rage was beginning to consume the attackers, and as a leader he should have imposed his moral will and authority, but he was too exhausted to lead his men back from the brink of atrocity. Between twenty and thirty of his original force of six hundred had been killed. There were old scores to settle, but the frightening weather imposed its own morality and cut the pursuit mercifully short: the wicked northeast wind threw razors of jagged ice into the faces of the pursuers, blinding them. The final audit of battle accounted for the true cost of the fight for the Turks: two Skoda mountain howitzers, twenty-seven machine guns, two hundred horses and mules, and nearly three hundred POWs. The Turks lost perhaps half the original force of almost twelve hundred troops. A heroic leader would have reveled in the victory, but Lawrence felt only a sense of futility: "A battle might be thrilling at the moment for generals, but usually their imagination played too vividly beforehand, and made the reality seem sham; so quiet and unimportant that they ranged about looking for its fancied core. This evening there was no glory left, but the terror of the broken flesh, which had been our own men, carried past us to their homes." And now a simple moral calculus emerged from the slaughter at Tafileh: "The Turkish wounded lay out, and were dead next day. It was indefensible, as was the whole theory of war: but no special reproach lay on us. We risked our lives in the blizzard (the chill of victory bowing us down) to save our own fellows; and if our rule was not to lose Arabs to kill even many Turks, still less might we lose them to save Turks."[4]

The severe weather continued its relentless assault on the victors. The men should have exploited their success and swept all the way to Kerak and even beyond to Amman, but cold and exhaustion had already settled in like the blanketing snow. Operationally, Lawrence saw the victory as a meaningless outcome. He sent over a report to Allenby's headquarters primarily for the interest of the planning staff.

Lawrence was later awarded the Distinguished Service Order by Allenby for his leadership at the battle of Tafileh, but despite the medal, he despised the tactical orientation of the heroic leaders and their fascination with battle. Yet he demonstrated again that his tactical acumen as a guerrilla leader extended to a conventional fight. Ironically, he had chastised Auda in the hills before Aqaba for his seeming unwillingness to engage the enemy in a conventional fight. It appeared to Lawrence that fighting, whether conventional or unconventional, was solely a necessary evil: that Sun Tzu was correct in his wisdom that the acme of a leader was to win without fighting. Such skill requires tremendous forethought and foresight that did not readily emerge from purely tactical considerations.

THE MATTER OF closing off Turkish shipping on the Dead Sea still remained. Lawrence contacted Arabs down along the warm shores of the sea for assistance. Here he found a willing ally among the Beersheba Bedouin. On January 28, 1918, a detachment of seventy of them under Abdullah el Feir attacked the small eastern shore port of El Mezraa. They thoroughly trashed the place, taking sixty prisoners and ten tons of corn and sinking six dhows and a motorboat. This effectively ended the active campaigning for the time being. They had achieved Allenby's objective in shutting down the Dead Sea commerce two weeks ahead of the general's timetable. They had also made inroads along the east coast of the sea, disrupting the Turkish grain supply, but to Lawrence's great regret they had not completely linked up with the British forces in Palestine north of the sea, near Jericho. But for the weather, they would have succeeded. For now, Lawrence would have to consolidate his gains around Tafileh and bring the villagers under the silken hand of Feisal.

Elsewhere, the dead hand of cold and darkness continued to press down upon the Arab garrison at Tafileh. The camels were worthless in the ice-encrusted snow and to their own embarrassment slid around like hulking wardrobes. Their natural fodder was under a hard heel of ice, impervious to the mouthings of their sensitive lips. As barley ran low in the town, even this ersatz feed was denied the beasts.

Lawrence was therefore forced to range the camels to grazing land five thousand feet below their present location by a long, circuitous route of dangerous switchbacks. Life in the town was no better for the men. The place was crawling with vermin chased by the howling winds. The sky was always a deathly slate gray, tinged with a mournful umber. Lawrence whiled away his time reading Malory's *Le Morte Darthur* and nursing another flesh wound to his hip, a memento of the recent battle.

Soon boredom, the true ghost of winter, stole in among the bodyguard, laying hold of the men in its usual disharmonious fashion. Awad, one of the Sherari, struck at Mahmas, a camel driver, and though not formally of the bodyguard, Mahmas fell under its law. The discordant clash of knives brought the two men under the severest punishment of the bodyguard. El Zaagi meted out the sternest retribution as Lawrence listened nearby. Through a tearful refusal, Mahmas resisted his manful punishment and slunk away from the fellowship highly disgraced. Awad had been a good fighter, and the incident upset Lawrence's sense of justice and "what's right."

Lawrence realized that the continued boredom would rot the moral cohesion of his "fellowship of the dagger." He decided, therefore, to disband the men temporarily and scatter them to their own devices until better weather prevailed. On February 4, Lawrence left Tafileh and headed south for Aqaba to get more gold for the spring campaign season. With a greatly reduced bodyguard, Lawrence slogged through the gooey ground aboard footloose camels that continually slid along the slushy trails toward his goal. The next day, they reached Maulud's camp at Aba el Lissan, feeling "filthy and miserable; stringy like shaven cats." The regulars in the camp had lost half their combat strength because of the hideous weather. Lawrence recalled: "These men of Maulud's had been camped in this place, four thousand feet above the sea, for two months without relief. They had to live in shallow dug-outs on the hillside. They had no fuel except the sparse, wet wormwood, over which they were just able to bake their necessary bread every other day. They had no clothes but khaki drill uniform of the British summer sort. They slept in their rain-sodden verminous pits on empty or half-empty flour-sacks, six or eight of them together in a knotted bunch, that enough of the worn blankets might be pooled for warmth." Though half the men had perished, the other half remained active and exchanged rifle fire with the Turkish outposts on a daily basis. Lawrence and the whole Arab effort on this front "owed much to them, and more to Maulud, whose fortitude stiffened them in their duty." Reflecting on Maulud's model of Arab leadership, Lawrence wrote: "The scarred old warrior's history in the Turkish army was a catalog of affairs provoked by his sturdy sense of Arab honor and nationality, a creed for which three or four times he had sacrificed his prospects. It must have been a strong creed which enabled him to endure cheerfully three winter months in front of Maan and to share out enough spirit among five hundred ordinary men to keep them stout-heartedly about him."[5]

As they pressed on toward Aqaba, a new, familiar scent was now in the air: the humid, salted breath of the Red Sea tugged warmly at their caked nostrils. The next day they reached Guweira; here Lawrence discovered Joyce and Alan Dawnay. They had been operating with Feisal to attack Mudowwara, but in the end the offensive failed for the usual reasons: failure to properly coordinate and synchronize operations between regular and irregular troops. Lawrence spent three nights with the officers discussing the new staff arrangements made to better integrate the Arab activities with Allenby's operations in Palestine. An intermediary headquarters group—the Hejaz Operations Staff—had just been established under Dawnay with the code name "Hedgehog."

MEANWHILE, FEISAL HAD sent gold in the sum of thirty thousand British pounds, saving Lawrence the full trip to Aqaba. He meant to get the gold back up to Tafileh as soon as possible. As security, Lawrence recruited the ever-useful Sheikh Motlog along with fourteen other retainers. The gold was stashed in one-thousand-pound bags, each bag weighing twenty-two pounds. Every man carried two bags, making the dense weight difficult for the camels slopping through the bottomless mud back to Tafileh. Motlog arrived ceremoniously riding atop the baggage of a Ford Model T. Because of the severe road conditions, the skid caused him to bounce off on his head. The driver, Private Marshall, jumped out of the car and apologized profusely, whereupon old Motlog, gaining his senses, said bemusedly, "Don't be angry with me. I have not learned to ride these things." After which he traded in the Ford for a used camel.

Lawrence left on February 8. Because of the ever-increasing elevation, the trudge back up to Tafileh was twice as hard as the trek down. Although ice-skating dangers were less likely, camel traction along the switchbacks became more difficult. They rode directly into the wind, now blowing hard like the Chicago "hawk," dipping and diving from ridge to ridge and digging its icy claws into flesh, always hoping to strike at an uncloaked eye. Lawrence pushed the party at a relentless, slush-bound pace: six miles in seven hours—unimaginable on the desert plain. He left Motlog by the wayside to rest his detachment, while he pressed on with the two Ateiba horsemen. Long out of their desert element, the horsemen soon collapsed, leaving Lawrence to plunge ahead on his own with his trusted camel, Wodheiha, camping several times along the way at various tribal garrisons and raising curious eyebrows at his cargo of 120 pounds of fifty-five hundred British gold pounds.

Toward the end of the journey, Lawrence encountered several frozen snowdrifts that Wodheiha bolted through like a snowplow. He finally reached Tafileh on the bright morning of February 11, tears streaming down his face from a case of encroaching snow blindness. There he found Emir Zeid and informed him of the boon of gold. Grateful, Zeid introduced him to a new English guest just recently arrived. Lieutenant Alec Kirkbride, sent by the inscrutable Wyndham Deedes to assist in the intelligence efforts among the Arabs, came to make use of his Arab-speaking skills. After a brief respite, Lawrence took him in tow and went on a recon mission to scout a passage toward the Jordan and Allenby's right flank. It appeared to Lawrence that as the weather improved, it would be possible to conduct a fighting linkup with the Palestine front in a month at most. He returned to Zeid to convey his plans. By now, Motlog had appeared with the rest of the gold. As Zeid listened to Lawrence, the prince slowly shook his head and shrugged. "But that will need a lot of money," he said.

And Lawrence replied, "Not at all," reminding the emir that he had just brought him thirty thousand pounds of British gold.

Zeid raised his hands upward in an outstretched, empty gesture.

"What gold?" After a pause, he mumbled sheepishly that he had spent it—all of it.

Lawrence's eyes grew wide, astonished. "You *must* be joking!"

"By Allah, it is true," said Feisal's half-brother. "I have given thousands to el Dhiab, the sheikh of Tafileh, thousands to the villagers; thousands to the Jazi Howeitat; thousands to the Beni Sakhr."

The more Lawrence listened, the more "aghast" he became. His entire plan had just been shot to pieces. Moreover, his promise to support Allenby had now been completely compromised. He ran to find Nasir, whom he found on his sickbed. Nasir explained the inner workings of tribal politics by offering that the young, inexperienced Zeid had been duped by his rapacious advisers, who certainly received some sort of kickback from the many beneficiaries of the emir's goodwill. As Lawrence pondered the situation throughout the night, he found no resolution short of getting the money back from all the recipients. He approached Zeid with the solution, but Zeid merely gave Lawrence a statement of the expenditures.

That was the last straw. Lawrence immediately decided to go to Allenby and ask to be relieved of his duties. He left that very afternoon with four bodyguards, riding hard for Beersheba, eighty miles distant. He reached the place by noon the next day, February 20. Here he learned that the British had just taken Jericho. On his way to Allenby's headquarters, he passed the train station and was amazed to find his old mentor, David Hogarth, just stepping off a train. He grabbed Hogarth and told him everything: "I had made a mess of things: and had come to beg Allenby to find me some smaller part elsewhere. I had put myself into the Arab business, and had come to wreck because of my sick judgment. . . . I now had no tricks left worth a meal in the Arab market-place, and wanted the security of custom: to be conveyed; to pillow myself on duty and obedience: irresponsibly."

Lawrence was at the moment of personal crisis. His belief in himself was being shattered by the failed trust he had placed in others: he expected them to act by the same standards meted out to himself. Once Lawrence started with Hogarth, the stream of disaffection became a seething torrent of leaders' anguish and grief: "I complained that since landing in Arabia I had had options and requests, never an order: I was tired to death of free-will, and of many things beside free-will. For a year and a half I had been in motion, riding a thousand miles each month upon camels: with added nervous hours in crazy airplanes, or rushing across country in powerful cars. In my last five actions I had been hit, and my body so dreaded further pain that now I had to force myself under fire. Generally I had been hungry: lately always cold: and frost and dirt had poisoned my hurts into a festering mass of sores."

Yet the physical pain was only secondary to the betrayal of his own self-respect that had been fraudulently engineered from the very beginning: "that pretense to lead the national uprising of another race, the daily posturing in alien dress, preaching in alien speech: with behind it a sense that the 'promises' on which the Arabs worked were worth what their armed strength would be when the moment of fulfillment came. We had deluded ourselves that perhaps peace might find the Arabs able, unhelped and untaught, to defend themselves with paper tools. Meanwhile we glozed our fraud by conducting their necessary war purely and cheaply. But now this gloss had gone from me. Chargeable against my conceit were the causeless, ineffectual deaths at [Tafileh]. My will had gone and I feared to be alone, lest the winds of circumstances, or power, or lust, blow my empty soul away."[6] There was more to mention: certainly the deaths of his two brothers, but the deadness in his soul could but conjure a silent cry that only the dead could hear.

Hogarth remained quiet, stunned and deeply moved. He took Lawrence by the arm and led him, carefully, to breakfast with Clayton. Slowly, unbeknownst to the protagonists, Lawrence was coming under the spell of an unknown illness that would take generations to recognize and many battles to acknowledge: post-traumatic stress disorder. Lawrence would struggle the rest of his life, single-handedly and alone, against this silent demon.

LAWRENCE'S GRIEF OPENS a further window onto an understanding of tactical leadership. He seems to assert that leadership is a fundamental human *need*: that every human being possesses both a desire to lead and a desire to follow, but these desires are never in balance. In fact, on balance most humans desire to follow. The Confucian project, for instance, was an effort to establish in the East a doctrine of *followership* as a way to order a just society. The West took a different path. Here the idea of heroic leadership came to reside at the center of Western culture, and the myth of the warrior king became its exemplar. In literature, the epic of Homer's *Iliad* and its two heroes, Achilles and Hector, express the heroic paradigm better than any other work, with this style of leadership dominating Western culture to this day. Essentially, the heroic leader is a man of quality whose worth and worthiness are reflected in his personal honor and reputation: a man of low honor has little worthiness, small esteem, no reputation. The hero is a physically strong man, for a weak man is an unworthy man. The heroic leader manifests all the exterior qualities that enable the force of his physical presence, and this presence represents his personal core identity, which he projects vigorously among his followers and protects with utmost savagery. He has little time for self-reflection, since reflex and passion dominate his action. Indeed, long reflection is counterproductive when immediate action dominates the idea of tactics. The projection of his identity as a kind of physical magnetism becomes registered among his followers as the leader's *charisma*. This, of course, has significant implications on a battlefield, and the premium leaders must pay is denominated in courage, valor, bravery, and, after the rise of Christianity, lip-service virtues like chivalry, fairness, and moderation. Self-identity through reputation thus serves a core human need. As followers, our identification with the leader serves the same psychological need and so completes an essential symmetry.

But there is an alternative to the heroic leader, which could be described as the *autonomous* leader who seeks to transcend the level of psychological need and gain personal autonomy from human desire. The idea is exemplified in the leadership of T. E. Lawrence. Again, literature offers a model in Homer's *Odyssey*. Here Odysseus breaks fundamentally with the heroic tradition. The human qualities that Odysseus strives to foster are interior and intellectual. This is not to say that he eschews physical prowess. Instead, his actions are shaped by due consideration and self-reflection, trying to hold reflexive action at bay through careful design and planning. Only then is action appropriate. It should come as no surprise, then, that

Lawrence would personally identify with Odysseus and spend over two years translating *The Odyssey* while on active duty with the RAF in India.

The autonomous leader asks the central question that the heroic leader chooses to ignore: *If I am to lead others, how do I first lead myself?* There is only one answer: He must overcome the leadership of his desires and passions and become independent—autonomous—of them. But practically, how does he accomplish this? For the heroic leader, there is no issue. He has been anointed to lead by right of succession or through some other social legitimation. The autonomous leader can overcome his desires only through learning and self-knowledge, hence the Socratic imperative "Know thyself." But this is a struggle of a lifetime, and it is precisely in this struggle that character and competence are built. As Lawrence said to Liddell Hart in 1932: "I was not an instinctive soldier, automatic with intuition and happy ideas. . . . When I took a decision, or adopted an alternative, it was after studying (doing my best to study) every relevant—and many an irrelevant—factor. Geography, tribal structure, religion, social customs, language, appetites, standards—all were at my fingertips. The enemy I knew almost like my own side. I *risked* myself among them a hundred times, *to learn*." The autonomous leader becomes an expert learner. The struggle to learn creates the dynamic tension between character and competence. And here character develops beyond the trivial sense of virtue as a checklist from a Boy Scout manual to mean *strength* of character and its natural corollary, strength of mind. Character is about respect and not reputation: it is society's signal and lasting embrace to the members of its community. Character revolves around living in accordance with certain key ethical and moral values, but in the enduring paradox and tragedy of our existence, war subverts this centrality and places martial competence at its heart. Thus the military leader gains respect in direct proportion to his prowess.

How did this paradox come to pass? In a peaceful and just society, ethics and morality create and preserve the very existence of peace. War is the ultimate breakdown of morality, and personal survival comes to the fore. At the social level, we turn to leaders who will guarantee our national survival. We are willing to accept the philandering leader as long as he gives us the best chance to exist. In war, this social compromise has already been made: men follow the most competent leader because he is the best guarantor of their lives; the competent sinner will always supplant the incompetent saint in tactical leadership. Yet in a further evolution or twist of the paradox, within the society of soldiers war often brings out the best character qualities among the combatants: self-sacrifice, self-discipline, generosity, initiative, hopefulness, spirit, camaraderie, responsibility, patience, determination. All these qualities were manifest throughout Lawrence's life, before and after the desert. The crucible of combat simply refined the metal and mettle of his humanity.

The autonomous leader, like Lawrence, seeks respect rather than reputation, for only the autonomous leader, who finds ultimate solace within himself, can find *self-respect* as meaningful, while "self-reputation" makes no sense. Reputation is always exterior to the self, dependent on the estimate and esteem of others. The autonomous leader also views charisma much differently. Where the heroic leader derives immense satisfaction from the adulation of his followers, who sense the gravity of his presence, the autonomous leader is more concerned with making others feel good about themselves. This sense of enabling helps to foster a spirit of empowerment. The subordinates feel self-actualized in their engagement with the world. Their identity shifts from the leader to the self and creates a sense of self-confidence, a willingness to assume responsibility, and a spirit of initiative. As an expert learner, the autonomous leader naturally becomes an expert teacher, further reinforcing conditions of empowerment. Within the context of conflict learning, mutual learning becomes crucial since the military milieu is so ambiguous, volatile, and dynamic.

Perhaps the best précis on Lawrence as an autonomous leader was penned by the commander who knew him best: Edmund "the Bull" Allenby. After Lawrence was killed, Allenby wrote: "He depended little on others; he had his private reasons for all he did, and those reasons satisfied him. Loyal pursuance of his own ideals, and the habit of independent thought, brought about a sound self-education; practice in analysis of character resulted in a full understanding of other men. His exceptional intellectual gifts were developed by mental discipline; and the trained mind was quick to decide and to inspire instant action in any emergency. Hence his brilliance as a leader in war."

In perhaps the final testament to Lawrence's leadership, almost sixty of his bodyguard died in his service—over half the original complement. They had formed a fellowship out of the sinews of leadership. As pariahs outcast by thirty or more desert tribes, they had developed into a firm union bound fast by a courage of despair, whose only hope was mutual trust. Only the intensity of mind-numbing activity seemed to transcend the loss of a personal identity, which they seemed always to rediscover in the freedom of the group. Over time, Lawrence's iron will and determination in creating his own tempered striking force challenged him to higher standards of leadership: "to live up to my bodyguard," he said, "to become as hard, as sudden, as heedless." Lawrence's ascetic self-abnegation had created a refined and efficient desert fighting machine and added yet another jewel to a never-ending chain of irony: the image of the ascetic Templar knight leading a band of renegade Muslim raiders in a holy war.

Thus, leader and led, in a dance of mutual self-respect, changed each other, slowly, irony by irony, the transformation bending to the will of Lawrence: "Into the sources of my energy of will I dared not probe. . . . The practice of our revolt fortified the nihilistic attitude in me. During it, we often saw men push themselves or be driven to a cruel extreme of endurance: yet never was there an intimation of physical break. Collapse rose always from a moral weakness eating into the body, which of itself, without traitors from within, had no power over the will. While we rode we were dis[em]bodied, unconscious of flesh or feeling; and when at an interval this excitement faded and we did see our bodies, it was with some hostility, and with a contemptuous sense that they reached their highest purpose, not as vehicles of the spirit, but when, dissolved, their elements served to manure the field."[7]

The autonomous leader, though, often pays a heavy psychological and emotional price. His predilection for self-reflection creates a self-awareness that, over time, can create the personal grief experienced by leaders like Lawrence, who refuse blithely to rationalize the moral ambiguities of their actions and the actions of their men and the doublespeak and even betrayal of their superiors.

CHAPTER EIGHT

Thief of Souls

Even to the creator himself, the earliest effect may seem to be a commerce with disorder. For the creative, which is an extension of life, is not an elaboration of the established, but a movement beyond the established, or at least a reorganization of it and often of elements not included in it. . . . This is the reason why, in order to invent, one must yield to the indeterminate within him, or, more precisely, to certain ill-defined impulses which seem to be of the very texture of ungoverned fullness which John Livingston Lowes calls, "the surging chaos of the unexpressed."

—BREWSTER GHISELIN, *The Creative Process*

Allenby's planning conferences had already begun by the time Lawrence arrived from Tafileh. Allenby had tried to get word to him in the Tafileh highlands, but the aircraft sent to bring word had dropped messages in the wrong place. He entered into the meetings just as deliberations had turned to strategic issues. In general, London was greatly satisfied with the outcome of the recent Palestine campaign and the capture of Jerusalem. The operations in Palestine were quickly becoming the only winning game in town, and Lloyd George was ready to ante up again at the gaming table of war. The slaughter at the third battle of Ypres that ended in November continued to drive strategic assessments to look for a military solution outside the western front and toward Germany's main allies. Practically, it meant that Allenby would be expected to pull more rabbits out of his military hat. True to the spirit of the Christmas season, visions of strategic sugarplums danced in the heads of the War Cabinet after the fall of Jerusalem. They saw Damascus and even far-off Aleppo as reasonable plums ripe for Allenby's taking. A quick seizure of Aleppo would finally knock Turkey out of the war and open a strategic route to allies like Russia and Romania.

By early 1918, the grand strategic situation of the war had changed dramatically. The Germans had signed a new armistice with the Russians, freeing up vast numbers of troops in the east that could be sent to the western front and even to the Middle East if need be. The Germans were planning a massive offensive in the spring before the American intervention could change the strategic calculus. The growing resurgence of Germany in the western theater gave "Westerners" like Robertson more ammunition to argue for a minimalist approach in the secondary theaters like Palestine. Lloyd George and the other "Easterners" argued that the protracted war in France had demonstrated decisively Clausewitz's principal dictum that defense is always the stronger form of war. As long as the Allies stood on the defense, they could withstand any onslaught the Hun might throw against them, at least until the American saviors arrived. Furthermore, the imminent collapse of Bulgaria would open up a new front against Austria in the region and directly threaten Germany's key ally.

As the debate continued into the new year, Lloyd George decided to turn the matter over to the Allied Supreme War Council at Versailles for resolution and advice regarding the military situation in the Middle East. The planning body was responsible for the coordination and integration of all Allied grand strategy and issued the findings of its study on January 21, 1918. Its conclusions were highly supportive to the position of the "Easterners." It recognized that Turkey was "the weakest point in the hostile coalition and should be the object of the attack." This meant, therefore, that the Allies should stand on the defensive in France, Italy, and the Balkans and exploit the weakness Turkey presented in Palestine. Robertson responded immediately, decrying his irrelevance as chief adviser to War Cabinet, which seemed bent on ignoring his military advice.

Lloyd George had come to feel that an impartial assessment was required now that the two sides of the argument had held their positions virtually unchanged since the beginning of the long debate. He sent General Jan Smuts, onetime nemesis of Allenby during the Boer War days, to Egypt in the first part of February. Smuts responded quickly on February 15 with a telegram to London stating that simultaneous offensives in Palestine and Mesopotamia would be infeasible without major reinforcement. In a more comprehensive report delivered on March 1, Smuts argued that the decisive front was in Palestine because of its strategic proximity and natural line of approach to Aleppo. He further recommended that because of its distance from Aleppo and primitive logistics infrastructure, the Mesopotamian Expeditionary Force should stand mainly on the defensive. Under these circumstances, the MEF could therefore relinquish two of its six infantry divisions as well as a cavalry brigade and send these units to reinforce Allenby along with an Indian cavalry division from France. These reinforcements would increase Allenby's offensive capability by at least 25 percent, while the Turkish balance would continue to deteriorate or remain the same.

Smuts was already privy to Allenby's plans, which began to consider the operational position more comprehensively for the first time by including the forces and operations east of the Dead Sea. This meant a fundamental reassessment of the Arab capabilities and Turkish intentions along the Hejaz from Deraa to Medina. The first phase of this plan meant tying in the British flank in Palestine with the Arab forces across the Dead Sea. In considering this move, Allenby naturally sought out the advice of Lawrence.

LAWRENCE WAS STILL recovering from the crisis of Zeid's profligacy in Tafileh when he met with Allenby. He could not refuse the general's request to continue what was, in effect, a charade, as much as he may have wanted to: "There was no escape for me. I must take up again my mantle of fraud in the East. With my certain contempt for half-measures I took it up quickly and wrapped myself in it completely. It might be fraud or it might be farce: no one should say that I could not play it. So I did not even mention the [moral and psychological] reasons which had brought me across [from Tafileh]; but pointed out that this was the Jordan scheme seen from the British angle. Allenby assented, and asked if we could still do it. I said: not at present, unless new factors were first discounted."[1]

The first factor was the Turkish garrison in Maan. In order for the Arab forces to range westward and link up with the British eastern flank, this position would first have to be isolated and then taken. Here the problem facing the Arabs was logistical. They needed more mobility if they were to advance to the northern side of Maan and cut the rail there. This meant reinforcements on the order of seven hundred baggage camels as well as more infantry guns and machine guns. Furthermore, the Arab rear and right flank would have to be covered from attacks coming south out of Amman. Allenby immediately approved the requests, ordering to Aqaba two elements of the Egyptian Camel Corps, a formation of Egyptians under Frederick G. Peake that had proved so effective throughout the war. With the new transport capability, the four thousand Arab regulars could now range eighty miles in advance of their base, well within the operational requirements for a successful assault on Maan. As for the Arab flank, Allenby expected to send an Indian brigade to Es Salt, which would pin Turkish forces in Amman.

On the next day, February 28, a corps commanders' conference was held to discuss the phasing of the campaign. The first phase would establish a secure British right flank with the aid of the Arab regulars. Lawrence would support the movements of this operation in a secondary role after the British and Arab regulars had made contact with each other and captured Maan. Afterward, with the help of the Egyptian Camel Corps, the Arab regulars would move their base of operations north, closer to Jericho. These general movements east of the Dead Sea would further encourage and expand the general scope of the Arab Revolt. Once the British eastern flank was secured, a general advance could begin along the Mediterranean coast. A first thrust would include the seizure of the plain of Esdraelon and the Jezreel Valley and then securing a line from Haifa to Tiberias. The next phase would carry the advance along the coast to Tyre and Sidon, with the final objective being the occupation of Beirut. The British right flank would keep pace with the left by moving through the Judean Hills and by advancing into the Yarmuk Valley. The advance in this sector would begin with a strike east out of Jerusalem on the road through Jericho and down to the Jordan River.

Allenby was making the best out of a difficult operational situation. The official history castigates him for a plan that was "stiff and mechanical, and it made transport master instead of servant." Liddell Hart continues the same facile criticism. The logistical reality was much less facile. The extension of the standard gauge of the Sinai railway could not be hastened at the flick of a marshal's baton. Serious engineering work had to be done at a deliberate pace. While Allenby was making his final preparations for the offensive, Lloyd George presented his plans to the Allied Supreme War Council back in Versailles. Once again, Robertson refused to support the plan, this time in front of the French, raising the ire of the prime minister to a new level. It was becoming apparent that Robertson as chief of the Imperial General Staff would soon find himself in a sack.

FOLLOWING THE MEETING with Allenby, Lawrence went down to Cairo for a few days of R&R. He then flew to Aqaba to reestablish his authority with Zeid's big brother Prince Feisal and explain how Zeid had diverted the money meant solely for the Dead Sea fight. Most likely Zeid was operating under a misunderstanding: to him gold was gold, to be spent on the immediate tasks at hand. The idea that gold would have a strategic value was something utterly alien to his understanding of military economics. Feisal, on the other hand, must have had some notion of its special allocation. More troublesome to Feisal was the Turkish threat to Tafileh. His gain in tribal and political status through its capture was more valuable to him than any amount of gold. Lawrence tried to convince him that under Allenby's new campaign strategy, Tafileh was irrelevant, "not worth losing a man over." In fact, if they took the place, the Turks would weaken their hold on both Maan and Amman, making everyone's job a whole lot easier. On March 4, the Turks did just that. Lawrence put a good face on the loss by relaying Allenby's generosity to Feisal in tangible terms: the camel train of seven hundred animals and three hundred thousand pounds of gold deposited directly into Lawrence's personal war chest for the upcoming campaign season more than made up for Zeid's losses. The regular Arab army was particularly pleased with the new transport, which finally made it a mobile field force. Now Joyce, Jaafar, and the others would have something real and lethal to work with.

After dispensing Allenby's largesse, Lawrence went on a four-day trip to Cairo to begin the staff coordination with Alan Dawnay's Hedgehog planning staff. Hedgehog was essentially a clone of Allenby's general staff: a shadowy presence of Allenby himself, along with his leadership and authority. Alan, an intelligence officer, was Guy's brother; Guy had planned the fall offensive that led to the fall of Jerusalem. Guy Dawnay was recalled to France, and Alan, as Allenby's archangel, became "Allenby's greatest gift to us—greater than thousands of baggage camels. . . . His was an understanding mind, feeling instinctively the special qualities of rebellion: at the same time, his war-training enriched his treatment of this antithetic subject. He married war and rebellion in himself; as, of old in Yenbo, it had been my dream every regular officer would. Yet, in three years' practice, only Dawnay succeeded." Greatly to Lawrence's disappointment, Dawnay's lack of spoken Arabic and the unfortunate state of his health (which had been shattered in Flanders Fields) meant that he could not command in the field. But for all that, Alan "had the gift, rare among Englishmen, of making the best of a good thing. He was exceptionally educated, for an Army officer, and imaginative. His perfect manner made him friends with all races and classes. From his teaching we began to learn the technique of fighting in matters we had been content to settle by rude and wasteful rules of thumb. His sense of fitness remodeled our standing."

The emergence of Dawnay and Hedgehog transformed the whole nature of Lawrence's guerrilla operation from a "wild-man show" to a fully integrated part of Allenby's conventional campaign and "removed it terrifyingly further from the sphere of joyous adventure." The broadened military role of Lawrence's raiders also broadened their responsibility to the total effort of the campaign. Increasingly, Allenby would count heavily on their success, and from this point further, Lawrence ceased to be a "sideshow." It was under Dawnay's intellectual leadership that the Arabs created their first major joint regular and irregular operation. The plan was meant to coincide with the first phase of Allenby's operations in Palestine and had three prongs of attack. The right prong with Joyce and his armored cars would sweep over to Mudowwara and finally cut the Hejaz railway, thus isolating Medina for good. The center prong of Arab regulars under Jaafar would circle north of Maan and strangle the garrison there at the rail line. Lawrence's leftmost prong would take the guerrillas and ride the farthest, linking up with Allenby around Es Salt. Since Lawrence would execute his move on March 30, he was free to dally a bit with Zeid and Nasir in Shobek.

Here the weather had changed considerably from the previous months, and Lawrence was able to enjoy the visit in relative comfort. He also received news from Ali ibn el Hussein el Harith at Azrak that Daud, close friend of Farraj, had died of disease. Word also came concerning the center prong of the Arab offensive under Feisal and Jaafar. Although the two leaders embraced the plan of cutting off Maan from the north, the Arab officers wanted to take the place through a direct assault. Joyce warned them that they lacked sufficient artillery and machine guns to make the attack succeed, and besides, their men were still untrained in urban combat. The main instigator was Maulud, who clamored for *attaque à outrance,* going so far as to write a long memo to Feisal urging this solution. Joyce continued to press his advice, but suddenly he was stricken with pneumonia and sent down to Suez. Next, Dawnay came over urgently to argue the case from the boot-polished staff position, but by then it was too late: the Arab cocktail of tribal honor and testosterone seized rational thought, thus ending the argument.

If the Arab army lacked the argument, they did, however, possess the military means to make the attempt, though in no manner were they a professional force: "In the regular Arab Army there was no power of punishment whatever: this vital difference showed itself in all our troops. They had no formality of discipline; there was no insubordination. Service was active; attack always imminent . . . men recognized the duty of defeating the enemy. For the rest they were not soldiers, but pilgrims, intent always to go the little farther." As a leader, Lawrence was willing to make practical compromises with his men, seeing the fundamental difference between conventional, reflexive discipline born and enforced during peacetime and its irregular variant, reflective discipline, whose utility emerged during war itself.

Discipline was a "stamp" that marked the peacetime recruit as a regular soldier but also "stamped" him into a conventional box of reliability and expectation. Guerrilla warfare, on the other hand, always demanded a kind of mental "trip wire" for self-reflection and reevaluation, because unconventional operations were in a constant state of dynamic emergence, subject to immediate review and challenge.

Perhaps because of his personal crisis after Tafileh, Lawrence considered another aspect of discipline beyond its role in normalizing corporate action and group reliability. Discipline had a binding effect on the human will to victory. In a modern, protracted war, discipline, like all the other military virtues, began a fundamental erosion: "Discipline was modified, supported, even swallowed up by an eagerness of the man to fight. This eagerness it was which brought victory in the moral sense, and often in the physical sense, of the combat. War was made up of crises of intense effort. For psychological reasons commanders wished for the least duration of this maximum effort: not because the men would not try to give it—usually they would go on till they dropped—but because each such effort weakened their remaining force. Eagerness of this kind was nervous, and, when present in high power, it tore apart flesh and spirit. . . . The Arab Army, born and brought up in the fighting line, had never known a peace-habit, and was not faced with problems of maintenance till armistice-time: then it failed signally."[2]

THE LATE WINTER brought essential changes to the two opposing sides in several fundamental ways. For Allenby, the capture of Jerusalem validated his command style as a generous but hard-driving taskmaster little willing to countenance incompetent subordinates. Among the local Arabs he had achieved almost biblical stature. The Arab rendering of his name, Allenby—"Allah en Nebi"—meant "the Prophet of God." By an extraordinary stroke of fate, he decided to enter Jerusalem on foot, fulfilling a Muslim prophecy that a holy man from the West would thus enter the holy city and free the Arabs from the Turks. Former inspector general of British cavalry, Allenby was beginning to appreciate the opportunities for mobile operations in the Palestine theater, and his campaign designs began to embrace maneuver warfare as its chief planning cornerstone. Field Marshal Earl Wavell of World War II fame, who served on Allenby's staff, regarded "the Bull" as the best British general of World War I.

As for the Turks, the beating administered them through the fall and winter had destroyed the entire offensive capability of their ground forces. In February 1918, the Turkish high command facing the British was shaken up and reorganized. The Yilderim ("Lightning") Army Group consisted of the Turkish Seventh and Eighth Armies, commanded by General Erich von Falkenhayn, who was sacked and replaced by General Otto Liman von Sanders, the victor of Gallipoli. Like Allenby, Liman was a horse soldier and loathed incompetency. His experience at Gallipoli taught him the power of a stubborn defense, but he turned this quality into a deficit by failing to recognize that every defensive position had a limited shelf life and every good defensive commander had to know when that life had expired. By most accounts, he was a "corpulent and charming gentleman" with wide political contacts throughout the Ottoman Empire. He was also the first real German commander to understand the psychology of the Turkish soldier, after having spent many months training him. He especially understood the resentment among the Turkish officer corps toward the many German leaders placed among the Turkish General Staff. Liman's first action was to replace German officers with Turkish officers, helping to restore confidence among the officer corps and eliminating unnecessary conflict among the staff. His initial arrival rejuvenated the flagging morale of the beaten Turks and animated them with a new sense of purpose and optimism.

Allenby began the operation to link up with Lawrence and the Arabs on February 19. Moving into the eastern Judean Hills brought very slow progress, for here the British encountered some of the worst terrain in the entire theater. The flank above the Jordan dropped precipitously toward the edge of the river and was dominated by ridges and steep ravines. Artillery batteries often took thirty-six hours to travel eight miles over the tortuous terrain. Despite these difficulties, Jericho was captured on February 21. The constricted nature of the terrain, however, prevented a complete and immediate breakout across the Jordan and an attack on Amman thirty miles to the northeast of Jericho. A lot of tactical "to-ing and fro-ing" had to take place before a sizable penetration could be achieved. Finally, on the night of March 21, at the same moment the Germans began their massive offensive on the western front, British troops began crossing the Jordan. But again mountainous terrain and bad weather intervened with heavy rains, causing difficulties in expanding the bridgehead. On March 25, men slogged and fought their way into Es Salt and reached Amman on the morning of March 27. During these delays, Liman von Sanders was able to reinforce the seriously weakened Amman garrison by rushing down troops on rail from Damascus and by redeploying troops from the recent recapture of Tafileh with as many as nineteen thousand men. For four days the British struggled to seize Amman, and all the while they controlled the key rail line passing through the area—yet they did nothing to damage it.

Lawrence called this failure "unpardonable carelessness," failing to break a single foot of rail line. The "raid" ended on April Fools' Day with the British forced to retrace their steps across the muddy Jordan Valley toward Jericho. From Allenby's perspective, the failure had the saving grace in creating in Liman von Sanders's mind an impression that the main effort of the British forces was being directed at Deraa and Damascus. The Allies captured a thousand prisoners but suffered as many casualties. Furthermore, the advance created an outpouring of hope among the civilians that was soon dashed during the retreat. The Turks, following in the wake of Allenby's withdrawal, used the subsequent opportunity to identify and punish the politically awakened Arabs.

AT THE SAME time, Lawrence continued to support the original plan, unaware of the British difficulties. After gathering his bodyguard, he left Aba el Lissan on April 2 with a caravan of two thousand baggage camels carrying enough gear to equip ten thousand guerrillas for an entire month and ignorant of the fact that the English had retreated from Amman two days earlier. On April 6, he reached Atara, where several wells were located southeast of Amman. According to the original plan, Lawrence with his supply caravan was to meet up with the Beni Sakhr and move westward to set up a main camp at Es Salt. From here, with the help of British cavalry, the entire force would move north against Madeba. As Lawrence was organizing the Arabs, conflicting messages flew about: first that Amman had been captured, then that the British were "falling back," and finally that they were fleeing from Es Salt. To clarify the situation, Lawrence sent out his trusty scout Adhub to the British headquarters. Adhub returned with bad news: the Turks were in control of Es Salt and were hanging the local Arabs, who had openly greeted the British. There was now fear that the Turks might even go on to recapture Jerusalem.

Lawrence was thoroughly confused and embarrassed by the sudden turn of events. Allenby's plan seemed feasible and easily executed. What could have gone wrong? Now he and the British had lost esteem in the eyes of the Arabs, while Turkish stock had soared under their new German commander. While trying to determine a new course of action, Lawrence conducted a personal reconnaissance of the city dressed as a gypsy. He realized just how strong the garrison had grown and determined that Allenby's original mission had indeed become impossible. The question now was, what to do? Lawrence decided to rejoin Feisal at Maan and perhaps reinforce him with the Indian machine-gun company wasting away at Azrak. Maan was one hundred twenty miles south of Amman.

Lawrence headed for Maan around April 11 with his small bodyguard. Along the way, he encountered a squad of Turks checking over the railway. The younger men of Lawrence's entourage wanted to assault the Turks immediately, while he cautioned restraint. When they began to gripe, he relented and they attacked instantly. The older men advanced in a wide arc, attempting to outflank the enemy, who had rushed for cover in a culvert. The sullen Farraj, still despondent from the loss of his friend Daud, charged directly at the position, and when he reached the embankment the enemy loosed a volley, whereupon he seemed to fly off his camel, disappearing into the undergrowth. After dispensing with the Turks, they all ran over to the embankment and found Farraj near his camel, shot through the stomach and back. A dead Turk was lying nearby, staring glassily at the wounded Arab. Farraj seemed dead, but when the men dismounted he greeted his comrades softly. In an instant a hush fell upon them: Farraj seemed to peer beyond the horizon and to withdraw within the last vestiges of his existence, "sunken in that loneliness which came to hurt men who believed death near." El Zaagi quietly told Lawrence that Farraj had just a few more hours to live. The men gathered around him and tried to stop his life's blood from seeping away into the sand. And as the red pool grew larger, they attempted to carry him away in his blanket, but the damage to his shattered spine was too great and he let out a piercing, heartrending scream. The raiders continued to fumble with him, and he finally asked to be set down and left alone, "for he was dying, and happy to die, since he had no care for life. Indeed, for long he had been so [since Daud's death], and men very tired and sorry often fell in love with death, with that triumphal weakness coming home after strength has been vanquished in a last battle."

Just then, Abd el Latif, one of Lawrence's bodyguards, yelled a warning. About a thousand yards up the line, he could see a detachment of Turks pacing an armored trolley in the raiders' direction. Farraj's agony could not stand any hasty movement, so now the ancient pledge was invoked: Leave no prisoner to a brutal enemy. His bodyguard had willingly embraced the old oath, but Lawrence never imagined the burden of Farraj's death would fall upon him. He crouched down next to the dying man, hiding his Webley in the folds of his robe. In an instant, Lawrence recalled all the petty punishments he had delivered Farraj and Daud since the early days of Aqaba; now he was about to relieve Farraj of the final punishment and deliver him into glory. He looked down at the dying Farraj, who suddenly "opened his eyes and clutched me with his harsh, scaly hand, the tiny hand of these unripe Nejd fellows." Lawrence paused, knowing that Farraj had guessed his purpose. The desert air seemed to stir and then to whisper: "Darkness . . . darkness . . . darkness." An old, familiar smile blossomed on Farraj's ashen lips. "Daud will be angry with you," he murmured.

"Salute him for me," Lawrence replied.

In a moment, as if to gather his final strength, Farraj said hoarsely, "Allah will give you peace." He closed his eyes, and then Lawrence covered Farraj's face with his bloody head scarf. After a pause Lawrence pulled the trigger, saluting Farraj with a bullet's song carried upon a chorus of wind.

BY NOW THE advancing Turks were very near, spraying machine-gun slugs among the mourners. The bodyguard wrapped Farraj in his blanket and shuffled hastily to the camels. Already as they rode off, they were murmuring over the best way to divide his belongings, especially Farraj's splendid camel. El Zaagi coveted the beast for himself. They camped at nightfall, and Lawrence's anger rose as his grief subsided: "I was bitter that these perfected dead had again robbed my poverty; and to cheapen the great loss with a little one I shot the poor beast with my second bullet."[3] When supper came they all feasted on Farraj's camel, his final comrade's legacy to share and share alike.

In the morning they rode out and stumbled across the Indians, still as inept at desert riding as when first they'd joined the Arabs. Lawrence helped them reload their camels and retie their sliding saddles. Finally, at sunset they were regroomed and moved off on their own under Hassan Shah, their gear and harnesses creaking and jingling into the sunset, observed by a lone cowering jackal. Lawrence pushed on toward Maan and Feisal; riding through the night, he heard the distant, muffled crump of artillery fire and saw the twinkling lights of artillery flares off in the distance. Next day, they passed through glimmering clouds of locusts beating their glinting wings against the heat of the day. The season had suddenly changed, causing Lawrence to reflect that he was now commencing his seventh straight summer in the desert.

They approached the mound surrounding Maan called Semna. A party of litter bearers was coming down the slope with a heavy load when one of the carriers gestured with a toss of his head and said, "Maulud Pasha."

Lawrence leapt off his camel and ran up, crying, "Is Maulud hit?" He was one of the most competent regular officers in Feisal's army. A man of the old school: honest and wise, direct, stalwart. He had been hit by shrapnel that shattered his leg above the knee. It would likely need amputation, if gangrene didn't kill him first.

The old lion, so small in the large litter, replied weakly: "Yes, indeed, Lurens Bey, I am hurt but thanks be to Allah, it is nothing. We have taken Semna." Despite the severe injury, he was proud of his military accomplishment outside of Maan. He leaned out of the litter, pointing out to Lawrence the key deployments he himself had made on Semna ridge. Lawrence then bade a hasty farewell and went to find Nuri Said, who had succeeded the wounded Maulud. Lawrence found Nuri positioned on a nearby hilltop just as Turkish artillery began to lob a desultory, poorly targeted barrage. As he spoke with Nuri, intelligence reports began to arrive from positions north and south of Maan: Jaafar had destroyed three thousand rails above the town, and the night before, Nuri had smashed the Ghadir el Haj station below Maan, wrecked its five bridges, and torn up a thousand rails. The Hejaz line would be useless for weeks. With the news, Lawrence hurried to the temporary field hospital to look in on Maulud. He found him under the care of a red-bearded doctor, Mahmud, who reassured Lawrence that the old warrior would survive without amputation. Much relieved, Lawrence went off to find Feisal, whom he spotted in the distance, etched black against the burning sun. As he approached closer, the prince's headband glittered brightly like a halo, even through the ever-present cigarette smoke. The sound of Lawrence's camel pulled Feisal from his reverie and he offered his hands to the Englishman, saying, "Please Allah, good [news]?"

Lawrence said, "The praise and the victory be to Allah." Feisal threw down his cigarette and grinned broadly, bundling Lawrence into his nearby headquarters tent. Here they exchanged the latest news. It was clear from the discussion that Feisal, in close contact with Dawnay, had the most up-to-date information. The emir was especially anxious to discuss his army and its new role in the reframed plan. Feisal explained the revised task organization of the Arab Northern Army, which fell under his command. It now consisted of four subordinate units: (1) the Arab regular army: a brigade of infantry, a battalion of mule-mounted infantry, a battalion of Egyptian Camel Corps, and a section of eight infantry guns; (2) the British detachment (commanded by Lieutenant-Colonel C. P. Joyce—still in the hospital with pneumonia): the Hejaz Armored Car Battery (three Rolls-Royce cars with mounted machine guns and two ten-pounder [2.75-inch, 70 mm] mountain guns mounted on Talbot trucks, a company of Egyptian Camel Corps, a flight of four airplanes, and logistical units; (3) the French detachment (commanded by Captain Rosario Pisani): two mountain guns, four machine guns, and ten automatic rifles; (4) the Arab irregular detachment (commanded by Major T. E. Lawrence): Ageyli bodyguard, various Bedouin and peasant formations as needed. The force was reorganized into three tactical columns: a center column under Maulud, reinforced by Auda abu Tayi's horse-mounted irregulars; a northern column under Jaafar, also of Arab regulars; a southern column under direct command of Alan Dawnay, comprising most of the ailing Joyce's force with additional Bedouin reinforcements. The French detachment was in reserve with Feisal along with his bodyguard. Lawrence learned the details of the fight for Maan thus far: Ghadir el Haj was the nearest station south of Maan and was seized successfully by Maulud on the night of April 11, the day before Lawrence's arrival. Jaafar had just stormed Jerdun, the station immediately to the north of the town. Dawnay with his southern column was at Guweira, readying to strike the Mudowwara station sixty miles farther down the line from Maan.

After the tactical briefing, matters turned to Nuri's complaint about Auda, that he had contributed nothing all day long to his attack in the south. At that moment, as if on cue, Auda entered the tent and denied Nuri's charge. Then Lawrence recalled the incident at Aba el Lissan, before Aqaba, and Auda's reluctance to charge the Turks, and how Lawrence had had to shame the old warrior into the attack after a series of mischievous taunts. Feisal was a bit surprised to learn of the incident, and Auda was deeply wounded by the dredging up of this old news: "He swore vehemently that he had done his best today, only conditions were not favorable for tribal work: and, when I withstood him further, he went out of the tent, very bitter." This rebuke seemed to mobilize Auda's men, who captured two nearby outposts the next day. By this time the positions dominating Maan had been captured by the Arabs, giving them great freedom of action to rove around the entire town and prepare for the final assault.

Lawrence had been moving around the battlefield in a Ford, flitting from one position to the next. He observed Jaafar massing his artillery on Semna ridge to the southwest of Maan and watched with Nuri as his men charged the sheds of the railway station. When the artillery fire suddenly abated, Nuri sent Lawrence back to Pisani with an urgent request for more fire. When Lawrence drove up to the artillery position, he found the Frenchman "wringing his hands in despair, every round had been expended. He said he had implored Nuri not to attack at this moment of his penury." As a consequence, the

Turks counterattacked and winkled the Arabs out of their positions around the rail yard. Despite the initial setback, an important lesson was learned concerning the improving quality of the Arab regular forces. It was now apparent from the fight that the Arab infantry was becoming better than its Turkish counterpart, requiring less British stiffening. Tactically, it meant that the force would be more flexible in employment and require fewer leaders.

On the morning of April 18, Jaafar decided to pull back to the Semna ridge to rest and recoup his losses from the previous week of fighting. He then urged the garrison to surrender, when he discovered that the commander was an old military college friend. The friend protested, and in the meantime Jemal Pasha was able to reinforce the garrison with a pack train of food and ammunition from Amman. But the railway remained smashed for weeks to come. Lawrence, anxious that Dawnay was out alone fighting his first battle with mixed guerrilla and regular troops, left the front at Maan and drove down to link up with Dawnay and his southern column near Tell Shahm. Here Lawrence diplomatically offered his services as an interpreter, since Dawnay had no command of the Arab language.

Lawrence was amazed to find everything deployed as though Dawnay were in the midst of a staff college field exercise. Dawnay continued to outline the elaborate plan, something Lawrence had never felt necessary during his entire raiding experience. The plan limited the natural chaos of guerrilla operations and constrained the scope for seizing unplanned and unforeseen opportunities. Dawnay, great planner that he was, was operating from the regular, pattern-induced paradigm of the conventional fighter: it was all that he knew. Lawrence then asked Sherif Hazaa, the Arab adviser to Alan Dawnay, if he knew what was expected of him. He looked dumbly at Lawrence and after much eye blinking confessed that he had no watch with which to synchronize his movements with the evolutions of the plan. Lawrence handed him his own timepiece and then crept off under a rock for a few brief winks of sleep.

At dawn, everything went into motion with the precision of steel vault doors slamming shut, one after the other. The first two posts surrendered almost immediately. Lawrence rushed on in the third Rolls-Royce, now playing the role of assistant engineer to Captain

Henry Hornby. The two watched Hazaa's Arabs assault the last post as though on a "steeplechase" instead of attacking in a series of covered rushes. The exhausted Turks quickly threw in the towel after witnessing the élan of the Arab charge. The final act of the battle was the attack on the station itself. After an initial air strike coordinated by Dawnay's plan, all the forces converged madly on the station house like iron filings to a magnet. Lawrence was one of the first to be drawn in, lifting the station bell as a worthy souvenir. Someone next copped the ticket punch, and last, Hornby grabbed the office stamp. All the while, the Turks looked on with chagrin and amazement as their prisoner status came to have less merit than these seemingly worthless trinkets of office. "A minute later, with a howl, the Bedouin were upon the maddest looting of their history. Two hundred rifles, eighty thousand rounds of ammunition, many bombs, much food and clothing were in the station, and everybody smashed and profited. An unlucky camel increased the confusion by firing one of the many Turkish trip-mines as it entered the yard. The explosion blew it arse over teakettle, and caused a panic."[4] While the Arabs were in their looting frenzy, the Egyptians found a food storehouse that they guarded as their own, causing consternation among Hazaa's Arabs. Weapons were drawn, and Lawrence offered to mediate the dispute to prevent an unnecessary gunfight. It was finally agreed that the Egyptians could have first dibs on the food stores and then turn the loot over to the guerrillas. Lawrence's role in mediation—"like the hypnotic influence of a lion-tamer"—may have saved several lives.

After the fall of Tell Shahm, the next station in line was Ramleh, but Dawnay's complex plan had not allowed for this opportunity. Many of the Bedouin had already bolted after the looting, and only Hazaa's men remained. Two armored cars were sent down to reconnoiter the station and found it abandoned. The place was turned over to Hazaa and his faithful Arabs for looting in recognition of their loyalty and fighting spirit. The rest of April 19 was spent tearing up the track toward Medina. The third day of the plan was devoted to the seizure of Mudowwara. This was just as problematic as Ramleh and for the same reason: not enough combat power available.

The hope appeared that perhaps the sudden rush of Arab success would stun the Turks into surrender. Though hope is seldom a method, it was the only plan available. On the morning of April 20, they set out in their vehicles toward the station, riding like Viking marauders through the sealike desert. As they stormed out of the east, the rising sun held them safely in its shadows until they were close enough to Mudowwara to see a long train huffing and puffing at the station. The smoking engine obscured most of the activity and left Lawrence and his party to wonder whether the place was being abandoned or reinforced. A few seconds later, their curiosity turned to consternation as a battery of Austrian mountain guns let loose with a barrage of high-explosive shells. With their question answered, the column swung on a wide arc out of range and proceeded to destroy as much of the track as possible, including the mining of the bridge Lawrence and Zaal had worked over the previous fall. The work ended the mission: eighty miles of line from Maan to Mudowwara was totally destroyed. From that moment forward, Medina was geographically and logistically isolated from the rest of the Turkish effort.

With the mission complete, Lawrence was about to leave for Aqaba and return to Allenby's headquarters when he received a new officer. Major Hubert Young had been sent from Mesopotamia to reinforce the effort in Syria. He had complete mastery of the Arab language and was selected to mirror the work of Lawrence in the broadening scope of operations. He was immediately sent to work with Zeid and Nasir to cripple the railroad north of Maan. The entire rail network from Deraa down to Medina had become a vulnerability for the weakening Turkish presence in Arabia.

THE ONE NIGHTMARE that stalked Allenby's waking dreams finally appeared on March 21, 1918. The Germans unleashed their great counteroffensive on the western front. Within a few days, the Allies lost a huge swath of territory in France and forced the War Cabinet to suspend all operations in the Middle East. Within two days of the assault, Allenby was ordered to swap out one of his British divisions with an Indian division and send it to France immediately. On April 9, the Germans launched a second great attack along the Lys River to broaden the scope of the offensive, making immediate and sustained progress. A week later, two more divisions were taken from Allenby and prepared for movement to Europe. Although most of the British units were eventually replaced by Indian units from Mesopotamia or France, they lacked the combat experience unique to the operations in Palestine. Moreover, the new units had to be reintegrated, reorganized, and retrained for assimilation into the larger Egyptian Expeditionary Force under Allenby. The upshot of the German attack was to force Allenby to abandon all plans for the late spring, early summer, phases of the campaign. Allenby was thus limited for the time being to small tactical actions that might set the stage for a larger campaign in the near future.

The general thread in Allenby's mind was to repeat the raid across the Jordan to feign a strike at the rail junction at Deraa and the seizure of Amman. Although the first raid was unsuccessful, it did divert significant attention and troops to that area. He was prepared to repeat the gambit, even with his limited resources, after a large emissary of Beni Sakhr arrived to offer a hand in the effort. While Lawrence was in Jerusalem visiting with Allenby, word was received that this second raid across the Jordan had failed. One reason for the failure was that the planning staff was incapable of coordinating the intricacies that Allenby demanded of the forces, especially in the joint arena of regular and irregular operations. With the departure of Guy Dawnay, architect of the Jerusalem plan, for Haig's staff in France, Allenby had lost his best planner. Another reason was that the Turks had heavily reinforced the whole Trans-Jordan sector. The actions of Lawrence's guerrillas, though largely unsuccessful at the tactical level, had finally convinced the Turks of the serious threat to the Amman area. From the Arab perspective, the British appeared fumbling in their efforts toward Amman, so much so that the Beni Sakhr considered withdrawing its support to Feisal's efforts east of the Jordan.

On May 5, Lawrence met again with Allenby to discuss the general's revised plans in light of the debacle in France. Insofar as the Arabs were concerned, it was Allenby's intent to maintain Arab pressure upon the Turks around Maan. He offered as much support as he could spare, including for the first time the promise of continuous aerial bombardment against the Hejaz railway and against Amman. This greatly uplifted Lawrence's spirit as an indication of the strength and commitment of Allenby's continued support for the Arab cause. During afternoon tea, Allenby idly mentioned that the Imperial Camel

Brigade operating in the Sinai would have to be disbanded because of the new manpower requirements. Unlike the Camel Corps manned mostly by Egyptians, the Camel Brigade was a mobile shock unit comprised of British and Australians mounted on the finest Sudanese camels. Lawrence casually asked, "What are you going to do with their camels?"

Allenby laughed and said, "I don't know; why not ask 'Q'?" "Q" was Sir Walter Campbell, Allenby's quartermaster-general. After a bit, Lawrence excused himself and strolled across a rather dusty garden walk and found Q filling out march tables. He repeated his question, and Campbell said that the camels were being assigned to the divisional transport of the newly arriving Indian divisions. Lawrence directly requested two thousand of them. Without looking up from his work, Q offered that Lawrence was out of his mind, and he should go bother someone else with a similar impairment.

Lawrence "returned to Allenby and said aloud, before his party, that there were for disposal two thousand two hundred riding-camels, and thirteen hundred baggage camels. All were provisionally allotted to transport; but, of course, riding-camels were riding-camels. The staff whistled, and looked wise; as though they, too, doubted whether riding-camels could carry baggage. A technicality, even a sham one, might be helpful. Every British officer understood animals as a point of honor."

That night, Allenby asked Sir Walter Campbell to dine with him, Lawrence, and the rest of the staff. Campbell sat at the general's right hand and Lawrence sat at his left. As soup was being served, Allenby casually opened a general disquisition on the nature of camels. Sir Walter immediately took up the theme and mentioned the fortuitous acquisition of hundreds of baggage camels from the old Imperial Camel Brigade that brought the Indian divisions' transport up to regulation strength. Allenby "cared nothing for strengths, the fetish of administrative branches." He cared instead about results, howsoever obtained.

Allenby then turned to Lawrence with a knowing gleam in his eye and asked: "And what do you want them for?" Lawrence leapt at the bait and replied with panache, "To put a thousand men into Deraa any day you please." The promise was shocking, and Lawrence meant every word of it, and by now Allenby readily believed him. He turned back to Sir Walter with a sad smile, paused, then said simply, "'Q,' you lose." For Lawrence, Allenby's boon was enormous: "It was an immense, regal gift; the gift of unlimited mobility. The Arabs could now win their war when and where they liked."

The very next day, Lawrence was off early to give Feisal the astonishing news back at Aba el Lissan. Lawrence could hardly contain himself in Feisal's tent after he arrived; he wanted desperately to spill the news but instead savored every second of his foreknowledge, like a parent about to spring a birthday surprise on a beloved child. He talked all around the subject, discussing "histories, tribes, migration, sentiments, the spring rains, pasture. . . ." Finally, Lawrence could no longer contain himself. He casually mentioned Allenby's gift of hundreds of riding camels. Feisal looked at him as if struck dumb, amid a "toke" on his ever-present cigarette: the butt dangling from the prince's lip, his mouth now wide-open in disbelief as he leaned and reached for Lawrence's knee as though to catch his balance. Then he stood up instantly, the cigarette falling, spilling ashes on his beard, down his robes. He embraced Lawrence quickly, energetically, pushing him away almost immediately to look in his eyes. "How?" Feisal rasped.

After Lawrence recounted the whole story, Feisal called for his black slave, Hejris, saying, "Hurry, call them."

"Who?" Hejris asked.

"Oh. Fahad, Abdullah el Feir, Auda, Motlog, Zaal . . ."

"And not Mirzuk?"

"Move!" Feisal shouted, and the black man disappeared.

Lawrence looked at Feisal with great affection and much satisfaction and said quietly, "It is nearly finished. Soon you can let me go." But Feisal would not hear of it.

In an instant, numerous feet slapped in the dust outside the tent. There was a brief stirring as the sheikhs put on their "game faces" for the audience with Feisal and then swept into the tent. They each passed through with, "Please Allah, good?" and Feisal replied, "Praise Allah!"

When they were all settled in, Feisal at last made the announcement. There was utter astonishment. The old warriors struggled inwardly to control their joy, trying to maintain a certain suave disdain at the news, all the while eyeing Lawrence in estimation of his role in performing the miracle. When Feisal finished, Lawrence said expansively, "The bounty of Allenby. . . ."

Zaal was first to regain his composure: "Allah keep his life and yours."

"We have been made victorious," Lawrence said dramatically, and then left the tent with a flourish to tell Joyce of the news.[5] As Lawrence retired, the entire tent erupted with elation. The leaders immediately began regaling one another with new promises of heroic deeds against the Turks and on behalf of their gracious benefactor, Allenby—Allah en Nebi, the Prophet of God.

Lawrence was now at the height of his personal cachet with Feisal, the tribesmen, and, for that matter, Allenby; the incandescence of his leadership never burned more brightly, shining upon the whole of the Arab Revolt. The dark tones of tribal culture created the conditions for this final fulmination. By now Lawrence was seen as a key benefactor, never mind that Allenby held the purse strings: it was Lawrence who *delivered* the goods. In a tribal culture, there was no government safety net, no social infrastructure, to fall back on in times of need. Self-reliance and the largesse of the tribal chief and one's own familial generosity dominated the orbit of personal existence. In this milieu, Lawrence had learned his special existential role, and he played it better than anyone else during the entire course of World War I. The enabling dimension of Lawrence's leadership— whether as material provider or teacher—always formed the core of his success and the source of his personal satisfaction.

LAWRENCE FOUND THE excitement contagious. He and Joyce spun webs of strategic fantasy as they started to plumb the full operational significance of their newfound mobility. Of course they would have to get the camels to Aqaba, where they would fatten them up and wean them from the Egyptian barley. The disbandment of the Camel Brigade meant more labor available for the final push in the fall. The entire supply system in Arabia would have to be revamped to account for the new mobility. Young took over as Arab quartermaster. Feisal now had more leverage to ratchet up the grip of the revolt. All that was needed was the time to prepare everything for the final offensive. The Arabs about the plateau above Aqaba had to be protected from any stray Turkish attacks while they reconstituted and reorganized. This meant that Nasir would have to continue to apply the high heat around Maan and draw all attention there. The railroad would have to be the main carriage of the raider as it had been for the Turk. The kind of reorganization Lawrence had in mind was the most significant since January 1917, when Feisal moved from Yenbo to Wejh.

Lawrence explained the timing to Feisal later in June. It would take a month for the Turks to stifle Nasir's actions around Maan and to the north. It would take two months more before the Turks were ready to attack south and recover the plateau around Aba el Lissan and strike at Aqaba. By then Allenby's riding camels would be ready for action. It was then that Lawrence suggested perhaps King Hussein would agree to transfer north the regular Arab units that had been operating with Ali and Abdullah for over a year. This would give Arab regular forces in the north a strength of nearly ten thousand rifles, which could be organized in three separate mobile groups. The first and largest group, perhaps six to seven thousand men, would operate as a covering force to maintain the siege of Maan. The second column of a thousand camels would strike the railway in the Deraa-Damascus sector. The third column of two to three thousand infantry, along with major reinforcements of Beni Sakhr, would try to link up with Allenby near Jericho.

When the idea was first floated past the king, jealousy toward Feisal poisoned his judgment and he refused to support the redeployment of the regulars from the south. Lawrence then went to see Allenby to seek his direct intervention in the matter. He arrived at GHQ on June 18 and found a very different command climate. William H. Bartholomew was now Allenby's chief of staff, and Lawrence laid before him the Arab plans. The chief smiled and said he was "three days too late." A major campaign scheme was in the making that would require the whole summer to develop. The Arabs would have to muddle through on their own in the meantime until the main army was ready. In the larger sense, the two plans simply moved to a state of hiatus. Allenby had approved the redeployment of Ali's and Abdullah's men, and it would take the whole summer to convince Hussein of its merits in any case. Lawrence would have plenty of time to recover and rest for the final push in the autumn.

OWING LARGELY TO Lawrence's leadership, the beginning of June found Turkish fortunes along the Hejaz railway again in dire straits. Rail service south of Amman was hanging by a seventy-five-mile thread of a shuttle service down to Al Hasa. During the period May 1 to 19, Lawrence, Young, Peake, Hornby, and others had destroyed twenty-five bridges. Rail operations were compounded by a severe fuel shortage that limited the number and speed of train movements. Virtually all coal supplies had been diverted to the western front, placing a greater burden on wood fuel. Steam engines often required as much as fifteen tons of wood a day, and the destruction of rail lines meant that more fuel had to be diverted to wooden-tie replacement. The Arab incursion onto the Maan plateau denied access to large stands of timber, while wide-ranging British bomber strikes drove off local woodchoppers. By the end of summer, olive trees and vineyards were being destroyed to feed the hungry iron monsters.

Water shortages were another problem affecting the thirsty trains. Lack of water affected train schedules. Drought and attacks on the railway also meant that more freight had to be carried as potable water rather than as critical military stores. Timetables were thrown out of whack as train movements became dependent on communications between the departure station and the arrival station. Trains were not cleared for departure until an all-clear message had been received from the receiving station. This could take several hours of coordination. If the message traffic was delayed or impeded, a security detachment had to be sent to clear that portion of the line, adding further inefficiencies.

Allenby was facing problems of a different kind. By June, stories floated around that King Hussein was becoming increasingly concerned about ibn Saud's threat to his hegemony in the region and that the king would sue for a separate peace and begin a private war of his own. Turkish and German propaganda was making the most of Allied losses and German gains in France. Rumors circulated that the British were about to evacuate Egypt and were planning to use Indian troops, many of whom were Muslim, as a sacrificial rear guard during the withdrawal. In mid-June, a detachment of Indian troops surrendered to the Turks, causing Allenby greater anxiety as he anticipated the long hot summer ahead. It was now clear to all sides that the culmination of the war in the Middle East was finally at hand. Every effort, every resource—material and mental—was being mobilized for the final struggle. No one was more aware of this than Lawrence, who was mobilizing the last measure of his personal will and stamina and wishing it were all over, finished for good.

CHAPTER NINE

The Hovering Dead

A true war story is never moral. It does not instruct, nor encourage virtue, nor suggest models of proper human behavior, nor restrain men from doing things men have always done. If a story seems moral, do not believe it. If at the end of a war story you feel uplifted, or if you feel that some small bit of rectitude has been salvaged from the larger waste, then you have been made the victim of a very old and terrible lie. There is no rectitude whatsoever. There is no virtue. As a first rule of thumb, therefore, you can tell a true war story by its absolute and uncompromising allegiance to obscenity and evil. . . . You can tell a true war story if it embarrasses you. If you don't care for obscenity, you don't care for the truth; if you don't care for the truth, watch how you vote. Send guys to war, they come home talking dirty.

—TIM O'BRIEN, *The Things They Carried*

By the end of May, sixty thousand troops had been redeployed to France from the Middle East, and these had been largely replaced by raw Indian drafts. Allenby was in the long process of integrating these new forces into his army. In his assessment, the quality of the infantry was thus degraded. The foot soldiers also took the brunt of the constant struggle against sickness and disease. By the high summer, malaria was approaching epidemic proportions, disrupting the army's training schedules. The general's cavalry, however, had been reorganized in a fashion that actually improved their quality by enhancing combat mobility and hitting power. Allenby's final stroke would rely, in the end, on his cavalry forces. Logistically, the situation had vastly improved since the winter. The Sinai railway was able to move two thousand tons of supply a day into Palestine, while tactical transport was able to efficiently and rapidly redistribute the matériel from the railhead throughout the army.

The long delay in reorganizing the force caused Allenby and Lawrence significant concern on two counts. First, the stalemate on the Maan plateau gave the Turks the opportunity to recover their strength and launch a decisive counterattack at the appropriate moment. Moreover, the ongoing stalemate could only sap the momentum of the entire Arab Revolt, which had been so painstakingly developed. Second, as time passed rumors began to circulate about the shape of the postwar Middle East. Knowledge of the Sykes-Picot Agreement and the Balfour Declaration was being used by the enemy for propaganda purposes and seemingly with some success. This placed great pressure on Lawrence to act and break the stalemate at Maan.

It was evident by the beginning of July that the great German spring offensive had collapsed, with the arrival of large American contingents having helped tip the scales. Despite the German failure, Allied strategists feared that the war in Europe would last well into 1919. Lloyd George, therefore, urged decision on the Palestine front and suggested British troops be sent there for a grand offensive during the forthcoming winter. This view was rejected as unrealistic: Allenby would have to make do with the troops he already had at hand. From the Turkish perspective, the activities east of the Jordan had convinced them that the next British strike would come there, and they continued to move troops from Palestine to address that eventuality. However, the collapse of Russia and the signing of the Treaty of Brest-Litovsk on March 3, 1918, drew Turkish strategic interests elsewhere, to the Caucasus.

Here there were old scores to settle with the Russians, who had seized Turkish territory after the Russo-Turkish War of 1877–78. These old territories were occupied, as were locations in northern Persia, initiating a new wave of pan-Turkish enthusiasm. While the acquisitions may have temporarily slaked Turkish regional ambitions, they were strategically meaningless. Worse, Turkish forces in

Palestine were tapped to occupy some of these distant posts. At the same time, the Germans were pulling out their national troops from the region and sending them back to the western front. The last major German combat unit was withdrawn on June 11, though German staff contingents and smaller detachments remained until the end of the war, typically operating at odds with their Turkish counterparts. As for the Turks, entering the fifth year of the war found their morale again virtually exhausted. Although they numbered a hundred thousand men along the front south of Damascus, these numbers were deceptive. In reality, the effective combat strength of these troops was much closer to thirty-two thousand infantry, four thousand cavalry, and 402 guns. Allenby's army had an effective advantage of over two to one: fifty-seven thousand infantry, twelve thousand cavalry, and 540 guns.

To conform with Allenby's deployment, the Turks had to spread their forces across a seventy-five-mile front running from the Mediterranean Sea east to Amman. When Liman von Sanders arrived, he sought to strengthen both the eastern and western flanks. Even as early as the middle of January 1918, it was evident to German planners that the Turks were unable to defend in depth anywhere along this front. Their best chance was to conduct a series of delaying actions all the way to Aleppo, if necessary, in order to maintain an army in being. By July, Liman, commanding from his headquarters still formed in the Yilderim "Lightning" Army Group at Nazareth, had reorganized his forces into the same three armies that had fought virtually from the beginning: the Seventh and Eighth Armies manned the line west of the Jordan, with the Fourth Army still standing fast about Amman as the nemesis of the Arabs east of the river. The two former armies defended a box some fifty-five miles wide and only twelve miles deep. In August, the Seventh Army received a new commander, General Mustafa Kemal Ataturk Pasha, "the greatest soldier and man that Turkey had produced in recent years." Liman had a small reserve in the so-called Asia Corps. Initially, Liman considered the possibility of withdrawing the Fourth Army to the Yarmuk Valley and around Deraa, but after careful consideration he rejected the idea in the belief that the already shaken army would utterly collapse if ordered to retreat.

Allenby's plan was wholly his own, unlike the inheritances of his last major operations. In the design of the campaign, there were several factors that he considered. First, he would have to launch the attack before the autumnal rains began. The likely date would be sometime in September. Second, he believed that creativity and novelty could enhance his general superiority of forces. Third, he knew the Turks could never achieve the kind of troop densities that the Germans had achieved on the western front. This meant he could achieve a significant breakthrough virtually anywhere he chose. Fourth, much of the enemy's rear area was in excellent cavalry country that could be exploited by his best arm, the Desert Mounted Corps, comprising three cavalry divisions. Finally, he anticipated that Liman would not withdraw any troop at the last moment but attempt to hold every inch of ground.

In the conceptualization of the campaign, Allenby was always concerned with joining up with Feisal's army east of the Jordan. In Allenby's record of the campaign, he wrote: "I was anxious to gain touch with the Arab forces east of the Dead Sea, but the experience, gained in the raids which I had undertaken against Amman and Es Salt in March and May, had proved that the communications of a force in the hills of Moab were liable to interruption, as long as the enemy was able to transfer troops from the west to the east bank of the Jordan. This he was in a position to do, if he controlled the crossing at Jist ed Damieh. The defeat of the Seventh and Eighth Turkish Armies, west of the Jordan, would enable me to control this crossing. Moreover, the destruction of these armies . . . would leave the Fourth Army isolated, if it continued to occupy the country south and west of Amman. I determined, therefore, to strike my blow west of the Jordan."

Naturally, Allenby recalled the vulnerability of the two westernmost armies to severed communications, as when Lawrence tried to destroy the Yarmuk bridges the previous fall. The linchpin of the Turkish railway was still located at Deraa station. Here one portion of the line veered south to become the Hejaz railway, and the other bent west, crossing the Jordan at Jist el Mejamie, continuing parallel in the rear of the Turkish front, and dropping down at Beisan in the Jezreel Valley, then jogging west again to El Afuleh in the plain of

Esdraelon, where there was a feeder line down to Haifa. Larry Addington had written that railroads are the "bones of strategy." This idea helped structure Allenby's use of his cavalry and mounted troops, including Lawrence's guerrilla forces. If the British could effect a wide enough penetration, they could slip through their mounted troops and seize El Afuleh and Beisan, trapping the Turkish Seventh and Eighth Armies against the Mediterranean Sea. Since both towns were within a day's march of the cavalry, it meant that the Turks would have to react immediately before the trap was sprung. If Allenby could develop an effective deception plan, this might prove successful enough to delay the Turkish decision making until it was too late. Lawrence's role, of course, would be crucial. In this case, rather than just seize Deraa or destroy bridges, his raiders would also demonstrate and harass along the area to fix and befuddle the Fourth Army.

On July 11, Lawrence met with Dawnay at Allenby's headquarters to discuss the planning concepts and the Arab role in the attack. Lawrence was impressed with Allenby's confidence, which he said was "like a wall." The deception plan was already in development. Again, Meinertzhagen would be the grand master of deceit. After his success at Gaza, Allenby began to appreciate "Meiner's" contribution to strategy. The plan was to set up near Jericho every useless tent and canvas remnant that could be found in Egypt. The veterinary and field hospitals would be relocated there to look like ordinary camps. Mock horses, camels, and troops would go through a daily charade of drills, creating clouds of obscuring dust. Bridges would be thrown up and taken down and thrown up again, all to create a great illusion of activity. At the precise moment, the Royal Air Force would launch an impenetrable cloud of counterreconnaissance formations to blind the Turkish high command. In all this, the Arabs would contribute as part of the deception plan.

Meanwhile, as Lawrence and Dawnay went back to Cairo for further deliberations, they learned that the Turks had just turned Nasir out of his position at Hesa, a train depot about fifty miles north of Maan. Turkish success here meant a likely strike at Aba el Lissan toward the end of August, just about the time that Lawrence's raiders would drive north to Deraa. This meant that the Turks would have to be delayed by at least two weeks. The only reserve available anywhere was a remnant of the disbanded Imperial Camel Brigade that had been consumed for its riding camels and offered up to Feisal. The one remaining battalion was under the command of Major Robin Buxton. He would take his three hundred men and destroy a bridge and tunnel near Amman and have enough time to return to Palestine and aid Allenby's preparations. This would provide the Arabs with a solid month with which to prepare their own two thousand camels for the final push. GHQ presented one difficult proviso for employment, however: Buxton's detachment must not incur any casualties.

Coincidentally, Young and Joyce had developed an elaborate logistics scheme that seemed divorced from the reality of Allenby's overall campaign design. As Lawrence saw it, the plan relied too much on chance, and its complexity made it that much more vulnerable to the vagaries of fate: "Allenby meant to attack on September the nineteenth, and wanted us to lead off not more than four nor less than two days before he did. His words to me were that three men and a boy with pistols in front of Deraa on September the sixteenth would fill his conception; would be better than a thousand a week before or a week after. The truth was, he cared nothing for our fighting power, and did not reckon us part of his tactical strength. Our purpose, to him, was moral, psychological, diathetic; to keep the enemy command intent upon the trans-Jordan front." But as a cross-cultural leader, Lawrence held views that were fundamentally divided: "In my English capacity I shared this view, but on my Arab side both agitation and battle seemed equally important, the one to serve the joint success, the other to establish Arab self-respect, without which victory would not be wholesome." The Arabs would have to *fight* in order to claim a hegemonic position in the Middle East.

As Lawrence continued to discuss it with Dawnay, the Deraa plan crystallized in his mind: "To reach Deraa from Aba el Lissan would take a fortnight: the cutting of the three railways and withdrawal to reform in the desert, another week. Our raiders must [therefore] carry their maintenance for three weeks. The picture of what this meant was in my head—we had been doing it for two years—and so at once I gave Dawnay my estimate that our two thousand camels, in a single journey, without advanced depots or supplementary supply columns, would suffice [along with] five hundred mounted infantry, the battery of French quick-firing '65 mountain guns, proportionate machine-guns, two armored cars, sappers, camel-scouts and two airplanes until we had fulfilled our mission. This seemed like a liberal reading of Allenby's three men and a boy."[1]

Lawrence still had to deal with Young and Joyce, who were furious at having their "top-heavy" plans ripped to shreds. Lawrence carefully argued that changes in Allenby's scheme had necessitated a change in their own plans, "competent" as they were. In particular, Lawrence's plan considered the role of Buxton's detachment in a spoiling attack that would buy time for the preparation of the Arab offensive on Deraa. Young and Joyce had made no consideration for Buxton. A heated debate ensued. "Lawrence," said Joyce, "you've clearly made a mistake. To introduce foreigners will only unman the Arabs; and to let Buxton go a month later will be even worse."

"Impossible!" Young said with defiance. "The Camel Brigade will only hinder the baggage camels, which otherwise might enable the Deraa force to reach its goal. By trying to do two greedy things we shall end in doing neither."

Lawrence pondered a long while, gazing steadily first at Young, then at Joyce, then back at Young, where his eyes finally rested. "Look: consider the whole deception element. First of all, Buxton will suddenly show up at Aqaba one fine day without any warning and quickly vanish on his way to Rumm. His force will be miles away from any Arab army unit and from any village. In the resultant vagueness the enemy intelligence can only conclude that the whole of the defunct camel brigade is now on Feisal's front. Such an accession of shock-strength to Feisal will make the Turks very tender of the safety of their railway: while Buxton's appearance at Kissir, apparently on preliminary reconnaissance, will only put credence into the wildest tales of our long-held intention shortly to attack Amman." Joyce began to nod thoughtfully but said nothing for the moment.

Lawrence turned to Young and regarded the transporter with veiled irony for a long time, his head cocked slightly to the right. Here was the logistician heaven-sent by the British gods to help the Arabs move. Lawrence was contemptuous of his staff obstinacy and planning pettiness: "He, a new comer, said my problems were insoluble: but I had done such things casually, without half his ability and concentration; and knew they were not even difficult." In Lawrence's assessment, Young was a typical "loggie": someone who "would never promise anything except that it could not be done, yet of course done it was, and two or three days before the necessary time." This contretemps with Young over logistics would simmer slowly until the very end of the campaign and cause some resentment between him and Lawrence. Even more contentious was the raid on Deraa itself.

"As for Deraa we can dispense with logistics once we reach Bair," Lawrence argued.

"I see. The camels must have grown more patient over the months," Young replied with heavy irony.

"Not at all. The pasturage has been spectacular in the region and the beasts have grown quite fat," Lawrence said casually. "In fact we can cut off the men's food for the attack on Deraa and live off the land on the return journey."

"Truly? The men will fight all the more, hungry in that desolate land," responded Young with even more irony. "The ten days' march home after the attacks will be quite a long fast indeed." But Lawrence had no intention of returning all the way back to Aqaba. Then Young said, "Are you sure you have victory in mind and not defeat?"

Lawrence winced; this last cut deeply, but he maintained his cool. "If each man has a camel under him, and if we kill only six camels a day the whole force will feed abundantly." Still, Young was dissatisfied. Then Lawrence began to point out that Young had estimated the fuel, ammo, and other matériel beyond the normal safe planning levels. He became angrier, overtaken by his planning fetishness.

Lawrence smiled now and began to pontificate on his guerrilla wisdom. He observed, "We've lived by our raggedness and beat the Turks by our uncertainty. Young, your scheme is faulty because it is precise." Lawrence had sufficient "slop" in his plans to account for virtually any eventuality and was agile enough to turn the circumstances into golden opportunities. Only one element of precision was required: the timing. Lawrence would "march a camel column of one thousand men to Azrak where their concentration must be complete on September the thirteenth. On the sixteenth we would envelop Deraa, and cut its railways. Two days later we would fall back east of the Hejaz Railway and wait events with Allenby. As a reserve against accident we would purchase barley in Jebel Druze, and store it at Azrak."[2]

Old Nuri Shaalan would provide reinforcement with a column of Ruwalla, along with contingents of Serdiyeh, Serahin, and Haurani peasants from the "Hollow Land" under Talal el Hareidhin. Young was now convinced that the whole plan was just a "deplorable adventure," but Joyce was excited and ready for any adventure, deplorable or not. Lawrence reminded them that Dawnay had loaned them the services of Major W. F. Stirling. His skill and knowledge of horses would provide entrée into the tents of Feisal and his sheikhs.

Nuri Said was selected to command the regulars in the Deraa operation, and he picked his four hundred best men. Allenby had also showered the Arab regulars with the baubles of victory and honor, while Lawrence's raiders merely wanted more gold. Pisani, the erstwhile French Lothario, had been awarded the Military Cross and now hungered after the Distinguished Service Order. He worked closely with Young to organize the four Schneider guns newly received from the departing Colonel Brémond.

The family spats were inevitable, but thanks to the professionalism of Young and especially Joyce, enough team cohesion was preserved to prevent a complete collapse of cooperation. Lawrence's arrogance appeared high-handed, even by his own admission. It was merely a manifestation of his own self-confidence and the long erosion of tolerance that led to his apparent posturing. Even before the war, Lawrence was never one to suffer fools gladly.

WHILE THE DERAA expedition was preparing for its early September debut, Lawrence hastened down to Aqaba to greet Buxton and his Imperial Camel Brigade remnant. He would guide them to Rumm. The march was uneventful, and Lawrence found his charge an amusing chap. Buxton was an old Sudan hand; he spoke Arabic fluently and understood the culture. He was also a good leader. Stirling came along, as did Dr. Marshall, the physician. After leading Buxton to Rumm, Lawrence headed back to Aqaba to organize his bodyguard. El Zaagi was in charge of organizing the band, numbering again near sixty men—mostly Ageyli. He put the singers and bards on the wings so that the singing kept the march to a musical cadence. He was disappointed, though, that Lawrence refused to have a banner grace his column. They rode for Guweira, Lawrence atop the heroic Ghazala and Abdullah alongside. When Lawrence arrived, planes were circling to speed him on to Jefer, where Feisal was urgently waiting.

Even after the long summer's rest, Lawrence had not completely regained his emotional stamina or, indeed, his former reckless courage. He wrote: "Death in the air would be a clean escape; yet I scarcely hoped it, not from fear, for I was too tired to be much afraid: nor from scruple, for our lives seemed to be absolutely our own, to keep or give away; but from habit, for lately I had risked myself only when it seemed profitable to our cause." Lawrence witnessed the internal war between instinct and reason, the turmoil within his mind as strong as ever. "Instinct said 'Die,' but reason said that was only to cut the mind's tether, and loose it into freedom: better to seek some mental death, some slow wasting of the brain to sink it below these puzzlements. An accident was meaner than deliberate fault. If I did not hesitate to risk my life, why fuss to dirty it? Yet life and honor seemed in different categories, not able to be sold one for another: and for honor, had I not lost that a year ago when I assured the Arabs that England kept her plighted word?" For over a year now, fate had tugged at that loose thread in Lawrence's character. The sense of justice or "what's right," in Jonathan Shay's phrasing, had snipped the integrity of Lawrence's character, and the long process of psychological unraveling began, exposing the fundamental paradox of leader's grief in modern combat: *The longer a leader successfully leads, the more exposed to emotional and psychological corrosion become the foundations of his leadership, competence, and most especially his character.*[3]

LAWRENCE ARRIVED AT Jefer on August 7. All the sheikhs were there in their finest robes, meeting with Feisal. At the great council, Feisal and Lawrence double-teamed to preach the prospective tribesmen to their revolutionary cause. The prince would conjure up the Arab history, tradition, and culture and work it before their eyes into a new amalgam of Arab nationhood. Against these ambitions, Feisal raised the specter of the Turk as evil incarnate and their true and sworn enemy. All through the discussions, Feisal the leader was made manifest for all to see and appreciate as he motivated the disparate Arabs toward a common and higher goal, Damascus and the Arab Revolt.

The great gathering of the tribes caused Lawrence again to confront his original sin, the guilt of deceiving the Arabs to their own cause. He continued the relentless and brutal self-recrimination. "It might have been heroic to have offered up my own life for a cause in which I could not believe: but it was a theft of souls to make others die in sincerity for my graven image. Because they accepted our message as truth, they were ready to be killed for it; a condition which made their acts more proper than glorious, a logical bastard fortitude, suitable to a profit-and-loss balance of conduct." Lawrence had sought a semblance of redemption in his struggle for Arab nationhood, but the more he contemplated his role through the perspective of historical distance, the more it all seemed a kind of personal vanity: "The self-immolated victim took for his own the rare gift of sacrifice; and no pride and few pleasures in the world were so joyful, so rich as this choosing voluntarily another's evil to perfect the self. There was a hidden selfishness in it, as in all perfections. . . . To endure for another in simplicity gave a sense of greatness. There was nothing loftier than a cross, from which to contemplate the world. The pride and exhilaration of it were beyond conceit. Yet each cross, occupied, robbed the late-comers of all but the poor part of copying: and the meanest of things were those done by example. The virtue of sacrifice lay within the victim's soul."

All original sin was a conspiracy, and Lawrence was at the center of it: he played Adam to the British Eve. In his guilt, so he believed redemption was denied, because "honest redemption must have been free and child-minded." When he set himself upon a cross of vanity, Lawrence denied a place of honor for a man worthy. His "thought-riddled" personal struggle increasingly set him apart from those he led. He wouldn't dare share his thoughts, his agony, his grief, with them. His shame was not their shame, his guilt was not their guilt; better "to incur the double punishment of ignorance." Drawing a deep, shuddering breath, he thought: "There seemed no straight walking for us leaders in this crooked lane of conduct, ring within ring of unknown, shamefaced motives cancelling or double-charging their precedents." At some point between his arrival to the Hejaz and his conquest of Aqaba, Lawrence moved from an accessory to his own guilt to its main culprit: "I bitterly repented my entanglement in the movement, with a bitterness sufficient to corrode my inactive hours, but insufficient to make me cut myself clear of it. Hence the wobbling of my will, and endless, vapid complaining."[4]

A DAY OR two later, Lawrence flew back to Guweira and slipped into Aqaba in the night to meet with Dawnay. They learned the next day of Buxton's extraordinary success on Mudowwara. Dawnay then continued on to meet with Feisal to deliver a warning order from Allenby's hand: Be cautious in the move to Damascus until we are on the proper side of the Jordan to link up. In that conversation, Feisal revealed to Dawnay a new vision of Arab desperation. Feisal said he would try to seize Damascus with or without British help: it would be the last real chance the Arabs would have for the rest of the year. If that attempt failed, then he would open negotiations with the Turks. Feisal had been negotiating with the Turks for months, through Jemal Pasha. Lawrence saw an opportunity here. Why not continue the negotiations and extend them into the anti-German cabal led by Mustafa Kemal? There was a certain paradox in Kemal's nationalism that could be exploited. As a true Turk, he could not logically deny the Arab claims beyond the traditional Turkish borders. There were other Turkish nationalists, mostly of a secular bent, who argued that Turkey was putting religious artifacts—like Mecca—before strategy. As the negotiations continued, Jemal offered Feisal control of the Hejaz, then Syria was thrown in to sweeten the offer, and finally—and without authority—he offered Hussein the crown of Mecca.

The Turkish staff had cards of its own to play. Soon after the Bolsheviks seized control of the Russian government, they released the contents of the Sykes-Picot Agreement. This perhaps more than anything forced Feisal to consider independent action if Allenby's coming offensive should fail. Of course, Lawrence had already forewarned Feisal of the existence of the treaty. He urged him to continue to press the fight, since force of arms would have greater merit in the end than words written on a scrap of paper. At around the same time, the War Cabinet offered that all Turkish territory seized by the Arabs should be theirs to keep. All this to-ing and fro-ing caused confusion and consternation among the Arabs. Old Nuri Shaalan asked Lawrence which of these pronouncements he should believe. Lawrence replied laconically, "The last in date." After the recent British defeat at Es Salt, Jemal sent down to Feisal Emir Mohammed Said, brother of their old nemesis Abd el Kader. Feisal said he would be happy to accept the peace offer, if only Jemal Pasha would evacuate Amman and turn over the province to Arab safekeeping. Thinking he had scored a tremendous diplomatic coup, Said rushed back and was nearly killed for his efforts.

Meanwhile, Mustafa Kemal, from the other side of the Turkish army, urged Feisal not to succumb to Jemal's blandishments. Instead he offered the Arabs an alliance that would help rid them of the Germans once and for all. All the while, Lawrence had a sneaking suspicion that the British were about to spring a separate peace of their own on the Turks, siding with the conservative-religious element like Jemal rather than the nationalist-secular faction of Mustafa Kemal. The fact that Lawrence gathered this information from private channels only reinforced his sense of betrayal and injustice: "It was only one of the twenty times in which friends helped me more than did our Government: whose action and silence were at once an example, a spur and a license to me to do the like."[5]

BY THE MIDDLE of August, Lawrence set out in a Rolls-Royce with Joyce to reconnoiter a secondary base should retreat from Azrak become necessary or the place be captured by the Turks. They chose Ammari. The reconnaissance also became a shakeout drive for the tenders and the armored cars, as they encountered virtually every sort of terrain and every imaginable mechanical difficulty. After traversing several hundred square miles of desert, they returned to the wells at Bair, where they found Buxton and his Imperial Camel Corps remnant resting triumphantly. Lawrence had to return Buxton back to Aqaba and thence to Allenby's safekeeping. Meanwhile, he would help Buxton and his men water their camels from the forty-foot wells.

The valley was crawling with the English, and the nearby Howeitat stared at them, never before seeing so many of Lawrence's kind in one place or even imagining so many existed. The tribesmen thought they were Lawrence's own slaves. They were dressed all alike—

uncomfortably for the desert in their shorts and boots and puttees. They ate meat from cans, uncooked and every day. They were all clean-shaven, indistinguishable, silent like automatons. To know one was to know no one, they were an irreducible manifold, a real army, and Lawrence was proud of them: "I was proud of my kind, for their dapper possession and the orderly busyness of their self-appointed labor. Beside them the Arabs looked strangers in Arabia. . . ."

It was now August 16, 1918, and Lawrence's thirtieth birthday. The realization sent him again into a mood of deep grief and rambling self-reflection, surely one of the most unique self-revealing passages in all of military literature. The thought of pride moved him to consider the basis of reputation, and he began to wonder "if all established reputations were founded, like mine, on fraud." If a fraud, Lawrence's later denials would no longer have any credibility or authenticity. "Any protestations of the truth from me was called modesty, self-deprecation; and charming—for men were always fond to believe a romantic tale. It irritated me, this silly confusion of shyness, which was conduct, with modesty, which was a point of view. I was not modest, but ashamed of my awkwardness, of my physical envelop and of my solitary unlikeness which made me no companion but an acquaintance, complete, angular, uncomfortable, as a crystal." Although fit to command, to lead, yet he felt himself ironically a misfit, something of an outcast: "With men I had a sense always of being out of depth. This led to elaboration—the vice of amateurs tentative in their arts. As my war was overthought, because I was not a soldier, so my activity was overwrought, because I was not a man of action. They were intensely conscious efforts, with my detached self always eyeing the performance from the wings of criticism." Here Lawrence is perhaps overly critical. Modern war is a thinking man's game, and he is judging himself by the long-irrelevant standard of the heroic leader.

Nonetheless, he speaks to the erosion of the integrity of his character and psyche brought on in part by the brutal operating environment: "To be added to this attitude were the cross-strains of hunger, fatigue, heat or cold and the beastliness of living among the Arabs. These made for abnormality. Instead of facts and figures, my notebooks were full of states of mind, the reveries and self-questioning induced or educed by our situations, expressed in abstract words to the dotted rhythm of the camels' marching." To the top of his list, though not mentioned, one must always add the corrosive fear that permeated every waking and sleeping moment. The constant dust of fear settled everywhere upon the psyche, grinding it down, wearing it away, so that one's character was always struggling to rebuild itself out of ever-diminishing stores of courage.

The social nature of combat builds strong bonds of trust and affection that replenish the soldier's courage when his own well has run dry. A man isolated from his comrades is a man, in truth, discouraged and disheartened. On his thirtieth birthday at the wells of Bair, Lawrence was at last confronting this truth as he struggled to explore and examine the deep sources of his own character. Lawrence's introspection was a violation of every Victorian and Edwardian tenet of personal behavior and orthodoxy. Deep self-reflection was a dangerous path that took individuals into a dark realm of second-guessing and confusion. Better to use these energies in prayer and religious contemplation, letting God worry about matters belonging to the soul.

Yet Lawrence could not help being "very conscious of the bundled powers and entities within me; it was their character which hid. There was my craving to be liked—so strong and nervous that never could I open myself friendly to another. The terror of failure in an effort so important made me shrink from trying. . . ."[6] Lawrence was a deeply lonely man who wanted to be liked. This introduced another paradox into his personal calculus: leaders must always act in ways that lead directly to being disliked, and often hated and despised.

The thirst for affection, perhaps rooted in some deep psychological Olduvai Gorge of his familial past, had within it its own riddle: "The disgust of being touched revolted me more than the thought of death and defeat: perhaps because one such terrible struggle in my youth had given me an enduring fear of contact: or because I so reverenced my wits and despised my body that I would not be beholden to the second for the life of the first. . . . To put a hand on a living thing was defilement; and it made me tremble if they touched me or took too quick an interest in me. This was an atomic repulsion, like the intact course of a snowflake. The opposite would have been my choice if my head had not been tyrannous. I had a longing for the absolutism of women and animals and lamented myself most when I saw a soldier with a girl, or man fondling a dog, because my wish was to be as superficial, as perfected; and my jailer held me back."[7] Under our modern science of psychiatry, Lawrence's expression of anguish might be assessed as some syndrome along the autism spectrum. But such speculation, perhaps insightful, offers little help to Lawrence after the fact. The disconnection with the other left him with no social compass, and much of this was of his own doing, whether wholly conscious and deliberate or not. Like a cat playing with a mouse, Lawrence saw the social plane of his existence. Was it no wonder, then, that he should lead among men alien to that existence? Impervious to the kind of manipulation that he had evolved among his native Englishmen?

A kind of deep intellectual boredom drove Lawrence to flit from one notion to another and to find the challenge of action a refuge for his turbulent mind: "True there lurked always that Will uneasily waiting to burst out. My brain was sudden and silent as a wild cat. . . . When a thing was in my reach, I no longer wanted it; my delight lay in the desire. Everything which my mind could consistently wish for was attainable, as with all the ambitions of all sane men, and when a desire gained head, I used to strive until I had just to open my hand and take it. Then I would turn away, content that it had been within my strength. . . . There was a special attraction in beginnings, which drove me into everlasting endeavor to free my personality from accretions and project it on fresh medium, that my curiosity to see its naked shadow might be fed. . . . I quickly out grew ideas. So I distrusted experts, who were often intelligences confined within high walls, knowing indeed every paving-stone of their prison courts: while I might know from what quarry the stones were hewn and what wages the mason earned. I gainsaid them out of carelessness, for I had found materials always apt to serve a purpose, and Will a sure guide to some one of the many roads leading from purpose to achievement. There was no flesh." Reminiscent of John Cardinal Newman, Lawrence had a sharp mind that was like a razor, often mining the stony rock of irresolvable ideas, coming close to bending and breaking, dulling its fine edge—or even worse: "It was only weakness which delayed me from mind-suicide, some slow task to choke at length this furnace in my brain."

Then Lawrence makes a remarkable revelation in view of his dominant role as a leader: "Self-seeking ambition visited me, but did not stay, since my critical self would make me fastidiously reject their fruits. Always I grew to dominate those things into which I drifted, but in none of them did I voluntarily engage. Indeed, I saw myself a danger to ordinary men, with such capacity yawing rudderless to their disposal." Yet still he "followed and did not institute; indeed, had no desire even to follow. . . . I had developed ideas of other men, and helped them, but had never created a thing of my own, since I could not approve creation. When other men created, I would serve and patch to make it as good as might be; for, if it were sinful to create, it must be sin and shame added to have created one-eyed or halt."

For Lawrence, the leader's grief was real and always stalked among the shadows of his dancing mind. And the shadows were as multivaried as life itself: all uniformly dark, hiding the shadow caster himself. The desire to serve others seemed the only dominant light capable of dispelling the darkened and turmoiled regions of his soul. "Always in working I had tried to serve, for the scrutiny of leading was too prominent. [While] subjection to order[s] achieved economy of thought, the painful, and was a cold storage for character and Will, leading painlessly to the oblivion of activity. It was part of my failure never to have found a chief to use me. . . . Instead of this, they gave me license, which I abused in insipid indulgence. Every orchard fit to rob must have a guardian, dogs, a high wall, barbed wire."

The assault on the very citadel of his moral and psychological existence was relentless and sapped every potential weakness. Even "the hearing [of] other people praised made me despair jealously of myself, for I took it as face value; whereas, had they spoken ten times as well of me, I would have discounted it to nothing. I was a standing court martial on myself, inevitably, because to me the inner springs of action were bare with the knowledge of exploited chance. . . . It was a revenge of my trained historical faculty upon the existence of public judgment, the lowest common denominator to those who knew, but from which there was no appeal because the world was wide." In the end, Lawrence's public life was left to the whims and vagaries of

history, the historian, and historical judgment. The historical Lawrence would always be a mere pale shadow of the living Lawrence,
and it seemed as though he lived for its deliverance. In the long summer of disquiet, Lawrence had found his own true self, the reflected
face of many battles. And it was a troublesome reflection: "Indeed,
the truth was I did not like the 'myself' I could see and hear."[8]

AROUND THIS SAME time, Major Stirling arrived to meet Lawrence.
His initial impressions of the leader were rather different from Lawrence's internal ecstasy of self-scrutiny. He found him "sitting in his
tent on a beautiful Persian rug looted from some unfortunate Turkish
train. He was dressed, as usual, in the most immaculate white robes
with the golden dagger of Mecca in his girdle. Outside lolled some of
his body-guard cleaning their rifles and crooning softly to themselves
and undoubtedly enjoying the quiet contemplation of some particularly devilish bit of work which they had [recently] perpetrated. They
were a remarkably interesting collection, numbering just under a hundred. Most of them belonged to the Ageyl and were hired soldiers by
profession. Not one of them but was famed for some daring deed, and
for hard living, hard riding and hard swearing, they were the pick of
Arabia. This bodyguard was a very necessary precaution, for there was
a price of £20,000 on Lawrence's head, and the Arabs are a treacher-
ous folk—unless they are your sworn and paid men. Any one of his
bodyguard, however, would have cheerfully died for Lawrence."

The one question that persisted in Stirling's mind, however, was
the crucial and fundamental one of leadership: "What was it that
enabled Lawrence to seize and hold the imagination of the Arabs? . . .
The Arabs are notable individualists, intractable to a degree and
without any sense of discipline, and yet it was sufficient for almost
any of us to say that [when] Lawrence wanted something done—it
was done. How did he gain this power? The answer may partly be
that he represented the heart of the Arab movement, and the Arabs
realized that he had vitalized their cause; that he could do everything
and endure everything just a little better than the Arabs themselves;
that, by his investment with the gold dagger of Mecca, he ranked
with Ashraf or the descendants of the Prophet, and the Emir Feisal
treated him as a brother, as an equal; that he seemed to possess

unlimited gold—for the average Arab is the most venal of all people. But chiefly, I think we must look for the answer in Lawrence's uncanny ability to sense the feelings of any group of men in whose company he found himself; his power to probe behind their minds and to uncover the well-springs of their actions." The force of Lawrence to plumb the depths of his own soul gave him the profound sensitivity and empathy to gaze behind the Bedouin mask of cultural inscrutability: he saw them much as he saw himself.

Stirling recounts another illustrative episode. When Buxton had arrived at Aqaba with the Imperial Camel Brigade task force after their 162-mile trek from the Suez Canal, Lawrence delivered a speech to Buxton's men who had gathered. Lawrence was about to lead them to Jefer and Feisal's camp. According to Stirling, "After supper Lawrence had the men collected round a large central blaze and gave them the straightest talk I have ever heard. He explained the general situation to them, told them that he was going to take them through a part of Arabia where no white man had ever set foot and where the Arab sub-tribes were none too friendly, that there was no need to worry about the Turks but every need to worry about our allies the Bedouin. They were mistrustful folk, he said, and would most certainly think that we had come to take their grazing-grounds. The essential thing was to avoid any cause of friction. If any were offended or insulted he begged of them to turn the other cheek—both because they were better educated and therefore less prejudiced and also because they were so few. The men were delighted and retired for the night, thinking that they were about to embark on the greatest rag in the history of war—as perhaps they were!"

ON AUGUST 20, Lawrence, his men, and Buxton's Camel Brigade task force reached the key bridge at Muaggar fifteen miles southeast of Amman. As they approached their target, the force was suddenly spotted by a low-flying Turkish biplane. Lawrence was faced with an immediate decision as to whether he should continue on with the mission and risk a severe repulse at the hands of an alerted enemy or wave off the strike altogether. To the great disappointment of Buxton, Lawrence decided to forgo the opportunity and instead raise a deception demonstration among the local villagers to the illusive effect that his detachment was the advance guard of a major Arab offensive aimed at Amman and beyond. The deception created dark rumors that flew among the enemy like ravens. Under the new moon, the Turks began to see things they had only imagined before.

Reluctantly, the large column peeled off from its target after dark and headed toward Azrak under a ghostly, glowing moon that seemed to awaken the denizens of the night. It became an eerie march as the sky thickened with clouds of large black birds that flitted among the night riders like the hovering dead. The gloom birds soared with bat-like agility and stillness, unnerving the men with their silent persistence. The flitting soon became a luminous black vortex that began to frighten the men, Arab and English alike. In terror, the raiders began to fire their rifles into the rushing, fluttering clouds of shadows. The men fought through the whirling vapor another two miles, when suddenly they disappeared as though drawn into the moon itself. In the shooting, Lieutenant Rowan of Buxton's troops was hit and killed by a stray bullet. He was buried in a small Mejaber graveyard with quiet dignity. Unnerved, the men stopped to camp by the beckoning wormwood bushes and rest in a sweet bed of fragrance. Lucky or not, the hail of birds likely kept Turkish aerial reconnaissance at bay that night.

On August 22, they reached Azrak and dug a great pit where they buried hundreds of pounds of explosives for the forthcoming raid on Deraa. With the digging completed, the Englishmen of the Camel Brigade took the showers Lawrence and Buxton had long promised them. After three days of relaxation, the column headed out for Aqaba, marching under the cadenced cries of "Are we well fed?" to be met with a thundering response of "No!" and the rhythmic "Do we see life?" met with a loud "Yes!" Bair was reached soon after. Here Lawrence decided to part with Buxton and head on to Aba el Lissan in an armored car. Buxton and his Cameleers were now in friendly territory, and their long trek had made them master riders of the desert and prime guerrilla raiders. They would serve Allenby well in his forthcoming campaign.

Lawrence reached the railroad station in Aba el Lissan on August 26. There he found Joyce, Young, and Dawnay about to leave. Joyce was readying to leave for Cairo for an unpleasant and long-delayed visit to the army dentist. While he went to relieve a toothache, Lawrence found himself with a new headache. Joyce's ship had just brought the mail up from Jidda, and it carried a news item in King Hussein's official gazette of Mecca concerning Jaafar Pasha. Hussein had learned that Jaafar had been awarded a military decoration by Allenby and in a fit of jealousy sought to undermine Jaafar's position as head of the Arab Northern Army. He did so through a proclamation that declared there was no rank among the Arabs higher than captain. The obvious inference was that Jaafar, as commanding *general,* was somehow illegitimately in command. The insult did not go unnoticed among Jaafar and his officers—division, regimental, and battalion commanders and staff officers—who immediately rushed to Feisal and tendered their resignations. This caused an immediate command crisis among Feisal's army and threatened the whole operation against Deraa, whereupon Lawrence interceded to remind Jaafar and his officers that the seventy-year-old Hussein was near barking mad and completely out of touch with reality. Feisal reminded them that he alone—not Hussein—had given the officers their commissions, and only he could accept their resignations—which he refused to do. Thus, it was Feisal who was the real target of the royal proclamation. The confusion stemmed from the fact that in late 1917, Feisal appointed Jaafar to head the Northern Army in Feisal's stead, but Hussein had never sanctioned the promotion.

With that argument in mind, Feisal telegraphed Hussein to explain his position, whereupon the old king replied with accusations, calling his son "traitor and outlaw." Feisal responded immediately by relieving himself of the command of the Aqaba front. Hussein countered by giving the authority over to Zeid, Feisal's half-brother, who refused the offer. Hussein's telegraphic dialogue became suffused with a seething anger that essentially shut down the entire Aqaba front. Dawnay delayed his return trip to Allenby, sensing that the emerging catastrophe was about to erupt. He begged Lawrence for a solution, and his only reply was "that things hung on chance." At this dark moment, Lawrence assessed the new situation and saw three courses of action that might resolve the crisis: "First, to get pressure put on King Hussein to withdraw his statement. The second, to carry on, ignoring it. The third, to set up Feisal in formal independence of his father. There were advocates of each course, amongst the English, as amongst the Arabs."⁹ The first thing that Lawrence did was to persuade Dawnay to have Allenby lean on Hussein for a resolution, but given Hussein's cunning and obstinacy, this could take weeks and Lawrence had no more than three days before the events would move forward and unleash the Deraa operation. Time was running out.

As leader and commander, Lawrence himself was under the gun to react swiftly before the whole plan completely unraveled. The first thing Lawrence did—since it was imperative that he remain at Aba el Lissan to sort out the situation—was to report immediately to Nuri Shaalan. Without providing complete details, he said that he would be unable to attend the great gathering of tribes at Kaf, preparatory to the launching of the offensive. This was a serious compromise, as it could possibly sow doubt in Nuri's mind about the commitment of Feisal's forces to the pending operation. The best that Lawrence could do was to promise Nuri that he would meet him in Azrak around September 16 to begin the final stroke. Lawrence also had to get the massive supply caravans launched on their way to Azrak. Major Young dealt with the issue in his usual efficient fashion, and despite the crisis, the departure was only a day late.

Just as the last supply columns of ammunition, fuel, food, and baggage trundled off to Azrak, the crisis turned more critical. Arab gunners, who heard rumors to the effect that Feisal had abandoned the army, decided to train their guns on the unit tents in apparent mutiny. Rasim, the artillery commander, had fortunately taken the precaution of stashing the breechblocks in his tent for safekeeping. Lawrence intervened and turned the emergency into his debut as a stand-up comedian, using the "high heads" as the brunt of his jokes and reminding them that victory lay in Damascus, not Mecca. If they were concerned about the whereabouts of Feisal, he would deliver the prince to them immediately and personally. Using clever stage management, Lawrence arranged to have his English driver, Bols, paint the Vauxhall sedan a bright green and pass through the gunners at the appropriate moment with Feisal and Zeid in the jump seat. The drive-by convinced the men of their indiscretion, and they readied themselves for the coming battle.

The fundamental challenge for Lawrence was to get the forces at

Aba el Lissan moving to Azrak on the appointed day. Here Stirling and Nuri Said, a future prime minister of Iraq, were instrumental in convincing the troops that it was in their own best interest to maintain their military bearing and cohesion. Lawrence reminded them that if they decided to abandon the Arab cause, they would be stranded in the middle of nowhere without proper food, supplies, and money. This side of the unemployment coin made them reconsider their situation and agree to remain under arms. Following all the negotiations, the Arabs were two days late in meeting their departure deadline.

Lawrence's final act was to reestablish Feisal in his rightful role as leader of the Arab Revolt. Feisal had to be in the fight, and after some persuasion he offered to come under Lawrence's direction. Meanwhile, Allenby and Wilson were doing their level best to pressure Hussein into issuing a formal apology to Feisal. If these efforts faltered, Lawrence pledged Feisal full support of the British government as sovereign leader in his drive on Damascus. This was an action of last resort. Up until now, the Arab Revolt had presented a common unified front, despite King Hussein's increasing obstinacy. To pluck Feisal from this common effort now would create serious, perhaps insurmountable, complications after the war. As the spat with Hussein continued, Lawrence took it upon himself to decode and translate the king's missives in less abusive terms, somewhat defusing the dialogue. "Finally, there came a long message, the first half a lame apology and withdrawal of the mischievous proclamation, the second half a repetition of the offense in a new form. I suppressed the tail, and took the head[ing] marked 'very urgent' to Feisal's tent, where we sat in the full circle of his staff officers." Lawrence proffered the cable to Feisal's secretary, who reworked the dispatch into proper form, and when it was ready he handed it to the prince, his hand shaking noticeably. There was now great tension settling upon them. Feisal sat quite still, without his customary cigarette, looking downcast but expectant. All eyes clicked in unison as the entourage turned nervously to look at Feisal. As he read the message, he became "astonished, and gazed wonderingly at me, for the meek words were unlike his father's querulous obstinacy. Then he pulled himself together, read the apology aloud, and at the end said thrillingly, 'The telegraph has saved all our honor.'" There was an audible gasp, which turned immediately into a cry of jubilation. In the tumult, Feisal whispered coyly into Lawrence's ear, "I mean the honor of nearly all of us."

Feisal's words struck Lawrence with such irony that his laugh turned into a giggle of immense emotional relief. He looked at Feisal and replied with a twinkle, ' I cannot understand what you mean."

"I offered to serve for this last march under your orders: why was that not enough?" he asked.

"Because it would not go with your honor," Lawrence said.

"You prefer mine always before your own," Feisal murmured. Then, all of a sudden he leapt to his feet, clapped his hands, and said almost gleefully, "Now, gentlemen, praise Allah and work."[10]

The final phase of the crisis was thus resolved in less than three hours. The entire camp burst into a frenzy of activity as everyone ran about their duties, making ready the massive move to Azrak. The planning schedules were quickly revised, and Feisal promised to meet Lawrence at Azrak no later than September 12. Lawrence then sped away in his Rolls-Royce to meet with Nuri Shaalan and mend fences with the Ruwalla.

ALLENBY WAS PLEASED to learn that the dispute between Hussein and his son Feisal had been resolved—at least for the time being. It meant he could move forward with his plans, which had fully matured to the point of operational execution. His unifying concept was to strike the Turks such a powerful blow as to shock, paralyze, and shatter them out of existence. A strong infantry stroke along the Mediterranean coast would open the attack and rupture the Turkish front. Here the elite Desert Mounted Corps would unleash a massive exploitation maneuver that would slash Turkish lines of communications as it cleaved into the Jordan Valley. The plan was the culmination of Allenby's months of discovery and learning, leading to the realization that simplicity trumps complexity and that violence of execution outbids naked force. Every detail received the minutest scrutiny; nothing was left to chance. Logistically, Allenby's forces were in much better shape than previously, especially with regard to water. Although the railhead from Egypt was strung as far as Lod, corps transport assets were necessary to redistribute supplies to the divisions. By the time the offensive began, nearly six hundred trucks were required to meet this need. In the case of Lieutenant-General Edward Bulfin's XXI Corps, difficult terrain meant that twenty-two hundred camels had to carry forty-four thousand gallons of water during the operations.

Crucial to Allenby's design of operational shock, the Royal Air Force would play a decisive role—first by striking at Turkish communications nodes and infrastructure and second by continuously harassing retreating enemy columns from the air. Finally, the RAF kept an impermeable shield of concealment over the Allied forces, preventing enemy aircraft from discovering Allenby's true operational form. The air force was thus a key component to the overall deception plan that confused and confounded Liman and his staff. Secrecy, the reverse side of the deception coin, was maintained at the highest levels since the war began. Mission objectives were not disclosed to division and brigade leaders until two or three days before D-Day. Allenby then cycled through the divisional headquarters personally to brief commanders and their staffs about the overall campaign design. This personal regard raised the morale and confidence of officer and soldier alike. If leadership, planning, and attention to detail meant anything at all, Allenby had already won the fight.

On Lawrence's front, things had finally begun to move toward Allenby's "three men and a boy with a revolver." The movement began according to the following order of battle. On August 30, Joyce sent out a caravan of six hundred camels on the long march to Azrak, escorted by thirty Gurkha machine gunners and thirty-five Egyptian camelry. On September 2, after quieting the troops because of Hussein's bold affront, a second caravan of eight hundred camels left Aba el Lissan. Lawrence, Nasir, and Lord Winterton, a useful remnant from Buxton's Imperial Camel Brigade, left on September 4 in Lawrence's Rolls-Royce. He was followed by 450 Arab camelry armed with twenty Hotchkiss machine guns, two English armored cars, five Rolls-Royce roadsters, two RAF aircraft, and Pisani's French mountain guns. Feisal and Joyce would bring up the rear.

As Lawrence raced off to meet with Nuri Shaalan and his Ruwalla tribesmen, he was seized by the exhilaration of the final culminating point of long months of hard work and moments punctuated by death, terror, and self-doubt: "For on this march to Damascus (and such it was already in our imagination) my normal balance had changed. I could feel the taut power of Arab excitement behind me. The climax of preaching of years had come, and a united country was straining towards its historic capital. . . . [B]y a momentary miracle we had truced all the feuds for this month, so that from Aqaba up to Damascus all was clear going."

CHAPTER TEN

Days of Wrath; O Days of Sorrow— the Road to Damascus

Our united forces entered Damascus unopposed. Some confusion manifested itself in the city. We strove to allay it; Allenby arrived and smoothed out all difficulties. Afterwards he let me go.

—T. E. LAWRENCE, *Seven Pillars of Wisdom*

September 6, 1918, found T. E. Lawrence in a Rolls-Royce speeding along from Aqaba on his way to Azrak. He was riding with Lord Winterton, lately of Buxton's Camel Brigade, and with the redoubtable Sherif Nasir. Much had changed since the triumph at Aqaba over a year ago. The Arab Revolt had expanded greatly, as had Lawrence's role in it. Formerly, he had been like a checkers player: on a small board with rather prosaic, one-dimensional playing pieces. Now, however, everything seemed transformed. His area of operations was now like a large chessboard and he was its master, working the complex pieces into intricate combinations and maneuvers. And Lawrence's board was now just one among several played under the deft hand of General Allenby over in Palestine. In the old days, Lawrence had prided himself on being able to ride hard from Aqaba to Azrak in three days, spending twenty-two out of twenty-four hours of the day mounted, braced in the saddle in a kind of rigid stupor, somehow maintaining sufficient awareness so as not to fall off the camel.

The expansion of the war had also transformed the desert landscape. There were now men everywhere: in columns, in files, in ranks, all moving steadily north over the Jefer plain, Lawrence's chessboard. They were advancing to keep pace with Allenby's successes to their west in Palestine. And Allenby was a hard taskmaster, constantly lunging and pressing the harassed Turks. The Turks, meanwhile, knew they were beaten, for even their German advisers said so. Yet somehow, perhaps through a perverted courage of despair, they clung on, having to be winkled out of their posts and positions at the point of the bayonet.

Corporal Green, Lawrence's experienced driver, had pushed the Rolls hard, sometimes racing past blurs of camels and columns at sixty-seven miles an hour. Nasir was astonished by the speed, and his salutations to the foot soldiers were always a few seconds too late. When they arrived at Azrak, it was already dark. They spent the night at the nearby airfield, sleeping under a large canvas hangar. A brisk, westerly wind threatened to bury the sleepers under a coating of blowing sand. By midnight the zephyr vanished, leaving in its wake a cloud of dagger-barbed camel flies that attacked them relentlessly. Near dawn, the camel flies were relieved by arriving waves of mosquitoes eager to have an early breakfast.

After the miserable night, Lawrence decided to move the camp to higher ground, up on the Mejaber ridge. On its rim he had a spectacular view of the Deraa-Amman road and the marshaling of the army below. Lawrence gazed upon the scene for some time, and as the sun set, he began to sense the new mood of the final campaign against Damascus: "I could feel the taut power of Arab excitement before me. The climax of the preaching of years had come, and a united country was straining towards its historic capital. In confidence that this weapon, tempered by myself, was enough for the utmost of my purpose, I seemed to forget the English companions who stood outside my idea in the shadow of ordinary war. I failed to make them partners of my certainty."[1] Yet Lawrence knew there could never be a full partnership, for who among the English shared his hopes and aspirations for the Arabs as he did? How silly: they had their own British and, yes, imperial interests at heart. It was Lawrence who was outside the circle; it was he who stood beyond the pale, outside its shadow.

But Allenby, the commander in chief, was not interested in shadows and contrasts. He wanted unity and homogeneity of action in order to accomplish his final mission: the seizure of Damascus. To that end, he saw Lawrence and his Arabs playing a pivotal role. First, they would demonstrate around Azrak as if to strike at Amman. Their very presence at Azrak had already accomplished as much. Next Lawrence would cut the rail at Deraa—and here Allenby was quite specific. As long as Lawrence was able to show up at Deraa with the proverbial "three men and a boy with pistols," that would suffice. Their presence would be like a lever, enough to threaten the Turks and their rail lifeline and help wedge them out of Palestine.

On September 11, Feisal arrived with the rest of the Arab army—an especially welcome sight to the hordes of camel flies, which darted after the two thousand camels with relish and determination. Next Nuri Shaalan turned up with the usual suspects: Auda abu Tayi, Mohammed el Dheilan, and Zaal. The recently mobilized tribes emerged with their leaders: ibn Bani, chief of the Serahin; ibn Genj of the Serdiyeh; Majid ibn Sultan of the Adwan; Fahad and Adhub, lords of the Zebn; and others. After exchanging a few pleasantries with Feisal, Auda, and Mohammed, Lawrence excused himself and left to be alone. He strolled down the valley to Ain el Assad, his old haunt by the dusky tamarisk. Yes, he thought, how things have changed: "I am tired of these Arabs; petty incarnate Semites who attained heights and depths beyond our reach, though not beyond our sight. They realized our absolute in their unrestrained capacity for good and evil; and for two years I had profitably shammed to be their companion! Today it came to me with finality that my patience as regards the false position I had been led into was finished. A week, two weeks, three, and I would insist on relief. My nerve had broken; and I would be lucky if the ruin of it could be hidden that long." But the underlying thread of the last two years had remained the same: the constant unwinding of shared deceit and trickery in obscuring British true intentions for the Arabs. The skein of betrayal hid the imperial interests, only now it promised to wrap Lawrence in its shroud of grief, guilt, and hopelessness. But the swindler's guilt was also compounded by the survivor's guilt: his two brothers had been dead now for over three years.

AT DAYBREAK ON the morning of September 14, Lawrence's column marched out. He stood above on a high cliff, watching the formation slowly depart. There were one thousand riders up from Aba el Lissan and three hundred nomad cavalry under Nuri Shaalan. The two thousand Ruwalla camelry would remain in reserve at Wadi Sirhan until needed, which was expected to be very soon. The horsemen consisted primarily of the elite nobility: sheikhs or their servants who could afford the expense of a horse and its kit. Lawrence was delayed a day in order to attend to political and strategic affairs with Feisal and Nuri Said. On the second day, Lawrence caught up with the column by fast car.

The initial attempt to cut the railway north of Amman had failed before he arrived. After Joyce explained the situation, Lawrence moved to the front of the spread-out force to find another approach more vulnerable than the site at the previous, failed location. While he was reconnoitering a position near three ancient Roman villages, Lawrence observed a dogfight between a Bristol fighter and a Turkish two-seater. After a long duel, the British pilot was successful, dropping the enemy in a ball of fire. But the British plane was now too shot up to provide adequate reconnaissance and air cover for Lawrence's column and so had to return to Ramleh in Palestine for repairs. After the brief distraction, Lawrence returned to his task and found a suitable site for demolition: a track running across two sturdy bridges that, when demolished, would occupy the Turks with several days of repair work. The size of the target required more dynamite than he had brought; the task would thus have to wait until morning.

Returning to camp, Lawrence now realized how the changes in the complexity of the campaign had also brought commensurate changes in the larger society of troops. The attachment of active British Army formations like the Gurkhas and other advisers had now created a segregated encampment. The quiet, sober British lay about the campfire discussing tomorrow's mission against the bridges; the Arabs, on the other hand, maintained their usual "babbling laughing turmoil" a few hundred yards away—the one somber and withdrawn, the other exuberant and extroverted.

During the next morning's breakfast, Lawrence laid down the mission before the Arab chieftains. The British with the support of the two armored cars would attack both bridges, the cars providing a base of fire if needed. Meanwhile, the Arab riders would break off and head to Tell Arar along the Damascus portion of the line. There they would wait four miles north of Deraa for Lawrence to return. Around two that afternoon, a motorized detachment consisting of the two armored cars and two jeeplike vehicles Lawrence refers to as "tenders" advanced toward the bridges. The tactical plan was simple: the two "jeeps" would wait under cover; Lawrence would advance with one of the armored cars, carrying his 150-pound loaf of explosives, and move on the bridges. The other armored car would cover the stone blockhouse with its machine gun. As the vehicles moved into position, seven or eight Turkish guards suddenly spotted the maneuver and in a panic advanced in the direction of the British. After a short burst of machine-gun fire from one of the armored cars, two of the enemy were hit and knocked out of action; the other group quickly surrendered. The blockhouse garrison, after witnessing the surrender of their comrades, threw in the towel as well.

Lawrence next turned his fine art of demolition toward the largest of the two bridges, some eighty feet long and fifteen feet high. He set the charges carefully, like a master painter preparing his palette. But where the painter's creation represented a melding of shadow and light, Lawrence's final composition was generated in the blast itself, the creation being in the destruction. The explosive medium of expression sought to create just enough damage to the bridge that the repair crews would first have to bring down the skeletal wreckage before they could actually start to rebuild a replacement bridge. The second span was dealt with in like fashion.

After the destruction, the men quickly left with their prisoners; some were released, as their intelligence value was deemed worthless. About three hundred yards from the bridges, one of the "jeeps" broke a strut, causing the bed of the vehicle to drop onto the rear wheels and brake to a sudden halt. The mishap created an immediate babel of consternation: the men kicked the tires, spat, and scratched their heads, all the while cursing the devil of technology, Rolls-Royce, in several languages. By an odd coincidence, the driver was Private Rolls—no relation, but an automotive genius in his own right nonetheless. After several minutes of pushing, prodding, shaking, and hammering, Rolls came up with an ingenious solution. He would use the vehicle's running boards, rope, and wooden balks to stabilize the bed and raise it off the rear tires. With a wary eye watching out for the inevitable Turkish patrols, the party quickly went to work. In several minutes the task was completed; after off-loading the cargo to the other vehicles, the convoy managed to make it back to Umtaiye, one of the three Roman villages, to spend the night. The rendezvous with the rest of the column would have to wait until morning.

Despite the wrecked vehicle, the mission had successfully cut the main route between Deraa and Amman. The destruction also had a second-order consequence farther south down the line: the Turkish force at Tafileh, which was expected to attack the Allied position at Aba el Lissan, would have to wait until the line was repaired. The stressed repair crews would need at least a week to do the work, and by then it would be too late.

THE DETACHMENT WAS off early that dawn, trying to overtake the Arab column at the rendezvous point. The terrain was rough going even for the heavy two-ton armored cars. The rouge-colored ground was splintered and split from a prolonged absence of rain. The party finally reached Tell Arar by eight o'clock in the morning. As Lawrence pulled up at the head of a ridge, he arrived just in time to witness the Arab forces attack the rail line just below his location. Trad led the Ruwalla cavalry, and Nuri Said deployed Pisani's artillery to suppress the Turks inside a nearby redoubt. The horsemen were quick to seize the position with only a single loss. By nine, the Arabs had captured the main rail choke point that led into both the Hejaz and Palestine; they had fulfilled their promise to Allenby to show up at Deraa with "three men and a boy with pistols." They did so with hardly a shot fired. From the position they commanded the entire area. The whole of Deraa itself, Mezerib, and perhaps even Ghazale could be theirs for the taking.

Surveying the entire scene, Lawrence thought: "I was seeing even further than this: northwards to Damascus, the Turkish base, their only link with Constantinople and Germany, now cutoff: southward to Amman and Maan and Medina, all cutoff: westward to Liman von Sanders isolated in Nazareth: to Nablus: to the Jordan Valley. Today was September the seventeenth, the promised day, 48 hours before Allenby would throw forward his full power. In 48 hours the Turks might decide to change their dispositions to meet our new danger; but they could not change them before Allenby struck."[2] It was too late; even with forty-eight hours to spare, it was over. The Turks were simply a few more moves from checkmate, and Lawrence's men, as Allenby's white knight, were the opening gambit that jumped them deep into the enemy's rear. Even as the knight was moved into position, the Turks had no inkling of their own immediate danger and approaching doom.

This did not, however, prevent them from reacting violently to Allenby's knight gambit. After the demolitions were blown, the Arabs and their allies pulled away. From his perch high on the ridge overlooking Deraa, Lawrence with his powerful binoculars was able to penetrate the midday haze and see a very unsettling scene. The Turks were rushing aircraft into action on the local airfield; as many as eight or nine planes were revving their engines on the flight line, spewing forth immense clouds of dust. The Turkish infantry manned their trenches and began to fire at the departing column. The reaction was largely ineffectual; by this time the column was already several miles distant. Several unarmored locomotives were preparing to depart as they rushed to gather steam. Beyond Deraa, though, everything else was "still as a map." Suddenly, out of the amber haze a Turkish aircraft dropped, as if readying to deliver a load of bombs. But as it came closer, Lawrence realized it was a Pfalz configured in an innocuous reconnaissance role. It flew over, high, attempting to discern the nature of the threat facing them at Deraa. Then eight more planes appeared, less docile and more aggressive than the first, bombing and strafing the tiny targets below. In response, Nuri Said opened up with his Hotchkiss machine guns, the tracers arcing lazily into the high heat. Pisani elevated his four mountain guns, setting his shrapnel shells on short fuses, hoping for a lottery strike. The last action drove the Turkish fliers higher, thinking they were now facing a serious antiaircraft defense. The higher they climbed, the less accurate their bombing and strafing became.

Elsewhere, more thorough demolitions were laid under the track by Peake and his Egyptians. While the actions continued, Lawrence met hastily with Nuri and Joyce. They considered the new challenge: the north-south section of track—from Damascus down through

Deraa to Maan and Medina—had been devastated. The question was how to obliterate the east-west portion of the line that ran from Deraa to Yarmuk and into Palestine. Lawrence's force would have to swing way around to the other, western side of Deraa to get at that portion of the rail. Under the circumstances, the Turkish aircraft would strafe and bomb the column throughout the entire evolution of its maneuver. At the same time, Peake's sappers would be dangerously exposed if the Turkish infantry screwed up enough courage and sallied from their trenches against the engineers.

As the three officers contemplated their next move, the gods of war unexpectedly smiled down upon them. Lieutenant Junor, the lone pilot left back at Azrak with his decrepit B E.12, suddenly appeared out of nowhere. He dove out of the sun upon the unsuspecting Turks with his two machine guns twinkling away. Though he was hopelessly outnumbered and outclassed, the shock of his sudden appearance and dead-eye accuracy made the enemy think they had been bounced by an entire squadron of Sopwith Camels. After his initial blazing pass, Junor flew westward across Deraa. Incredibly, the Turkish pilots followed him in hot pursuit. Junor's heroic action completely removed the air threat to Lawrence's plans. With the newfound freedom of maneuver, he detached two of Pisani's guns along with 350 of Nuri's regulars and sent them west to Mezerib and the western part of the rail line.

Moving rapidly through the cover of cornstalks and thistle, Nuri's detachment reached the position in half an hour. Lawrence was about to follow them with his Ageyli bodyguard when he again heard the deep thrum of aircraft engines. To his amazement, Junor materialized out of the afternoon mirage with his escort of Turkish fighters peppering after him with a deadly hail of fire. They now had his slower machine hemmed in on three sides, but their numerical advantage became a disadvantage in their fear of shooting one another out of the sky. Junor zoomed overhead, dropping a quick message on Lawrence's head: "My fuel is shot!" Lawrence immediately took his men to clear a makeshift landing strip to get his pilot safely down. As Junor floated in, the wind suddenly intervened on behalf of the enemy and flipped the plane into the ground. The craft cartwheeled across the strip at a sharp angle and came to rest on a pile of boulders. The

Turks witnessed the crash, and with their honor thus salved, they skulked back to Deraa. Lawrence rushed up to the crash, imagining the worst. As he came to the other side of the wreck, he was astonished to find Junor grinning painfully from a slash to the jaw but otherwise unhurt.

Major Young drove up from behind in his Model T just as a die-hard Turk spilled his last bomb on the wreckage. But still Junor was not finished. He off-loaded his Lewis and Vickers machine guns with ammo drums and requisitioned Young's Ford to offer his service to Peake's sappers.

THE TASK STILL remained to cut the track at Mezerib and destroy the lucrative bridge below Tell el Shehab, where Lawrence had failed twice before. Joyce remained back at Tell Arar, leading the supply trains and a reserve detachment of Nuri's Arab regulars. The Ruwalla horsemen, the Gurkhas, and the motorized troops under Peake also remained there. Lawrence would use his bodyguard as the striking force against the bridge, moving as fast as possible against the target. Initially, his party made good progress, moving widely dispersed like common Bedouin. All of a sudden a Turkish fighter-bomber, which had crept up on them, dropped a stick of bombs in their midst, taking out two of the camels. Their riders, unhurt, quickly leapt on two nearby beasts and continued on. Then another machine floated in silently, with its engine turned off, and dropped two more bombs. One of them wounded Lawrence in the right elbow, striking near the ulnar nerve and numbing his arm. The sight of blood running down his arm and onto his wrist and hand momentarily unnerved him. The first plane had by now circled back to begin another strafing run, knocking Lawrence out of his initial shock. It was the first time he had been wounded from the air; what disturbed him more than the sting of shrapnel and sight of his mortal blood was the emotional assault to his nerves.

The Turks soon flew off without pressing their advantage, demonstrating again their preference for inflicting random acts of violence on unsuspecting local tribesmen over engaging in a coherent tactical fight. Lawrence finally reached Mezerib and learned that the remainder of Nuri's troops was still two miles behind. While they waited, his men watered their camels and quenched their thirst after the long day of heavy action. By now the whole area was alive with news of their arrival—the first time Allied troops had been in the location since Lawrence's abortive raid in the fall. The local Haurani peasants now began to stage a virtual uprising, with many approaching Lawrence's campsite in a mood of jubilation, bringing useful intelligence about the nearby Turks. The Turkish railway station was just over three hundred yards to their front, seemingly on the verge of surrender. Tallal, one of Lawrence's retainers who hailed from the area, said he knew the stationmaster personally and could persuade him to capitulate. The pair walked cautiously toward the station; suddenly the guards opened up with a heavy blast of rifle fire. The two quickly found themselves flat on the ground in a thatch of tall weeds. They slowly withdrew back to their supports when Nuri arrived with his regulars and Nasir. A quick leadership council was held: Should they bypass the station and simply take out the more important bridge?

Peake's earlier demolition would suffice in the north-south direction; blowing the bridge would sever the east-west route. Why bother with the station at all? As they continued to discuss the matter, the nearby hordes of Haurani—men, women, and children—had been taunting the Arabs to attack. To Lawrence, it seemed likely that the peasants themselves were readying to storm the station at any moment. That decided the issue: Pisani was ordered to deploy his two remaining mountain guns and began pumping rounds into the Turkish defenses; Nuri unloaded with a score of machine guns. At that, a huge cheer exploded from the crowd, and at the sound, the soldiers swiftly advanced and carried the position without loss. Forty prisoners were quickly rounded up and offered to Nuri to crown his victory.

Soon after the capture, a mob of peasants descended, along with the night, upon the station and began a frenzied plunder. By now Young had come up with the reserves. He and Lawrence found two railcars crammed with German PX goodies. The Arabs were especially suspicious of the canned goods. One enterprising plunderer had opened a tin and discovered to his horror that its contents contained pickled pig's feet, a prized German delicacy. The mob found trucks topped off with gas and tried to drive them over the railroad tracks. In the process, several of the trucks tipped over and burst into flames.

The resulting conflagration spread to the wooden outbuildings, and hungry flames licked high into the air, even above the nearby water tanks.

While the marauding continued, Lawrence and Young ran off and cut the main telegraph line at Deraa: the most important communications node in the entire theater of operations. It connected the whole theater back to Damascus and thence to Constantinople. In a highly centralized and directed force like the Turkish army, loss of higher control meant a sudden paralysis and collapse that would occur by the time Allenby launched his offensive. From his perch high atop a telegraph pole, Lawrence gazed down upon the rampant pillaging and looting. He witnessed a scene as lurid as it was apocalyptic. All was by now aflame; the peasants in their hitched-up white robes flashed and flickered about the burning plunder like silver piranhas feasting on the spoils, their faces a frenzied red, reflecting a long-denied rage and hunger for Turkish wealth. At the edges of this incandescent turmoil, streams of peasants came pouring down from the nearby hills, attracted by the fiery commotion and the opportunity to loot. But for some others, the conflagration became an uncertain beacon of freedom, signaling a time to rejoice at the impending destruction of the Turkish yoke.

The town elders of Deraa soon came forth, begging Lawrence and Nasir to accept the keys to the town, if only they would act on their behalf against the Turks in the city. Yet once again Lawrence and Nasir demurred, deferring the decision to the principles of responsible leadership: the attainment of the local tactical prize of Deraa could not stand against the strategic reward that stood beyond the flames at Damascus.

BUT THE NIGHT was far from over. Around nine o'clock, another would-be celebrant showed up. He was a young boy, the son of the headman of Tell el Shehab. His father, the sheikh, had recently been killed, so Lawrence became suspicious when the lad described the defenses at the bridge in great detail. The suspicion was somewhat allayed when he offered to bring the garrison commander into the discussions within the hour. At the appointed time the boy returned with the commander, an Armenian captain, who, like all Armenians, hated the Turks and was willing to settle old scores. He warned, however, that the garrison contained a number of hard-core diehards. He promised to neutralize the main sentry posts as long as Lawrence would bring up a detachment swiftly in order to seize the sleeping camp.

At eleven, Lawrence moved out with a mixed column; Nasir and Nuri were in tactical command. Tell el Shehab was deep in the Yarmuk Valley. The one-hundred-twenty-foot bridge crossed the Wadi Khalid, which fed into the Sea of Galilee. As they approached the bridge from above, they could hear the powerful rushing waters. The sound dampened their movement as they crept into the ravine. The sleeping garrison was hidden by an evening mist that rose from the river and obscured the position. As Lawrence sank into the fog, one of his men suddenly grabbed his arm and pointed to a dim cloud of smoke rising through the mizzle a short distance to the west: a train! By the time the column had moved farther into the valley, the train had reached the garrison station, huffing and puffing as it began to take on water. Although the garrison was now essentially cut off from the east, it still had communications to the west, into Palestine. Since the train had taken such a long time to brake itself to a halt, Lawrence guessed it was quite large, probably bringing reinforcements to Deraa. Lawrence, Nasir, and Nuri decided to halt the attack.

By now it was past midnight, and the wet air began to seep into the raiders' wool cloaks. Soon the men were shivering under their sodden wraps as they waited for events to unfold and watched the unusually active Turks move around the locomotive. Soon, Lawrence caught a speck of white moving through the damp darkness, coming ever closer to his position. Dancing through the mist, the fleck became the boy of Shehab. Breathless, he whispered that the plan had gone awry. The train was German and had just brought over a relief force under the command of a colonel, probably a full regiment. It had come from Afuleh, sent by the wily General Liman von Sanders to reinforce Deraa. The Germans had also arrested the Armenian captain. He also warned that a strong picket had been deployed not more than a hundred yards to their front. The changed situation now created another reframing exercise.

In consultation, Nuri believed he and his regulars could still storm the place under the advantage of surprise and preparation. Even though the German force may have been stronger, they were all most likely still aboard the train, resting and probably asleep. Even Lawrence had to admit to himself, "It was a fair chance: but I was at the game of reckoning the value of the objective in terms of life, and as usual finding it too dear."[3] In the end he voted against the plan. After all, they had already slit the rail line in two places, also cutting off the lines of communication of two armies facing Allenby in Palestine and effectively isolating and trapping the Fourth Army in Amman. On top of that, Lawrence had pulled at least a regiment-sized force from the defenses directly facing Allenby: all in all, not too bad for an evening's work. In the end Nuri and Nasir agreed, and the column slowly began to back its way out of the ravine.

As they disengaged, two demolition parties were detached and blew up portions of the track west of Tell el Shehab. The act of vengeance helped somewhat to lift the fatigue of the men, who had been fighting steadily for almost twenty-four hours.

SHORTLY BEFORE DAWN, after a brief rest the entire Arab army moved eastward through the ashen rubble of Mezerib. The army was indistinguishable from the horde of peasants that followed in its wake. This brought confusion to the Turkish recon pilots, who reported the strength of the army as upward of nine thousand troops. To confuse them even further, Lawrence and Nasir urged the peasants to return to their homes and await the arrival of Allenby's coming liberation. The subsequent hiving off of the peasants from the main body thoroughly confounded the enemy as to the Arabs' size, direction, and location: Lawrence seemed to be everywhere, going nowhere. While passing through Mezerib station, Pisani's gunners shot up the large water tower, leaving their final calling card. The commotion of Lawrence's retreat forced the German column that was advancing to the relief of Deraa to hightail it back to the bridge at Shehab, expecting an attack there at any moment.

At four in the afternoon, Lawrence had reached the station at Nisib, a few miles down the line south of Deraa. Pisani immediately opened up on the garrison with his French artillery. Lawrence planned to fix the garrison in position under Pisani's fire and maneuver with his mounted troops to destroy the bridge just to the north. The Arabs had the advantage of moving with the sun at their backs, obscuring them and making it difficult for the Turks to see their full intentions. The bridge was defended by a small but heavily fortified blockhouse. Pisani worked over the bridge house with two of his pack guns and six of the machine guns. A heavy fire was also directed at the main garrison, which was located near the village. By now Lawrence had nineteen machine guns firing into the garrison, attempting to pin and suppress the Turks from aiding the defense by the bridge itself. Village elders soon came out of the town, gesticulating wildly for the Arabs to stop the firing. Nasir spoke with them briefly and agreed to their entreaties provided the headmen could persuade the Turks to surrender. They agreed and returned to the village.

By later in the afternoon, the relentless hammering at the bridge drove off the occupants of the stone blockhouse. With the elders bartering for their safety, the battlefield suddenly went eerily silent. The only motion was the setting sun, casting long fingers of shadow and light across the landscape, seemingly creating a silent sound of its own. The departing sun reflected obliquely into the western faces of the rock, which dazzled and sparkled in smoky brilliance like Sinbad's lost treasure. The unearthly scene had a strange effect on Lawrence's bodyguard. When at last he roused himself from the uncanny mood and ordered them to advance against the bridge, they shockingly refused; now for the first time Lawrence's own handpicked men lost their nerve in a fight. The enemy had again opened up from the village after paying little heed to the village chiefs. Bullets were flying about as Lawrence tried to tease his retainers into action, but still they refused. Finally giving up, Lawrence chose the young and frightened Hemeid to join him. Hemeid shivered in fear, barely able to climb on his camel, but he stayed close to his leader as the pair rode down to the approaches of the bridge. Here they found Nuri chewing thoughtfully on the stem of his pipe. He began to discuss tactical theory with Lawrence, arguing the next best course of action. For the following ten minutes, the three stood there as silhouettes against the twilight sky, drawing upon them stinging bullets like bees to honey.

But instead of extracting nectar, the rounds impaled themselves on the nearby chert, loosing loud screams of extinction: *brazeeroww . . . phuckeewow!*

At length, Nuri agreed to cover Lawrence's advance closer to the bridge. Before moving to get a closer inspection of the blockhouse, he gave Hemeid his camel and told him to go back to the camp and return with the shirkers. He informed Hemeid that if they didn't join him at the bridge, they would face a wrath greater than death. At that, Hemeid lunged away with the two camels, happy to get off the ridgetop unscathed.

While Lawrence was examining the structure of the bridge in the waning light, the two leaders of his bodyguard raced down: Abdullah, the Robber, and el Zaagi. Both were apologetic and furious at the unfortunate lapse of military virtue displayed by the others and now eagerly sought redemption. The two gathered up demolition charges and blasting caps and with Lawrence headed toward the nearest bridge abutment. The abutments were five feet thick and almost twenty-five feet high. They quickly stacked dynamite against the structures, while Nuri and his men covered them from his higher position. After the charges were laid, Nuri's Arabs began a retreat toward Umtaiye a few miles to the east. The withdrawal of Nuri's troops to a place of safety from the blast seemed interminably long: Lawrence and his sappers were waiting underneath the bridge, where a sudden sally by the Turks from the other side would easily seal their fate. Lawrence had cut six-inch fuses that would offer a thirty-second burn. If the enemy suddenly advanced, he would have to light the fuses immediately, whether or not Nuri and his men got away.

After nearly an hour of waiting, Nuri fired a flare that cracked open the night sky, signaling he had gotten to safety. Lawrence quickly rechecked the eight hundred pounds of explosives, lit the fuses, and ran with the others into the shelter of the abandoned bridge redoubt. At that instant, the whole earth recoiled and lifted the bridge from its pier, raining boulders and debris on Lawrence's position. The titanic concussion knocked out Lawrence and his fellows. Their last moment of consciousness was a collage of dust, shock . . . and joy, for Lawrence had just destroyed his seventy-ninth bridge and, strategically, one of his most important.

Soon Lawrence awoke—or, rather, was awakened by a heavy yet gentle hand. He looked up, peering through dancing stars in a snow globe of confusion and concussion, to see the face of . . . God. The stars quickly settled and a mortal Nuri squinted back, his bearded visage coming alive in a tobacco-stained grin.

LAWRENCE'S BAND REJOINED the main column and rested the night near Umtaiye, just off the rail line. But sleep did not come easily, for all through the night more visitors continued to wander into the encampment. The Arab fighters had had little sleep the last three nights and were now subjects of slavering oaths of fealty from the native peasants. However, some of these peasants seemed disheartened, different from those at Mezerib. Some sort of discontent had shattered their initial enthusiasm, and it seemed to emanate especially from the village of Taiyibe. Apparently, the settlement had gotten into a shooting scuffle with Joyce's armored cars the day before. After a chat with Nasir, Lawrence decided to ride directly and unannounced into Taiyibe and settle the situation. They arrived at the sheikh's tent well after midnight just as a major confab was taking place among the elders. Fearing the chance encounter with Joyce would now escalate into full-scale hostility, the peasants were debating whether or not to approach the Turks for mercy and protection. The sudden arrival of Lawrence with armed men decided the matter, as it became clear to the headmen that the Turks were a losing horse, and despite yesterday's unfortunate incident, backing the Arab cause would be in the villagers' own best interest. After an hour of tea and idle conversation, the sheikhs vowed to support the revolt.

Lawrence returned to his bivouac just before dawn to try to steal some sleep. As he dozed off, a large explosion shook him awake. The Turks had just sent down from Deraa an armored train carrying a field gun. This intrusion sent the entire camp scurrying into action out of range of the piece. Up above, an airplane was spotting for the train and dealing an accurate, observed fire on the Arabs, killing two of the camels. The plane then suddenly slewed out of the air to land. With its "eyes" gone, the cannon began pounding the nearby village of Taiyibe with fifty well-placed rounds until its ammunition ran out and the train withdrew.

At that moment, Joyce returned with the armored cars. Lawrence informed him of the suspicious landing that might indicate an airfield nearby. After a quick breakfast—their first in days—Joyce and Lawrence with Junor in the second car went off on the hunt. They drove five miles over rugged terrain and entered a still valley where the aircraft appeared to have landed. The drivers turned off their engines and began to coast quietly down into the canyon about a thousand yards from the railway. The path bent into a small meadow, where they discovered a covey of three Turkish aircraft. Astonished to find their quarry, they fired up the engines and raced to get into machine-gun range. Unfortunately, a direct path to the enemy was blocked by a deep and impassable ravine, forcing them to drive a course tangent to the aircraft. At about twelve hundred yards they were spotted, and two of the planes made a dash to escape. The cars immediately began plastering them with fire, but the range was too great for accuracy, so the fliers made good their getaway. The third bird wasn't so lucky: its balky engine refused to start, probably the reason it had landed in the first place. The crew tried valiantly to get the engine fired up but were eventually driven off by the machine guns. As the gunners found the range, the plane went into a shuddering dance as it was hit repeatedly by fifteen hundred rounds of .303-caliber ammo. Satisfied that the sieved fuselage was useless, Lawrence and the two cars drove off. As they left the valley, they heard a muffled explosion and turned back to see black smoke billowing from the wreckage.

The two lucky planes went back to Deraa to rearm and refuel and soon returned to become the hunters, seeking out Lawrence and his cars. The planes found their targets, and each began dropping a string of four bombs on the vehicles. A near miss blew off the front tire of the lead vehicle. Despite the damage, all returned safely to Umtaiye, where Lawrence was soon fast asleep under one of the armored cars. Although a desultory bombing continued throughout the rest of the afternoon, it failed to rouse him from his deep slumber.

When at last he did awaken, Lawrence's first thought concerned the vulnerability of the Arabs to air attack. The Turks had at least a full squadron of planes operating against him, probably eight or nine aircraft. The constant bombing and strafing was beginning to unnerve the Arab irregulars, and he knew that without his guerrilla raiders, the entire Arab army would be blind. What was clear was that Lawrence would have to see Allenby and request sufficient air cover to save his force. It was now September 18. If he left immediately, he could be back by September 22 and resume the drive on Damascus. The force could continue their cat-and-mouse game until he returned. Yet at the same time, the Arabs must still exercise some positive initiative and maintain their freedom maneuver through continuous attacks against the Turks.

For now, the rail line into Deraa from the north and the line leaving town to the west had both been cut. The track to the south needed attention next. The bridge at point 149 was already repaired and had to be struck again. A site just farther to the south had to be severed as well, so that repair parties couldn't come up from the south to reach the bridge and restore it. The first task was for Nuri's regulars. Lawrence would take his bodyguard and strike the second location.

Still, a further question lingered. The incident at the Shehab bridge made it evident that the morale of his private bodyguard was shattered. And while Lawrence was away that morning hunting Turkish airplanes, Abdullah and el Zaagi had administered a heavy dose of Bedouin punishment. This only made the men more fearful, lowering their morale even further. Lawrence had self-styled his bodyguard as a model of the Persian Immortals of antiquity, so-called because the guard maintained a constant strength, with each loss being replaced immediately with new blood. Lawrence's personal force had been stable at ninety men, but over the last several months sixty had been killed. Now the constant attrition was rendering his bodyguard virtually ineffective and beyond his abilities as a tactical leader to rally them.

Lawrence would have to discuss the situation with Nasir and Nuri: the air cover issue, the continuous bombing of Taiyibe, and the moral collapse of his retainers. During the brief council of war, a reframing emerged: Lawrence would personally request air support from Allenby; meanwhile, any village that had suffered damage from Turkish air attacks would be recompensed in English gold and in gratitude for its loyalty; and Lawrence's bodyguard would stand down and recover its honor.

There still remained the task to support the demolition of the bridge at point 149. Denied employment of his bodyguard, Lawrence chose Junor with his Ford and one of the armored cars. The mission quickly turned into a fiasco. Without the pathfinding skills of his retainers, Lawrence's party became hopelessly lost in a maze of canyons and wandered about the stony echo chambers for three hours. Finally, they heard Peake's demolition at point 149 and drove to the sound, discovering a train hastily backing away from the destruction. Lawrence's group opened up with machine guns; the Turks rejoined with an ineffectual fire from the train. At that moment, however, one of the enemy had perhaps the luckiest day of his life. A lottery ticket shot struck the only unarmored portion of the armored car. A bullet hit a rock and then ricocheted upward into the belly of the car, puncturing the gas tank. The round just as easily could have pierced Lawrence between the eyes. It took an hour to repair the hole, and with dawn breaking, the hapless mission was scrubbed.

THE DETACHMENT ARRIVED back at Azrak in early afternoon. During the return, Lawrence was able to snatch three hours of dreamless sleep following the abortive night mission. At Azrak he found Feisal and Nuri Shaalan waiting to hear the latest news, which Lawrence was able to provide, speaking well into the evening. After daybreak the next day, an aircraft arrived with the first news of Allenby's astonishing victory. He had smashed through the Turkish defense as through a house of cards. After making the stunning proclamation, the pilot was about to head back to GHQ in Ramleh. Lawrence seized the opportunity to fly back as well and confer with Allenby.

After reaching Ramleh, Lawrence immediately went to Allenby's headquarters. Afterward Lawrence described the meeting: "There I found the great man unmoved, except for the light in his eye as [Louis] Bols [chief of staff] bustled in every fifteen minutes, with news of some wider success. Allenby had been so sure, before he started, that to him the result was almost boredom: but no general, however scientific, could see his intricate plan carried out over an enormous field in every particular with complete success, and not know an inward gladness: especially when he felt it (as he must have felt it) a reward of the breadth and judgment which made him conceive such unorthodox movements; and break up the proper book of his administrative services to suit them; and support them by every moral and material asset, military or political, within his grasp."[4]

Now Allenby roused himself from his moment of self-reflection and, taking Lawrence by the elbow, strode over to the large operations map mounted on the wall. The advancing red arrows showed the true magnitude of Allenby's success better than words could describe. And there was more punishment to come for the Turks: Beirut was now added to the agenda of military objectives along with Damascus. The coup de grâce would be delivered by Allenby's swift cavalry forces: Major-General Edward Chaytor and his New Zealanders would jump the Jordan River and drive for Amman; Major-General George Barrow's Indians would cross the Jordan farther north and thrust at Deraa; and finally, Chauvel's Aussies would strike across the Jordan at Kuneitra near the Golan Heights. Barrow and Chauvel, after seizing their intermediate objectives, would ride on Damascus and, then, *checkmate*. Lawrence was to assist all three axes of attack and not seize Damascus, the crown jewel of the entire campaign, on his own hook; it was to be a combined effort. Lawrence next explained the situation with respect to air cover for the Arabs: there was none. At this Allenby rushed over to his desk and pressed a button. Almost immediately General Geoffrey Salmond, commander of British air forces in the Middle East, hustled in with his aide, Brigadier-General Amyas Borton. The presence of the air commander reminded Lawrence of another aspect of Allenby's leadership genius: "The perfection of this man who could use infantry and cavalry and artillery and Air Force, navy and armored cars, deception and irregulars, each in its best fashion!" Lawrence reiterated the air situation to Salmond, who only smiled enigmatically and said, "So much the better." All the enemy planes on the Palestine front had been annihilated in the air or captured on the ground during the furious advance. Salmond would now have fresh meat to grind beyond the Jordan and promised to send over a couple of Bristol fighters. Then Allenby interrupted: "I say, Salmond, how do you propose to support these devils? We have no significant refueling and rearming capability with the Arabs."

"Not a difficulty," was Salmond's response. "We'll supply the lot by air, including the petrol."

Lawrence thought to himself, "Only by air? An air-contained fighting unit? Unheard of!" Even before he completed the thought, Salmond and Borton sat down with a stubby pencil and paper and worked out a logistics load table for a D.H.9 and a Handley Page. Of the scene Lawrence would later write: "Allenby sat by, listening and smiling, sure it would be done. The cooperation of the air with his unfolding scheme had been so ready and elastic, the liaison so complete and informed and quick. It was the RAF, which had converted the Turkish retreat into a rout, which had abolished their telephone and telegraph connections, had blocked their long columns, scattered their infantry units."

The question then emerged concerning the single Handley Page bomber, one of the largest planes flying at that time and the only one in the theater: Could it land out in the desert? Lawrence was certain it could but requested an expert's opinion at the landing site itself. After a quick review of the bidding, the staff meeting broke up and Lawrence went off to find breakfast in the HQ garden. Soon he began to appreciate the civilized quality of Allenby's headquarters—and it made him feel guilty: "I felt immoral, enjoying the white table-cloths, and coffee, and soldier servants, while our people at Umtaiye lay like lizards among the stones, eating unleavened bread, and waiting for the next plane to bomb them."[5] Lawrence continued to sip his fresh-brewed coffee, increasingly aware of how the garden's fecund growth startled him with a sudden wind-driven movement; the vegetation "seemed to fidget," unnerving him in a way the desert never did. At length he was joined by some of Allenby's staff, who for the moment distracted his unease.

BEFORE DAWN ON September 22, Lawrence stood by at an Australian airfield for his flight back to Umtaiye. In a few moments Ross Smith, his pilot, taxied over in the D.H.9 and Lawrence hopped aboard. Two other planes would complete the flight as well. The passage was uneventful and took about an hour. When the three planes arrived at Umtaiye, they were waved off and sent to a new bivouac at Um el Durab a few miles away. The continuous bombing had forced the displacement of the camp, and even after the relocation the Turks continued to bomb the empty campsite.

Ross Smith examined the new landing strip and certified it serviceable for the heavy Handley Page. The sight of the three British aircraft did much to boost the morale of the Arab army. Even Lawrence's chastened bodyguard appeared renewed, exhibiting a fresh fire in their hearts and blood in their eyes. While all were distracted by a breakfast of hot sausages, the alarm was sounded to warn of another aerial attack; this time the Germans were leading the assault. Two of the British planes were scrambled and made ready to meet the attack. Peters, one of the pilots, looked invitingly at Lawrence, as if to present him a backseat to the forthcoming dogfight. Lawrence considered the offer but in the end thought better of it: "No: I was not going up to an air-fight, no matter what caste I lost with the pilot. He was an Australian, of a race delighting in additional risks, not an Arab to whose gallery I must play." Peters turned away and flew up into the fray. In five minutes, Smith shot down one of the German scouts, much to the exultation of the onlooking Arabs. After the rest of the Germans had been chased away, the pilots landed and resumed their meal of cold sausages and tepid tea.

For Smith, the time at the front was growing short. He still had to return to Ramleh after shuttling the bomber over to Azrak. With that task in mind, he would fly Lawrence to Azrak and continue on to GHQ in one of the scouts. Feisal and Nuri Shaalan were waiting just as the huge beast dropped effortlessly from the sky. The Arabs were overjoyed at its arrival and at its size, saying, "Indeed and at last they have sent us *the* airplane, of which these smaller planes are its foals." One of the tribesmen ran about flapping his arms, saying repeatedly, "The biggest plane in the world!" Before dark, rumor had spread throughout the entire area of the new bomber that had come to be placed under the hand of Feisal. Salmond's chief of staff, Borton, had come along as well to help integrate the huge bomber into the Arab army. A ton of fuel was carried in the bomb racks and in the fuselage, which like some flying titan began to disgorge its cargo of spare parts for the fighters, food, medicine, letters, and communications. At nightfall, the huge plane rose from the desert, a black dragon winging its way into the setting sun toward Ramleh. There it would rearm with real bombs and begin night bombing runs on the garrisons at Deraa and Mafrak.

Lawrence spent the rest of the evening informing Feisal and Nuri Shaalan of his recent visit to Allenby's headquarters. The Arab army would continue to harass the Turkish Fourth Army around Amman and wait to link up with Chaytor's New Zealanders. It was Lawrence's view that the Turkish front had so catastrophically collapsed that Feisal's army could be in Damascus in a week. Wrapped in a black broadcloth cloak, Nuri's eyes lit up at the news, and he immediately offered his Ruwalla Camel Corps to support the advance. This meant that Feisal's liberation army would now number over four thousand men, three-quarters of whom were guerrillas. Nuri's unique brand of hard, tight leadership would be especially useful during the mad pursuit to Damascus.

BY SEPTEMBER 24, the Turks had given up trying to reestablish the rail link between the Fourth Army and the communications plexus at Deraa. At the moment this was all unknown to Lawrence, who continued his efforts toward the railway, leading an attack against the station at Mafrak. Here he was met with enormous resistance by a German machine-gun company. An attempt to reach the nearby bridge and blow it was countered with such a fierce hail of bullets and grenades that even with armored car protection, the sortie was beaten back. Puzzled by the stiff defense, Lawrence withdrew to Um el Durab for regrouping.

News greeted him that the Handley Page was scheduled to make a bombing run on Mafrak that very night. Lawrence remained skeptical of a completely successful night raid but agreed to wait; he could always police up whatever the bomber missed with his mounted raiders. At precisely midnight, a deep-throated rumble could be heard coming out of the west. Under a desert moon, the huge bomber materialized into its dragonlike hulk. Finding its target all lit up and astir with rail activity, the bomber began dropping its sticks of large hundred-pound bombs, which slammed into the jammed rail sidings. The packed freight immediately caught fire, causing a serious panic among the Turks. The station burned fiercely through the whole night and well into the next day.

During the afternoon, it became apparent that the entire Turkish Fourth Army had been shattered and was falling like loose bird shot into a full-scale retreat. At last their great nemesis had been shattered. The Beni Hassan reported that the enemy was no longer a cohesive army but a band of "gypsies" in complete rout. The tribesmen tore into the fleeing Turks, trapping stragglers and disorganized remnants. The collapse of the Fourth Army caused Lawrence to call a hasty council and gather his captains: Nasir, Nuri Said, Nuri Shaalan, and Tallal. Major Young also attended to offer logistical advice. Lawrence argued that with the collapse of the Turks near Amman, their mission was accomplished. He told them: "Our new endeavor should be to force the quick evacuation of Deraa, in order to prevent the Turks there reforming the fugitives into a rearguard. I propose that we march north, past Tell Arar, and over the railway at dawn tomorrow, into Sheikh Saal village. It lies in familiar country with abundant water, perfect observation, and a secure retreat west or north, or even southwest, if we're directly attacked."[6] Once his listeners understood that the maneuver would decisively cut off Deraa from Damascus, the group unanimously assented to his proposal. though Lawrence sensed that somehow Young harbored reservations about the plan.

In its execution, it meant that they would lose their armored car support for the time being, as well as their air cover. As the Bristol fighters flew back to Palestine to relay Lawrence's intentions, they spotted a large column of Turkish cavalry heading toward the Arab position. At this turn of events, one of the fighters peeled off and flew over Lawrence's camp, dropping a note that warned of the mounted element charging from the west. Lawrence read the message and ran off to find Nasir. Nasir was standing with Nuri Said on a heap of ash, discussing the forthcoming maneuver, when Lawrence pounded up beside them. Should they stay and fight the new threat or simply disengage and head north? A quick decision was required. As they pondered the new circumstances, Nuri Shaalan arrived and offered to use his horsemen as a rear guard to delay the Turks long enough for Lawrence to get the main body on the march north. They also received word that the armored cars, which had been sent back to Azrak, had spotted the huge dust cloud spewed forth by the enemy horse and sped back to reinforce Lawrence. Joyce's reinforcements decided the issue.

When Joyce arrived with the armored cars, Nuri Shaalan charged out to meet the Turkish cavalry. His force closed rapidly upon the enemy, and much to his surprise, the entire detachment immediately surrendered. As it turned out, the "cavalry" was merely rear echelon stragglers who had mounted transport animals bareback in an attempt to escape to Damascus. The "cavalry charge" was simply the continuation of the massive rout of the Fourth Army. Meanwhile, Lawrence continued north with the main body, hoping to meet up with Nuri Shaalan later.

As Lawrence continued his advance, it became increasingly apparent to him that the chance encounter with the Turkish rabble had upset his new timetable. Besides, by now his raiders were all bedecked in captured Turkish khaki. He would have to detour in order to avoid frightening the local peasantry, who were in full revolt against their former masters. The circumstances caused Lawrence to camp just before twilight to await Nuri Shaalan and his horsemen.

Around midnight, Major Young appeared for a private conversation with Lawrence.[7] Young was now convinced that the Arab Revolt was successful, its main missions accomplished. They had followed Allenby's orders and had maintained a harassing presence against the Fourth Army; but now that it no longer existed, the work was done. Furthermore, Young argued, "we can honorably fall back to Bosra, twenty miles out of the way to the east; there Nesib el Bekri is gathering more forces. We can wait with them for Allenby's troops to march into Deraa and wait a just reward there." Lawrence was a bit taken aback by Young's proposal. First, it would put an added burden on Allenby's forces. After all, Lawrence's forces at Sheikh Saad would operationally be the best positioned of all of Allenby's troops on the east side of the Jordan. It would prevent the Turks from establishing any sort of coherent defense south of Damascus. He told Young, "Damascus means the end of this war in the East and, I believe, the end of the general war, too; because the Central Powers being interdependent, the breaking of their weakest link—Turkey—would swing the whole cluster loose. Therefore, for every sensible reason, strategic, tactical, political, even moral—we are driving on." There was another reason he had to continue, but this reason Lawrence kept to himself. Arab honor demanded that the Arabs seize Damascus with their own sword. Seizure of the capital by dint of their own efforts would help seal the freedom they had fought and died for these many

months. Lawrence was not about to turn his back on Arab honor; to
do so would destroy his own.

But Young persisted with his reasoning, bringing Pisani and Winterton into the argument as well: "Tomorrow it will be madness to
cross west over the railway. The line will be guarded from end to end
by tens of thousands of Turks pouring out of Deraa. If they let us
cross over, we will only be in still greater danger." [8] By now Young's
audience was tired and had grown weary of his pestering. Lawrence
simply turned over on his carpet and wondered aloud, "What was
keeping Nuri Shaalan and Tallal?" With that, the decision was made
final: Lawrence's irregulars would continue to drive the sword into
the back of the routed enemy. Tomorrow the campaign would continue as planned.

NASIR, NURI SHAALAN, and Tallal had missed the rendezvous point
and didn't link up with Lawrence until morning. After a brief breakfast they all headed north, buoyed by the heady atmosphere of impending victory. All along the march they continued to attract village
peasants to their column. Outside Deraa, they encountered two
Aussie pilots whose Bristol fighter had been shot through the radiator. Lawrence and his band helped repair it as the celebratory mood
continued with women from a nearby village bringing water for the
radiator as though to a wedding festival.

At noon the Arabs marched through a melon field, the front of
their formation now extending nearly two miles wide. Advancing
through the field, they once again came upon the railway extending
north from Deraa to Damascus. A long train chugging up toward the
old capital indicated that a spur of the track had been repaired again.
As the locomotive puffed off beyond the bright horizon, the entire
column advanced upon the railway and began a rabble-inspired demolition, with hundreds of Arabs trying their rookie hands at dynamite. Their actions evoked more the image of young boys with
fireworks at a Fourth of July celebration than a military operation.
But the ease with which these amateurs had broken a long swath of
rail revealed to Lawrence how vulnerable and ineffectual the Turks
had become.

After pondering the thought, Lawrence decided to convene a brief war council with Nasir and the others. He was surprised and pleased to find Auda abu Tayi present as well. Auda had just returned from his own bit of freelancing and freebooting along the Druze Mountains. The large force would now reorganize itself into four main attack columns: Tallal would lead one in an assault against the large grain depot at Ezraa. Auda would attack Khirbet el Ghazala, a station to the south. Nuri was ordered to sweep the roads for Turkish stragglers coming out of Deraa. Lawrence would continue on with his detachment to Sheikh Saad.

Lawrence's column soon departed, making slow progress through a moonless night, though it reached Sheikh Saad with the sun's rising. Here they encountered the clan of ibn Smeir, a sworn blood enemy of Nuri Shaalan. But since ibn Smeir himself was not in camp, the column would be the respected guests of ibn Smeir's family. For two years Feisal, Nasir, and Lawrence had struggled, more or less successfully, to keep the blood feuding at a minimum. Even though victory was near at hand, the tribal tensions would likely get worse as each clan clamored for its share of the spoils of war. Lawrence precisely captured the military implications of the feuding when he later wrote: "The strain of keeping them in play, and employing their hot-heads in separate spheres, balancing opportunity and service that our direction might be esteemed as above jealousy— all that was evil enough. Conduct of the war in France would have been harder if each division, almost each brigade, of our army hated every other with a deadly hatred and fought when they met suddenly."[9]

The other three attack columns rejoined Lawrence that evening with the great news of their success. All were laden with booty, so much so that they were unable to pursue the fleeing enemy. Tallal was successful at Ezraa; Auda captured a decrepit train, artillery, and two hundred prisoners, some of whom were German; Nuri seized four hundred prisoners, mules, and machine guns. The bulk of the Turkish rabble was handed over to the local villagers as valuable day labor. While the plunder was being divided up, a British aircraft swooped low and dropped a message. Young readied the recognition panels and ran out to get the note: Bulgaria had surrendered! The Arabs had no knowledge of the faraway place but drew the obvious implications: the war would soon be over.

Later that evening, Feisal arrived with Nuri Said and the bulk of the Arab regular army. The villagers of Sheikh Saad were duly impressed. More mobs of enemy-routed troops continued to roll past like dark clouds of ash from a dying volcano. Zaal went out against one of these clouds with the Howeitat. An hour later he returned in riotous laughter. "We gave them to the boys and girls of the village for servants," he told Lawrence with a scornful hoot. News also arrived that Chauvel's Aussies were driving up from the southwest into the nearby villages, helping to precipitate a mass uprising all along the entire front. Within two days' time, Lawrence speculated, another sixty thousand armed men would have joined the revolt.

Additional intelligence arrived from Allenby via aircraft that helped to clarify further the operational situation for Lawrence. The Germans had torched the military facilities at Deraa; the airfields and magazine stores were ablaze in towering flames; the Germans were now part of the detritus of defeat, drifting north with the Turks. The message also indicated that the entire Turkish Seventh Army had been smashed and was rolling in two waves along with the remnants of the Fourth Army toward the Arabs: one column of six thousand men, the other a fragment of two thousand. Now, it seemed, the real slaughter was about to begin.

THE ARAB ARMY along with two of Pisani's pocket guns would go after the two thousand remnant. Tallal was becoming worried because the Turkish vestiges were moving directly toward his home village at Tafas. Lawrence rode to Tafas with his detachment, hoping to fight a delaying action until the main body came up. About halfway to the objective, Lawrence met some mounted tribesmen shepherding a herd of prisoners stripped to the waist. They had been beaten mercilessly, the welts on their backs oozing a crimson tide of blood. But the victims were members of the hated police battalion from Deraa, and Lawrence allowed the beatings to continue. It was an ominous sign: the day was beginning with a new aura and mood Lawrence had never experienced or witnessed before. This was going to be a day of wrath and vengeance. The angry Arabs also reported that one of Jemal Pasha's lancer regiments had already entered Tafas. The lancers were an elite unit that still maintained its cohesion and could be expected to put up a stiff fight: not a good omen.

When Lawrence reached the outskirts of Tafas, he saw columns of smoke rising among the huts and shacks. Near the ascending ground he saw a clutch of villagers huddled among some thorny bushes. They told of unspeakable horrors perpetrated by the death's-head lancers only an hour earlier. Lawrence then deployed his column in an ambush position at the north edge of the village. Soon the Turks emerged, heading for Mishin; the lancers were deployed in the front and rear, with a rabble of composite units and transport in the center. Machine guns provided flank security. The enemy column continued to advance into Lawrence's fire sack, and when it reached an open area, the Arabs unleashed a torrent of fire and steel. Nuri Said and Pisani were there; Auda was ready to launch against the Turkish flank; Tallal was glancing back anxiously at his village. The Turkish reaction was slow and ineffectual. They turned two field guns against the ambushers, but as usual the shrapnel had its fuses set too long, so the shells screamed over Lawrence's head without doing damage. The Turks quickly hustled out of the ambush, and Pisani began to pump high explosive rounds into the rear of the retreating column. Lawrence was unable to press home his ambush because of the urgent need to aid the village.

The Arabs returned and entered Tafas cautiously, stepping carefully over the dead that lay all around. Lawrence would later recall the scene: "The village lay stilly under its slow wreaths of white smoke. . . . Some gray heaps seemed to hide in the long grass, embracing the ground in the close way of corpses. We looked away from these knowing they were dead; but from one a little figure tottered off, as if to escape us. It was a child, three or four years old, whose dirty smock was stained red over one shoulder and side, with blood from a large half-fibrous wound, perhaps a lance thrust, just where the neck and body joined.

"The child ran a few steps, then stood and cried to us in a tone of astonishing strength (all else being very silent), 'Don't hit me, Baba.' Abd el Aziz, choking out something . . . flung himself off his camel, and stumbled, kneeling, in the grass beside the child. His suddenness frightened her, for she threw up her arms and tried to scream; but, instead, dropped in a little heap, while blood rushed out again over her clothes." Then, she died.

The men found more dead, including four babies. Near the out-walls, they found a pregnant woman, dead with a wicked saw-toothed bayonet stuck between her outstretched bare legs. There were twenty more dead who lay with her in as many grotesque shapes and poses. Lawrence's bodyguard stood around, silently trying to comprehend the slaughter. Then, suddenly, el Zaagi burst into a horrific spasm of mad laughter, at last breaking the surreal silence and completing the sensory mood of senselessness.

The effect on Lawrence was overwhelming. The mindless slaughter pushed him over the brink toward depravity. He hesitatingly turned to his men: "The best of you brings me the most Turkish dead."[10] At the order they all regrouped and raced after the receding enemy, while Lawrence remained back with the inconsolable Tallal.

Tallal slowly surveyed the wreckage of his village and soon gave out a wail like a wounded child. He urged his horse forward through the devastation to higher ground. From here he could see the routing Turks; then he began to shiver fiercely, uncontrollably. Lawrence sidled near him to speak, but Auda caught his arm and reined him back. Very deliberately and carefully, Tallal tugged his head cloth across his face and drew it tight behind his head, softly uttering some secret oath. Then he suddenly lurched forward on his mount, driving steel spurs deep into her flanks. The mare leapt into a fast gallop and, with Tallal bent low in his saddle, charged straight at the center of the retreating enemy.

The charge was down a gentle slope and quickly gathered momentum as Lawrence and the others watched in stunned and hushed silence. The shooting had stopped, and the only sound came from the pounding of the horse's hooves, which seemed strangely and mockingly loud. As Tallal drew near his target, he suddenly screamed forth his battle cry in a piercing shout: "Tallal! Tallal!" At that moment, the entire Turkish force unleashed upon him with every weapon a scything fire. The fusillade riddled and staggered his gallant steed; Tallal flew off the falling animal and fell dead, impaled upon the Turkish lances.

Auda turned to Lawrence, stony cold and grim, shouting: "Allah give him mercy; we will take his price!" He jiggled his horse's reins and slowly began to advance upon the dust-shrouded enemy horde: the sword of the prophet was now unsheathed again. After Tallal's charge of retribution, the peasants from the village rallied. Everyone now began to follow Auda's lead. Using an adroit maneuver, Auda was able to drive the Turks into bad terrain, forcing them to split apart into three vulnerable groups. The third element was the smallest, comprising mostly German and Austrian machine gunners and a few mounted troops. They assembled around three cars and fought in brilliant desperation, beating back the mad, relentless charges of the enraged Arabs. For the first time in the war, Lawrence personally gave the order "Take no prisoners!" At that instant, its moral construction gone, the Arabs ceased being an army and Lawrence stopped being a leader, his moral compass gone. Now the full consequences of his leader's grief took control, finally snuffing out the last flickering flame of his moral identity. Instead of leadership, he could offer only berserker incitement. All melded into one boiling, uncontrollable force of retribution. No longer men, they fought like devils with the rage of hatred inflaming their hearts and vengeance searing their souls.

Soon they left the redoubtable Germans behind and sought easier pickings among the other remnants. By now the peasants had recovered weapons from the battlefield wreckage, some even riding abandoned mules. The madness of Tafas rampaged well into the night. The Turks were murdered, then killed—again and again. Finally, through sheer exhaustion and the fall of night, the execution stopped.

LAWRENCE RETURNED TO Sheikh Saad, physically, spiritually, and emotionally savaged. All he could think about was the day of wrath. After a while his mind turned to the Germans, the first time he had fought against them. The Germans were a marked distinction beside the Turks, and Lawrence further wondered how the revolt would have fared against this different and more implacable enemy.

He arrived in camp after midnight, his fourth night in a row of riding, with little if any sleep. After a brief rest, Lawrence found a third camel, the great-hearted Baha, and rode back to Deraa, which he reached at dawn. Nasir had occupied the mayor's mansion and began to consolidate his hold on the city. The Indians under General Barrow had just arrived and were about ready to make a full-scale attack upon the town. Lawrence immediately rode out with el Zaagi to inform the general that the town was already in friendly hands. As the two riders approached, the Indians readied their weapons on the unlikely pair, uncertain of their intentions. At about the same time, a flight of British planes flew off to bomb the town in preparation for the ground assault. The unfortunate Nuri Said bore the brunt of the bombing, as his regulars were just arriving from Sheikh Saad into the far side of Deraa. Lawrence hastened to find Barrow to explain that the Arabs had already been in control of the town since the previous evening. Lawrence was also trying his utmost to ensure that Arab autonomy was maintained in as many captured places as possible in order to strengthen their position during any forthcoming armistice negotiations. At first Barrow was unsure of Lawrence's claims, but eventually Lawrence managed to convince the general that just for the sake of expediency, it was best to let the Arabs hold the places they had seized by force of arms. In the end, Barrow asked for food and other supplies and continued on toward Damascus for his rendezvous with Chauvel's Australians.

Feisal arrived the next day from Azrak with a jubilant entourage, celebrating the first great tangible result of the Arab Revolt since the capture of Aqaba. The triumph was punctuated by a mild earthquake, which was greeted as an auspicious omen. Lawrence remained in Deraa another night, holding his place at the airfield, for he held the town in contempt after its long association with the Turks. After having dinner with his bodyguard, he contemplated his recent triumph: "I tried in the blankness to think forward: but my mind was blank, my dreams puffed out like candles by the strong wind of success. In front was our too-tangible goal: but behind lay the effort of two years, its misery forgotten or glorified. Names rang through my head, each in imagination a superlative: Rumm the magnificent, brilliant Petra, Azrak the remote, Batra the very clean Yet the men had changed. Death had taken the gentle ones; and the new stridency, of those who were left, hurt me."[11] At last the end had crossed upon the horizon and come into view. Yet somehow, if only for an instant, Lawrence refused to accept it. He wanted to continue, perhaps for-

ever; for an end meant a new and uncertain beginning. After the revolt, then what?

He could not sleep, so he roused Major Stirling and his drivers
early at dawn. They all piled into Blue Mist, the Rolls-Royce tender,
and headed out for Damascus, at last to put everything to a final rest.
The bodyguard followed. By noon they had caught up with Barrow
and his headquarters. Here Lawrence traded his car for a camel. Barrow, shocked to see Lawrence ride up, asked, "When did you leave?"

"This morning," Lawrence replied.

Barrow had expected to reach Damascus in three forced marches
and was astonished by Lawrence's speed. He asked him, "Where will
you stop tonight?"

"In Damascus."

Lawrence's jaunty reply left Barrow a bit dumbfounded. He had
no choice but to continue his careful, deliberate pace to Damascus
while Lawrence simply rushed ahead.

Meanwhile, Nasir, Nuri Shaalan, and Auda were well out ahead,
trying to smash up another Turkish column of remnants, perhaps as
many as seven thousand. Lawrence finally caught up with his comrades and informed them that the Indians were at least three miles to
the rear. The main body of Turks was walled up in a farmstead and
would be difficult to root out on the fly. Stirling suggested they go
back to Barrow for reinforcements to help overcome the defense. In
a short time an Indian cavalry squadron came up with its English
colonel, a rather decrepit man more concerned with maintaining
rank-and-file order on the march than thriving on the chaos of attack. He approached the enemy but was quickly driven off by a few
rounds from a mountain gun. Stirling and Lawrence became incensed
at his performance, but the old colonel refused to shift from his
safe distance and engage the defenders. The two then went to
Brigadier-General C. L. Gregory, commander of the 10th Cavalry
Brigade in Barrow's 4th Cavalry Division, who offered a formidable force: horse artillery and British troops from the Middlesex
Yeomanry Regiment. They drove forward among the Arabs and
pushed into the rear of the Turkish position. By nightfall, the whole
column was crushed and forced to abandon all its equipment as it
streamed toward Damascus. Only Auda maintained pressure through-

out the night, driving the remnants of the Fourth Army to its shallow grave near Kiswe.

BY SEPTEMBER 30, the Arab Revolt was essentially over. Lawrence and most of his men spent the night in Kiswe, trying to stay out of the way and out of trouble. Meanwhile, the Australians enveloped Damascus to the north and west. Feisal began to implement his Damascus plan, which sought to wrest political control of the city when the Turks retreated with their German allies. By that evening, the Arab flag was waving to the departing enemy from the top of the Town Hall. Lawrence tried to dissuade Nasir from entering the town that evening amid all the confusion. A formal entry ceremony was planned for dawn on October 1. Still, by midnight on September 30 there were already four thousand men, mostly Ruwalla tribesmen, in Damascus.

The Germans left the city as the rear guard, setting all the military stores and ammo dumps alight: setting a beacon for all of Syria to see. Lawrence arrived outside the gates of the city at dawn and expected to find the worst after all the demolition. From atop a ridge, he saw to his surprise that the emerald gardens were tranquil beneath a dewy river mist. A citadel was set in the center of the gardens like a crown jewel to Arab freedom. Only a few wisps of smoky sentinels stood guard over the treasure. A dispatch rider now approached Lawrence and said, "Good news: Damascus salutes you!" Nasir was up ahead, waiting outside the gate with Nuri Shaalan. Nasir was given the privilege of entering the city first, with Nuri at his side. Nasir's fifty battles earned him the honor. Lawrence went with Stirling to shave in a nearby stream, certain that today of all days, presentation would matter. An Indian noncom tried to arrest them for their outlandish uniforms, but their total lack of concern told the would-be jailer that he had made a serious mistake.

After a critical duel with their razors, the pair drove off slowly along the bank of the Barada. Long delays finally brought them to City Hall, where they crashed their way into the antechamber. Here serious Arab politicking was under way, especially now that Nasir and Nuri Shaalan had joined the government. Lawrence tried to speak with Nasir in order to gain a tenor of the conversation. Then, all of a sudden the room convulsed, as though an elephant were trying to force its way through the throng of politicians. The source of the convulsion soon became evident: Auda abu Tayi and Sultan el Atrash, sheikh of the Druzes, were locked in a violent hand-to-hand, hand-to-gland struggle, throwing each other around the room. Lawrence and Mohammed el Dheilan tried to break the two apart and after much effort were able to drag Auda into a large ceremonial ballroom, incongruent for its high decadence and adornment. Zaal and Hubsi were called in as reinforcements, ushering Auda into a large stuffed chair. By now Auda had gone thoroughly mad in rage over Sultan's unknown insult. After almost half an hour, Auda calmed down enough to hear the spoken word again. Auda's clenching wrath had cracked his Allied false teeth, the ones he'd received after Aqaba. He finally stopped lurching for his pistols, and slowly his twitching fits subsided. He wiped the seething foam from his crooked mouth and blood from his battered face. His hair was a tangled mat stuck to his bare head. At last he spoke, offering Lawrence and Mohammed three days to seek revenge upon Sultan. Without another word, Lawrence left to seek out Sultan and escort him secretly and safely from the city.

When Lawrence returned after disposing of Sultan, he was shocked to find how quickly the city's population had increased. There must have been well over a quarter of a million souls teeming about in wild celebration. The crowds began to chant names from the pantheon of rebel heroes: Feisal, Nasir, Shukri, Aurans—as Lawrence was known to the Arabs.

Then Chauvel arrived and, like Barrow, had no clue what to do with a captured city, a particular blind spot among the cavalrymen. Lawrence told Chauvel that he was responsible for public order and requested that he leave his horsemen outside the city for the night, as the greatest celebration in six hundred years was about to begin. Chauvel's chief of staff found this very agreeable, and Lawrence decided to escort the two through the ecstatic throng. There was some discussion of protocol for tomorrow's march of Chauvel's men, but Lawrence was hardly listening. All he heard were the cries of history that had stood silent for so long: the Middle East was about to become boisterous again.

. . .

THE POLITICAL SITUATION was evolving quickly, with new players moving up to the international table all the time. All the breezy promises made to the Arabs were now coming home to roost, and this time the control of Damascus would drive those promises toward fulfillment. Lawrence was determined to help the Arabs consolidate their political gains and was convinced that the next twenty-four hours would be decisive in that process. After dispensing with Sultan, he snuck back into the Town Hall. During the chaotic transition of the past few days, an Algerian faction, under the old nemesis Abd el Kader and former Aqaba trail mate and brother Mohammed Said, had seized a loose control of the political circumstances in the capital. The Algerians were nothing more than opportunists who had filled a power vacuum after the Turks relinquished control of the city. Up until that point, they had been quite loyal to their former masters. Now the situation was growing delicate. The altercation between Auda and Sultan was the beginning of a potentially dangerous coalescence of counteralliances. Lawrence needed to buy time for Feisal's formal arrival and installation in the seat of government, but at the moment he had no real military force: his bodyguard was too blunt an instrument for political infighting. He could ask the British to intervene, but then they would never leave; best to keep them at arm's length. At present, Nasir was still a figurehead until Feisal's arrival. It was then decided that Shukri should be appointed head of state until Feisal appeared. The issue turned on how the decision was to be enforced. Nuri Shaalan immediately offered his horsemen, telling Lawrence, "You shall have the Ruwalla if you do all your will, and quickly."[12] Nuri quickly deployed his tribe, taking the first decisive steps to counter the emerging Algerian threat. At the same time, Nuri Said's regulars had consolidated control over the central government district and the Town Hall. When Abd el Kader and Mohammed Said met with Lawrence to clarify relationships, he was careful to place his retainers in conspicuous places and poses.

Late on October 1, Lawrence, as Feisal's duly constituted deputy, formally abolished the civil government of Damascus. He appointed Shukri el Ayubi as acting military governor, Azmi as his adjutant-general, and Jemil as Lawrence's chief of security. It came as no surprise, then, that Mohammed Said thoroughly denounced Lawrence, calling him the most abominable of names: "a Christian and an Englishman." Next, Mohammed Said and Abd el Kader began to pressure Nasir to exert himself on their behalf. Nasir was a simple soldier without a political bone in his body and was vulnerable to the false plea of Arab solidarity that the Algerians were using to cloak their naked grab for personal power. For Nasir, the political tension was worse than the ordeal of combat. As the negotiations continued in the ballroom, the rancor and acrimony began to weigh heavily upon him. At one point, Abd el Kader suddenly leapt to his feet and confronted Lawrence with a particularly vituperative and violent outburst. He was now beyond reason, driven by an irrational lust for power that was beginning to slip from his hands. Lawrence simply ignored the outburst and tried to step around the seething politician. As Lawrence tried to avoid him, the Algerian lunged forward with his dagger. At half-stride, Auda pounced on him like a cougar and indelicately planted him into the heavy carpet. Auda was ready to slit the man's throat in an instant after his morning frustrations with Sultan, but Nuri Shaalan intervened immediately to return Auda to the nether borders of sanity. Nuri reminded the Algerians again that the Ruwalla and the others were sworn to Lawrence. Any more trouble from the two would lead to their sudden execution. For an instant, Lawrence considered giving Auda his head and letting him dispatch the pair, but his high aspirations for model Arab governance stayed the temptation.

After the Algerians were run out of the Town Hall, the process of consolidation continued. Feisal was being delayed for having to deal with his increasingly embarrassing "war-friends." He had an urgent need to replace them with more reliable men who would make trusted governors. Lawrence and the others continued to shuttle emissaries between themselves and the levers of government. A core staff was quickly fielded and put to work addressing the mundane business of government: police and public safety—uniforms, regulations, pay, precincts, chains of command; water—the water supply was currently befouled with the bodies of men and animals; power supply—the powerhouse had to be tended to, and the resumption of street lighting would be the first clear and sure sign that order was being restored and a functioning government in place; sewage and refuse—typhus, dysentery, and cholera traveled in the wake of defeated armies and had to be contained; fire safety and prevention—the debris of war had made the streets tinderboxes, ready to fulminate with awesome consequences; prisons and detention—jails had to be restored and provisioned, though Shukri's generosity and amnesty had emptied most of them for the time being; the former rebels, now citizens once again, had to be disarmed and returned to hearth and home; human services—the people had been starving for days, and if the economy became confident in the new government, supplies would again begin to flow in from the local villages. The problem, however, was transportation. The Turks had carried off their own—or killed what they left behind; the British couldn't—or wouldn't—share their own, so the rebels disbanded their transport to help feed the people.

To bind Damascus to the rest of the evolving Arab kingdom, one essential was needed more than anything else: an operational railway. It cemented the people to the new nation and made the broader economy run. Like the station clock in the center of any town, it added a sense of normalcy and dependability to an otherwise chaotic moment in history. Everything would turn out all right because the trains were running, and even the mail would flow again. As for the currency, it was in terrible shape. The Aussies and other Allies were using the money as little more than toilet paper after looting millions in Turkish notes. Prices had to be fixed so as to encourage spending rather than hoarding, and an acceptable currency had to be established to further drive the battered economy. Lawrence put Major Young to the task; he used up the last of the Aqaba gold to prop up the new scrip. Young also ensured that the old Turkish property and fiscal records were secured and preserved.

All these issues could take weeks to resolve. The most immediate concern, however, was forage for all of Allenby's cavalry and transport: nearly forty thousand horses were milling about the outskirts of Damascus. If Lawrence couldn't solve this one problem, nothing else would matter, at least in the critical eyes of the British. Young, Stirling, and Kirkbride performed yeoman work in aiding Lawrence to solve the English logistics crisis. By the end of the first night, he had established a rudimentary façade of Arab government that would stand the next two years without any outside foreign interference.

This was all an extraordinary achievement, perhaps the least known of Lawrence's many successes. He had helped win the Arab Revolt, but only sound government could secure the peace and freedom that had been so hard won by so many. October 1, that day of incredible crisis resolution, problem solving, improvisation, and innovation, had finally answered Nasir's profound question on the way to Aqaba: Would this struggle be worth it in the end? That day, peace and freedom redeemed the long sacrifice.

Late that night, Lawrence was alone in his rooms. He had just now come to realize the one central tenet of good government. In the Arab world, good governance meant the opportunity to practice one's chosen religion. The sound of the *Muedhdhin's* cry to prayer reminded him of what he had forgotten all day. For the Arab, life without religion was a life not worth living, no matter how free or ordered. He let the crier's call to worship lift his weary mind above the spires of the mosques: "Allah alone is great: I testify there are no gods, but only Allah: and Mohammed is His Prophet. Come to prayer: come to security. Allah alone is great: there is no god—but only Allah." Then, after a long pause, the crier dropped his voice a couple of octaves and cried: "And He is very good to us this day, Oh people of Damascus." Lawrence's last thought before drifting to sleep was his sense of overpowering existential detachment, the slaughter at Tafas for now forgotten: "The clamor hushed, as everyone seemed to obey the call to prayer on this their first night of perfect freedom. While my fancy, in the overwhelming pause, showed me my loneliness and lack of reason in their movement: since only for me, of all the hearers, was the event sorrowful and the phrase meaningless."[15]

ON THE EARLY morning of October 2, Lawrence was rudely roused by a citizen with news that Abd el Kader had returned again and was fomenting rebellion in the streets of Damascus and in the countryside. The foolish Algerian had incited the standoffish Druzes with the help of Sultan. The Druzes had been riding the fences, waiting to see which side would win. They saw their new game as a chance for plunder by launching an anti-Christian jihad against the Maronite Christians. They attacked shops and other easy targets under the political whip of Abd el Kader and Mohammed Said. But Nuri Said soon discovered the true tepidness of the uprising. Once he began cordoning off long swaths of streets with machine-gun sections, the plundering Druzes dropped their booty and ran away down dark alleys. Chauvel offered a troop of cavalry as a roving constabulary to help brace the local security. The press got wind of the violence and in rumor and repetition blew the episode into an epic of blood and destruction. Soon the echo of events reached the sensitive ears of Allenby, who enjoined calm and order in the capital.

By the afternoon, the Druzes had been driven from the city with the help of the lately mobilized city militia. The town soon returned to its celebration of liberty, taking new delight in the candies, iced drinks, and Hejaz freedom flags lining all the major boulevards. Lawrence was once again enjoying the return to the carnival atmosphere when an Australian doctor rushed up to him, almost dislodging his cold tea. The doctor wanted to know why the Arabs had not secured the Turkish hospital. Lawrence was momentarily confused. All three hospitals—the military, the civilian, the missionary—were secure and in good hands; which one could he mean? Discussion with the doctor revealed that the "hospital" in question was in fact the infirmary in the Turkish military barracks, now guarded by two Australian infantry companies. After looking dully into each other's eyes for some moments, Lawrence and the doctor hastened to the site to investigate.

The Aussies had indeed secured the *exterior* of the massive building. The pair passed through the huge threshold and entered into an oppressive and stony silence inside. The great courtyard was filled with rubbish left by thousands of prisoners who had abandoned the place only the day before. Beyond the courtyard was the dark, shuttered infirmary itself. It seemed to suck the blazing light and dry heat out of the forecourt. Lawrence hesitated and then stepped inside. Never in his life had he experienced such a nauseating odor. Like spectral fingers of death, the foul mephitis cloyed his nostrils, seeking to assault his brain and corrode his senses. Only after his eyes adjusted to the dungeon-black corridor did the shock of the dead bodies break his nausea: "The stone floor was covered with dead bodies side by side, some in uniform, some in underclothing, some stark naked. There might be 30 there, and they crept with rats, who had gnawed wet galleries into them. A few were corpses nearly fresh, perhaps only a day or two old: others must have been there for long. Of some the flesh, going putrid, was yellow and blue and black. Many were already swollen twice or thrice life-width, their fat heads laughing with black mouths across jaws harsh with stubble. Of others the softer parts were fallen in. A few had burst open, and were liquescent with decay."

Beyond this point—this essence of putrescence—was a large dressing gallery where Lawrence heard a moan: "I trod over to it, across the soft mat of bodies, whose clothing, yellow with dung, crackled dryly under me. Inside the ward the air was raw and still, and the dressed battalion of filled beds so quiet that I thought these too were dead, each man rigid on his stinking pallet, from which liquid muck had dripped down to stiffen on the cemented floor." Lawrence moved silently among the cots until he found the man who had moaned, "Pity . . . pity." Others suddenly seemed to become conscious. "There was a brown waver as several tried to lift their hands, and a thin fluttering like withered leaves, as they vainly fell back again upon their beds." These living ghosts had no one voice through which to communicate; their hoarse whispers sounded like reedy rustling, undulating through the corridor, where meaning was out of time, out of place. The patients were badly wrapped mummies, somehow displaced between dawn and darkness, life and death, quietly awaiting entombed extinction.

The thought's horror pressed Lawrence into action. He raced from the charnel house through the courtyard into the arbor and asked the Aussies for a labor party. They declined. They had no tools, they said; they had no doctors. Then Kirkbride rushed in to say he had found the infirmary doctors; they were upstairs, in pajamas, brewing coffee. Quickly, the most fit prisoners in the barracks were rounded up and started to dig a mass grave by the garden. The Turkish doctors began a rough triage and found fifty-six dead, two hundred dying, and seven hundred undying. The last, these seeming apparitions, began digging but were stymied when they struck a stone subfloor under the vegetation. They could only manage to widen the margins of the pit, enough to embrace and bury the dead. Soon clouds of quicklime were sprinkled on the bodies, almost as a token ritual of farewell. The powdery shroud cloaked the liquefying corpses in a jellied whiteness.

By midnight it was all over and Lawrence collapsed in his bed. He had not slept more than three hours at a time since leaving Deraa four days and many graveyards ago.

THE NEXT DAY brought the old Arab army together again, for the last time, in Damascus. Pisani was there with the artillery, Joyce with the armored cars. Order had been restored again throughout the city after Abd el Kader's abortive coup. Chauvel complained that the Arab soldiers were not properly saluting his Australian officers. Such quotidian banality mattered less to Lawrence than the immediate fact that the barracks hospital had been resurrected, even partially restored. As he was contemplating his proud achievement, a British medical officer burst in upon his reverie: "You in charge?" After a wary hesitation, Lawrence offered a casual nod of assent.

The medico then broke out with, "Scandalous . . . disgraceful . . . outrageous . . . ought to be shot . . ." He was obviously referring to the conditions at the infirmary. Abruptly, after all the months of intense combat, Lawrence's highly strung nerves came unwired. He let out a loud cackling giggle; shuffling, he bent backward as though struck in the chest. The officer glared at him: "Bloody brute!"[14] Then Lawrence let out another strained squawk, whereupon the doctor smacked him upside the head and shoulders and stalked off in a muttering dither.

At that moment, Lawrence knew the revolt was over, and more precisely, his role in it was finished. Feeling more ashamed than angry, he suddenly realized the meaning of the desolate sadness that had lurked and stalked him these many months. At that instant, he comprehended that he was like a young stepfather and the Arab Revolt the hopeful stepson he had so carefully nurtured, encouraged, supported, and sustained during its formative years. Now, at the moment of adulthood, the son was about to meet his true father, Emir Feisal, on his way up from Deraa. Lawrence, the cast-aside stepfather, had just received his ironic thanks under the generic hand of a British officer. The blow was a reminder of the duplicitous role Lawrence had played in the upbringing of the revolt in the knowledge it would likely be indentured to British imperialism. All that now remained to fill the sudden emptiness were the remnants of crushed pride and staggering loss. There would be no final closure for Lawrence, because the wholeness and fullness of his emotional investment could never be salvaged.

The idea that began while a student at Oxford City High School for Boys, that he could somehow free an enslaved people, meant a personal kind of commitment that was both audacious and presumptuous beyond imagination. Like the loving stepfather who believes he can embrace as his own a child of another's blood, Lawrence thought he could adopt a remote race as his own true son. The long period of accommodation, already begun at Carchemish, would accelerate in the Hejaz. Though the burden of reconciliation would fall most heavily upon Lawrence as the foster father of the revolt, it would transform him, change him in ever-increasing turns of commitment until he no longer recognized himself. The conformity and congruence of father to son became too extreme, so in time Lawrence's heart and soul would warp and bend beyond self-recognition.

Allenby knew that the distance between fatherhood and leaderhood was too small to notice. Perhaps he saw this at the end, when he tried to persuade Lawrence to remain for a time with his stepchild. But for Lawrence the remorseless grief was too great, and after the war his temperament could no longer recover its misshapen identity. Thus began the journey through Lawrence's grief: a lifelong departure; a farewell to comrade; a goodbye to self. And the end of one odyssey would beget another.

For Lawrence, his leader's grief and personal guilt continued toward Damascus and beyond. But finally, on the late morning of May 13, 1935, along the road to his cottage at Clouds Hill, T. E. Lawrence found his redemption. Here he sped to his death, as he had sped through life: driven by some creative impulse that seemed blind in its direction yet purposive in its motivation. Lawrence had lived guru-philosopher Alan Watts's principle that "you don't sing to get to the end of the song." Lawrence might have said, "You don't live to die; you live to create." What he *did* say, however, was: "As far as harnessing to my go-cart the eternal force—well, no: I pushed my go-cart into the eternal stream, and so it went faster than the ones that are pushed cross-stream or up-stream." It was his genius that showed him to push the "right way" through the eternal creative stream; though in the end, like his great hero Odysseus, he would take the long way home.

Lawrence's intense psychological struggle in the desert brought him to a profound moral conversion that would lead ultimately to his personal redemption. He saw the central paradox of military art: *In order to create one must destroy.* Such a paradox can lead to only one possible conclusion: *Military art by its very nature leads to its own abnegation and to the abnegation of the military artist as well.* He realized at some point that in order to salvage the creative force of military art *as art,* some *thing* had to be created in the end. For Lawrence, the resolution to the paradox became obvious: a generative military art had to create a *lasting peace.* No other solution was possible; no other symmetry could emerge. Yet today the world waits in vain for Lawrence's vision of peace in the Middle East.

Acknowledgments

Following the 2003 debacle in Iraq, our learning institution (the U.S. Army School of Advanced Military Studies [SAMS] in the Command and General Staff College at Fort Leavenworth, Kansas) underwent a major curriculum review to better prepare our officers intellectually for what was proving to be a long, drawn-out war. In my reflections on the problem, I began to be attracted to the tutor/student method of instruction, which demonstrated great utility in advanced military education and seemed to offer a possible solution to the army's postinvasion concerns with officer education. Coincidentally, in April 2004, I happened to attend a conference on learning and education at Oxford University, where the tutor/student method—known as the Oxford method—originated. I was also aware that T. E. Lawrence (of Arabia) had studied there and realized he would make the perfect "poster child" for the kind of officer education I had envisioned. With that in mind, I began serious research in the Lawrence archives at Oxford in September 2004. Here I also attended a conference conducted by the T. E. Lawrence Society and was able to meet the leading experts on Lawrence, including Jeremy Wilson, Malcolm Brown, and others. I was especially intrigued by Harvard psychiatrist John E. Mack, who wrote a Pulitzer Prize–winning biography of Lawrence entitled *A Prince of Our Disorder*. I was able to have several personal conversations with Mack about my research, and his generous response encouraged me to continue with my research. Tragically, however, Mack was killed by a drunk driver in London the day after the conference ended.

After further research, I began seriously to propose that the Oxford method of instruction be formally adopted into the SAMS curriculum, but for various reasons this proposal was rejected. Nonetheless, I continued to pursue my conviction that advanced military education of the sort that informed Lawrence was crucial to leader development in the kinds of wars we were fighting in Iraq and Afghanistan. By 2006, I decided to write a book using Lawrence as an example of the successful educated, intellectual leader in action. This became the basis for an article I published in *Army* magazine entitled, "T. E. Lawrence and the Mind of an Insurgent." In March 2008, I retired from SAMS and began to write the first draft of the book.

Apart from the profound debt of gratitude I owe the late John Mack for his initial insights, kindness, and encouragement, there are many others I wish to thank as well: Tom Ricks, Jim Dubik, Shimon Naveh, Huba Wass de Czege, Mike Steele, Mike Pearlman, Deborah Charles, Bruce Menning, Jake Kipp, Leah Stevens, Bruce Reider, Tim Challans, L. D. Schneider, Ellen Kaplan, Bob Kaplan, Mark Bowden, Bob Epstein, Rolly Dessert, Dan Schneider, Maria Clark, Sadaf Ardestani, Bob Berlin, Dave Hable, Ken Gams, Dan Paulick, Tom Bennett, Dave Paulick, Bob Mayes, Jeff LaFace, Kevin Benson, Michéle Robien, Robin Swan, Jim Greer, E. J. McCarthy, Jonathan Jao, John Flicker, Nabil Barghouti, Ofra Graicer, Ron Davids, C. C. Franché, and Orrick White; Letta, Kevin, Jason, Jenifer, Julie, Joey, Cameron, and especially my late parents and my students; the staff of the Bodleian Library, Oxford University; the staff of the Liddell Hart Center for Military Archives, King's College, London; the Imperial War Museum, London; the staff of the Combined Arms Research Library, Fort Leavenworth, Kansas; the staff of the Library of Congress, Washington, D.C.; the staff of the university library, University of Kansas, Lawrence, Kansas; the staff of the Harry Ransom Humanities Research Center, University of Texas, Austin, Texas; and the T. E. Lawrence Society.

Notes

Chapter 1: Arrival

1. Philip B. Davidson, *Vietnam at War* (Oxford: Oxford University Press, 1991), 15.

Chapter 2: Pale Rider

1. T. E. Lawrence, *Seven Pillars of Wisdom* (New York: Anchor Books, July 1991), 65.
2. Ibid., 67.
3. Ibid., 76.
4. Ibid., 84.
5. Ibid., 91.
6. Ibid., 96–97.
7. Ibid., 122–23.
8. Ibid., 136–37.
9. Ibid., 157.
10. Ibid., 163.

Chapter 3: A Flash of Genius

1. Thomas S. Kuhn, *The Structure of Scientific Revolution* (Chicago: University of Chicago Press, 1970, 2nd ed.), 198–204.
2. Lawrence, *Seven Pillars of Wisdom,* 167–68.
3. Ibid., 175–76.
4. Ibid., 182–83.
5. Ibid., 183–84.
6. See Chapter 33, *Seven Pillars of Wisdom,* and T. E. Lawrence, "The Evolution of a Revolt," *Army Quarterly* (November 1920), for Lawrence quotes. James J. Schneider, "T. E. Lawrence and the Mind of an Insurgent," *Journal of the Royal Artillery* 1, no. 133 (spring 2006): 13–16.

7. Lawrence, *Seven Pillars of Wisdom*, 208.
8. Ibid., 216.

Chapter 4: Aqaba!

1. Lawrence, *Seven Pillars of Wisdom*, 246.
2. Ibid., 250.
3. Ibid., 253–54.
4. Ibid., 256.
5. Ibid., 273–74.
6. Ibid., 277–79.
7. Ibid., 290.
8. Ibid., 302–05.
9. Ibid., 314.

Chapter 5: Lawrence in LEGO-land

1. Lawrence, *Seven Pillars of Wisdom*, 321–22.
2. Ibid., 328.
3. Ibid., 337.
4. Ibid., 339–40.
5. Ibid., 355–57.
6. Ibid., 367–69.
7. Ibid., 374–75.

Chapter 6: To Whom the Gods Pray

1. Lawrence, *Seven Pillars of Wisdom*, 378.
2. Ibid., 407–08.
3. Ibid., 412–13.
4. Ibid., 419.
5. Ibid., 422–23.
6. Ibid., 423–24.
7. Ibid., 431.
8. Ibid., 437.

Chapter 7: The Grief of Leaders

1. Lawrence, *Seven Pillars of Wisdom*, 472.
2. Ibid., 475–76.
3. Ibid., 479.
4. Ibid., 481.
5. Ibid., 492.
6. Ibid., 502.
7. Ibid., 468.

Chapter 8: Thief of Souls

1. Lawrence, *Seven Pillars of Wisdom*, 503.
2. Ibid., 510–11.
3. Ibid., 517.
4. Ibid., 523.
5. Ibid., 526–28.

Chapter 9: The Hovering Dead

1. Lawrence, *Seven Pillars of Wisdom*, 539–40.
2. Ibid., 540–41.
3. See Jonathan Shay, *Achilles in Vietnam* (New York: Scribner, 1994) and *Odysseus in America* (New York: Scribner, 2002).
4. Ibid., 548–52.
5. Ibid., 556.
6. Ibid., 562–63.
7. Ibid., 562, 563.
8. Ibid., 564–66.
9. Ibid., 576.
10. Ibid., 578–79.

Chapter 10: Days of Wrath; O Days of Sorrow—the Road to Damascus

1. Lawrence, *Seven Pillars of Wisdom*, 583.
2. Ibid., 594.
3. Ibid., 604.
4. Ibid., 615.
5. Ibid., 615–16.
6. Ibid., 622.
7. In *Seven Pillars,* Lawrence refers to Young as "Sabin."
8. Lawrence, *Seven Pillars of Wisdom*, 623–24.
9. Ibid., 627.
10. Ibid., 631.
11. Ibid., 638.
12. Ibid., 648.
13. Ibid., 651–52.
14. Ibid., 659.

Index

NOTE: Lawrence is represented by his initials, TEL, throughout this index.

ABOUT THE AUTHOR

JAMES J. SCHNEIDER is Professor Emeritus of Military Theory formerly at the School of Advanced Military Studies, U.S. Army Command and General Staff College, Fort Leavenworth, Kansas. A recognized international expert in his field, Schneider has taught and written extensively on military theory, having helped develop some of the key theoretical and pedagogical underpinnings to contemporary operational art for a whole new generation of military officers. Schneider served in Vietnam with the First Infantry Division and received his Ph.D. in history at the University of Kansas. He is currently a consultant on military affairs for a global strategy firm and working on his next book, *How Generals Think*.

ABOUT THE TYPE

This book was set in Sabon, a typeface designed by the well-known German typographer Jan Tschichold (1902–74). Sabon's design is based upon the original letter forms of Claude Garamond and was created specifically to be used for three sources: foundry type for hand composition, Linotype, and Monotype. Tschichold named his typeface for the famous Frankfurt typefounder Jacques Sabon, who died in 1580.